STRUCTURE

NEW YORK · CHICAGO

ANGUAGE AND LITERATURE

FRESHMAN YEAR

THE
GOLDEN ECHO

Sister Mary Rosenda

O.S.F., Ph.D.
ALVERNO COLLEGE
MILWAUKEE, WISCONSIN

W. H. SADLIER, INC.

Grateful acknowledgment is made to the following publishers, agents, and individuals for permission to reprint material in copyright:

☐ Bank of America: *The Serpent and the Mouse*, translated by Arthur W. Ryder, from THE PANCHATANTRA. ☐ Elswyth Thane Beebe: *Brothering Fish*, William Beebe. ☐ Brandt & Brandt, New York: *The Devil and Daniel Webster*, Stephen Vincent Benét. ☐ Burns & Oates, Ltd., London: *The Legend of St. Christopher, Breaker of Men*, C. C. Martindale, S. J. ☐ Coward-McCann, Inc., New York: *A Lady Comes to an Inn*, Elizabeth Coatsworth, from THE CREAKING STAIR by Elizabeth Coatsworth; reprinted by permission of Coward-McCann, Inc.; copyright 1929; copyright renewed 1955 by Elizabeth Coatsworth. ☐ E. E. Cummings and Liveright Publishing Corporation, New York: *hist wist*, E. E. Cummings, from TULIPS AND CHIMNEYS by E. E. Cummings; copyright 1923 by E. E. Cummings. Reprinted with permission of the author. ☐ Dodd, Mead & Company, New York: *Cerelle*, Margaret Bell Houston; copyright 1930 by Margaret Bell Houston. *The Cremation of Sam McGee*, Robert W. Service, from THE COLLECTED POEMS OF ROBERT SERVICE. *The Skater of Ghost Lake* and *Jesse James*, William Rose Benét, from GOLDEN FLEECE by William Rose Benét; copyright 1933, 1935 by Dodd, Mead & Company. ☐ Dorrance & Company, Inc., New York: *Forest Fire*, Edna Davis Romig, from BLUE HILLS by Edna Davis Romig; reprinted with permission of the publishers. ☐ E. P. Dutton & Company, Inc., New York: *Tact*, Arthur Guiterman, from LYRIC LAUGHTER by Arthur Guiterman; copyright 1939 by E. P. Dutton & Company, Inc.; reprinted with permission of the publisher. ☐ Mrs. Arthur Guiterman: *Pershing at the Front* and *The Vizier's Apology*, Arthur Guiterman. ☐ Alice Hamilton, M. D.: *English Is a Queer Language*, Alice Hamilton; reprinted by permission of the author. ☐ Harcourt, Brace & World, Inc., New York: *I Get a Colt to Break In*, Lincoln Steffens, from THE AUTOBIOGRAPHY OF LINCOLN STEFFENS; copyright 1931 by Harcourt, Brace & World, Inc.; copyright renewed 1959 by Peter Steffens; reprinted by permission of the publishers. *anyone lived in a pretty how town*, E. E. Cummings; copyright 1923, 1951; reprinted from POEMS 1923–1954 by E. E. Cummings by permission of Harcourt, Brace & World, Inc. ☐ Harvard University Press, Cambridge, Massachusetts: *Geary's Rock* from BALLADS AND SONGS OF THE SHANTY-BOY collected and edited by Franz Rickaby; copyright 1926 by Lillian Rickaby Dykstra. ☐ Rufina McCarthy Helmer: *St. Brigid*, Denis A. McCarthy. ☐ Holt, Rinehart & Winston, Inc., New York: *Out, Out*, Robert Frost; copyright 1916, 1921, 1930, 1939 by Holt, Rinehart and Winston, Inc.; copyright renewed 1944 by Robert Frost; reprinted by permission of Holt, Rinehart & Winston, Inc. ☐ Houghton Mifflin Company, Boston: *Ballad of the Oysterman*, Oliver Wendell Holmes. ☐ John F. Kennedy: *Inaugural Address*. ☐ Alfred A. Knopf, Inc., New York: *Masculine Protest*, Frank O'Connor, from MORE STORIES by Frank O'Connor; copyright 1952, 1954 by Frank O'Connor. *The Black Duck Dinner*, James Stevens, from PAUL BUNYAN by James Stevens; copyright 1925, 1947 by Alfred A. Knopf, Inc. *Matilda*, Hilaire Belloc, from CAUTIONARY VERSES by Hilaire Belloc; published in 1941 by Alfred A. Knopf, Inc. Verse fragment, David McCord, from SAY IT WITH WORDS by David McCord. *Sea Lullaby*, Elinor Wylie, from COLLECTED POEMS OF ELINOR WYLIE; copyright 1921, 1932 by Alfred A. Knopf, Inc. ☐ J. B. Lippincott Company, Philadelphia: *The Highwayman*, Alfred Noyes, from COLLECTED POEMS OF ALFRED NOYES, VOLUME I; copyright 1913, 1941 by Alfred Noyes; published by J. B. Lippincott Company; Canadian permission, Hugh Noyes. *The River Is a Piece of Sky*, John Ciardi, from THE REASON FOR THE PELICAN by John Ciardi; copyright 1959 by John Ciardi; published by J. B. Lippincott Company. ☐ Little, Brown & Company, Boston: *Eletelephony*, Laura E. Richards, from TIRRA LIRRA by Laura E. Richards. ☐ Lothrop, Lee & Shepard Co., New York: *Words To Take Along*, Eloise Lambert, from OUR LANGUAGE by Eloise Lambert; copyright 1955 by Lothrop, Lee & Shepard Co., Inc. ☐ The Macmillan Company, New York: *The Lady of the Tomahawk*, Robert P. Tristram Coffin; copyright 1933 by The Macmillan Company. *Lazybones* and *The Means Massacre*, Robert P. Tristram Coffin; copyright 1938 by The Macmillan Company. *Simon Legree—A Negro Sermon*, Vachel Lindsay; copyright 1917 by The Macmillan Company; copyright 1945 by Elizabeth C. Lindsay. *The Crow and the Pitcher, The Dog and the Shadow, The Dog in the Manger, The Fox and the Crow, The Fox and the Grapes, The North Wind and the Sun, The Old Man and Death, The Shepherd Boy and the Wolf, The Wolf in Sheep's Clothing*; reprinted with permission of the publisher from AESOP'S FABLES, edited by Joseph Jacobs; copyright 1950 by The Macmillan Company. ☐ Virgil Markham: *How the Great Guest Came*, Edwin Markham. ☐ Ann Blyth McNulty: *In the Beginning Was the Word*, Ann Blyth. ☐ The New Yorker Magazine, Inc., New York: *What Do You Mean It Was Brillig?* James Thurber; copyright 1939 by The New Yorker Magazine, Inc. ☐ Oxford University Press, London: *The Godson* and *How Much Land Does a Man Need?* Leo Tolstoy, translated by Louise and Aylmer Maude. ☐ Idella Purnell: *A Shot at Night*, Idella Purnell; reprinted with permission of the author. ☐ Selma Robinson: *Ballad of the Huntsman*, Selma Robinson. ☐ Scholastic Magazines, Inc., New York: *What Is Poetry?* Paul Engle, from LITERARY CAVALCADE; copyright 1956 by Scholastic Magazines, Inc.; reprinted by permission. ☐ The Viking Press, Inc., New York: *The Creation*, James Weldon Johnson, from GOD'S TROMBONES by James Weldon Johnson; copyright 1927 by The Viking Press, Inc.; copyright 1955 by Grace Nail Johnson; reprinted by permission of The Viking Press, Inc.

☐ The Horn Book, Inc., Boston: *A Company of Mine Is Nature*, Kim Dang Sig. ☐ A. D. Long: *A Ballad of Marjorie*, Dora Sigerson.

☐ We have tried in every way to obtain permission to reprint these three selections in this volume, but we have been unable to reach the authors. The selections and authors are *St. Swithin*, Daniel Henderson; *An American Hercules*, James Stevens; *Pecos Bill and the Willful Coyote*, William C. White.

TABLE OF CONTENTS

Christmas

UNIT 3

The Bard and His Lyre   THE LONG NARRATIVE

UNIT 4

Songs of Twilight   THE SHORT VERSE NARRATIVE

UNIT 1

A Handful of Pennies

WORKING

WITH WORDS

A Handful of Pennies

WORKING WITH WORDS

Words in Large Structures

If you would like to study painting or music or architecture or engineering or woodworking or designing, you have, though you may not realize it, a special readiness for this book. For somehow you are interested in man's arranging materials into structures. Whether someone builds with glass or wood or steel or sound, he has much in common with the man who builds with words. He has learned the secret of putting parts together so that they function or delight as a whole. He fits them. He varies. He balances. And the special privilege of his fellowmen, who rejoice at what they see or hear, is to use their minds for the discovery of what, how, and why the final arrangement is.

Before you can sincerely ask how something is put together, however, you must be convinced that the whole is worth examining. For a time, therefore, you and your fellow students will look at several very different things that man has made from words. Let your curiosity and your response to each piece lead you through the directions for a more thorough look at it.

Reading, Writing, and Discussion

Be sure to read this—and every other poem, for that matter—aloud. If you have never before realized some of the basic fun you can have with words, you will find it here. Watch what happens when the elephant's trunk and your tongue get twisted in the telephone wires.

Eletelephony

LAURA
RICHARDS

Once there was an elephant,
Who tried to use the telephant—
No! No! I mean an elephone
Who tried to use the telephone—
(Dear me! I am not certain quite
That even now I've got it right.)

Howe'er it was, he got his trunk
Entangled in the telephunk;
The more he tried to get it free,
The louder buzzed the telephee—
(I fear I'd better drop the song
Of elephop and telephong!)

1. What is the main device that makes this poem fun to read?
2. Humor involves a balance between the familiar and the unexpected. How do the two elements enter this poem? **3.** Is this verse pure nonsense and fun with words, or is it also an enjoyment of common experience?

Read this poem to find what a child sees from a bridge above a river and to discover how a poet places words to convey the sight.

The River Is a Piece of Sky

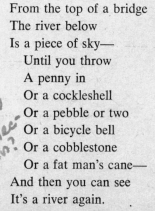

From the top of a bridge
The river below
Is a piece of sky—
   Until you throw
   A penny in
   Or a cockleshell
   Or a pebble or two
   Or a bicycle bell
   Or a cobblestone
   Or a fat man's cane—
And then you can see
It's a river again.

The difference you'll see
When you drop your penny:
The river has splashes,
The sky hasn't any.

JOHN CIARDI

1. Does the delight of this poem lie in a contrast, in a comparison, or in a combination of both? **2.** Does your answer to number **1** lead you to the discovery of a similarity between humor and delight? **3.** What elements of a child's song does the first stanza embody? **4.** Does the difference expressed in the last stanza fit every other aspect of the poem? Discuss.

Here is a piece of prose to help you read poetry more intelligently. The poem accompanying it was written by a Korean high school boy after he had learned a little English. It is printed here just as he wrote it.

Notice how Mr. Engle helps you discover the beauty of the poem.

A Company of Mine Is Nature
(ON MORNING OF FIRST OF OCTOBER)

When was opened the window,
A song of bird called the name of mine
When I stand at the window,
Out of doors, nature gives to me lovely her smile;
And, in the blue sky, the sun-light
Is soft as mother's hand kindly put on my head.
So soon have I to run out,
And take their joy with all mine.
When I was laid down on the grasses colored,
A song of grasshopper called the name of mine—,
When I walk about and about and see
Fall coming over and over the mountain,
 while loneliness there;
And when I breathe a song sweetly and cheerfully;
The light wind blows blending with them.
So soon have I to follow the breeze,
And take their joy with all mine.

KIM
DANG
SIG

WHAT IS POETRY?

Poetry lives wherever anyone uses words—for speaking or for writing. The motion of language belongs to the youngest child shaping words for *hurt, hungry, mother, scared.* Any expression of any emotion by any person of whatever age is usually put into rhythmical language, even if the expression is nothing more than, "Ouch! That hurts!"

Kim Dang Sig's poem (see page 3) proves that poetry does not come out of some remote area of human life called "art," but rather out of whatever in a person's life moves him. There is nothing strange about the reason for poetry, nothing, as people use to believe, odd about the writer of poetry.

"A company of mine is nature," says the poet, and therein he simply states what we all have said many times in our own less interesting way—"You *have* to feel good on a day like this." We live in the natural world of light and air and landscape and bird, and are one "company" with all of these things.

In reminding us that poetry is an instinctive way of expressing human excitement, Kim Dang Sig's poem has the great advantage over a more grammatically correct poem in that it sounds like the spontaneous sort of cry which we give at times when we are aroused by strong feelings. In this sense, Kim's poem is close to the original notion of poetry as inspired song. The directness and quick awkwardness of Kim's language is appropriate to the subject, which is a direct awareness of our sudden sense of belonging to all the earth.

Perhaps the most expressive lines in the poem are these:

4 A HANDFUL OF PENNIES

When I walk about and about and see
Fall coming over and over the mountain,
while loneliness there;

The feeling of that onrush of autumn which is like the strong
and ever-onward driving quality of life itself is finely suggested
in the line, "Fall coming over and over the mountain." The important thing is that fall does come on, even while loneliness is
there, almost as if it were coming because of the loneliness, and
seeking out the poet for company. Who has not known that
loneliness himself, and tried to find relief in association with
Nature?

Poetry is not about rare states of mind which are experienced
only by unique people called poets. It is about the most ordinary
sensations of our daily lives, put into words that make other
people feel the same sensations.

The extraordinary thing about poetry is the shape it gives to
those sensations in words. That is what is extraordinary about
Kim's poem: it truly reproduces the urgent attitude that must
have been in the poet's mind when he wrote the poem.

There is an old German poem by one of the troubadours
(called *Minnesingers,* because *minne* was the medieval word
for *love*) in which there is the line, "A straw-stem made me
glad today." That is the sort of quick perception which is the
whole quality of this Korean boy's poem.

Even a grasshopper's chirping seems to call his name—which
is a poet's way of saying that his mind is so full of the wonder
of the day that even this humble sound belongs to him. And the
line about the "grasses colored" does not get its success from
the delightful shock of reversing the order of the noun and adjective. If the poet had written, "When I was lying on colored
grass," he would have had the same fine effect. For the pleasure
in the poem is not in the refreshing quaintness of the language,
but in the emotional sweetness of the poet's mind as it comes
through the language.

In a sense, anyone who ever raises his voice for emphasis, in
rage or in joy, is using the method of poetry. For what makes
poetry possible is exactly the same thing that makes human life

possible: the fact that we are living creatures who feel, and who try to put those feelings into words, even if the sensation involved is no more than saying, about music—"I hate that noise." This sensible Korean boy has realized this, and it is the poem's special quality. His poem makes us more aware of life, not only aware of the poem, and that is the end of all art.

1. Is *What Is Poetry?* an analysis of poetry or of one specific poem? **2.** List all the general qualities of poetry treated in this essay and discuss by what means the author makes them clear to us. **3.** Show these qualities in operation in the parts of the poem that are not discussed in the essay. **4.** Using *The River Is a Piece of Sky* as a concrete example, write a short account of what you learned from Paul Engle.

As you read this poem, notice the sights and sounds and stillness that the poet selects to emphasize the bird's plight.

A Widow Bird Sate Mourning for Her Love

A widow bird sate mourning for her love
Upon a wintry bough;
The frozen wind crept on above,
The freezing stream below.

There was no leaf upon the forest bare,
No flower upon the ground,
And little motion in the air
Except the mill-wheel's sound.

PERCY
BYSSHE
SHELLEY

1. What one word does the first stanza of this poem suggest to you? The second stanza? **2.** Pick out all the words in each stanza that suggested the answer to number **1**. **3.** What is the only motion in the first stanza? How does it contribute to the impression created? Is there any sound in this stanza? **4.** What is the only sound in the second stanza? How does it contribute to the impression created? Is there any movement in this stanza? **5.** How does the rhyme pattern—*love above—bough below; bare air—ground sound*—move with the meaning of the poem?

As you read this next poem, give full swing to the lines as they unfold the situation of *anyone*, who may be someone you already know. Expect to find words in surprising places.

anyone
lived
in a pretty
how town

anyone lived in a pretty how town
(with up so floating many bells down)
spring summer autumn winter
he sang his didn't he danced his did.

Women and men (both little and small)
cared for anyone not at all
they sowed their isn't they reaped their same
sun moon stars rain

children guessed (but only a few
and down they forgot as up they grew
autumn winter spring summer)
that noone loved him more by more

when by now and tree by leaf
she laughed his joy she cried his grief
bird by snow and stir by still
anyone's any was all to her

someones married their everyones
laughed their cryings and did their dance
(sleep wake hope and then) they
said their nevers they slept their dream

stars rain sun moon
(and only the snow can begin to explain
how children are apt to forget to remember
with up so floating many bells down)

one day anyone died i guess
(and noone stooped to kiss his face)
busy folk buried them side by side
little by little and was by was

all by all and deep by deep
and more by more they dream their sleep
noone and anyone earth by april
wish by spirit and if by yes.

Women and men (both dong and ding)
summer autumn winter spring
reaped their sowing and went their came
sun moon stars rain

e e cummings

1. Do you know *anyone?* Who is he? Could Cummings have called him by a better name? **2.** Is *no one* a person? If so, who is he? If not, what does Cummings suggest by making him sound like one? **3.** Notice that almost all the lines in this poem swing like bells. Which lines do so especially well? Which ones don't at all? What does their movement suggest? Why are bells important to the poem? **4.** In every stanza there is a line similar to the line *spring summer autumn winter* or to the line *when by now and leaf by tree.* To what essential impression do these lines contribute? **5.** Does Cummings' unusual use of words make you feel annoyance or delight? Discuss. **6.** What special meanings does he create by the following lines?

> *he sang his didn't he danced his did.*
> > *they sowed their isn't they reaped their same*
> > > *and down they forgot as up they grew*
> > > > *that noone loved him more by more*

when by now and tree by leaf
bird by snow and stir by still

7. There are only two periods in the poem. Account for them.
8. Charles Hamm has set this poem to music. Track down the score and see if you can convince one of your classmates, a music student, or the school chorus to perform it.

If you do not take the conflict of hero and foe in this poem too seriously, you might end up finding sense in the nonsense.

Jabberwocky

'Twas brillig, and the slithy toves
    Did gyre and gimble in the wabe:
All mimsy were the borogoves,
    And the mome raths outgrabe.

"Beware the Jabberwock, my son!
    The jaws that bite, the claws that catch!
Beware the Jubjub bird, and shun
    The frumious Bandersnatch!"

He took his vorpal sword in hand:
    Long time the manxome foe he sought—
So rested he by the Tumtum tree,
    And stood awhile in thought.

And, as in uffish thought he stood,
    The Jabberwock, with eyes of flame,
Came whiffling through the tulgey wood,
    And burbled as it came!

One, two! One, two! and through and through
    The vorpal blade went snicker-snack!
He left it dead, and with its head
    He went galumphing back.

"And hast thou slain the Jabberwock?
    Come to my arms, my beamish boy!
O frabjous day! Callooh! Callay!"
    He chortled in his joy.

'Twas brillig, and the slithy toves
    Did gyre and gimble in the wabe:
All mimsy were the borogoves,
    And the mome raths outgrabe

LEWIS CARROLL

1. In spite of the surface of nonsense this poem has, you should be able to follow it as a story with setting and action. Describe the setting and trace the line of action. **2.** This poem is a kind of nonsense adventure poem. What elements suggest the adventure aspect? **3.** Some of the nonsense words connected with these elements especially reveal that the author is not taking the adventure too seriously. For instance, the monster is called a *Jabberwock* so that all the horror he might have is removed by the *Jabber* in his name. The hero stands *in uffish thought,* which comes so close to being *oafish* that it carries the same suggestion. Find all the other words like this and discuss the effect of their association. **4.** In THROUGH THE LOOKING GLASS, where *Jabberwocky* first appeared, Humpty Dumpty compares one kind of word in the poem to *portmanteau.* **-a** Investigate the origin and meaning of the word *portmanteau* and discuss the aptness of the comparison. **-b** Find all the words in *Jabberwocky* that seem to be portmanteau words. **-c** Find some actual English words that originated as portmanteau words or, as linguists call them, blends. *Dandle,* for instance, is a combination of *dance* and *handle.* **5.** Try a nonsense adventure story of your own about a Sniffelant, a Cringerator, a Blinkeneer, or a creation of your own.

Read this piece and you will see what a prose writer can do with the Jabberwock he finds in actual life.

What Do You Mean It *Was* Brillig?

JAMES THURBER

I was sitting at my typewriter one afternoon several weeks ago, staring at a piece of blank white paper, when Della walked in. "They are here with the reeves," she said. It did not surprise me that they were. With a colored woman like Della in the house it would not surprise me if they showed up with the toves. In Della's afternoon it is always brillig; she could outgrabe a mome rath on any wabe in the world. Only Lewis Carroll would have understood Della completely. I try hard enough. "Let them wait a minute," I said. I got out the big Century Dictionary and put it on my lap and looked up "reeve." It is an interesting word, like all of Della's words; I found out that there are four kinds of reeves. "Are they here with strings of onions?" I asked. Della said they were not. "Are they here with enclosures or pens for cattle, poultry, or pigs; sheepfolds?" Della said no sir. "Are they here with administrative officers?" From a little nearer the door Della said no again. "Then they've got to be here," I said, "with some females of the common European sandpiper." These scenes of ours take as much out of Della as they do out of me, but she is not a woman to be put down by a crazy man with a dictionary. "They are here with the reeves for the windas," said Della with brave stubbornness. Then, of course, I understood what they were there with: they were there with the Christmas wreaths for the windows. "Oh *those* reeves!" I said. We were both greatly relieved; we both laughed. Della and I never quite reach the breaking point; we just come close to it.
Della is a New England colored woman with nothing of the

South in her accent; she doesn't say "d" for "th" and she pro-
nounces her "r"s. Hearing her talk in the next room, you might
not know at first that she was colored. You might not know till
she said some such thing as "Do you want cretonnes for the
soup tonight?" (She makes wonderful cretonnes for the soup.)
I have not found out much about Della's words, but I have
learned a great deal about her background. She told me one day
that she has three brothers and that one of them works into a
garage and another works into an incinerator where they burn
the refuge. The one that works into the incinerator has been
working into it since the Armitage. That's what Della does to
you; she gives you incinerator perfectly and then she comes out
with the Armitage. I spent most of an hour one afternoon trying
to figure out what was wrong with the Armitage; I thought of
Armistead and armature and Armentières, and when I finally
hit on Armistice it sounded crazy. It still does. Della's third and
youngest brother is my favorite; I think he'll be yours, too, and
everybody else's. His name is Arthur and it seems that he has
just passed, with commendably high grades, his silver-service
eliminations. Della is delighted about that, but she is not half so
delighted about it as I am.

Della came to our house in Connecticut some months ago,
trailing her glory of cloudiness. I can place the date for you
approximately: it was while there were still a great many
fletchers about. "The lawn is full of fletchers," Della told me one
morning, shortly after she arrived, when she brought up my
orange juice. "You mean neighbors?" I said. "This early?" By
the way she laughed I knew that fletchers weren't people; at least
not people of flesh and blood. I got dressed and went downstairs
and looked up the word in the indispensable Century. A fletcher,
I found, is a man who makes arrows. I decided, but without a
great deal of conviction, that there couldn't be any arrow-makers
on my lawn at that hour in the morning and at this particular
period in history. I walked cautiously out the back door and
around to the front of the house—and there they were. I don't
know many birds but I do know flickers. A flicker is a bird
which, if it were really named fletcher, would be called flicker
by all the colored cooks in the United States. Out of a mild

curiosity I looked up "flicker" in the dictionary and I discovered that he is a bird of several aliases. When Della brought my toast and coffee into the dining room I told her about this. "Fletchers," I said, "are also golden-winged woodpeckers, yellowhammers, and high-holders." For the first time Della gave me the look that I was to recognize later, during the scene about the reeves. I have become very familiar with that look and I believe I know the thoughts that lie behind it. Della was puzzled at first because I work at home instead of in an office, but I think she has it figured out now. This man, she thinks, used to work into an office like anybody else, but he had to be sent to an institution; he got well enough to come home from the institution, but he is still not well enough to go back to the office. I could have avoided all these suspicions, of course, if I had simply come out in the beginning and corrected Della when she got words wrong. Coming at her obliquely with a dictionary only enriches the confusion; but I wouldn't have it any other way. I share with Della a form of escapism that is the most mystic and satisfying flight from actuality I have ever known. It may not always comfort me, but it never ceases to beguile me.

Every Thursday when I drive Della to Waterbury in the car for her day off, I explore the dark depths and the strange recesses of her nomenclature. I found out that she had been married for ten years but was now divorced; that is, her husband went away one day and never came back. When I asked her what he did for a living, she said he worked into a dove-wedding. "Into a what?" I asked. "Into a dove-wedding," said Della. It is one of the words I haven't figured out yet, but I am still working on it. "Where are you from, Mr. Thurl?" she asked me one day. I told her Ohio, and she said, "Ooooh, to be sure!" as if I had given her a clue to my crazy definitions, my insensitivity to the ordinary household nouns, and my ignorance of the commoner migratory birds. "Semantics, Ohio," I said. "Why, there's one of them in Massachusetts, too," said Della. "The one I mean," I told her, "is bigger and more confusing." "I'll bet it is," said Della.

Della told me the other day that she had had only one sister, a beautiful girl who died when she was twenty-one. "That's too bad," I said. "What was the matter?" Della had what was the matter at her tongue's tip. "She got tuberculosis from her teeth," she said, "and it went all through her symptom." I didn't know what to say to that except that my teeth were all right but that my symptom could probably be easily gone all through. "You work too much with your brain," said Della. I knew she was trying to draw me out about my brain and what had happened to it so that I could no longer work into an office, but I changed the subject. There is no doubt that Della is considerably worried about my mental condition. One morning when I didn't get up till noon because I had been writing letters until three o'clock, Della told my wife at breakfast what was the matter with me. "His mind works so fast his body can't keep up with it," she said. This diagnosis has shaken me not a little. I have decided to sleep longer and work less. I know exactly what will happen to me if my mind gets so far ahead of my body that my body can't catch up with it. They will come with a reeve and this time it won't be a red-and-green one for the window, it will be a black one for the door.

1. Which of these best identifies the nature of *What Do You Mean It* Was *Brillig?:* a story about Della; an account of Della's background; a study of Della's activity at Mr. Thurber's house; an account of Della's misuse of words; an analysis of Della's sense of humor? **2.** Discuss how the title fits the piece. **3.** How would you describe Mr. Thurber's attitude toward Della? To support your answer, give evidence of the piece itself. **4.** *What Do You Mean It* Was *Brillig?* is made up of a series of incidents which are not at all arranged in the order in which they occurred. Be prepared to defend the lack of actual time order. **5.** Compare and contrast the humor created by word play in this prose piece with that in *Eletelephony* and *Jabberwocky*.

Read this piece of prose to share the fresh view of a foreigner looking upon aspects of the English language which you take for granted.

ENGLISH IS A
QUEER LANGUAGE

ALICE HAMILTON, M.D.

To realize how queer it is, one must follow the struggles of an intellectual foreigner trying to learn English. That has been our experience since Bohus Petrzelka, a doctor of laws from Prague, with his wife and little daughter, took up his abode in the roomy ell of our house. Both Petrzelka and his wife knew German well (and hated it), but during the six years of the German occupation English was forbidden, and they forgot what they had learned in school and had to start from scratch. While little Jane lapped it up as a kitten laps milk, her parents struggled along, trying to reason out the why of many strange usages which we had never realized were strange. We tried to explain, but we found it surprisingly difficult.

Jarmila came to me with this puzzle. "Mrs. Green told me her mother is coming to visit her, and she is going to stay a week. How can she stay if she is going? How can she go if she is staying?" I could not explain, because never before had I realized that "going" may have nothing to do with the verb "to go," though the latter has its own present participle which seems identical. This other "going" deals only with the future: I am going to see this matter through; he is going to lose his job; she is going to be tired out. None of these examples have anything to do with "to go." All I could say was a helpless, "Well, it is idiomatic."

The next was also a surprise and also beyond my capacity to explain. Jarmila said, "Somebody asked me if I would not miss Clara while she is away. I know what it means when you say you miss the bus, but how can I miss her when she is not here?"

The next problem was much worse. Jarmila said, "Is it true that it means the same thing if you say, 'The house burned down' or 'The house burned up'? Surely if it burned up, that means the fire started in the cellar and worked up, while if it burned down, it started in the attic and worked down."

"No," I said, "it does not. You can say it either way and it means the same thing."

Jarmila sighed. "I do not understand this 'up.' I thought I knew the difference between up and down, but they tell me it is the same if I slow up my car or slow it down. And there are so many 'up's' that seem quite unnecessary. Why do they tell me to hurry up when I am not going upstairs? And why must I clean up the mess, wrap up the parcel, tidy up my desk? What has 'up' to do with it all?"

"Well," I began, rather helplessly, "perhaps 'clean up' seems more thorough than just 'clean.' "

Jarmila looked skeptical, and after a period of meditation she came back in triumph. "No," she said. " 'Up' has nothing to do with thoroughness. Look now. There are four ways you can use 'make up.' I make up the bed. I make up my mind. I make up my face when I put on rouge and lipstick. And Jane makes up with Anne when they have quarreled."

"Yes," I said, "and there is a fifth. I make up a story to entertain Jane."

Of course there was no explanation I could give her, and it sent me and the rest of the family on a search for the unnecessary "up's" we use all the time. You can put yourself to sleep chasing them down the alphabet from "add up" to "wake up," and you will find queer things, such as "up to now" and "it's up to you" and two "look up's," one meaning to raise one's eyes, the other to seek information from the encyclopedia. I gave up trying to explain "up."

What about "must"? There too the problem was quite new to me. Jarmila said, "Does not 'must' carry the meaning of compulsion or command, from oneself or somebody else? But the other day I was telling some of the neighbors how long it took me to drive to Hammonnassett Beach, and one of them said, 'You must have lost your way,' and then another said, 'You must have been pretty tired by the time you reached home.' Now nobody commanded me to lose my way or to get tired. So why 'must'?"

The next problem was a tough one. Bohus came back from work (a Czech doctor of laws cannot practice law in this country because his study has been based on Napoleonic law) saying that a man had told him that if he learned all the ways there are in English of using the word "get" he would have mastered the language. That started us on a hunt for "get," which yielded a more abundant harvest than did Jarmila's "up."

Just try to follow "get" down the alphabet from "get along with somebody" to "get well." Of course we get sick, too, we get ahead of somebody, get behind in our work, get even with somebody, get homesick, get cold feet, get discharged, get rich, and so on ad infinitum. We can even, if inelegantly, "get going," and as a final triumph, we can "get our comeuppance," thus combining the two troublesome words in a very useful but quite unexplainable expression.

Jarmila and Bohus became experts at finding English words that mean three or four or more different things. Take "fall," for instance. We fall in love, we fall sick, we love the fall of the year, we fear the fall-out from the atom bomb, Christmas Day falls on a Friday. And if we are old-fashioned enough to say "it fell out," we mean "it came to pass." We keep house, we keep books, we keep silence, we keep the Sabbath day holy. We put on a hat, put off till tomorrow, put out a fire, put up with disagreeable people.

Even so simple an expression as "back and forth" arouses criticism, because it is illogical. "One can not go back if one does not first go forth. Why do you not say 'forth and back'?"

Our Czech friends tell us that the Czech language is logical and that one can explain it reasonably. English, I find, is not.

1. Like *What Do You Mean It Was Brillig?,* this essay is composed of a series of situations concerning language problems. Here, however, they are arranged in the order of occurrence.

Show how the first sentence of *English Is a Queer Language* lays the plan for this arrangement. Contrast the problem of Della with that of the Petrzelkas to see if the nature of each requires the arrangement provided for it. **2.** Which provides the essential enjoyment in *English Is a Queer Language*—the content or the method of telling the situations? Compare or contrast it with Thurber's essay in regard to the source of enjoyment. **3.** Have you learned enough of any language to encounter problems similar to the Petrzelkas' problems with English? If so, write an account of your own discovery of a *queer language*. **4.** Find some oddities of the English language which the Petrzelkas missed. Write about them in a verse similar to this verse by Katherine Buxbaum:

> I came beneath a pinetree bough
> When I was searching for my cough.
> I could not reach the pine cones, though,
> The branch was high and I was lough.
> "Ah, me," I cried, with rueful laugh,
> "Would that I were a tall giraugh."
> Just then a wind came hurtling through,
> The branches cracked, so fierce it blough.
> This blast, so shrill it made me cough
> Dislodged the cones, which tumbled ough,
> And on it went with angry sough;
> I put my treasure in my mough
> And started home across the slough
> Forgetting what I'd come to dough.
> Bossy was standing by her trough;
> Did I mistake, or did she scough?

Read this chapter from Eloise Lambert's OUR LANGUAGE to see how a writer arranges facts interestingly.

Words To Take Along

ELOISE LAMBERT

Whenever people plan to go on a trip, one of the first questions they ask themselves is: "What shall I take with me? What clothes will I need?" Especially if they are going by air, they will need to travel light. So they sort out their things carefully; old blue jeans and loafers that they wear only in the house will be left at home; ski clothes will be left behind if they are going to Bermuda or some tropical resort; sun suits, on the other hand, will be left behind if they are going to the north woods. If they're going on a long trip around the world, they'll try to pick out one of their most conservative outfits to take along, things that will look right almost any time and place. If they find they need other things, special things for special places along the way, they will pick them up where they are needed; perhaps they'll buy native things that will fit in with whatever the style of the place may be.

What applies to clothes can apply also to words. Before you set out on your trip to see the world of your language, you might find it worth while to sort out your words just as you sort out your clothes. For just as you have comfortable old jeans and loafers that you wear only around the house, so you have words that you use only at home. If you doubt that you have such "old blue jeans" words, stop and think a minute. All families have words that they use only among themselves. Sometimes we use them so naturally and unconsciously that we aren't aware of them, but they are there.

They come into being in lots of ways.

Sometimes they are family words that are coined by some member of the family just for fun, like the word "galumpus" that one family uses to refer to their electric mixer. Sometimes they are shortened words, like the "Cue" and "Come" that are used by one family for "Thank you" and "You're welcome." Sometimes families give proper names to family belongings, like "Suzabella" for the family sedan; or sometimes they give one to a pest, like "Amos" for "A mosquito." All of these words are perfectly good words within the family, where everyone knows them and understands what they mean, but they wouldn't be much good anywhere else or with other people.

All of this brings us back to the secret of language that you discovered for yourself when you saw that you'd have to shift from "abbadabba" to "dog." It isn't the word itself, or the sound, that is important. The only really important thing is that the group in which it is to be used should agree that that particular word means one certain thing. It can be a large group of 250 million English speakers who all agree that "shoe" means something you wear on the foot, or it can be a small family group of four (or even two) who agree that "galumpus" will mean "electric mixer" to them. What your own family words are, only you and your family will know, but look at them, and the way they came into being will show you better than anything else how words begin.

Once you have looked over these "old blue jeans" words, you will probably decide not to take them along, because they wouldn't be of much use to you even as far away as across the street. So you look a little farther and you find that you have some "casual" words. These are words which, just like your "casual" clothes, look all right to wear in your own home town and places near by, but you're not sure they would be just right anywhere else. What these casual words are will depend on where you live, just as where you live determines whether your casual clothes are woolen slacks and sweaters or shorts and tropical shirts and blouses. You will have to pick them out of your own vocabulary.

Here are samples of what these words may be like. If you

live in or near Boston, one of them will almost surely be "tonic"; you use this word naturally and easily to mean "soft drink" and it's a perfectly good word for it in that area, but it won't get you what you want in Texas, California, or any other place in the country. In other localities, you would have to ask for "soft drink," "soda," "pop," or "soda-pop." If you live in or near Philadelphia, one of your casual words may be "hoagy," which you and everyone else in that area knows and understands to mean a very large sandwich; but if you hope to get that kind of sandwich in New York, you'll have to ask for a "hero sandwich"; in Pittsburgh, for a "submarine sandwich"; and in other sections of the country, for a "jumbo," or a "Dagwood," or any of a dozen other terms. Practically every community in the country has its own local words of this sort. Sometimes you don't realize you are using strictly local words until you go to some distant place and find you are misunderstood or not understood at all when you try to use one.

These "casual" or local words start in much the same way as the family words. One person coins the word, others hear it, and if it catches their imagination they adopt it and pass it on to others. Soon everyone in that community will be in general unspoken agreement that that word means that one thing, and it will be an accepted local word. Occasionally a word coined in this way gets publicity and catches the imagination of the whole country, as was the case with "hot dog," which grew very fast from a local word into an all-American word. However, many of the local words remain strictly local. It's a good idea, then, to look into your five-thousand use words and pick out the "casual" words and leave them behind with your "at home" words. They can travel short distances, but on a long trip they could lead to misunderstanding and confusion.

In addition to your "at home" words and your "casual" local words, you will find that just as you have a lot of clothes that are well suited to your section of the country, you also have a lot of words that belong especially in your part of the nation. In fact, the whole general tone of both your wardrobe and your vocabulary is determined by the part of the country you live in. If you live in the South, you will have a predominance of warm-weather clothes, shorts, swim suits, sandals and tropical sport shirts, all of which are what you need in the South, but which wouldn't do you much good in the Maine woods, where you'd find a Mackinaw lumber jacket, high-lace boots and flannel shirts much more suitable. If you live in the ranch country of the West, you'll probably have levis, cowboy riding boots, and maybe even ten-gallon hats, and these are very good for that section of the country; but they would look a little odd on the New York subways, where most people would be wearing business suits and street clothes suited to commuting and the business world.

It's the same way with your words. If you live in the South you'll have in your list words like "spoonbread," "grits," "corn-pone," "chess-pie," "praline," "black-eyed peas"; you'll have "bayou" and "levee"; you'll have "dragline" for a steam shovel; and you'll probably have "tote" for "carry" and "poke" for "paper bag." These words are fine for the South, but you won't find them very usable in the western ranch country, where words for general use include "pan-bread," "arroyo," "mesa," "mesquite," "sagebrush," "roundup," "pinto," "corral," and "dogie." Neither will you find either of these sets of words usable in New York, where you'll need "Palisades," "subway," "El," "Hudson tubes," "pizza," "borscht," "bagels," "lox," "strudel," and "stoop."

A look at these words gives you some idea of how sectional words come into being. Some of them (like "bayou," "mesa," "Palisades") are sectional because they refer to some geographical feature which exists in one section and not in another. Some are sectional because they refer to things that grow in one section and not in another, like the "mesquite" bush of the Southwest. Some refer to a food that may be popular and much used in one section and not in another, like the "black-eyed peas" of the South. Some may be local coinages that have spread over a whole section, like "tote" for "carry."

There is one thing that it is good to know about these sectional words. Just as your clothes bear American trademarks, regardless of whether they are swim suits for the South, Mackinaws for the North, levis for the West, or business suits of New York, so your words bear American trademarks. They will be recognized as American wherever you take them. A New Yorker will recognize and understand "bayou," "mesquite," and "corral," and a person from New Orleans will understand "Palisades" and "El," and a Nevadan will understand "levee" and "subway." Practically every American will have all of these sectional words in his recognition vocabulary (that is, they will be among the thirty or forty thousand words he knows and recognizes), but they may not be among the five thousand that he uses freely and easily in his everyday speech. A man in New York doesn't really need to use the word "pinto" very often, neither does a man in dry, arid Arizona need the word "levee" very often. However, you can take most of your sectional words and expressions almost anywhere in the country. Some of them might call for a little explaining here and there; and some of them might sound a little odd and out of place, like cowboy clothes on New York's Fifth Avenue; but you can make do with them if they are all you have.

Luckily, however, they are not all you have, because after you have looked over all your words, and sorted out the "at home" and the "casual" home-town words, and the sectional ones, you will discover that you have a lot that are not in any one of these special groups. These will be your general American words, and you will have more of them probably than any other kind. Words for all of the things that we all know about and use in common, wherever we may happen to live in the United States; words like "shoe," "hat," "dress," "suit"; words like "bread," "water," "train," "television"; words like "book," "newspaper," "dictionary"; and tens of thousands of similar words. These are the solid English words which, like our more conservative clothes, are suitable and usable any time and anywhere. They are the words we want most of all to take along. They will see us through a trip not only around the entire United States, but around the entire English-speaking world.

1. Though *Words To Take Along* is also concerned with the use of language, how does it differ essentially from the preceding prose pieces—in fact, from all the writing studied so far? **2.** How does this difference affect the division of material? Is the division of events or of ideas? How does it affect the way the author expresses herself? **3.** Make a small guidebook to supplement the English dictionary for a foreigner coming to live at your house. Make three divisions in the book: at home words, casual local words, and regional words. Make them peculiar to your own family, to your neighborhood, to your section of the country.

Have you recently reread these two addresses by presidents of the United States? Read them now and you will discover what results when a government official also knows how to build with words.

INAUGURAL ADDRESS

JOHN F. KENNEDY

We observe today not a victory of party but a celebration of freedom—symbolizing an end as well as a beginning—signifying renewal as well as change. For I have sworn before you and Almighty God the same solemn oath our forebears prescribed nearly a century and three-quarters ago.

The world is very different now. For man holds in his mortal hands the power to abolish all form of human poverty and to abolish all form of human life. And yet the same revolutionary beliefs for which our forebears fought are still at issue around the globe—the belief that the rights of man come not from the generosity of the state but from the hand of God.

We dare not forget today that we are the heirs of that first revolution. Let the word go forth from this time and place, to friend and foe alike, that the torch has been passed to a new generation of Americans—born in this century, tempered by war, disciplined by a cold and bitter peace, proud of our ancient heritage—and unwilling to witness or permit the slow undoing of those human rights to which this nation has always been committed, and to which we are committed today.

Let every nation know, whether it wish us well or ill, that we shall pay any price, bear any burden, meet any hardship, support any friend or oppose any foe in order to assure the survival and success of liberty.

This much we pledge—and more.

To those old allies whose cultural and spiritual origins we share, we pledge the loyalty of faithful friends. United, there is little we cannot do in a host of new co-operative ventures. Divided, there is little we can do—for we dare not meet a powerful challenge at odds and split asunder.

To those new states whom we now welcome to the ranks of the free, we pledge our word that one form of colonial control shall not have passed merely to be replaced by a far more iron tyranny. We shall not always expect to find them supporting our every view. But we shall always hope to find them strongly supporting their own freedom—and to remember that, in the past, those who foolishly sought to find power by riding on the tiger's back inevitably ended up inside.

To those peoples in the huts and villages of half the globe struggling to break the bonds of mass misery, we pledge our best efforts to help them help themselves, for whatever period is required—not because the Communists are doing it, not because we seek their votes, but because it is right. If the free society cannot help the many who are poor, it can never save the few who are rich.

To our sister republics south of our border, we offer a special pledge—to convert our good words into good deeds—in a new alliance for progress—to assist free men and free governments in casting off the chains of poverty. But this peaceful revolution of hope cannot become the prey of hostile powers. Let all our neighbors know that we shall join with them to oppose aggression or subversion anywhere in the Americas. And let every other power know that this hemisphere intends to remain the master of its own house.

To that world assembly of sovereign states, the United Nations, our last best hope in an age where the instruments of war have far outpaced the instruments of peace, we renew our pledge of support—to prevent its becoming merely a forum for invective—to strengthen its shield of the new and the weak—and to enlarge the area to which its writ may run.

Finally, to those nations who would make themselves our adversary, we offer not a pledge but a request: That both sides begin anew the quest for peace, before the dark powers of destruction unleashed by science engulf all humanity in planned or accidental self-destruction.

We dare not tempt them with weakness. For only when our arms are sufficient beyond doubt can we be certain beyond doubt that they will never be employed.

But neither can two great and powerful groups of nations take comfort from their present course—both sides overburdened by the cost of modern weapons, both rightly alarmed by the steady spread of the deadly atom, yet both racing to alter that uncertain balance of terror that stays the hand of mankind's final war.

So let us begin anew—remembering on both sides that civility is not a sign of weakness, and sincerity is always subject to proof. Let us never negotiate out of fear. But let us never fear to negotiate.

Let both sides explore what problems unite us instead of belaboring the problems that divide us.

Let both sides, for the first time, formulate serious and precise proposals for the inspection and control of arms—and bring the absolute power to destroy other nations under the absolute control of all nations.

Let both sides join to invoke the wonders of science instead of its terrors. Together let us explore the stars, conquer the deserts, eradicate disease, tap the ocean depths, and encourage the arts and commerce.

Let both sides unite to heed in all corners of the earth the command of Isaiah—to "undo the heavy burdens . . . (and) Let the oppressed go free."

And if a beachhead of co-operation can be made in the jungles of suspicion, let both sides join in the next task: Creating, not a new balance of power, but a new world of law, where the strong are just and the weak secure and the peace preserved forever.

All this will not be finished in the first 100 days. Nor will it be finished in the first 1,000 days, nor in the life of this administration, nor even perhaps in our lifetime on this planet. But let us begin.

In your hands, my fellow citizens, more than in mine, will rest the final success or failure of our course. Since this country was founded, each generation has been summoned to give testimony to its national loyalty. The graves of young Americans who answered that call encircle the globe.

Now the trumpet summons us again—not as a call to bear arms, though arms we need—not as a call to battle, though embattled we are—but a call to bear the burden of a long twilight struggle, year in and year out, "Rejoicing in hope, patient in tribulation"—a struggle against the common enemies of man: Tyranny, poverty, disease, and war itself.

Can we forge against these enemies a grand and global alliance, north and south, east and west, that can assure a more fruitful life for all mankind? Will you join in that historic effort?

In the long history of the world, only a few generations have been granted the role of defending freedom in its hour of maximum danger. I do not shrink from this responsibility—I welcome it. I do not believe that any of us would exchange places with any other people or any other generation. The energy, the faith, and the devotion which we bring to this endeavor will light our country and all who serve it—and the glow from that fire can truly light the world.

And so, my fellow Americans: Ask not what your country will do for you—ask what you can do for your country.

My fellow citizens of the world: Ask not what America will do for you, but what together we can do for the freedom of man.

Finally, whether you are citizens of America or of the world, ask of us the same high standards of strength and sacrifice that we shall ask of you. With a good conscience our only sure reward, with history the final judge of our deeds, let us go forth to lead the land we love, asking His blessing and His help, but knowing that here on earth God's work must truly be our own.

THE GETTYSBURG ADDRESS

ABRAHAM LINCOLN

Fourscore and seven years ago our fathers brought forth on this continent a new nation, conceived in liberty and dedicated to the proposition that all men are created equal.

Now we are engaged in a great civil war, testing whether that nation, or any nation so conceived and so dedicated, can long endure. We are met on a great battlefield of that war. We have come to dedicate a portion of that field, as a final resting-place for those who here gave their lives that that nation might live. It is altogether fitting and proper that we should do this.

But, in a larger sense, we cannot dedicate—we cannot consecrate—we cannot hallow—this ground. The brave men, living and dead, who struggled here, have consecrated it, far above our poor power to add or detract. The world will little note, nor long remember, what we say here, but it can never forget what they did here. It is for us the living, rather, to be dedicated here to the unfinished work which they who fought here have thus far so nobly advanced. It is rather for us to be here dedicated to the great task remaining before us—that from these honored dead we take increased devotion to that cause for which they gave the last full measure of devotion—that we here highly resolve that these dead shall not have died in vain—that this nation, under God, shall have a new birth of freedom—and that government of the people, by the people, for the people shall not perish from the earth.

INAUGURAL ADDRESS, JOHN F. KENNEDY

1. Although *Words To Take Along* is also addressed directly to an audience, it has an approach that is different from this inaugural speech. Identify and describe the difference. **2.** What is the common effect of words and phrases like *beginning, renewal, new generation of Americans, proud of our ancient heritage*? After you have discovered it, find all the other expressions that contribute to it. **3.** The body of this speech is made up of a series of pledges and of exhortations. Examine them to see how they broaden and deepen the appeal to the audience. **4.** Find sentences which you think are the kind that will often be quoted. Exactly what aspects do you think give them a quotable quality? **5.** Find the limerick about the young lady from Niger and bring it to class. Be prepared to discuss the force of Mr. Kennedy's reference to it.

THE GETTYSBURG ADDRESS

1. Almost every idea in this address is a form of beginning, or of end, or of both in balance. Classify all the ideas accordingly and discuss the aptness of these unifying ideas to the general time, the specific occasion, and the purpose of Lincoln's speech. **2.** Anything that is beautiful involves a pleasing combination of repetition and variety. Discuss how the movement of Lincoln's sentences is created by this kind of combination. **3.** List and explain all the specific choices of idea and vocabulary that you think would especially inspire Lincoln's audience.

Read *Brothering Fish* and investigate how the author manages to carry you so far away from where you really are.

Brothering Fish

WILLIAM BEEBE

You are standing on a metal ladder in water up to your neck. Something round and heavy is slipped gently over your head, and a metal helmet rests upon your shoulders. Thus were the knights of old helmed by their squires for the grim business of war. Instead of a slotted vizor, however, you find two large frames of glass before your eyes. Turning your head, you see emerald waves breaking upon the distant beach of ivory, backed by feathery palms waving in the sunlight against a sky of pure azure.

You wave good-by to your grinning friend at the pump, and slowly descend, climbing down step by step. For a brief space of time the palms and the beach show intermittently through waves which are now breaking over your very face. Then the world changes. There is no more harsh sunlight, but delicate blue-greens with a fluttering of shadows everywhere. Huge pink and orange growths rise on all sides—you know they are living corals, just as you know that the perfect clouds in the sky visible in the earliest light of dawn from Darjeeling are not clouds, but the snow peaks of the distant Himalayas. The first little people of this strange realm greet you—a quartet of swimming rainbows—four gorgeously tinted fish who rush up and peer in at you. You reach out for them, and they vanish.

Now your feet touch ground and you walk slowly about on the cleanest white sand in the world. An ostrich feather of a sea-plume as tall as yourself sweeps against you; it is royalpurple and might well be some weird fern from Mars. On a mound of sand you gently seat yourself, sand-colored crabs and small fish skittering just out of the way. You lean against a fretwork of purest marble while at your elbow is a rounded table of lapis lazuli on which are blossoming three flowers—flowers unearthly and which lean toward you of their own free will. Their petals are resplendent in hues of gold and malachite, and are fluted and fringed like some rare and unknown orchid. You reach forward to pluck one, and, faster than the eye can follow, the blossoms disappear beneath the fur of lapis velvet from which they seemed to sprout.

Dozens of fishes, all strange, all graceful and beautiful, play about you, nibbling at the coral, rushing toward the sponge which you have lifted from its place, hoping for some disturbed tidbit. When you sit quietly, they gather closer and peer in through the glass at you again and again. Their absurd mouths forever open and close, and if you are a good lip-reader, you cannot fail to decipher the syllables which seem to issue in watery waves. They say, "Oh! Oh! Brother! Brother! Oh! Oh!" And you answer them in kind, speaking from the safe, dry, airy room of your helmet. They are so friendly, so curious, so utterly unlike the nervous, useless-lived inmates of our aquariums.

Your attention swings from wonders to marvels and back again. You begin to say things to yourself, gasps of surprise, inarticulate sounds of awe; you are troubled with a terrible sense of loss that (as the case may be) twenty, thirty, or fifty years of your life have passed and gone without your knowing of the ease of entry into this new world. *Are* you under water? There is no sense of wetness; the air you breathe is, if anything, better than that in the motorboat rocking overhead. You hold up your hand and see little washer-woman's wrinkles on the soles of your fingers, and you realize you are where you are. A great blue enameled fish glides past, then suddenly stands straight upon his head and mumbles something; a skein of fairy lace drifts against your helmet; to your friends in the boat it is merely a school of jellyfish.

Only a moment has passed since you left the world overhead, or was it many hours? A gentle tug comes along the hose, and you resent this reminder of an existence which you had almost forgotten. But you rise and half walk, half float to the swaying ladder, and regretfully mount it. You find that you have been down forty minutes and another impatient adventurer is waiting to take your place. You had planned to tell the others all about it, but you suddenly find yourself wordless. You exclaim something bromidic which sounds like Marvelous! Great! Wonderful! then relapse futilely into silence and look helplessly into the distance where the emerald waves still break and the palms wave as if fairyland had not intervened in your life since you saw them last.

All I ask of each reader is this— Don't die without having borrowed, stolen, purchased, or made a helmet of sorts, to glimpse for yourself this new world. Books, aquaria, and glass-bottomed boats are, to such an experience, only what a timetable is to an actual tour, or what a dried, dusty bit of coral in the whatnot of the best parlor is to this unsuspected realm of gorgeous life and color existing with us today on the self-same planet Earth.

1. Who or what is the center of this account? Give evidence from the beginning situation, the continued movement, and the final plea. **2.** Can you see a relation between your answer to **1** and the primary effect of this piece? **3.** How does the ending of *Brothering Fish* return the reader to the beginning in regard to every concrete detail? **4.** By reference to a knight's helmet, what does Beebe suggest about the experience he describes? **5.** Examine each underwater sight Beebe presents and discuss how he makes it vivid.

Read *I Get a Colt to Break In* to discover how a writer can look back on childhood experience and, with increased delight and wisdom, rebuild it with words.

I Get a Colt to Break In

LINCOLN STEFFENS

Colonel Carter gave me a colt. I had my pony, and my father meanwhile had bought a pair of black carriage horses and a cow, all of which I had to attend to when we had no "man." And servants were hard to get and keep in those days; the women married, and the men soon quit service to seize opportunities always opening. My hands were pretty full, and so was the stable. But Colonel Carter seemed to think that he had promised me a horse. He had not; I would have known it if he had. No matter. He thought he had, and maybe he did promise himself to give me one. That was enough. The kind of man that led immigrant trains across the continent and delivered them safe, sound, and together where he promised would keep his word. One day he drove over from Stockton, leading a two-year-old which he brought to our front door and turned over to me as mine. Such a horse!

She was a cream-colored mare with a black forelock, mane, and tail and a black stripe along the middle of her back. Tall, slender, high-spirited, I thought then—I think now—that she was the most beautiful of horses. Colonel Carter had bred and reared her with me and my uses in mind. She was a careful cross of a mustang mare and a thoroughbred stallion, with the stamina of the wild horse and the speed and grace of the racer. And she had a sense of fun. As Colonel Carter got down out of his buggy and went up to her, she snorted, reared, flung her head high in the air, and, coming down beside him, tucked her nose affectionately under his arm.

"I have handled her a lot," he said. "She is as kind as a kitten, but she is as sensitive as a lady. You can spoil her by one mistake. If you ever lose your temper, if you ever abuse her, she will be ruined forever. And she is unbroken. I might have had her broken to ride for you, but I didn't want to. I want you to do it. I have taught her to lead, as you see; had to, to get her over here. But here she is, an unbroken colt; yours. You take and you break her. You're only a boy, but if you break this colt right, you'll be a man—a young man, but a man. And I'll tell you how."

Now, out West, as everybody knows, they break in a horse by riding out to him in his wild state, lassoing, throwing, and saddling him; then they let him up, frightened and shocked, with a yelling bronco-buster astride of him. The wild beast bucks, the cowboy drives his spurs into him, and off they go, jumping, kicking, rearing, falling, till by the weight of the man, the lash, and the rowels, the horse is broken—in body and spirit. This was not the way I was to break my colt.

"You must break her to ride without her ever knowing it," Colonel Carter said. "You feed and you clean her—you; not the stable man. You lead her out to water and to walk. You put her on a long rope and let her play, calling her to you and gently pulling on the rope. Then you turn her loose in the grass lot there and, when she has romped till tired, call her. If she won't come, leave her. When she wants water or food, she will run to your call, and you will pet and feed and care for her." He went on for half an hour, advising me in great detail how to proceed. I wanted to begin right away. He laughed. He let me lead her around to the stable, water her, and put her in the stable and feed her.

There I saw my pony. My father, sisters, and Colonel Carter saw me stop and look at my pony.

"What'll you do with him?" one of my sisters asked. I was bewildered for a moment. What should I do with the little red horse? I decided at once.

"You can have him," I said to my sisters.

"No," said Colonel Carter, "not yet. You can give your sisters the pony by and by, but you'll need him till you have taught the colt to carry you and a saddle—months; and you must not hurry. You must learn patience, and you will if you give the colt time to learn it, too. Patience and control. You can't control a young horse unless you can control yourself. Can you shoot?" he asked suddenly.

I couldn't. I had a gun and I had used it some, but it was a rifle, and I could not bring down with it such game as there was around Sacramento—birds and hares. Colonel Carter looked at my father, and I caught the look. So did my father. I soon had a shotgun. But at the time Colonel Carter turned to me and said:

"Can't shoot straight, eh? Do you know what that means? That means that you can't control a gun, and that means that you can't control yourself, your eye, your hands, your nerves. You are wriggling now. I tell you that a good shot is always a good man. He may be a 'bad man' too, but he is quiet, strong, steady in speech, gait, and mind. No matter, though. If you break in this colt right, if you teach her her paces, she will teach you to shoot and be quiet."

He went off downtown with my father, and I started away with my colt. I fed, I led, I cleaned her, gently, as if she were made of glass; she was playful and willing, a delight. When Colonel Carter came home with my father for supper, he questioned me.

"You should not have worked her today," he said. "She has come all the way from Stockton and must be tired. Yes, yes, she would not show fatigue; too fine for that, and too young to be wise. You have got to think for her, consider her as you would your sisters."

Sisters! I thought; I had never considered my sisters. I did not say that, but Colonel Carter laughed and nodded to my sisters. It was just as if he had read my thought. But he went on to draw on my imagination a centaur: the colt as a horse's body —me, a boy, as the head and brains of one united creature. I liked that. I would be that. I and the colt: a centaur.

After Colonel Carter had gone home, I went to work on my new horse. The old one, the pony, I used only for business: to go to fires, to see my friends, run errands, and go hunting with my new shotgun. But the game that had all my attention was the breaking in of the colt, the beautiful cream-colored mare, who soon knew me—and my pockets. I carried sugar to reward her when she did right, and she discovered where I carried it; so did the pony, and when I was busy they would push their noses into my pockets, both of which were torn down a good deal of the time. But the colt learned. I taught her to run around a circle, turn and go the other way at a signal. My sisters helped me. I held the long rope and the whip (for signaling), while one of the girls led the colt; it was hard work for them, but they took it in turns. One would lead the colt round and round till I snapped the whip; then she would turn, turning the colt, till the colt did it all by herself. And she was very quick. She shook hands with each of her four feet. She let us run under her, back and forth. She was slow only to carry me. Following Colonel Carter's instructions, I began by laying my arm or a surcingle over her back. If she trembled, I drew it slowly off. When she could abide it, I tried buckling it, tighter and tighter. I laid over her, too, a blanket, folded at first, then open, and, at last, I slipped up on her myself, sat there a second, and as she trembled, slid off. My sisters held her for me, and when I could get up and sit there a moment or two, I tied her at a block, and we, my sisters and I, made a procession of mounting and dismounting. She soon got used to this and would let us slide off her rump, but it was a long, long time before she would carry me.

That we practiced by leading her along a high curb where I could get on as she walked, ride a few steps, and then, as she felt me and crouched, slip off. She never did learn to carry a girl on her back; my sisters had to lead her while I rode. This was not purposeful. I don't know just how it happened, but I do remember the first time I rode on my colt all around the lot and how, when I put one of the girls up, she refused to repeat. She shuddered, shook, and frightened them off.

While we were breaking in the colt, a circus came to town. The ring was across the street from our house. Wonderful! I lived in that circus for a week. I saw the show but once, but I marked the horse trainers, and in the mornings when they were not too busy I told them about my colt, showed her to them, and asked them how to train her to do circus tricks. With their hints I taught the colt to stand up on her hind legs, kneel, lie down, and balance on a small box. This last was easier than it looked. I put her first on a low big box and taught her to turn on it, then got a little smaller box upon which she repeated what she did on the big one. By and by we had her so that she would step up on a high box so small that her four feet were almost touching, and there also she would turn.

The circus man gave me one hint that was worth all the other tricks put together. "You catch her doing something of herself that looks good," he said, "and then you keep her at it." It was thus that I taught her to bow to people. The first day I rode her out on to the streets was a proud one for me and for the colt, too, apparently. She did not walk, she danced; perhaps she was excited, nervous; anyhow I liked the way she threw up her head, champed at the bit, and went dancing, prancing down the street. Everybody stopped to watch us, and so, when she began to sober down, I picked her up again with heel and rein, saying, "Here's people, Lady," and she would show off to my delight. By constant repetition I had her so trained that she would single-foot, head down, along a country road till we came to a house or a group of people. Then I'd say, "People, Lady," and up would go her head, and her feet would dance.

But the trick that set the town talking was her bowing to anyone I spoke to. "Lennie Steffens' horse bows to you," people said, and she did. I never told how it was done—by accident. Dogs used to run out at us, and the colt enjoyed it; she kicked at them sometimes with both hind hoofs. I joined her in the game, and being able to look behind more conveniently than she could, I watched the dogs until they were in range, then gave the colt a signal to kick. "Kick, gal," I'd say, and tap her ribs with my heel. We used to get dogs together that way; the colt would kick them over and over and leave them yelping in the road. Well, one day when I met a girl I knew I lifted my hat, probably muttered a "Good day," and I must have touched the colt with my heel. Anyway, she dropped her head and kicked—not much; there was no dog near, so she had responded to my unexpected signal by what looked like a bow. I caught the idea and kept her at it. Whenever I wanted to bow to a girl or anybody else, instead of saying, "Good day," I muttered, "Kick, gal," spurred her lightly, and—the whole centaur bowed and was covered with glory and conceit.

Yes, conceit. I was full of it, and the colt was quite as bad. One day my chum Hjalmar came into town on his Black Bess, blanketed. She had had a great fistula cut out of her shoulder and had to be kept warm. I expected to see her weak and dull; but no, the good old mare was champing and dancing, like my colt.

"What is it makes her so?" I asked, and Hjalmar said he didn't know, but he thought she was proud of the blanket. A great idea. I had a gaudy horse blanket. I put it on the colt, and I could hardly hold her. We rode down the main street together, both horses and both boys, so full of vanity that everybody stopped to smile.

We pranced, the black and the yellow, all the way down J Street, up K Street, and agreed that we'd do it again, often. Only, I said, we wouldn't use blankets. If the horses were proud of a blanket, they'd be proud of anything unusually conspicuous. We tried a flower next time. I fixed a big rose on my colt's bridle just under her ear and it was great—she pranced downtown with her head turned, literally, to show off her flower. We had to change the decoration from time to time, put on a ribbon, or a bell, or a feather, but, really, it was not necessary for my horse. Old Black Bess needed an incentive to act up, but all I had to do to my horse was to pick up the reins, touch her with my heel, and say, "People"; she would dance from one side of the street to the other, asking to be admired. As she was. As we were.

I would ride down to my father's store, jump off my prancing colt in the middle of the street, and run up into the shop. The colt, free, would stop short, turn, and follow me right up on the sidewalk, unless I bade her wait. If anyone approached her while I was gone, she would snort, rear, and strike. No stranger could get near her. She became a frightened, frightening animal, and yet when I came into sight she would run to me, put her head down, and as I straddled her neck, she would throw up her head and pitch me into my seat, facing backward, of course. I whirled around right, and off we'd go, the vainest boy and the proudest horse in the state.

"Hey, give me a ride, will you?" some boy would ask.

"Sure," I'd say, and jump down and watch that boy try to catch and mount my colt. He couldn't. Once a cowboy wanted to try her, and he caught her; he dodged her forefeet, grabbed the reins, and in one spring was on her back. I never did that again. My colt reared, then bucked; and, as the cowboy kept his seat, she shuddered, sank to the ground, and rolled over. He slipped aside and would have risen with her, but I was alarmed and begged him not to. She got up at my touch and followed me so close that she stepped on my heel and hurt me. The cowboy saw the point.

"If I were you, kid," he said, "I'd never let anybody mount that colt. She's too good."

That, I think, was the only mistake I made in the rearing of Colonel Carter's gift-horse. My father differed from me. He discovered another error or sin, and thrashed me for it. My practice was to work hard on a trick, privately, and when it was perfect, let him see it. I would have the horse out in our vacant lot doing it as he came home to supper. One evening, as he approached the house, I was standing, whip in hand, while the colt, quite free, was stepping carefully over the bodies of a lot of girls, all my sisters and all their girl friends. My father did not express the admiration I expected; he·was frightened and furious. "Stop that!" he called and he came running around into the lot, took the whip, and lashed me with it. I tried to explain; the girls tried to help me explain.

I had seen in the circus a horse that stepped thus over a row of prostrate clowns. It looked dangerous for the clowns, but the trainer had told me how to do it. You begin with logs, laid out a certain distance apart; the horse walks over them under your lead; and whenever he touches one, you rebuke him. By and by he will learn to step with such care that he never trips. Then you substitute clowns. I had no clowns, but I did get logs, and with the girls helping me, we taught the colt to step over the obstacles even at a trot. Walking, she touched nothing. Ready thus with the logs, I had my sisters lie down in the grass, and again and again the colt stepped over and among them. None was ever touched. My father would not listen to any of this; he just walloped me, and when he was tired or satisfied and I was in tears, I blubbered a short excuse: "They were only girls." And he whipped me some more.

My father was not given to whipping; he did it very seldom, but he did it hard when he did it at all. My mother was just the opposite. She did not whip me, but she often smacked me, and she had a most annoying habit of thumping me on the head with her thimbled finger. This I resented more than my father's thoroughgoing thrashings, and I can tell why now. I would be playing Napoleon and as I was reviewing my Old Guard, she would crack my skull with that thimble. No doubt I was in the way; it took a lot of furniture and sisters to represent properly a victorious army; and you might think, as my mother did, that a thimble is a small weapon. But imagine Napoleon at the height of his power, the ruler of the world on parade, getting a sharp rap on his crown from a woman's thimble. No. My father's way was more appropriate. It was hard. "I'll attend to you in the morning," he would say; and I lay awake wondering which one of my crimes he had discovered. I know what it is to be sentenced to be shot at sunrise. And it hurt, in the morning, when he was not angry but very fresh and strong. But you see, he walloped me in my own person; he never humiliated Napoleon or my knighthood, as my mother did. And I learned something from his discipline, something useful.

I learned what tyranny is and the pain of being misunderstood and wronged, or, if you please, understood and set right; they are pretty much the same. He and most parents and teachers do not break in their boys as carefully as I broke in my colt. They haven't the time that I had, and they have not some other incentives that I had. I saw this that day when I rubbed my sore legs. He had to explain to my indignant mother what had happened. When he had told it his way, I gave my version: how long and cautiously I had been teaching my horse to walk over logs and girls. And having shown how sure I was of myself and the colt, while my mother was boring into his silence with one of her reproachful looks, I said something that hit my father hard.

"I taught the colt that trick, I have taught her all that you see she knows, without whipping her. I have never struck her; not once. Colonel Carter said I mustn't, and I haven't."

And my mother, backing me up, gave him a rap: "There," she said, "I told you so." He walked off, looking like a thimble-rapped Napoleon.

1. How does Lincoln Steffens use words and incidents to suggest that every method of breaking—his father's walloping, his mother's thimble rapping, and his own gentle leading—had limitations and had aspects that complemented one another. **2.** Find all the ways Steffens suggests a change from boy to man in the narrator. **3.** Explain in your own words how this piece of prose differs essentially from the others studied thus far. **4.** The following ideas in themselves have nothing to do with the main stream of thought of *I Get a Colt to Break In*. Discuss how Steffens enriches the piece by bringing them in:

kitten   glass   centaur   Napoleon

5. Examine all the parts where Steffens describes the colt. Does he describe her as vividly as Beebe describes the fish in *Brothering Fish*? Discuss.

As you read *Masculine Protest,* notice that it is different from *I Get a Colt to Break In*. Here the author imaginatively shapes an experience which may or may not have actually happened.

MASCULINE PROTEST

FRANK O'CONNOR

For months things had been getting worse between Mother and me. At the time I was twelve, and we were living in Boharna, a small town twenty miles from the city—Father, Mother, Martha, and I. Father worked in the City Council and we didn't see much of him. I suppose that threw me more on Mother, but I could be perfectly happy sitting with her all day if only she let me. She didn't though. She was always inventing excuses to get rid of me, even giving me money to go to the pictures, which she knew Father didn't like because I wasn't very bright at school and he thought the pictures were bad for me.

I blamed a lot of it on Martha at first. Martha was sly, and she was always trying to get inside me with Mother. She was always saving, whereas I always found money burned a hole in my pocket, and it was only to spite her that I kept a savings bank at all. As well as that, she told Mother about all the scrapes I got into. They weren't what you'd really call scrapes. It was just that we had a gang in our neighbourhood, which was the classy one of the town, and we were always having battles with the slummy kids from the other side of town who wanted to play in our neighbourhood. I was the Chief Gang Leader, and it was my job to keep them from expanding beyond their own frontiers.

Martha let on not to understand why I should be Chief Gang Leader. She let on not to know why we didn't want the slum kids overrunning our locality. Though she knew better than to tell Mother when I made Viking raids on the housekeeping money, she was always at me in a low, blood-curdling voice, following me round like a witch. "You'll be caught yet, Denis Halligan. You'll be caught. The police will be after you. You took three shillings out of Mummy's purse. God sees you!" Sometimes she drove me so wild that I went mad and twisted her arm or pulled her hair, and she went off screeching, and I got a licking.

I had managed to kid myself into the belief that one day Mother would understand; one day she would wake up and see that the affection of Dad and Martha was insincere; that the two of them had long ago ganged up against her, and that I, the black sheep, was the one who really loved her.

This revelation was due to take place in rather unusual circumstances. We were all to be stranded in some dangerous desert, and Mother, with her ankle broken, would tell us to leave her to her fate, the way they did in storybooks. Dad and Martha, of course, would leave her, with only a pretence of concern, but I, in my casual way, would simply fold my hands about my knees and ask listlessly: "What use is life to me without you?" Nothing more; I was against any false drama, any raising of the voice. I had never been one for high-flown expressions like Martha: just the lift of the shoulder, the way I pulled a grass-blade to chew (it needn't be a desert), and Mother would realize at last that though I wasn't demonstrative —just a plain, rough, willing chap—I really had a heart of gold.

The trouble about Mother was that she had a genius for subjecting hearts of gold to intolerable strain. It wasn't that she was actively unkind, for she thought far too much of the impression she wanted to make to be anything like that. It was just that she didn't care a damn. She was always away from home. She visited friends in Galway, Dublin, Birr, and Athlone, and all we ever got to see of her was the flurry between one foray and the next, while she was packing and unpacking.

Things came to a head when she told me she wouldn't be at home for my birthday. At the same time, always conscientious, she had arranged a very nice treat for Martha and me. But the treat wasn't the same thing that I had been planning, when I proposed to bring a couple of fellows along and show Mother off to them, and I began to bawl. The trouble was that the moment I did, I seemed to have no reasons on my side. It was always like that with Mother; she invariably had all the reasons on her side, and made you feel contrary and a pig, but that was worse instead of better. You felt then that she was taking advantage of you. I sobbed and stamped and asked why she hadn't done that to Martha and why she was doing it to me. She looked at me coldly and said I was a pretty picture and that I had no manliness. Of course, I saw she was in the right about that too, and that there was no excuse for a fellow of my age complaining against not being treated like his younger sister, and that only made me madder still.

"Go on!" I screamed. "Who's trying to stop you? All you want is people to admire you."

I knew when I had said it that it was awful, and expected her to give me a clout, but she only drew herself up, looking twice as dignified and beautiful.

"That is a contemptible remark, Denis," she said in a biting tone. "It's one I wouldn't have expected even from you."

The way she said it made me feel like the scum of the earth. And then she went off for the evening in a car with the Clarkes, leaving Martha and me alone. Martha looked at me, half in pity, half in amusement. She was never really disappointed in Martha, because she expected less of her. Martha was born sly.

"What did I tell you?" she said, though she hadn't told me anything.

"Go on," I said in a thick voice. "You sucker!" Then I went upstairs and bawled and used all the dirty words I knew. I knew now it was all over between Mother and me; that no circumstances would ever occur which would show how much I loved her, because after what had happened I could not live in the same house with her again. For quite a while I thought about suicide, but I put that on one side, because the only way I could contemplate committing suicide was by shooting, and my air pistol was not strong enough for that. I took out my post-office book. I had four pounds fifteen in the bank. As I've said, it was purely out of spite against Martha, but that made no difference now. It was enough to keep me for a month or so till I found some corner where people wanted me; a plain rough-spoken chap who only needed a little affection. I was afraid of nothing in the way of work. I was strong and energetic. At the worst, I could always make for Dublin, where my grandfather and Auntie May lived. I knew they would be glad to help me, because they thought that Dad had married the wrong woman and never pretended to like Mother. When Mother had told me this I was furious, but now I saw that they were probably clev-erer than I was. It would give me great satisfaction to reach their door and tell Auntie May in my plain straightforward way: "You were right and I was wrong." For the last time I looked round my bedroom and burst into fresh tears. There is some-thing heartrending about leaving for the last time a place where you have spent so much of your life. Then, trying to steady my-self, I grabbed a little holy picture from the mantelpiece and a favourite story-book from the bookshelf and ran downstairs. Martha heard me taking out my bike and came to see. It had a dynamo lamp and a three-speed gear; a smashing bike!

"Where are you off to?" she asked.

"Never mind!" I said as I cycled off.

I had no particular feelings about seeing Martha for the last time.

Then I had my first shock, because as I cycled into Main Street I saw that all the shops were shuttered for the weekly half-holiday and I knew the post office would be shut too and I could not draw out my savings. It was the first time I felt what people so often feel in after life, that Fate has made a plaything of you. Why should I have had my final quarrel with Mother on the one day in the week when I could not get away from her? If that wasn't Fate, what was? And I knew my own weak-ness of character better than anyone. I knew that if I put it off until next day, the sight of Mother would be sufficient to set me servilely seeking for pardon. Even setting off across Ireland without a penny would be better than that.

Then I had what I thought was an inspiration. The city was only twenty miles away, and the General Post Office was bound to be open. I had calculated my time to and from school at twelve miles an hour; even allowing for the distance, it wouldn't take me more than two hours. As well as that, I had been to the city for the Christmas shopping, so I knew the look of it. I could get my money and stay in a hotel or have tea and then set off for Dublin. I liked that idea. Cycling all the way up through Ireland in the dark, through sleeping towns and villages; seeing the dawn break over Dublin as I cycled down the slopes of the Dublin mountains; arriving at Auntie May's door in the Shelbourne Road when she was lighting the fire—that would be smashing. I could imagine how she would greet me—"Child of grace, where did you come from?" "Ah, just cycled." My natural modesty always came out in those day-dreams of mine, for I never, under any circumstances, made a fuss. Absolutely smashing!

All the same, it was no joke, a trip like that. I cycled slowly and undecidedly out the familiar main road where we walked on Sunday, past the little suburban houses. It was queer how hard it was to break away from places and people and things you knew. I thought of letting it go and of doing the best I could to patch it up with Mother. I thought of the gang and at that a real lump rose in my throat. Tomorrow night, when my absence was noticed, there would be a new Chief Gang Leader; somebody like Eddie Humphreys who would be so prim and cautious that he would be afraid to engage the enemy which threatened us on every side. In that moment of weakness I nearly turned back. At the same moment it brought me renewed decision, for I knew that I had not been chosen Chief Gang Leader because I was a little sissy like Eddie Humphreys but because I was afraid of nothing.

At one moment my feet had nearly stopped pedalling; at the next I was pedalling for all I was worth. It was as sudden as that, like the moment when you find yourself out of your depth and two inclinations struggle in you—to swim like hell back to the shallows or strike out boldly for the other side. Up to that I had thought mainly of what was behind me; now I thought only of what was ahead of me, and it was frightening enough. I was aware of great distances, of big gray cloud masses on the horizon, of the fragility of my tires compared with the surface of the road, and I thought only of the two-hour journey ahead of me. The romantic picture of myself cycling across Ireland in the dark disappeared. I should be quite content to get the first stage over me.

For the last ten miles I wasn't even tempted to look at the scenery. I was doubled over the handlebars. Things just happened; the road bent away under me; wide green rivers rose up and slipped away again under me, castles soared from the roadside with great arches blocked out in masses of shadow.

Then at last the little rocky fields closed behind me like a book, and the blessed electric-light poles escorted me up the last hill, and I floated proudly down between comfortable villas with long gardens till I reached the bridge. The city was stretched out on the other side of the river, shining in the evening light, and my heart rose at the thought that I had at least shown Mother whether or not I had manliness. I dismounted from my bicycle and pushed it along the Main Street, looking at the shops. They were far more interesting than the shops at home, and the people looked better too.

I found the post office in a side street and went up to the counter with my savings-bank book.

"I want to draw out my money," I said.

The clerk looked at the clock.

"You can't do that, sonny," he said. "The savings-bank counter is shut."

"When will it open again?" I asked.

"Not till tomorrow. Any time after nine."

"But can't I get it now?"

"No. The clerk is gone home now."

I slouched out of the post office with despair in my heart. I took my bicycle and pushed it wearily back to the Main Street. The crowds were still going by, but now it looked long and wide and lonesome, for I had no money and I didn't know a soul. Without a meal and a rest, I could not even set out for Dublin, if I had the heart, which I knew I hadn't. Nor could I even return home, for it was already late and I was dropping with weariness. One side of the Main Street was in shadow; the shadow seemed to spread with extraordinary rapidity, and you felt that the city was being quenched as with snuffers.

It was only then that I thought of Father. It was funny that I had not thought of him before, even when thinking of Grandfather and Auntie May. I had thought of these as allies against Mother, but I hadn't even considered him as an ally. Now as I thought of him, everything about him seemed different. It wasn't only the hunger and panic. It was something new for me. It was almost love. With fresh energy I pushed my bicycle back to the post office, left it outside the door where I could see it, and went up to the clerk I had already spoken to.

"Could I make a telephone call?" I asked.

"You could to be sure," he said. "Have you the money?"

"No, sir."

"Well, you can't make a call without the money. Where is it to?"

"Boharna," I said.

At once his face took on a severe expression.

"That's one and threepence," he said.

"And I can't ring unless I have the money?"

"Begor, you can't. I couldn't ring myself without that."

I went out and took my bicycle again. This time I could see no way out. I dawdled along the street, leaving my bicycle by the curb and gazing in shop windows. In one I found a mirror in which I could see myself full-length. I looked old and heartbroken. It was just like a picture of a child without a home, and I blinked away my tears.

Then, as I approached a public-house, I saw a barman in shirt sleeves standing by the door. I remembered that I had seen him already on my way down and that he had looked at me. He nodded and smiled and I stopped. I was glad of anyone making a friendly gesture in that strange place.

"Are you waiting for someone?" he asked.

"No," I said. "I wanted to make a phone call."

"You're not from these parts?"

"No," I said. "I'm from Boharna."

"Are you, begor?" he said. "Was it on the bus you came?"

"No," I replied modestly. "I biked it."

"Biked it?"

"Yes."

"That's a hell of a distance," he said.

"It is long," I agreed.

"What did you come all that way for?" he asked in surprise.

"Ah, I was running away from home," I said despondently.

"You were what?" he asked in astonishment. "You're not serious."

"But I am," I said, very close to tears. "I did my best, but then I couldn't stick it any longer and I cleared out." I turned my head away because this time I was really crying.

"Oh, begor, I know what 'tis like," he said in a friendlier tone. "I did it myself."

"Did you?" I asked eagerly, forgetting my grief. This, I felt, was the very man I wanted to meet.

"Ah, indeed I did. I did it three times what's more. By that time they were getting fed up with me. Anyway, they say practice makes perfect. Tell me, is it your old fellow?"

"No," I said with a sigh. "My mother."

"Ah, do you tell me so? That's worse again. 'Tis bad enough to have the old man at you, but 'tis the devil entirely when the mother is against you. What are you going to do now?"

"I don't know," I said. "I wanted to get to Dublin, but the savings bank is shut, and all my money is in it."

"That's tough luck. Sure, you can't get anywhere without money. I'm afraid you'll have to go back and put up with it for another while."

"But I can't," I said. " 'Tis twenty miles."

" 'Tis all of that, begor. You couldn't go on the bus?"

"I can't. I haven't the money. That's what I asked them in the post office, to let me ring up Daddy, but they wouldn't."

"Where's your daddy?" he asked, and when I told him: "Ah, we'll try and get him for you anyway. Come on in."

There was a phone in the corner, and he rang up and asked for Daddy. Then he gave me a big smile and handed me the receiver. I heard Daddy's voice and I nearly wept with delight.

"Hullo, son," he said in astonishment. "Where on earth are you?"

"In the city, Daddy," I said modestly—even then I couldn't bring myself to make a lot of it, the way another fellow would.

"The city?" he repeated incredulously. "What took you there?"

"I ran away from home, Dad," I said, trying to make it sound as casual as possible.

"Oh!" he exclaimed and there was moment's pause. I was afraid he was going to get angry, but his tone remained the same. "Had a row?"

"Yes, Dad."

"And how did you get there?"

"On the bike."

"All the way? But you must be dead."

"Just a bit tired," I said modestly.

"Tell me, did you even get a meal?"

"No, Dad. The savings bank was shut."

"Ah, blazes!" he said softly. "Of course, it's the half day. And what are you going to do now?"

"I don't know, Dad. I thought you might tell me."

"Well, what about coming home?" he said, beginning to laugh.

"I don't mind, Dad. Whatever you say."

"Hold on now till I see what the buses are like. . . . Hullo! You can get one in forty minutes' time—seven ten. Tell the conductor I'll be meeting you and I'll pay your fare. Will that be all right?"

"That's grand, Dad," I said, feeling that the world was almost right again.

When I finished, the barman was waiting for me with his coat on. He had got another man to look after the bar for him.

"Now, you'd better come and have a cup of tea with me before your bus goes," he said. "The old bike will be safe outside."

He took me to a café, and I ate cake after cake and drank tea and he told me about how he'd run away himself. You could see he was a real hard case, worse even than I was. The first time, he'd pinched a bicycle and cycled all the way to Dublin, sleeping in barns and deserted cottages. The police had brought him home and his father had belted hell out of him. They caught him again the second time, but the third time he'd joined the army and not returned home for years.

He put me and my bicycle on the bus and paid my fare. He made me promise to tell Dad that he'd done it and that Dad owed me the money. He said in this world you had to stand up for your rights. He was a rough chap, but you could see he had a good heart. It struck me that maybe only rough chaps had hearts as good as that.

Dad was waiting for me at the bus stop, and he looked at me and laughed.

"Well, the gouger!" he said. "Who ever would think that the son of a good-living, upright man like me would turn into a common tramp."

All the same I could see he was pleased, and as he pushed my bike down the street he made me tell him all about my experiences. He laughed over the barman and promised to give me the fare. Then, seeing him so friendly, I asked the question that had been on my mind the whole way back on the bus.

"Mummy back yet, Dad?"

"No, son," he said. "Not yet. She probably won't be in till late."

What I was really asking him, of course, was "Does she know?" and now I was torn by the desire to ask him not to tell her, but it choked me. It would have seemed too much like trying to gang up against her. But he seemed to know what I was thinking, for he added wtih a sort of careful casualness that he had sent Martha to the pictures. I guessed that that was to get her out of the way so that she couldn't bring the story to Mother, and when we had supper together and washed up afterwards, I knew I was right.

Mother came in before we went to bed, and Father talked to her just as though nothing had happened. He was a little bit more forthcoming than usual, but that was the only indication he gave, and I was fascinated, watching him create an understanding between us. It was an understanding in more ways than one, because it dawned on me gradually that, like myself and the barman, Dad too had once run away from home, and for some reason—perhaps because the bank was shut or because he was hungry, tired, and lonely—he had come back. People mostly came back, but their protest remained to distinguish them from all the others who had never run away. It was the real sign of their manhood.

I never ran away after that. I never felt I needed to.

1. Discuss all the ways in which the story resembles *I Get a Colt to Break In.* 2. Discuss all the ways in which it differs. 3. Line up the words and actions in the story that make the following statements especially humorous: -a . . . *Mother would realize at last that I wasn't demonstrative—just a plain, rough, willing chap—I really had a heart of gold.* -b *I knew now it was all over between Mother and me; . . .* -c *She was never really disappointed in Mother, because she expected less of her.* -d *My natural modesty always came out in those day-dreams of mine, for I never, under any circumstances, made a fuss.* -e *It would give me great satisfaction to reach their door and tell Auntie May in my plain straightforward way: "You were right and I was wrong."* 4. Can you account for the blending of two attitudes, that of an adult and that of a twelve-year-old boy, in the presentation of Denis? Give evidence of both from the story. 5. The narrator describes very little of his surroundings in this story, but when he does, there is always a very good reason. Find all the parts where he does describe them and discuss the effect of the description on these parts of the story. 6. After reading *I Get a Colt to Break In* and *Masculine Protest,* do one of the following: -a Write an account of an incident which reveals the ideas that you and your parents have on discipline. -b Write an account of an incident which reveals conscious or unconscious growing up in a young person.

Words in Themselves

WORD ANCESTRY: Language is a curious thing. Even when we believe we are learning a new word, it is likely that we are not, for there are few words that are really new. Many of our words have come to us from centuries ago. Almost all of them have their roots in the speech of our ancestors.

The Greek and Roman mythologies left a lasting impression on our words and phrases. Take the expression *to work like a Trojan*. Most people know that *to work like a Trojan* is to work with great industry and endurance, as did the Trojans when they defended their city from the Greeks after Paris had stolen Helen from Menelaus. But how many of us know what it means to be a *Cassandra?* You may be surprised to learn that Winston Churchill was called a Cassandra when he predicted the rising power of the Nazis in the 1930's. Why? Because thousands of years ago Cassandra, the daughter of Priam, was given the gift of prophecy by Apollo (so runs the myth). Later she offended the god and he saw to it that, although she could still prophesy, no one believed her. And so, a Cassandra is one who prophesies evil that will actually happen but which no one believes will.

Many of our geographical names have their roots in the past too. The name *Atlantic Ocean* comes from the legend of the nymphs, the Atlantides and the Oceanides. *Europe* has its name from a beautiful girl named Europa, the first human being to reach the island of Crete. The story goes that she was carried there on the back of a white bull, who really was Zeus in disguise.

Twins, Castor and Polydeuces, are found among the constellations. Another set of twins, *Gemini* in Latin, prove that we still show a trace of old Roman respect for them when we say *by Jimminy*.

THE WORD BOOK: Even if we did not know any myths, even if we had never read the ILIAD and the ODYSSEY, we could still reach into the mythological treasure of words through a great book only an arm's reach away. This is our modern word book, the dictionary.

Have you ever looked long enough and carefully enough into a standard dictionary to find all the help it offers us for building meaning with words? You will find in your dictionary how to pronounce words, how to define them, how to spell them. You will learn the part of speech a word may function as, its origin, its current usage. In the dictionary you will find the synonyms and antonyms of words, the areas of interest in which they are used, the geographical areas in which they function. To learn what a dictionary can teach you, study yours carefully. Here is a series of assignments on words used in the literature you've studied thus far. Find the information indicated for each word in boldface type.

1. Take part in a class workshop to study these words for: **-a** spelling **-b** syllabication **-c** accent **-d** pronunciation.

Every Thursday when I drive Della to Waterbury in the car for her day off, I explore the dark depths and the strange recesses of her **nomenclature**.

"She got tuberculosis from the teeth," she said, "and it went all through her **symptom**.*"*

All I could say was a helpless, "Well, it is **idiomatic**.*" . . . to seek information from the* **encyclopedia**.

Jarmila looked **skeptical**, *and after a period of meditation she came back in triumph.*

. . . the torch has been passed to a new generation of Americans, . . . proud of our ancient **heritage** . . .

To that world assembly of sovereign states, the United Nations, we renew our pledge of support—to prevent its becoming merely a forum for **invective** . . .

Let us never **negotiate** *out of fear.*

The trouble about Mother was that she had a genius for **subjecting** *hearts of gold to intolerable strain.*

"That is a **contemptible** *remark, Denis," she said in a biting tone.*

2. Continue your class workshop to study: **-a** derivation **-b** meaning of the words in boldface type.

The more he tried to get it free,
The louder **buzzed** *the telephee.*

We keep house, we keep books, we keep silence, we keep the **Sabbath** *holy.*

This has been our experience since Bohus Petrzelka . . . took up his abode in the roomy **ell** *of our house.*

Can we forge against these enemies a grand and global **alliance** *. . . ?*

But in a larger sense, we cannot dedicate—we cannot consecrate—we cannot **hallow**—*this ground.*

Instead of a slotted **vizor**, *however, you find two large frames of glass before your eyes.*

. . . feathery palms waving in the sunlight against a sky of pure **azure**.

. . . a rounded table of **lapis lazuli** *on which are blossoming three flowers . . .*

3. Conclude the class workshop in a study of levels of usage. Concentrate on the words in boldface type.

A widow bird **sate** *mourning for her love*

Beware the **Jabber***wock, my son!*

. . . she is not a woman to be put down by a **crazy** *man with a dictionary.*

. . . a dried, dusty bit of coral in the **whatnot** *of the best parlor . . .*

You exclaim something **bromidic** *which sounds like Marvelous!*

. . . our neighbourhood, which was the **classy** *one . . .*

. . . she told Mother about all the **scrapes** *I got into.*

4. Look up these words in your dictionary. Syllabicate, mark accents, and show the diacritical marks. Be ready to pronounce each word aloud.

Until you throw a penny in . . .
Or a **cobblestone**.

*Coming at her **obliquely** with a dictionary only enriches the confusion . . .*

*. . . and looked up the word in the **indispensable** Century.*

*. . . the strange recesses of her **nomenclature**.*

*. . . get discharged, get rich, and so on **ad infinitum**.*

*. . . the sponge . . . hoping for some disturbed **tidbit**.*

*Books, **aquaria**, and glass-bottomed boats . . .*

*. . . they break in a horse by riding out to him . . . **lassoing**, throwing . . .*

*I held the long rope and the whip (for **signaling**) . . .*

*Let all our **neighbors** know that we shall join with them . . .*

5. There is a compound word in each of the following sentences. Listed after it are other compounds of the same word. Use your dictionary to check on these terms. Which should be written as one word? Which as two?

*I was sitting at my **typewriter** one **afternoon** several weeks ago . . .*

type setting	after dinner (adjective)
type metal	after effect
type script	after math

*. . . as if I had given her a clue to my crazy definitions, my insensitivity to the ordinary **household** nouns . . .*

house boat	house party
house coat	house top

*If you live in the South you'll have . . . "dragline" for a **steam shovel** . . .*

steam boat	steam roller
steam engine	steam ship

*My natural modesty always came out in those **day-dreams** of mine . . .*

| day bed | day coach |
| day break | day light |

6. Test your skill in the use of the dictionary on these words:

Let both sides explore what problems unite us instead of **belaboring** *the problems that divide us.*

Their petals are **resplendent** *in hues of gold and* **malachite** . . .

For a brief space of time the palms and the beach show **intermittently** *through waves* . . .

You lean against a **fretwork** *of purest marble* . . .

She was a careful cross of a **mustang** *mare and a thoroughbred stallion* . . .

I had seen in the circus a horse that stepped thus over a row of **prostrate** *clowns.*

It had a **dynamo** *lamp and a three-speed gear; a smashing bike!*

Was it on the **bus** *you came?*

. . . *though I wasn't* **demonstrative** . . . *I really had a heart of gold.*

7. Be a TV announcer and sell a specific modern dictionary.
8. Evaluate the commercials your classmates present. Lay particular stress on imaginative presentation. Show how imagination helps salesmen as well as English students. Pick out for special mention the important aspects of the dictionary mentioned in the commercial.

WORD PERSONALITY: Words have identity and they have personality in their own word world. They are easily identified and distinguished from each other by the way they are spelled and pronounced, and by their exact meaning, or denotation. Their personality is expressed by their power to evoke emotion, by their ability to make people see and hear and feel and taste and smell, by their wide associative or connotative meanings, and by their imaginative appeal.

There are times when a writer must keep words within the bounds of exact denotation. Scientific writing, philosophical treatises, and mathematical problem solving find use for only strict denotative language. Words with emotional and imaginative appeal would block rather than help communication.

Poetry, in fact all imaginative writing, is patterned in language that keeps the specific denotation but extends its meaning richly and effectively through connotation and imagery. To read poetry with appreciation and enjoyment, the reader must recognize the power of words to denote, to connote, and to create images.

WORD ASSOCIATION: What we call connotation is simply word association. The words we use have a crowd of associations linked to them because of our past experience in relation to them. A man who remembers the odor of carnations as the cloying smell around the casket of his mother may ever after link carnations with death and find every reference to carnations unpleasant. A woman may remember carnations as the flowers of her first corsage and in later life associate this flower with happiness. The same word, *carnation,* is associated with death for one and with life for another. This is called individual connotation.

Another level of connotation is group connotation. It is the kind of connotation that enables the people of the same culture to enjoy the allusions in the literature they share. When Hamlet says that his mother is *like Niobe, all tears,* any competent reader knows the connotation of *Niobe:* the mother of mythology who was punished by the gods and turned into a perpetually weeping rock. In the first line of the sonnet on his blindness, *When I consider how my light is spent,* Milton takes it for granted that his readers know the meaning of *light* with all its connotations in relation to seeing.

A third class of connotative words are what we call general. These are words with associations that are widely shared. Most people are attracted to words like *mother, country, orchid;* and they are repelled by words like *snake, vulture, offal, scavenger.*

1. Notice how words are used in these lines by Elizabeth Barrett Browning:

> Earth's crammed with heaven,
> And every common bush afire with God;
> But only he who sees takes off his shoes—
> The rest sit round it and pluck blackberries.

Each word in this lovely poem means something specific on the denotative level. *Earth* and *crammed* and *heaven* and *bush* and *afire* and *shoes* and *blackberries* have the exact meaning in the poem you will find for them in the dictionary. If they did not there would be something defective about this poem. But we know we are not reaching the meaning of the poem itself when we control only the denotative meaning of each word. It is the connotative level of meaning that unlocks for the reader the actual meaning of the poem.

The speaker finds earth so full, so rewarding, so richly endowed with love, so overflowing with beauty, so stunning with meaning that she imagines immense heaven crammed into our small earth. Because the poet's experience with life is so rich and meaningful for her, each experience is a burning bush; and it is a burning bush for others, too, but only for those who see. And these *take off their shoes*. The rest, those who do not see— those who have no spiritual vision, no insight, no spiritual aspirations, no awareness of intellectual values, no perception of beauty—*sit round it and pluck blackberries.* **-a** What is the connotation of *bush afire*? **-b** What is the connotation of *see* in the third line? **-c** Why do those who see *take off their shoes*? **-d** Can you tell the Bible story that is suggested in lines 2 and 3? **-e** Why does the poet have *the rest round it and pluck blackberries*?

If you can answer these questions, you have some understanding of connotation.

2. Did you see Ann Blyth in the film *Student Prince*? You may be surprised to know that she is interested in the personality of words, too. Here is something she said about words in an address to representatives of the press:

In the beginning was the Word, and the Word was with God, and the Word was God. Since these words were first written a million billion words have been penned and spoken. There are words that sing and jump and skip and dance; little-girl words. And there are words with fun in their eyes and things in their pockets and their hair mussed; little-boy words.

There are young words, and there are wise old words with a glint in their eyes. There are words wide-eyed with wonder, soft as a baby's feet, strong as a baby's twining fingers.

There are steel words and iron words: thrusting, stinging, lancet words; cruel blades of words. And there are sweet words; soothing, unguent words; father-, mother-words; the words that raise you like a child again and hoist you on their shoulders.

Words are everything that man is; everything he can be— they are everything he should not be. They are his slave; they are his master. In a world of mercy, man is at the mercy of words.

In the beginning was the word—all the infinite wonder and beauty and truth and love and life that God is—uttered in one divine word. This is the truth. And by its nature every word should be a reflection of the Divine Truth.

I plead with you, gentlemen of the press, to remember that words are written about men and read by men. I plead that infidelity is not new—it isn't even news. To recount broken commandments on the front page helps no one and hurts many. Sensationalism and emotionalism and carnalism are a direct appeal to man's baser part and the betrayal of a trust.

You are the light bearers, men of the press. Don't burlesque man; lead him. You have the words. You have the truth. Lead not the child of God into darkness.

3. Which of these words have a pleasant association for you? Which have unpleasant associations?

For the pleasure in the poem is not in the refreshing **quaintness** *of the language* . . .
And why must I clean up the **mess**, *wrap up the parcel,* . . .
So you look a little farther and you find that you have some **"casual"** *words.*

. . . we pledge our word that one form of colonial control shall not have passed merely to be replaced by a far more iron **tyranny**.

And if a beachhead of co-operation can be made in the **jungle** *of suspicion . . .*

You hold up your hand and see little washer-woman's **wrinkles** *on the soles of your fingers . . .*

. . . like some **rare** *and unknown orchid.*

. . . without your knowing of the **ease** *of entry into this new world.*

While we were breaking in the colt, a **circus** *came to town.*

I liked the way she . . . went **dancing**, *prancing down the street.*

4. What kind of connotation do these words have—group, general, or both?

*. . . poetry does not come of some remote area of human life called "***art***" . . .*

A **widow** *bird sate mourning for her love . . .*

This **diagnosis** *had shaken me not a little.*

. . . it will be a **black** *one for the door.*

We keep house; we keep books; we keep silence; we keep the **Sabbath** *day holy.*

For just as you have comfortable old **jeans** *and loafers . . . so you have words that you use only at home.*

Sometimes families give proper names to family belongings, like "Suzabella" for the family **sedan**; *. . .*

But we shall always hope to find them strongly supporting their own **freedom** *. . .*

. . . ask what you can **do** *for your country.*
You are standing on a metal **ladder** *in water up to your neck.*

5. In five strong sentences develop one of the words used in number **3** or **4** (above) through its group and general connotative meanings.

WORD IMAGERY: Words also have the power to appeal to the senses. We call this kind of appeal the image-making power of words. Poetry, of course, is the language of imagery. But we use images continuously, even if we are not poets. We are speaking with word images when we say *a plane swoops; a boy zooms down the street; a kettle sings; a train tears down the tracks.* We are making use of image-making words when we call a rainy day *an umbrella day,* when we say that *the sun glints cold* or use expressions like *to beat around the bush, to walk a chalk line, to keep the ball rolling, to heap coals of fire on one's head.*

1. Notice all the interesting word images in this delightful poem by E. E. Cummings:

hist whist
little ghostthings
tip-toe
twinkle-toe

little twitchy
witches and tingling
goblins
hob-a-nob hob-a-nob

little hoppy happy
toads in tweeds
tweeds
little itchy mousies

with scuttling
eyes rustle and run and
hidehidehide
whisk

whisk look out for the old woman
with the wart on her nose
what she will do to yer
nobody knows

for she knows the devil ouch
the devil ouch
the devil
ach the great

green
dancing
devil
devil

devil
devil
　　　wheeEEE

Cummings creates sound and sight images that go hand in hand with the lighthearted, gaily mysterious, nonsensical meaning. Write five sentences using specific words from the poem which have sight and sound appeal.

2. Write five sentences in which you use word images of sight and sound. Create a picture of one of the following: **-a** your mother bustling around the kitchen preparing for guests **-b** your father painting the garage **-c** your pup romping with a ball.

SIMILARITY AND CONTRAST: Some words have such precise and limited meaning that there are no other words that have meaning within their range. But for most words there are other words that have almost the same meaning. These are their synonyms.

There are words, too, for which there are other words that contrast them with opposite meaning. Antonyms are of this kind. Some words can be changed into their antonyms by prefixing to them *in, un, dis,* or any other negative prefix. Other words have antonyms unrelated to them in sound or pronunciation.

1. Find the synonyms of the words in boldface type, without changing the part of speech:

There was no leaf upon the forest bare, . . . and little **motion** *in the air . . .*

. . . it sounds like the **spontaneous** *sort of cry which we give at times when we are aroused by strong feelings.*

In a sense, anyone who ever raises his voice for emphasis, in **rage** *or in joy, is using the method of poetry.*

Perhaps the most **expressive** *lines in the poem are these: . . .*

I could have avoided all these **suspicions**, *of course, . . .*

. . . it never ceases to **beguile** *me.*

English is a **queer** *language.*

Let both sides, for the first time, formulate serious and **precise** *proposals . . .*

. . . we are the heirs of that first **revolution**.

. . . the unfinished work which they who fought here have thus far so **nobly** *advanced.*

2. List the antonyms of the words in boldface type:

The **difference** *you'll see/ when you drop your penny:*

Poetry is not about rare states of mind which are experienced only by **unique** *people called poets.*

. . . **special** *things for special places along the way, . . .*

*. . . and you find that you have some "***casual***" words.*

. . . the whole centaur bowed and was covered with glory and **conceit**.

I was strong and **energetic**.

. . . the sight of Mother would be sufficient to set me **servilely** *seeking for pardon.*

. . . somebody like Eddie Humphreys who would be so prim and **cautious** *that he would be afraid to engage the enemy which threatened us on every side.*

THE LIBRARY: Knowing people and places can give you hints about knowing books. The more you become interested in them, the more you will want to know them. In reverse, the proposition is just as true. But books will remain strangers to you until you become familiar with their make-up, until you feel at home in the libraries where they are stored. And personal investigation is the only method. You wouldn't say you know your way around Greece after merely looking at a map and reading a guide book. Similarly, no explanation by a teacher or direction from your book can substitute for hours spent in the library by yourself, exploring all of its corners and discovering the solutions it provides to many of your problems.

Supplement the following work in your school library with a few trips to the public library:

1. In preparation for an oral talk, make a trip to the library to get twelve different books. Do not use the card catalogue, but browse through every section of the library according to the Dewey decimal system classification. Choose from each section a book that tempts you to closer examination. Working in the library, take notes on interesting aspects of each book and notes for a comparative explanation of the parts of a book. After all the class members have turned in notes, your teacher will choose one or more of you to give your talk. If you are chosen, sign out some of the books to use for illustration of the points you make about them.

2. On a day stipulated by the teacher, bring to class a book you signed out of the library—preferably a book suggested by something you have studied thus far. Make a test on the parts of a book so that every member of the class can answer the questions in terms of the book he brings to class.

3. *What Do You Mean It* Was *Brillig?* is printed in a collection of essays by James Thurber called THE THURBER CARNIVAL. Look in the card catalogue to see if the book is in the library. If it is not, find another book by Thurber. Find author and title cards. Try the subjects *Essays* and *Humor*. Is there a cross reference to the book? Is there a subject card for it? Are there any subject cards on any books about the same subject? Write a report of your findings.

4. Alice Hamilton has two sisters who have also done some writing. Investigate the work of the three of them in five different volumes of the READER'S GUIDE. Keep a record of the articles by each, the articles about each, the reviews of books they've written. In your record, indicate how many entries (subject, title, and author) there are for each article. Find three of the articles in magazines and write a brief report of each.

5. Have you ever seen a map on which the journey of some explorer is plotted? Make a similar map of the school library—labeling all important areas and plotting the path of one or more of your library investigations.

6. Do some investigating on John F. Kennedy's inaugural address. What periodicals listed in the READER'S GUIDE reprinted it in whole or in part? Which ones printed commentaries on it? Check the vertical file for pictures and clippings related to the inauguration of President Kennedy.

7. Beginning with *History,* check in the card catalogue under any topics that would include references to Lincoln's *Gettysburg Address* or the Battle of Gettysburg. Make a report of your discoveries, including the arrangement of the card catalogue in regard to specific topics. Check the vertical file for pictures or pamphlets on the Civil War.

8. Browse for a period in the *General Works* section of the library and track down all the avenues of information on someone like E. E. Cummings, or on any aspect of poetry.

9. Write a letter to your little sister explaining how she might find more poetry like John Ciardi's *The River Is a Piece of Sky.*

10. Keep a journal of all the new library discoveries you make throughout this year. As a freshman in college you may appreciate what you learned from making mistakes and misusing the tools of research as a freshman in high school.

Words in Basic Relationships

Have you ever tried to say something you wanted to say well and discovered that your listeners were not at all impressed or did not really understand what you were trying to say? You knew you had failed to communicate your thoughts, but did you take time to find out why you failed? If you did, you discovered that you used excellent words, perhaps, but did not succeed in putting them in the kind of logical and effective sequence that ensures communicated meaning.

To communicate with others we need words and we need a knowledge of the power of words. But that is not enough. We need to know how to arrange these words in well-planned sentences, because meaning exists not only in the words themselves but in the new meanings that are made by relating words logically to each other. This kind of logical relationship words have in sentences we call the syntax of the sentence, or the grammar of the sentence. When we fail to communicate clearly, it is because we do not know how to establish the correct relationship between words in sentences. We do not know the grammar of the sentence.

If we wish to be able to speak well and write well, the place to start is with sentences. If we can structure correct and effective sentences; that is, if we can make our sentences say what we want them to say, we will have little difficulty relating sentence to sentence in meaningful paragraphs, and in relating well-made paragraph to well-made paragraph in a whole piece.

Words function in sentences in four ways. They name, they predicate, they modify, and they join. Nouns and pronouns are naming words, verbs are predicating words, adjectives and adverbs are modifying words, conjunctions and prepositions are joining words. In studying and writing effective sentences we will find that the verb is the core. It alone has the strength to hold up the whole weight of the sentence. Its power to assert or affirm something about the subject we call predication. This is the first and most important function of words in sentences. You will find that a verb alone can express thought completely. No other part of speech can carry so much meaning.

You will also find that verbs are not all alike in their ability to express meaning. Some verbs express what we call *seen action*. These help move the meaning of the sentence along through time and space. *The missile hurtled through the sky*. The word that moves the missile and suggests its velocity is the verb. Other verbs express *unseen action* that does not suggest movement through time and space. *The children slept.* The action of this verb is in the subject. Still other verbs serve only as equal signs. They merely join a noun to a noun or pronoun, or a noun to an adjective. *Mary is the secretary. Mary is she. Mary is tall.*

SENTENCE PATTERNS: Making good sentences is a building process. You must know what you are building with and the shape of the finished structure. If you keep in mind these simple basic structures, you will find sentence making an orderly process.

> N–V (Noun-Verb)
> N–V–N (Noun-Verb-Noun)
> N–LV–N (Noun-Linking Verb-Noun)
> N–LV–A (Noun-Linking Verb-Adjective)

When you understand these basic patterns of the simple sentence, you will be ready to make additional patterns by adding adjective and adverbial modifiers. You will know how to join phrase and clause modifiers and how to join clause to clause.

Writing is grammar in action. As you carry out your writing assignments, you will be making an intelligent beginning to effective writing. You will get greater and greater control of the basic unit of structure in all writing, the sentence. You will learn that the structuring of prose as well as of poetry starts with the grammar of the sentence. And you will grow, especially in power to write strong narrative sentences.

WORDS FOR THE NARRATIVE WRITER: The narrative writer is alive to the stir and movement of life. He sees and hears and feels the human experience that is making a moment-by-moment impact on his senses. But while he is seeing and listening, he is also thinking. And, because he thinks, his mind pierces the outer rim of reality to find the meaning at its core.

He is not one who just lets things happen to him. He is vibrantly part of the movement of life. He is able to view life imaginatively and see himself caught up into human experience or detached from it. He is able to hold experience away from himself, so to speak, and look at it intently. He sees people, really looks at them, in groups or alone, the young and the old. He is conscious of the shades, the intensities, and the varieties of motives. He is aware of the texture of things, whether the odd or the commonplace. He lives thoroughly aware of reality.

He is a worker with words and can look as intently and penetratingly at them as he can at people and things. He knows how to use the meaning power, the image-making power, the emotional charge of words to create with them new imaginative worlds like the concrete one he lives in. But, above all words, he cherishes the verb for its power to create the sense of movement through time and space that is the essence of narration.

Grammar in Action

The following work enables you to utilize your grammatical knowledge in your own writing and to relate it to your reading. Thus you will turn fact and recognition into a full understanding of the grammar of your language.

Predicating—The Verb and the Verb Phrase

INDEPENDENT PREDICATION

1. Make some simple declarative statements telling what you might do if you met the Jabberwock in the corridors of your school. Then change the statements according to the following directions and be ready to discuss the different effects. **-a** Move each subject into an unusual but acceptable position. **-b** Double the action of each statement, making a series of compound verbs. **-c** Change each statement to a question addressed to your teacher. **-d** Change each statement to a request or command with an understood subject addressed to the Jabberwock. **-e** Change each statement to an exclamation addressed to your friend.

2. Write five sentences in which you place at least three of the subjects in an unusual place: **-a** running a power mower **-b** peeking into secret preparations **-c** planning an unusual party **-d** rushing away for an appointment **-e** avoiding a dental appointment **-f** preparing to leave for school.

3. In a series of about seven sentences combine all the subject techniques of questions **1** and **2**. Identify. In one or two sentences about these topics, use understood subjects.

an old shoe   a quiet time at home
   an unwanted job   an impossible assignment
     the other side of a joke   noses you have known

4. Be a reporter at an imaginary trial. Record a section of the trial in which the four types of sentences are used: **-a** You are on trial for speeding in the corridor. **-b** You are on trial for parking your helicopter too close to the TV antenna. **-c** You are on trial for tying up telephone communications every night. **-d** You are on trial for avoiding income tax on baby sitting.

5. Many everyday situations include all four types of sentences. Make up a conversation for such a situation, using all four types of sentences: **-a** Your mother is leaving for the weekend. **-b** Your dad is explaining how to change a tire. **-c** You are going to take an IQ test. **-d** You are getting ready for a game (football, baseball, basketball).

DEPENDENT PREDICATION

1. Write dependent clauses to accompany each of the following: **-a** Once there was a kangaroo . . . **-b** Once there was a dinosaur . . . **-c** Once there was a chimpanzee . . . **-d** Once there was a buffalo . . . **-e** Once there was a crocodile . . .

2. Write a dependent clause to establish a situation for each of these:

She screamed   She wheezed   He snorted

He laughed   He winked   He sneezed   He fumed

She chuckled   She whispered   She gurgled

3. Write five different replacements for the second line of the following couplet of the poem *Eletelephony* to express, in the form of dependent clauses, different kinds of confusion.

> *Dear me! I am not certain quite*
> *That even now I've got it right.*

1. Write an account, in simple sentences, of some humorous word usage you have heard, like that which Thurber recalls in *What Do You Mean It* Was *Brillig?*   **2.** Rewrite the account from number **1** by combining the statements, wherever possible, into compound sentences. Examine all the words you used to connect the clauses and analyze them to make certain that they express the proper relationships. Be prepared to contrast the accounts from numbers **1** and **2** to determine how the change in sentence type affects the style. Change the sentences to complex sentences and determine the effect on style.   **3.** Finally rewrite the account, giving each sentence the individual form you think best for it. Contrast the effects of the different types of sentences on the clearness, emphasis, and interest of the ideas.   **4.** Reread the first paragraph of *What Do You Mean It* Was *Brillig?* and classify each sentence as simple, compound, complex, or compound-complex. Analyze the aptness of the type of one of them in relation to its contribution to the entire paragraph. Experiment with some of the sentences by changing their structure in regard to sentence type and in regard to position of ideas; compare and contrast the effects of the changed forms with the original form.

5. Discuss the following in reference to the second paragraph of *What Do You Mean It* Was *Brillig?*:

-a SENTENCE ONE: Would the sentence be more effective if the first clause were subordinated? the second? Why or why not? Would the thought be more effective expressed as two simple sentences? Why or why not?

-b SENTENCE TWO: Would the sentence be more effective if the introductory phrase were changed to an independent clause? Why or why not?

-c SENTENCE FIVE: Is a compound sentence the most effective form for these two ideas? Why or why not?

-d SENTENCE SIX: How does the accumulation and stretching out of dependent clauses in this sentence contribute to the humor?

-e SENTENCE TEN: Would this idea be more effective if it were attached to the preceding or the following sentence as a dependent or independent clause? Why or why not?

-f SENTENCES TWELVE AND THIRTEEN: Are these two sentences simple, compound, complex, or compound-complex? Compare and contrast the effects created by the same types of clauses in the two sentences.

6. Write some short conversations: **-a** In simple sentences: a conversation between two children discussing an adult situation like a wedding, a political election, or a family budgeting. **-b** In compound sentences: a conversation between two women hanging up wash in their back yards and gossiping about one of the situations suggested in **a**. **-c** In complex sentences: a conversation between two college students discussing their plans for the future.

7. Write one simple, one complex, one compound, and one compound-complex sentence on: **-a** My first ride on the roller coaster or ferris wheel. **-b** The horseback ride on which I nearly got thrown. **-c** My strategy for swatting mosquitoes in the dark. **-d** What I would do if my inner tube collapsed and I didn't know how to swim.

KINDS OF VERBS AND VERB PHRASES

1. Action verbs can show either seen or unseen action. Pantomime certain actions while the members of the class write the proper verb. **2.** Find all the verbs in paragraph 2, page 40 (*I Get a Colt to Break In*) and classify them as verbs of seen action, verbs of unseen action, or linking verbs. What three strands of thought are carried through the paragraph by these three kinds of verbs? **3.** Notice that there are only three verbs in the poem called *A Widow Bird Sate Mourning for Her Love* by Shelley—one linking verb, one of seen action, one of unseen action. Classify each. Discuss how these three types contribute to the basic mood and contrast in the poem. **4.** Read paragraphs 1 and 2, page 33 (*I Get a Colt to Break In*) without the verbs. Analyze how the omission affects the meaning. By comparing the effects of omitting different kinds of verbs in individual sentences, analyze which kinds make the greatest contribution to the meaning of a sentence. In paragraph 2, for instance, which sentences are hardly affected at all by the omission of verbs? What kind of ideas do they express? **5.** Tell an abbreviated story in sentences using verbs alone. EXAMPLE:

Sing. Stop. Dance. Stop. Whistle. Stop. Play. Stop. Start. Stop. Stop. Stop. Go.

SUGGESTED SUBJECTS:

freshmen at a dance
first freshman days
getting a meal

lining up
meeting your teachers
high school at last

6. Analyze the first paragraph from a newspaper article that reports some very exciting event. Make a list of all verbs. Label them as seen or unseen action. If they are linking verbs, identify them as such. **7.** Take an editorial from the newspaper and analyze the verbs in a similar manner. **8.** Write five sentences on these topics, using verbs of seen action:

learning to drive
a pizza party

getting the family together
the last football game

9. Write six sentences in which each of the following performs an action that can be seen:

cab driver	basketball	poet
submarine	announcer	wheel

10. Write five sentences using unseen action verbs. Change the verbs to seen action.

getting a book from the school library
visiting a friend in the hospital
going on a fishing trip
getting to school on time

11. Use three different verbs for each of the subjects listed below. Make each verb as lively as possible. EXAMPLE: a car skids, speeds, glides.

girl   traffic officer   dog   train   my uncle   hall

12. Some verbs of seen action are very general in nature; e.g., *to walk, to talk, to sit, to run, to kill.* Effective writing uses specific verbs; e.g., *to shuffle, to amble, to chatter, to slump, to dash.* For each general verb above give three specific verbs.

13. Find an advertisement having a minimum of fifty words. Underline all action verbs, seen or unseen. Clarify them as specific or general.

14. Write an advertisement using only specific verbs for:

handy homework kit   school chorus, band, orchestra
     school baseball team   personalized elevator
       gold plated paper clips   a cure-all for algebra

15. The most common linking verb is *to be.* Others are *to seem, to appear, to feel, to become.* To be certain that you have a linking verb, substitute a form of the verb *to be.* Write five sentences with linking verbs. Using the same sentences, change the linking verbs to action verbs.

school rules   pantry shelf
     our championship   plan to build a hot rod
       being a freshman   my allowance

16. Without using any linking verbs, write five sentences on some autumn free day. **17.** Some forms of the verb *to be* are used as auxiliary verbs rather than linking verbs. Make a list of ten verb phrases in which you use an auxiliary plus a specific action verb. Forms of other verbs (*do, can, may, shall, will*) are also auxiliaries. **18.** In the safety signal which says *curve,* the verb is understood. This is often true in road signs and danger signals. Make up five safety signals to be used in school. Write them first with the linking verb expressed and then without. Which is more effective? Why? **19.** Write five sentences with linking verbs to describe the calm after a storm or any other quiet aspect of nature. **20.** Using at least one linking verb in each sentence, compose five sentences about a famous painting. **21.** Write a short conversation of about six sentences in which the first speaker uses a single verb, and the second speaker answers using the same verb in a verb phrase. **22.** In no more than five sentences using transitive verbs, describe the essential action of your favorite sport. **23.** Find all the sentences with coined words that function as transitive verbs in Lewis Carroll's *Jabberwocky*. Write similar sentences with real English words functioning the same way. Write similar sentences with your own coined nonsense verbs. **24.** Classify as transitive or intransitive all the action verbs in paragraph 2, page 34 (*I Get a Colt to Break In*). Notice the difference between the verbs which complete the action within themselves and verbs that need an object to complete it. Would *lassoing* be more expressive here if it were used transitively? What effect is achieved by its intransitive use? Contrast the use of *drives* in the second sentence and *break* in the third sentence to decide whether the object is essential in both. If not, what does the transitive use of the verb contribute to the sentence?

VERB IN RELATION TO SUBJECT

1. Pretend you are watching a baseball game from a knothole in the fence. Describe the game in the present tense. **2.** In the past tense tell about your first day in high school. **3.** Pretend you are a fortune teller. Foretell the future of:

your best friend	your younger sister or brother
your teacher	your favorite baseball player
your rival	your favorite movie star

4. Using the irregular verbs *lie, lay, sit, set, rise, raise,* write seven sentences about one of the following: **-a** summer at the beach **-b** my operation **-c** part-time work **-d** working on night shift

5. Identify the basic tense used in *I Get a Colt to Break In* and the one in *Brothering Fish*. Compare the use of each tense in terms of subject matter and effect. **6.** Analyze the pattern of tenses in Lincoln's *Gettysburg Address*. Be prepared to discuss the effectiveness of the movement from one tense to another as Lincoln achieves it. **7.** Focus your understanding of the distinction between tenses and time by contrasting the use of present tense in *Brothering Fish* with its use in some parts of *I Get a Colt to Break In*.

Naming—The Noun and Pronoun

NATURE AND FUNCTION OF THE NOUN

1. Put yourself in a certain place. Write five sentences in which you use all the names for the things you can touch from the position: **-a** at your dressing table **-b** at your desk in your bedroom **-c** an easy chair in your living room **-d** in the bleachers during a basketball game

2. List all the nouns in paragraphs 1 and 2, page 30 (*Brothering Fish*). Name their function in the sentence.

3. Select, from your list in number **2**, all the words functioning as nouns that could also function as verbs. Write two sentences for each to illustrate the distinction between its usage as a noun and as a verb. In each case, make one sentence compound and the other complex.

4. Take some of the words James Thurber's Della misuses and use them correctly in complex sentences of your own, illustrating as many noun uses as each one can be made to illustrate.

5. Write a series of sentences on skills you could teach to your younger brothers and sisters or to various little children on your block. Use as many indirect objects as you can. Identify the specific function of all the other nouns in your paragraph.

6. Write sentences with objective complements which are: **-a** a noun denoting a person **-b** a noun denoting a thing **-c** a collective noun **-d** a proper noun **-e** an abstract noun.

7. Use each of the following verbs with the five types of objective complement in number **6** (above): **-a** consider, **-b** name, **-c** elect.

8. Locate the following in the dictionary or some other reference book and identify them in sentences using appositives:

James Thurber	Percy Bysshe Shelley
William Beebe	E. E. Cummings	Lewis Carroll

9. In sentences using appositives identify any of the following names as belonging to literary characters that you've met in your reading experiences of the past. If you haven't met at least ten of them, find out about some of them from your classmates.

Alice	Tom	Mary	King	Peter
Heidi	Jo	Dick	Queen	George
Winnie	Arthur	David	Chief	Captain
Johnny	Betty	Polly	Jack	Joe

10. Many nursery rhymes begin with proper names. List the first lines of at least ten of them and indicate whether the name is used as the subject of the sentence or as a noun of direct address. Indicate which ones are followed by appositives. Identify the uses of the other nouns in each line.

11. List all the different things you've ever wanted to be. Do the same with two of your friends who have told you of their dreams. Then write a sentence expressing each idea with a subjective complement and with a different verb for each sentence.

12. Write ten compound sentences similar to the following, in which you use the same word as an object in one clause and as the subjective complement of a negative verb in the next clause: **-a** I can easily eat a large anchovy pizza, but I wouldn't like to be a large anchovy pizza. **-b** In our school play I impersonated Goliath, but I am no Goliath in size or strength. **-c** After spending several summers on the farm, I can handle a stubborn mule, but I am no stubborn mule.

13. In sentences express as many relationships as you can in the form of prepositional phrases for each of the following:

skyscraper	sea	paper	bicycle
basket	door	border	crowd

14. Answer the following questions in sentences using prepositional phrases: **-a** What can you be before but not behind? **-b** Whom would you want to be below but not above? **-c** What would you want to be with but not without? **-d** What would you like to be on but not off? **-e** What would you like to be under but not over? **-f** What would you like to be over but not under? **-g** What would you like to be in but not out of? **-h** What are you against but not for? **-i** What would you want to be away from but not beside? **-j** What would you like to be going to but not from? **15.** Explain the American way of life to an exchange student. Include five sentences in which you use abstract nouns.

16. In seven sentences discuss the values of a high school education. Use abstract nouns. Identify. **17.** List and identify all the nouns in the *Gettysburg Address* as concrete or abstract. Is one kind of noun most common in this selection, or is there something of a balance? Discuss the effect of this predominance or balance on the style. Do the same for paragraphs 1 and 2 of *Brothering Fish.* **18.** Write a series of sentences on liberty or death using all abstract nouns. Then write a series of sentences on the same subject using all concrete nouns. Which of these two pieces is more interesting? Why? **19.** Write a series of playful sentences using as many compounds as you can from the following list. Check the dictionary to make certain that the expression you use is considered as a single compound noun in its function.

house   street   water   school   floor   air   fire

EXAMPLE: Through the skylight of the top floor of the skyscraper I thought I saw a skylark on fire in the sky. Or was some sky pilot doing luminous skywriting at night and erasing it immediately? Neither. It was merely some little boy's skyrocket illegally anticipating the Fourth of July.

20. From *I Get a Colt to Break In, Brothering Fish,* and *What Do You Mean It* Was *Brillig?* pick out all the capitalized nouns. Decide which of them would always be proper nouns when they are used as nouns. For those that could be used as common nouns, illustrate the distinction. When a rule of capitalization other than that of the proper noun is operating, indicate the rule. **21.** Find sentences in which you can replace all the common nouns by proper nouns. This may necessitate the removal of other words in the sentence. **22.** Look up five news items in today's paper and write the essential facts of each one in a single sentence making good use of proper nouns. Then rewrite the sentences by replacing the proper nouns with common nouns. Discuss what happens to the expression of the idea when this change takes place. **23.** List at least ten words that were originally used only as proper nouns, either in history or in mythology, but are now most often used as common nouns. Illustrate the two uses of each in sentences. EXAMPLES:

James Watt was the British engineer who invented the steam engine.

The 100-watt bulb was so bright for her weak eyes that she covered them almost completely with their lids.

Mercury, the messenger god, had a staff that could become a snake when necessary.

It was so cold that I was expecting the mercury in the thermometer to freeze into a silver icicle.

24. Contribute to a class collection of words that can function as collective nouns, but are not used very often. Check the dictionary to see how limited their use is. Write a sentence for each word in which you also practice using compound verbs.
EXAMPLES:

brace   covey   band

QUALITIES OF NOUNS—NUMBER

1. Write two sentences for each word using number **23** of the preceding section, illustrating the use of singular and plural verbs with collective nouns.

2. Write a series of sentences involving individual members of the group in number **1**. Show how various complications of the subject (e.g., compound subjects with *and, or;* subjects with modifiers, etc.) affect the number of the verb.

3. Track down the problem of number connected with each of the following words:

scissors	data	parenthesis	athletics
news	dues	trousers	politics
compasses	basis	economics	mumps

Then use them in a little word play in verse, after you read David McCord's verse which promotes a campaign for obsolete positive forms of negatives that are in use:

> I know a little man, both ept and ert,
> An intro? Extro? No, he's just a vert.
> Shevelled and couth and kempt, pecunious, ane;
> His image trudes upon the captive brain.

When life turns sipid and my friend is traught
The Spirit soars as I would sist it ought.
Chalantly then, like a gainly goof,
My digent self is sertive, choate, loof.

4. Go through *Jabberwocky* and change all the plural nouns to singular and all the singular nouns to plural. Change all the verbs to agree in number. How does this change affect the non-sensical situation in the poem?

QUALITIES OF NOUNS—CASE

1. Tell the case of all the nouns in *Jabberwocky*. Identify the function of each.

2. Tell the case and function of each noun in *A Widow Bird Sate Mourning for Her Love* by Shelley.

3. In *anyone lived in a pretty how town,* pick out all the unusual uses of words as nouns. Tell the case and function of each one.

4. Try some verse of your own, using as nouns words that are ordinarily used as other parts of speech. Some possible first lines: **-a** The young boy swam in a sea of can't **-b** She lost her was but found her will be **-c** He constantly came with his if's and when's

Identify the case and function of each noun in your completed verse.

5. Try to write five varied sentences each of which makes use of all the functions of the noun. Is it possible to accomplish this usage in an ordinary simple sentence? In a simple sentence with a compound predicate? For the content of your sentences, write about famous people you're meeting in your study of history, science, or some other subject.

6. Answer each of the following questions with a series of answers, illustrating as many different possessive forms as you can (regular singular, singular ending in *s*, regular plural, irregular plural, compound posssessives, etc.) **-a** Whose life was lost in a war? **-b** Whose words do you treasure? **-c** Whose case has been tried in court? **-d** Whose work has contributed to our cultural history? **-e** Whose writings would you like to read?

-f Whose life seems to have been a great adventure? **-g** Whose goals would you like to adopt? **-h** Whose activities have greatly influenced the movement of world events?

7. Make use of as many problem plural and possessive forms as you can in a series of sentences about the in-laws of any of the following couples. If they never married, imagine that they did when they grew up. If you haven't read the stories of any of the literary couples, choose one of the historical or biblical couples and find the necessary facts through research.

David Copperfield and Agnes Wickfield   Heidi and Peter
Tom Sawyer and Becky Thatcher   Ulysses and Penelope
Amy March and Laurie   Isaac and Rebecca
Samson and Delilah   Ruth and Booz
Jacob and Rachel   Anna and Joachim
Tobias and Sara   Abraham and Mary Lincoln
George and Martha Washington

8. Write a sentence using a simple appositive for each of the following:

my favorite book   the work most boring to me
my first friend   the earliest historical date I remember
my most difficult subject   my favorite month
my favorite hideout   the song I can sing the best

Identify the functions of the other nouns in each sentence.

9. Write a series of sentences about one of the *firsts* you've experienced in high school (your first homecoming, your first gym class, your first study period, your first try with a locker, or the like). Use as many appositives as you can, some restrictive and some nonrestrictive, to illustrate the difference in the use and punctuation of the two kinds.

10. **-a** Examine John Kennedy's inaugural address for the use of complex appositives. Determine in which cases the dash and the colon could be used interchangeably. **-b** Write your own sentences modeled on the structure of each of these and expressing similar ideals either for your family, your neighborhood, or a club of which you're a member.

1. In the second paragraph, page 40 (*I Get a Colt to Break In*), find all the verbs that have objects or subjective complements. Decide which of these single nouns could be replaced by noun clauses. Then, keeping the same subject and verb and as much of the original idea as possible, rewrite each sentence that can be changed, using a noun clause. Do you think any one of your rewritten sentences is more effective than the original sentence with a single noun?

2. In complex sentences, express as noun clauses: **-a** five of your wishes **-b** five of your dreams **-c** five facts you've learned **-d** five things you don't understand.

3. How many of the noun clauses you expressed in answer to number **2** can you reduce to single nouns? What is the difference in effect?

4. Can a noun clause function in all the ways that a single noun can? Illustrate each use, if possible, with a single noun in a simple sentence and then with a noun clause in a complex sentence.

5. Lest you think that a noun clause is recognizable by its introductory word, write sentences with noun clauses using each of the following as an introductory word:

that	how	when	where	why	what
whatever	who	whom		no introductory word	

USE OF QUOTATION MARKS

1. Write a conversation between James Thurber and Della that might begin with Della's telling him that the new towels Mrs. Thurber bought for the kitchen are not observant or that she can't stand that parrot because he keeps mimeographing her. First use indirect quotations; then rewrite using direct quotations. Which is more effective? Why? Check to see that your punctuation is perfect. Identify the function of every noun clause.

2. Write a conversation between the boy Lincoln Steffens and his father about methods of discipline. Try to involve the use of single quotation marks, of the question mark within and without quotation marks, of the exclamation point within and without quotation marks.

3. Write a conversation between the Jabberwock and the owner of the vorpal blade. Though you may use unconventional diction, use conventional punctuation illustrating the rules for quotation marks.

4. From tonight's newspaper and from any current magazine, collect as many examples as you can of different uses of quotation marks and of italics. Bring them to class tomorrow for a discussion of both the interchangeable and the distinct use of the two.

5. Write a series of original sentences in which you try to illustrate all the usage you discovered regarding quotation marks and italics. SUGGESTED TOPICS:

> A Visit to the Library
>> The Extent of My Cultural Experience
>>> Life with a Schoolteacher

NATURE OF THE PRONOUN

1. Using only pronouns write a five-sentence biography of a famous person. Indicate the function and classification of each pronoun. Read it aloud to the class and have the students' guess who the person is.

athlete   musician   actor   teacher

2. Write six sentences using no pronouns. Rewrite the sentences, using pronouns. Indicate the function and classification of each pronoun. The first day of school: **-a** a mother's viewpoint **-b** a student's viewpoint **-c** a teacher's viewpoint **-d** a bus driver's viewpoint.

3. From any of the literature at the beginning of this book find sentences that use no pronouns and that illustrate each of the possible functions of the noun. Rewrite each sentence as many times as you can make substitutions to illustrate the different kinds of pronouns.

4. Rewrite paragraph 1, page 33 (*I Get a Colt to Break In*), changing all the pronouns to nouns to reveal the importance of pronouns. From the resulting piece, be prepared to discuss what the proper use of pronouns can contribute to your writing.

5. Rewrite paragraph 1, page 33 (*I Get a Colt to Break In*), changing all the nouns in the original piece to pronouns to reveal that, important as the pronoun is, it is only a substitute. Identify the function and type of each noun or pronoun in the paragraph.

6. In a question-answer conversation between the narrator of *Masculine Protest* and his father, illustrate the distinction between: **-a** relative and interrogative use of *who* **-b** relative and interrogative use of *what*.

QUALITIES OF PRONOUNS—PERSON

1. What persons are the personal pronouns that carry the basic line of thought in *I Get a Colt to Break In,* Kennedy's inaugural address, *Brothering Fish,* and *What Is Poetry?* Discuss the relative effects of each in its particular context.

2. Write a series of sentences on some exciting experience you've had. Use third person pronouns throughout. Then change the pronouns to first person, and finally to second person. Discuss the relative effects of each change.

QUALITIES OF PRONOUNS—CASE

1. Write a short verse using no nouns and as many cases of different personal pronouns as you can. Identify the function of each one. EXAMPLE:

We!

Sometimes I wish that I were he;
I wish that I would not be me.
But then I also think, you see,
That he might wish that he were me.
So then of course if I were he,
I'd sometimes wish that I were me.
And this in truth could never be,
For, being he, I'd still be me,
And I'd still wish that I were he.

JOHN GENKE

2. Write a series of questions that you might include in a questionnaire for newcomers to a scout troop if you were made the leader. Aim the questions to get a picture of a boy's or girl's interests and social life in particular. In the questions, illustrate all the nominative, objective, and possessive uses of *who*.

3. Forms of *who* and *whoever* used at the beginning of noun clauses functioning as objects provide a particular case problem. Get practice in solving it by completing the following with noun clauses illustrating the proper use of *who* and *whom, whoever, and whomever*. Identify the function of each one: **-a** Everyone in our class is willing to vote for . . . **-b** For the job of collecting dues I suggest . . . **-c** For a good companion on a walk I want . . . **-d** For a good companion at a plant I insist on . . . **-e** For a shopping companion I won't tolerate . . . **-f** On the first day of school I saw . . . **-g** By the end of the first day of school I heard . . . **-h** To assure an interesting conversation at the banquet, I'll invite . . . **-i** For an intelligent discussion of the material we had in class today, I'll phone . . . **-j** As soon as I glanced through the window in the door of the classroom, I felt like Alice in Wonderland, for I noticed . . .

QUALITIES OF PRONOUNS—NUMBER

1. Write sentences using each of the following as subjects. Use one pronoun in each sentence to refer to the subject.

fitchew	cormorant	bison
philanthropist	ecologist	neurologist
stallion	bibliophile	semantics

2. Rewrite the sentences in number **1**, replacing each noun subject with a suitable personal pronoun. Indicate subject-verb agreement.

3. Cope with the problem pronouns by writing a series of sentences telling how:

everyone . . .	someone . . .	many . . .	anyone . . .
no one . . .	either . . .	some . . .	neither . . .

. . . does or do his or their studying.

Underline the subject, verb, and possessive pronouns that agree in each sentence and mark them singular or plural.

4. Write a series of warning signs (like *Everybody should keep his seat*) for one of the following situations. Illustrate the agreement of pronouns like *everybody* and *nobody* with possessive pronouns.

a tour of a cave   a trip in a balloon
   a tour up a mountain   a trip through a zoo

Modifying and Joining

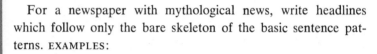

MEANING OF MODIFICATION

For a newspaper with mythological news, write headlines which follow only the bare skeleton of the basic sentence patterns. EXAMPLES:

N–V	Phaëton Perishes
N–V–N	Prometheus Snatches Fire
N–LV–N	Daphne Becomes Tree
N–LV–A	Ceres Is Kind

By adding details in the form of modifiers that describe and limit, develop the sentences into complete, informative sentences.

ADJECTIVES

1. Write a commentary that an imaginary guide might use on an imaginary tour of the underworld or of Olympus. Use the best single adjective you can think of to describe each of the mythological characters he meets. In the commentary involve the following terms, as well as any others you are acquainted with.

FOR THE UNDERWORLD:

Phaëton   Pandora   Prometheus
Midas   Baucis   Philemon   Ceyx

FOR OLYMPUS:

Apollo   Diana   Cupid   Jupiter
Latona   Venus   Minerva .   Psyche   Mercury

2. The following words, which have mythological origins, can be used as adjectives. Use them as predicate adjectives in sentences in which you account for their origin:

vulcanized	saturnine	mercurial
aeolian	psychic	Olympic
hygienic	jovial	chaotic
panicky	herculean	echoing
titanic	protean	labyrinthine

3. Combine practice in predicate adjectives with a review of linking and action verbs by writing sentences using the same verb first as linking with a predicate adjective and then as transitive. Use your imagination to involve mythological characters and geography in your sentences by telling how Mt. Helicon looks, how the golden apples taste, how the Minotaur sounds, how the hair of Cerberus feels, how Tartarus smells, how Arcadia appears, how the narcissus grows.

EXAMPLE: Patting one of Cerberus' three heads, I felt the hair on his snout. The hair felt coarse and snarled.

4. In different aspects, compare the following characters from Norse mythology by writing sentences with adjectives in different degrees of comparison:

Audhumbla	Heidrum	Urdur	Ymir	Vili	Ve
Verdandi	Munin	Fenris	Loki	Thor	Tyr
Schrimner	Heimdall	Freya	Odin	Hugin	Aske
Nidhogge	Skunir	Embla	Skuld	Bragi	Frey
Utgard-Loki	Skrymir	Iduna	Hela	Thrym	

EXAMPLES: Hugin is as small as Munin; Geri and Freki are larger than Hugin and Munin; Audhumbla is larger than all of them. Thyrm is sly; Loki is slyer; and Utgard-Loki is slyest.

5. In sentences using pronominal adjectives to suggest the appropriate gender, write the most important fact or event you connect with each of the characters in number **4**.

6. Write a rhyme about the seven days of the week in terms of classical or Norse mythology (see page 180). Use different degrees of adjectives.

7. In sentences using proper adjectives, reveal the home city of twenty mythological characters.

EXAMPLE: Like most women, Niobe, the Theban queen, had to make her own fatal mistake instead of learning from Arachne's.

8. Make an investigation of which names of Greek gods and goddesses are the root of modern words that are used as adjectives. (You have already met some of these words in number **2.**) After you have as complete a list as you can make, check in the dictionary to find out whether they would be used as proper or as common adjectives today.

ADJECTIVE PHRASES

1. Take the titles of the fables you've read and rewrite them:
-a By adding a single adjective to describe each noun.

EXAMPLE: The (Frustrated) Fox and the (Inaccessible) Grapes

-b By adding a prepositional phrase used as an adjective

EXAMPLE: The Fox (with Designs) and the Grapes (Beyond Reach)

(Do not use adjectives or adjective phrases that are already used in the body of the story.)

2. Go through three fables that you've read and find all the single adjectives and the adjective phrases in them. **-a** Indicate whether each is limiting or descriptive. **-b** How many of the single adjectives could be changed to adjective phrases? Draw some conclusions on the effectiveness of the change. **-c** How many of the adjective phrases could be changed to single adjectives? Draw some conclusions on the effectiveness of the change.

3. After you have investigated Thurber's FABLES FOR OUR TIMES, make a list of titles, using other adjective prepositional phrases, to suggest kinds of fables that different members of your class might write. EXAMPLES:

Fable for a Zoo Keeper
  Fable for Parents
    Fable for Ancient Greeks

Fable without Finish
Fable in French

4. For an imaginary literary banquet write a speech you could use to announce the arrival of any authors or characters you've met in your studies thus far. Use adjective prepositional phrases after each name to characterize the persons. EXAMPLES:

James Thurber of the Witty Word
Cupid of the Amorous Arrow

ADJECTIVE CLAUSES

1. In *The Prodigal Son* there is just one adjective clause. Find it. In *The Godson* there are just about as few adjective clauses in proportion to the length. Find them. Can you see anything in the nature and style of these two stories that would account for the scarcity of adjective clauses?

2. In sentences using adjective clauses, identify the role of each of the following characters in the action of the story:

THE PRODIGAL SON:
 the father   the younger son   the older son

THE GODSON:
 the poor peasant   the godmother
  the son   Vasili Kudryashov
   the godfather   the robber
    the rich tradesman   the hermit

HOW MUCH LAND DOES A MAN NEED?:
 the elder sister   the stranger from beyond the Volga
  the younger sister   the innkeeper
   Pahom   the Bashkirs
    the lady landowner   the Bashkir Chief
   the steward   Semyon

EXAMPLE: The father in *The Prodigal Son* is the character who loves his son enough to forgive him completely.

3. Distinguish between restrictive and nonrestrictive adjective clauses in a series of sentences reviewing the authors you have studied. In each sentence include the piece the author wrote and one other fact you can find out about him. Pay careful attention to the punctuation of the restrictive and nonrestrictive clause in each sentence.

EXAMPLE: Leo Tolstoy, who wrote *The Godson,* was a Russian who also wrote great novels.

4. Recall or find the old nursery rhyme called *This Is the House That Jack Built.* You'll notice that the rhyme is made up of a series of sentences using adjective clauses. Are they restrictive or nonrestrictive? Write two similar verses, one with restrictive and one with nonrestrictive clauses. Base each one on a parable which you read as extra reading.

ADVERBS

1. Find all the adverbs in *Peter Klaus* and identify them as adverbs of time, manner, place, degree, frequency, affirmation, negation. Identify what word each modifies.
2. Rewrite each of these in four different ways telling **-a** when **-b** how **-c** where, and **-d** how often the action is done. Add a single adverb to express each idea.

Peter Klaus pastured his flock.
Peter watched his favorite goat.
Peter obeyed the groom.
Peter took a draught of wine.
Peter opened his eyes.

3. Go through the first four paragraphs of *The Sleeping Beauty in the Wood:* **-a** Find all the adverbs that modify either adjectives or other adverbs. **-b** Experiment with the use of such modifiers by inserting some of them before adjectives and adverbs without modifiers in this paragraph. **4.** List thirty fairy-tale characters and write sentences comparing their actions. Use adverbs in comparative and superlative forms. **5.** In *The Iron Stove* there aren't many adverbs that can be compared. Find those that can, tell what word each modifies, and write the comparative and superlative form of each. **6.** Make out a quiz for oral class practice on the usage of troublesome adjectives and adverbs. Use characters and events from *The Constant Tin-Soldier* for the content. Adjectives and adverbs to use:

sure—surely	good—well	careful—carefully
any other	bad—badly	where
less—fewer	beautiful—beautifully	somewhat
most—almost	straight	this kind of

ADVERBIAL PHRASES

1. Throughout the short legend *How Arthur Gets His Sword from the Lady of the Lake,* find the adverbial phrases that tell **-a** to what place Arthur and Merlin came **-b** where Arthur saw some object (note intervolvement of two adverbial phrases) **-c** what it was that Arthur became aware of **-d** how the object was clothed **-e** where Merlin predicted there would be a rock **-f** where the damsel sent Arthur **-g** how far Arthur was to row **-h** where Arthur and Merlin tied their horses **-i** how Arthur grasped the sword **-j** where the arm and hand went **-k** where Merlin advised Arthur always to keep the scabbard. **2.** Write a conversation between Arthur and Merlin as they ride along toward the lake. Have Arthur question Merlin about things that will happen in the future. Merlin's answers should be incomplete sentences which are adverbial phrases. **3.** Do any of your older relatives tell family legends? If so, retell one in your own words. If not, invent one for someone in your relationship. Make conscious use of adjective and adverbial phrases. When you have finished the story, underline all of these phrases, identify them as adjective or adverb, and encircle the word each modifies.

ADVERBIAL CLAUSES

1. In *The Legend of St. Christopher, Breaker of Men,* find two adverbial clauses that modify by telling **-a** when **-b** why **-c** how **-d** under what condition. Did you find any that tell *where?* Discuss. Point out several adjective and noun clauses that one might mistake for adverbial if he didn't examine them carefully. **2.** Use the following sentences as independent clauses in complex sentences. By writing several sentences for each, add adverbial clauses expressing every possible condition for the action. **-a** Kidd, the pirate, buried a great amount of treasure. **-b** Tom Walker married a tall termagant. **-c** Tom met a stranger. **-d** Tom shared his secret. **-e** Tom's wife disappeared.

3. In a short verse based on any legend you've read, pile up adverbial clauses expressing a different condition in each line until they reach a final climax in an independent clause for the last line. EXAMPLE:

> *When* autumn squirrels dodged his gun
> *Where* Kaatskill Mountains reach the sun,
> (*Although* he should have left the spot
> *As quickly as* he shot a shot
> *Because* his wife might box his ears)
> Rip fell asleep, and slept for years.

4. In *Rip Van Winkle* find five single adverbs and five adverbial phrases that could be changed to adverbial clauses. Make the change in each case and compare the effects. **5.** Write five sentences for each of the following conditions. Then move the adverbial clause in each sentence to several different places to study the effect of placement on punctuation and on the idea itself. **-a** If I were Paul Bunyan . . . **-b** When I dreamed I was Pecos Bill . . . **-c** Although I'm not Davy Crockett . . . **6.** In Pecos Bill's *Beat the Drums* song, find all the adverbial constructions. Would they be set off by commas if their position in the sentence were changed? **7.** Create another pet for Paul Bunyan comparable to the Blue Ox. Tell about him in a series of sentences that demonstrate the use and punctuation of adverbial constructions.

CONJUNCTIONS

1. One stylistic characteristic of the epic is the cataloguing of men, armies, armor, weapons. The conjunction as a joining word is a necessary element in such catalogues. In the ILIAD find examples of: **-a** list of warriors' names, joined by *and* **-b** list of armor and weapons joined by *and* **-c** list of places.
2. Find examples in MORTE D'ARTHUR of *and* used to connect dependent clauses. Bring at least one example of each of the following: **-a** adjective clauses joined by *and* **-b** adverb clauses joined by *and* **-c** noun clauses joined by *and*.
3. Co-ordinating conjunctions can also join independent clauses. Such a construction (two or more independent clauses joined by *and, but, or, nor*) is called a compound sentence. Find several

examples of compound sentences in any given chapter of the ILIAD. Experiment with restating or rewriting these sentences substituting *and* for *but* or *or*. **4.** Using the names from number **1**, construct a series of sentences in which you use *and* to connect phrases and clauses. Underline and identify these constructions. In class restate these sentences, substituting *or* or *but* for *and*. How does this change the meaning? **5.** Sometimes, in addition to its grammatical function, the conjunction has a stylistic function also. Find in Watson's version of the ILIAD sentences that begin with *and, or,* or *but*. What is the effect of this in the paragraph as a whole? **6.** Write a series of sentences that end with: *and I didn't know what to do*. Use *and* in its correct grammatical sense at least three times—to join words, phrases, and clauses. **7.** Write a series of simple sentences with compound subjects. Use one of the following titles:

Achilles Arms for War
   A Court Feast at Camelot
      Penelope and the Suitors Wait

8. Write a series of sentences without using co-ordinating conjunctions in any way. Try one of the following titles:

The Background of the Trojan War
   A Day in Helen's Life
      A Day in Guinevere's Life
         Lancelot at the Tournament

9. Take a paragraph from any page of the ILIAD and make a list of the sentences with adverb clauses. In class be able to explain the use of the subordinating conjunction.
10. Write five epic similes using adverb clauses to express the following:

how Hector approached the Greek camp
   how Andromache protected Astyanax
      how Priam grieved for Hector
         how Odysseus showed his anger at the suitors

Underline each subordinating conjunction you use.

11. In the ILIAD and ODYSSEY you will notice long sentences with series of adverb clauses that add a formal tone to the writing. Find several examples of these series and read and analyze them for the class.

12. Using correlative conjunctions (*both . . . and, either . . . or, neither . . . nor, not only . . . but also*) write five sentences discussing one of the following topics:

> If I were Telemachus
>> Advice to Achilles
>>> What Andromache will tell Astyanax about his father
>>>> Was Lancelot loyal to Arthur?

13. Regarding the stories you've read, tell the class which ones you enjoyed, which ones were humorous, which ones were adventurous, which ones were fast-moving, etc. Use *and* to connect series of words and elements. At your dictation the class should write this list, substituting a comma for the conjunction wherever it would improve the style.

14. Using a series of phrases, describe:

> King Arthur's throne room
>> King Arthur's banquet table
>>> Queen Guinevere's garden

15. Begin a sentence with a series of adverb clauses. Relate a humorous incident that could have happened at Arthur's court. Punctuate correctly.   **16.** In a series of sentences explain the work of some of the gods and goddesses. Wherever possible use words and phrases in a series to show the use of the comma and the semicolon with a series.   **17.** In a series of compound sentences using co-ordinating conjunctions to separate the clauses, compare or contrast individual Greek and Trojan warriors. Revise the sentences, first using the period to separate the two clauses and then the semicolon. In class discuss how the variation of the punctuation aids or hinders the meaning.   **18.** Find several compound sentences in MORTE D'ARTHUR. Rewrite these sentences by subordinating one clause to another. Underline the subordinating conjunction.

19. Tell what relationship the following conjunctive adverbs express. Then use them in compound sentences to relate ideas about King Arthur's knights.

accordingly	furthermore	moreover	thus
besides	however	consequently	therefore
otherwise	hence	nevertheless	instead

20. Add an independent clause to each of the following to create a compound sentence that would best be punctuated by a colon. **-a** Arthur had an idea . . . **-b** Guinevere had a dream . . . **-c** Lancelot had one desire . . . **-d** Merlin accomplished one thing that night . . . **-e** All the knights had something in common . . . **-f** Uther Pendragon kept his promise to Merlin . . . **-g** King Arthur had a special custom at Pentecost . . . **-h** One seat at the Round Table always stood empty . . . **-i** On the serpent's tomb was a prophecy about Lancelot and Galahad . . . **-j** King Arthur acquired his sword in a strange manner . . .

21. Write fifteen compound sentences eliminating punctuation. Vary your use of the following rules:

> comma and co-ordinating conjunction
>> semicolon and conjunctive adverb
>>> semicolon without conjunction
>>>> semicolon with clauses that have commas
>>>>> colon

Exchange your sentences with another student who will punctuate each sentence correctly. Have him identify the rule he used each time.

22. Ask a classmate, a brother, or a sister to give you a dictation test on punctuation. While he dictates, write and punctuate as you write. This will help you to make correct punctuation a habit. When you finish the dictation, see if you can justify by rule every punctuation mark you used.

PREPOSITIONS

1. In oral drill show the function of the preposition by establishing as many relationships as you can between the following sets of words:

sword—shield		knight—horse
stone—castle	window—tower	fountain—garden

2. Find examples of prepositional phrases in Morte D'Arthur. In class identify these phrases as adjective or adverb.

3. The function of a preposition can easily be seen by changing the preposition in a given sentence. In oral drill change the prepositions in the following sentences, using as many different prepositions as you can. As the relationship changes, the meaning changes also.

> *Now a strange thing happened at Arthur's birth.*
> *We will have Arthur for our King!*
> *Arthur called his barons to a Council.*
> *Arthur put the sword back into the stone.*
> *Then the hermit departed from the Court of King Arthur.*

4. Using adverbial and adjective prepositional phrases, explain one of the following to a new student in your school:

> how to get a library book
>> how and when to report an absence
>>> how to get on the freshman football team
>>>> how to organize a study period

Underline the preposition in each sentence and circle the object of the preposition. In the margin identify the word the prepositional phrase modifies.

Non-Grammatical Elements

INTERJECTIONS

1. Examine the ballads you've read thus far for examples of the use of interjections. Do you see any similarity between the interjection and the refrain in a stanza? Discuss.

2. Write the story of a dream in which the following characters meet in strange situations. With the proper interjections, express their responses to each other and to the situations.

the three Billy Goats Gruff	the serpent	⎫
the troll	the mouse	⎬ from the fable
Sir Lancelot	the three little pigs	St. Swithin
Elaine	Sir Galahad	the wolf	Babylon
Sir Bors	Sir Percival	Babylon's three sisters

3. Suggest some refrains using interjections for a ballad of your own in imitation of *Babylon.* Your opening lines without the refrain might be one of the following or one of your own:

There were three freshmen sharing a locker;
One of the three saw the other two mock her.

There were three students caught in the rain;
They thought that raincoats were for the inane.

There are three athletes comparing their muscles;
Along comes the coach—away each one hustles.

DIRECT ADDRESS

1. Many refrains also make use of direct address. Suggest some other refrains for your ballad in number **3** above, this time illustrating the varieties of direct address. **2.** After you've read *Lazybones,* write a verse made up entirely of dialogue between Dan Yancey and Abel Leigh. Alternate the two names as nouns of direct address in this manner:

Abel, help me out of this lurch.
Dan, you saw your own white birch.

INTRODUCTORY WORDS

1. Examine *Jesse James, De Boll Weevil,* and *The Battle of Blenheim* for the use of non-grammatical introductory words. Try to determine what function they do have in each case, since it is not a grammatical one. **2.** After you have read *Binnorie,* imagine a situation in which someone in the court calls the harpist and questions him about the story behind his last tune: *Woe to my sister, false Helen!* Illustrate the usage and punctuation of non-grammatical introductory words by making use of a variety of them in the answers of the harpist. Write the dialogue in verse form.

PARENTHETICAL EXPRESSIONS

1. Expressions like *I believe, I am sure, for example, in my opinion, I hope, after all, by the way, to tell the truth, on the contrary,* and *of course* are often used parenthetically. You will notice that you cannot find many of them in the narrative poems you read. Be prepared to account for this in a discussion. **2.** Insert some parenthetical expressions in the first stanza of some narrative poems already studied. Be prepared to comment on and demonstrate the effect. **3.** Write ten sentences illustrating the use and punctuation of parenthetical expressions. In them, review the characters of narrative poetry by commenting on their major traits.

Dates and Addresses—Uses of Commas and Colons in Letter Writing

1. After finding out the exact date of birth of ten authors from the section on narrative poetry, write an account of them, using the title *Birthdays of Some Narrative Poets*. Be sure to avoid monotony in your sentences and to use proper punctuation.
2. Write any or all of the following friendly letters. Illustrate the punctuation of dates and addresses in the heading and within the body of the letters: **-a** from Edward's wife to his mother after he *gang oure the sea.* **-b** from the wife of one of the Scots lords to the King of Dumferling after the shipwreck. **-c** from Casey to his wife after he struck out. **-d** to your cousin, telling about your first experience with narrative poetry. **-e** to your father, telling him why you need some money to buy a book of narrative poems. **-f** to your mother, telling her about some of the mothers you've met in narrative poetry—Edward's, Hanna Dustin, Mrs. Yancey, etc.
3. Write any or all of the following business letters. Illustrate the proper punctuation of dates and addresses in sentences in the body of the letter as well as in the heading. Find the correct addresses in the library: **-a** a letter to William H. Sadlier, Inc., the publishers, commenting on your English textbook. **-b** a letter to some publisher ordering a copy of some book of narrative poetry for your library. **-c** a letter to the publisher of one of your textbooks, making suggestions for a revision that is being contemplated.

Review

1. Make a grammatical analysis of *The Wreck of the Hesperus* by studying: **-a** the clause structure: the kinds of clauses and, in each case, the respective contributions of subordination and co-ordination to the movement of the story. **-b** The nouns: their grammatical functions and their structural role in the narrative. **-c** the verbs: their classification and their structural role in the narrative. **-d** the single and phrase modifiers: their classification and their structural role in the narrative. **-e** the prepositions and conjunctions (other than subordinating) and their structural role in the narrative.

2. Notice how the author of *The Means Massacre* has insects, birds, and other animals react to the situation in strong sentences of action. Build a series of narrative sentences in which individual aspects of nature react to a different situation. Be able to analyze each sentence grammatically and be prepared to explain how each grammatical element contributes to the movement of the action.

SUMMING UP

I. Identify these terms in reference to the dictionary:

—A

dictionary	denotation
unabridged	connotation
abridged	association
vocabulary	derivation
definition	etymology

—B

prefix	pronunciation
suffix	diacritical mark
root word	accent
hyphenation	phonetic
syllabication	variant spelling

—C

slang	homonym
colloquialism	restrictive labels
obsolete	thesaurus
synonym	grammar
antonym	

II. Identify these terms in reference to the library:

—A

endpaper	introduction
title page	preface
copyright	foreword
frontispiece	glossary
index	appendix

—B

library	cross reference
bibliography	magazine
card catalogue	pamphlet
Dewey decimal system	newspaper
vertical file	reference book
READER'S GUIDE TO PERIODICAL LITERATURE	
encyclopedia	handbook
atlas	

III. Identify these grammatical terms:

—A

predication	verb
independent predication	verb phrase
dependent predication	finite verb
subject	compound verb
expletive	utterance

—B

sentence pattern	sentence structure
declarative sentence	simple sentence
interrogative sentence	compound sentence
imperative sentence	complex sentence
exclamatory sentence	compound-complex sentence

—C

action verb	person
transitive verb	number
linking verb	tense
auxiliary verb	irregular verb
intransitive verb	principal parts of verb

—D

noun	objective complement
object	noun phrase
subjective complement	noun clause
indirect object	common noun
appositive	proper noun

—E

collective noun   personal pronoun
abstract noun   relative pronoun
concrete noun   interrogative pronoun
compound noun   gender
case   antecedent
pronoun

IV. Identify these grammatical terms: (to be studied with second unit)

—A

modification   pronominal adjective
description   proper adjective
limitation   adjective phrase
adjective   adjective clause
comparison of adjectives restrictive/nonrestrictive

—B

adverb   adverb of manner
comparison of adverbs   adverb of place
adverb phrase   adverb of degree
adverb clause   adverb of frequency
adverb of time   adverb of affirmation/negation

V. Identify these grammatical terms: (to be studied with third unit)

conjunction   preposition
correlative conjunction   series (of words, phrases, clauses)
co-ordinating conjunction subordinating conjunction

VI. Identify these grammatical terms: (to be studied with fourth unit)

interjection
direct address
parenthetical expressions

Singing Winds and Talking Beasts

THE
SHORT PROSE TALE

Singing Winds and Talking Beasts
THE SHORT PROSE TALE

The Past Meets the Present

Our literature began with folklore. Starting with myths and beast stories and fables and parables and fairy tales, it has widened like a river with many tributaries. From folklore it has moved along in a steady stream to become the novels, poems, and plays that are leaving our presses at this moment. Not only are our literary beginnings in folk tales of thousands of years ago, but all through the ages these old stories have been told and retold and woven into the living texture of our literature. At a turn of the page you may meet any of the gods and heroes of antiquity—Apollo, Vulcan, Cupid, Mercury, Aeneas, Hector, Achilles. You read a modern novel like Lewis' TILL WE HAVE FACES and find the old allegorical myth *Cupid and Psyche.* You go to the theater to enjoy the musical comedy MY FAIR LADY and discover that it is a retelling of the ancient pagan myth *Pygmalion.*

Folk stories do not stay within the pages of our books. They ramble about in every area of life. We meet them in medicine, astronomy, biology, chemistry, physics, industry—anywhere, for mythology is not just a treasury of story. It is also a word treasure chest. Today we call a circus organ a *calliope.* A person who gives excellent advice is a *mentor.* One who tries to browbeat us we call a *hectoring* bully. One who attempts anything very difficult has a *herculean* task on his hands. Industry uses the *vulcanizing* process. *Uranium,* a radioactive metallic chemical element, plays an important part in today's technology. How many people who use these words day after day know that each gets its name from a mythological being: Calliope, Mentor, Hector, Hercules, Vulcan, Urania?

In the Beginning

Thousands of years ago primitive men watched the wind bending the grass and the trees and wondered what the wind was and where it came from. Because they could feel it but could not see it, they imagined it was a god. They invented a name for the god who controlled all the winds and called him **Aeolus**. The rough north wind became **Boreas**. The kindest of winds, the west wind, was **Zephyrus**. These people of old watched the sun move across the sky in a blaze of light so brilliant their eyes could not look into it, and they said the sun god was driving his flaming chariot over the heavens from east to west. They named the god of the sun **Phoebus Apollo**. At night they looked at the moon with its soft light and invented a moon goddess, **Diana**.

In this way, the storytellers of long ago, in times before science had unlocked the knowledge of man in his world, gave imaginative life to thousands of mythological beings. Every force of nature—in the heavens, on earth, and under the earth—had its deity. From these stories, which took the form of myths, legends, fables, parables, and fairy tales, we learn of the complex mythology of pagan times. These old tales weave for us the religion of paganism, on which the literature of the Greeks and the Romans was built.

We learn that these pagan people believed that the gods and goddesses lived on the summit of **Mount Olympus**. The heavenly beings could pass back and forth from earth to Olympus through a gateway of clouds guarded by goddesses called the **Seasons**.

Jupiter, the Olympian king of all the gods, lived in a magnificent palace. Here the gods met to discuss the affairs of men and to feast daily on ambrosia.

Minerva and the **Graces** were believed to weave the robes of the gods. Everything solid was made of metal forged by **Vulcan** or under his direction. He was the artist who made the brass houses of the gods. He made their golden shoes. He constructed their chariots and shod their horses.

Neptune (Poseidon) and Pluto, brothers of Jupiter, shared the universe with him. Jupiter's portion was the heavens, Neptune's the ocean, Pluto's the underworld, or the realms of the dead. Earth and Olympus they held in common. Other important gods and goddesses were:

Juno (Hera), queen of the gods
Iris, her attendant, goddess of the rainbow
Mars, the god of war
Phoebus Apollo, the god of archery, prophecy, and music
Diana, the goddess of the moon
Venus, the goddess of beauty and love
Cupid (son of Venus), the god of love
Minerva (Pallas Athena), the goddess of wisdom
Mercury (Hermes), the god of commerce and of everything requiring skill
Ceres (Demeter), mother of Proserpine, presided over agriculture
Proserpine, queen of the underworld
Bacchus (Dionysus), the god of wine, and promoter of civilization, the law giver, a lover of peace
The Muses (daughters of Jupiter and Mnemosyne, memory) presided over the area of the arts and sciences
Calliope, the muse of epic poetry
Clio, the muse of history
Euterpe, the muse of lyric poetry
Melpomene, the muse of tragedy
Terpsichore, the muse of choral dance and song
Erato, the muse of love poetry
Polyhymnia, the muse of sacred poetry
Urania, the muse of astronomy
Thalia, the muse of comedy

The Fates, Clotho, Lachesis, and Atropos, spun the thread of life, or human destiny. They always had at hand the shears with which to cut the thread of life at will.

The **Erinnyes**, or **Furies**, punished those who escaped from human justice or defied it. The heads of the **Furies** were wound with snakes.

Nemesis was the goddess of vengeance, or the expression of the righteous anger of the gods.

Pan was the god of shepherds and flocks. He lived in Arcadia.

The **Satyrs** were gods of the fields and woods. They were hairy, horned, and goat-footed.

Stories that Explain the Work—Myths

Human beings have always been curious. They have always wanted to know the *what* and the *why*. This natural curiosity brought explanatory myths into existence. Primitive people asked *What is the world?* and *What is man?* but they could find no rational explanation. For what could be explained only by scientific study they gave a poetic account. The hundreds of stories, coming to us from the far, far past, that account imaginatively for the phenomena of nature, we call explanatory myths.

The most common of the explanatory myths tell the story of a human being transformed into a river or a flower or an animal, in fact, into any sort of animate or inanimate creature. These are the delightful tales that account for the origin of frogs and spiders and laurel trees and birds and weeping stones.

Other myths are good adventure stories. They seem to have been invented by excellent storytellers to amuse their friends. These stories, entertaining rather than explanatory, are called aesthetic myths. Tales about the adventures of Aeneas, the wanderings of Ulysses, the love affairs of the gods and goddesses are aesthetic myths.

Reading, Writing, and Discussion of Myths

Each kind of folklore has its own structure. Each may be identified by the way the storyteller looks at the experience of his story and the way he patterns it. Myth, fable, parable, fairy tale, legend, and tall tale are all distinct story forms.

We will start with the most common class of myth, the explanatory. Because these myths are told by and for the common, uneducated people, they are simple and direct. They offer folk explanations of the world, in which reality is seen imaginatively. A single line of action for meaning shapes a story without character development or descriptive setting.

Like all well-told stories, explanatory myths have a threefold structure. They are made up of an introductory section, a development, and a conclusion. The introductory section contains a short exposition and the starting incident. The development consists of incident added to incident until the point of the story is reached. The conclusion is often just the point of the story.

In some myths exposition consists of one sentence which gives either setting or identification of the character involved. Then one incident starts a series of events that make up the development. The last event of the development is a kind of climax in which the main character is transformed or dies as a result of an earlier transformation. When there is variation in any or all of the three parts of the basic structure, new patterns of storytelling arise. This method of storytelling, in which incident is added to incident without concern for causal relationships until the point of the story is reached, may be called linear.

1. Look for the linear structure as you read the following transformation myth:

DIANA AND ACTAEON

It was midday when young Actaeon, son of King Cadmus, said to the young men who were hunting stags in the mountains with him, "Our nets and our weapons are wet with the blood of our victims. We have had enough sport for today. Now while Phoebus parches the earth, let us put aside our weapons and rest."

There was a valley thick with cypresses and pines that was sacred to the huntress queen, Diana. In this valley was a cave. A fountain flowed from one of its sides, with an open basin bounded by a grassy rim. Here the goddess of the woods came when weary with hunting to bathe in the sparkling water.

This day, having gone there with her nymphs, she handed her javelin to one, her quiver and bow to another. One took her robe and another unbound the sandals from her feet. While the goddess was refreshing herself, Actaeon came to the place, led there by his destiny. When the nymphs saw a man at the entrance of the cave, they screamed and rushed to hide the goddess.

Diana reached on a sudden impulse for her arrows. As they were not at hand, she dashed water into the face of the intruder, saying, "Now go and tell if you can that you have seen Diana bathing."

Immediately a pair of branching horns grew out of Actaeon's head, his neck gained in length, his ears grew sharp-pointed, his hands became feet, his arms long legs, his body was covered with a hairy spotted hide. Fear took the place of his former boldness and he fled.

He admired his own speed until he saw his horns in the water. "Wretched me," he tried to say, but no sound came. He groaned, and tears flowed down the face that had taken the place of his own. Yet his consciousness remained and he tried to make plans. Should he go home to the palace or stay in the woods?

While he hesitated, his dogs caught sight of him and rushed after him swifter than the wind. Over rocks and cliffs, through mountain gorges he fled and they followed. Where he had often chased the stag and cheered on his pack, his dogs now chased him, cheered on by the huntsmen. He longed to call out, "I am Actaeon," but the words did not come at his will.

Presently one dog fastened its teeth in his back, another seized his shoulder. While they held their master, the rest of the pack came up and buried their teeth in his flesh. His friends and huntsmen cheered on the dogs calling on Actaeon to come and join in the sport.

At the sound of his name he turned his head and heard them regretting that he was not present. Soon the dogs were all around him, rending and tearing; and it was not until they had torn his life out that the anger of Diana was satisfied.

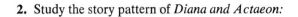

2. Study the story pattern of *Diana and Actaeon:*

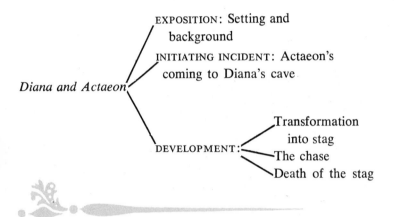

Diana and Actaeon

EXPOSITION: Setting and background

INITIATING INCIDENT: Actaeon's coming to Diana's cave

DEVELOPMENT:
Transformation into stag
The chase
Death of the stag

For a study of myths which have more complex structure, read *Minerva and Arachne* and *Niobe*.

MINERVA
AND ARACHNE

There was a contest, in which a mortal dared come in competition with Minerva. That mortal was Arachne, a maiden who had attained such skill in the arts of weaving and embroidery that the nymphs themselves would come from their groves and fountains to gaze upon her work. It was not only beautiful when it was done, but beautiful also in the doing. To watch her, as she took the wool in its rude state and formed it into rolls, or separated it with her fingers and carded it till it looked as light and soft as a cloud, or twirled the spindle with skilful touch, or wove the web, or, after it was woven, adorned it with her needle, one would have said that Minerva herself had taught her. But this she denied, and could not bear to be thought a pupil even of a goddess. "Let Minerva try her skill with mine," said she; "if beaten I will pay the penalty." Minerva heard this and was displeased. She assumed the form of an old woman and went and gave Arachne some friendly advice. "I have had much experience," said she, "and I hope you will not despise my counsel. Challenge your fellow-mortals as you will, but do not compete with a goddess. On the contrary, I advise you to ask her forgiveness for what you have said, and as she is merciful perhaps she will pardon you." Arachne stopped her spinning and looked at the old dame with anger in her countenance. "Keep your counsel," said she, "for your daughters or handmaids; for my part I know what I say, and I stand to it. I am not afraid of the goddess; let her try her skill, if she dare venture." "She comes," said Minerva; and dropping her disguise stood confessed. The nymphs bent low in homage, and all the bystanders paid reverence. Arachne alone was unterrified. She blushed, indeed; a sudden colour dyed her cheek, and then she grew pale. But she stood to her resolve, and with a foolish conceit of her own skill rushed on her fate. Minerva forbore no longer nor interposed any further advice. They proceed to the contest. Each takes her station and attaches the web to the beam. Then the slender shuttle is passed in and out among the threads. The reed with its fine teeth strikes up the woof into its place and compacts the web. Both work with speed; their skilful hands move rapidly, and the excitement of the contest makes the labour light. Wool of Tyrian dye is contrasted with that of other colours, shaded off into one another so adroitly that the joining deceives the eye. Like the bow, whose long arch tinges the heavens, formed by sunbeams reflected from the shower, in which the colours where they meet seem as one, but at a little distance from the point of contact are wholly different.

Minerva wrought on her web the scene of her contest with Neptune. Twelve of the heavenly powers are represented, Jupiter, with august gravity, sitting in the midst. Neptune, the ruler of the sea, holds his trident, and appears to have just smitten the earth, from which a horse has leaped forth. Minerva depicted herself with helmed head, her Aegis covering her breast. Such was the central circle; and in the four corners were represented incidents illustrating the displeasure of the gods at such presumptuous mortals as had dared to contend with them. These were meant as warnings to her rival to give up the contest before it was too late.

Arachne filled her web with subjects designedly chosen to exhibit the failings and errors of the gods. One scene represented Leda caressing the swan, under which form Jupiter had disguised himself; and another, Danaë, in the brazen tower in which her father had imprisoned her, but where the god effected his entrance in the form of a golden shower. Still another depicted Europa deceived by Jupiter under the disguise of a bull. Encouraged by the tameness of the animal Europa ventured to mount his back, whereupon Jupiter advanced into the sea and swam with her to Crete. You would have thought it was a real bull, so naturally was it wrought, and so natural the water in which it swam. She seemed to look with longing eyes back upon the shore she was leaving, and to call to her companions for help. She appeared to shudder with terror at the sight of the heaving waves, and to draw back her feet from the water.

Arachne filled her canvas with similar subjects, wonderfully well done, but strongly marking her presumption and impiety. Minerva could not forbear to admire, yet felt indignant at the insult. She struck the web with her shuttle and rent it in pieces; she then touched the forehead of Arachne and made her feel her guilt and shame. She could not endure it and went and hanged herself. Minerva pitied her as she saw her suspended by a rope. "Live," she said, "guilty woman! and that you may preserve the memory of this lesson, continue to hang, both you and your descendants, to all future times." She sprinkled her with the juices of aconite, and immediately her hair came off, and her nose and ears likewise. Her form shrank up, and her head grew smaller yet; her fingers cleaved to her side and served for legs. All the rest of her is body, out of which she spins her thread, often hanging suspended by it, in the same attitude as when Minerva touched her and transformed her into a spider.

NIOBE

The fate of Arachne was noised abroad through all the country, and served as a warning to all presumptuous mortals not to compare themselves with the divinities. But one, and she a matron too, failed to learn the lesson of humility. It was Niobe, the queen of Thebes. She had indeed much to be proud of; but it was not her husband's fame, nor her own beauty, nor their great descent, nor the power of their kingdom that elated her. It was her children; and truly the happiest of mothers would Niobe have been if only she had not claimed to be so. It was on occasion of the annual celebration in honour of Latona and her offspring, Apollo and Diana,—when the people of Thebes were assembled, their brows crowned with laurel, bearing frankincense to the altars and paying their vows,—that Niobe appeared among the crowd. Her attire was splendid with gold and gems, and her aspect beautiful as the face of an angry woman can be. She stood and surveyed the people with haughty looks. "What folly," said she, "is this!—to prefer beings whom you never saw to those who stand before your eyes! Why should Latona be honoured with worship, and none be paid to me? My father was Tantalus, who was received as a guest at the table of the gods; my mother was a goddess. My husband built and rules this city, Thebes, and Phrygia is my paternal inheritance. Wherever I turn my eyes I survey the elements of my power; nor is my form and presence unworthy of a goddess. To all this let me add I have seven sons and seven daughters, and look for sons-in-law and daughters-in-law of pretensions worthy of my alliance. Have I not cause for pride? Will you prefer to me this Latona, the Titan's daughter, with her two children? I have seven times as many. Fortunate indeed am I, and fortunate I shall remain! Will any one deny this? My abundance is my security. I feel myself too strong for Fortune to subdue. She may take from me much; I shall still have much left. Were I to lose some of my children, I should hardly be left as poor as Latona with her two only. Away with you from these solemnities,—put off the laurel from your brows,—have done with this worship!" The people obeyed, and left the sacred services uncompleted.

The goddess was indignant. On the Cynthian mountain top where she dwelt she thus addressed her son and daughter: "My children, I who have been so proud of you both, and have been used to hold myself second to none of the goddesses except Juno alone, begin now to doubt whether I am indeed a goddess. I shall be deprived of my worship altogether unless you protect me." She was proceeding in this strain, but Apollo interrupted her. "Say no more," said he; "speech only delays punishment." So said Diana also. Darting through the air, veiled in clouds, they alighted on the towers of the city. Spread out before the gates was a broad plain, where the youth of the city pursued their warlike sports. The sons of Niobe were there with the rest,—some mounted on spirited horses richly caparisoned, some driving gay chariots. Ismenos, the first-born, as he guided his foaming steeds, struck with an arrow from above, cried out, "Ah me!" dropped the reins, and fell lifeless. Another, hearing the sound of the bow,—like the boatman who sees the storm gathering and makes all sail for the port,—gave the reins to his horses and attempted to escape. The inevitable arrow overtook him, as he fled. Two others, younger boys, just from their tasks, had gone to the playground to have a game of wrestling. As they stood breast to breast, one arrow pierced them both. They uttered a cry together, together cast a parting look around them, and together breathed their last. Alphenor, an elder brother, seeing them fall, hastened to the spot to render assistance, and fell stricken in the act of brotherly duty. Only one was left, Ilioneus. He raised his arms to heaven to try whether prayer might not avail. "Spare me, ye gods!" he cried, addressing all, in his ignorance that all needed not his intercessions; and Apollo would have spared him, but the arrow had already left the string, and it was too late.

The terror of the people and grief of the attendants soon made Niobe acquainted with what had taken place. She could hardly think it possible; she was indignant that the gods had dared, and amazed that they had been able to do it. Her husband, Amphion, overwhelmed with the blow, destroyed himself. Alas! how different was this Niobe from her who had so lately driven away the people from the sacred rites, and held her stately course through the city, the envy of her friends, now the pity even of her foes! She knelt over the lifeless bodies, and kissed now one, now another of her dead sons. Raising her pallid arms to heaven, "Cruel Latona," said she, "feed full your rage with my anguish! Satiate your hard heart, while I follow to the grave my seven sons. Yet where is your triumph? Bereaved as I am, I am still richer than you, my conqueror." Scarce had she spoken, when the bow sounded and struck terror into all hearts except Niobe's alone. She was brave from excess of grief. The sisters stood in garments of mourning over the biers of their dead brothers. One fell, struck by an arrow, and died on the corpse she was bewailing. Another, attempting to console her mother, suddenly ceased to speak, and sank lifeless to the earth. A third tried to escape by flight, a fourth by concealment, another stood trembling, uncertain what course to take. Six were now dead, and only one remained, whom the mother held clasped in her arms, and covered as it were with her whole body. "Spare me one, and that the youngest! O spare me one of so many!" she cried; and while she spoke, that one fell dead. Desolate she sat, among sons, daughters, husband, all dead, and seemed torpid with grief. The breeze moved not her hair, no colour was on her cheek, her eyes glared fixed and immovable, there was no sign of life about her. Her very tongue cleaved to the roof of her mouth, and her veins ceased to convey the tide of life. Her neck bent not, her arms made no gesture, her foot no step. She was changed to stone, within and without. Yet tears continued to flow; and borne on a whirlwind to her native mountain, she still remains, a mass of rock, from which a trickling stream flows, the tribute of her never-ending grief.

1. Study the story patterns of *Minerva and Arachne* and of *Niobe:*

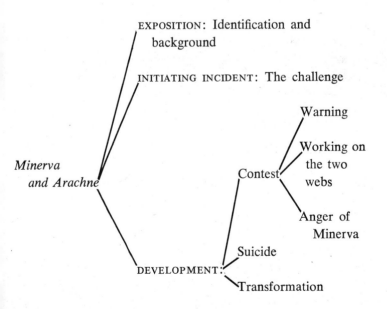

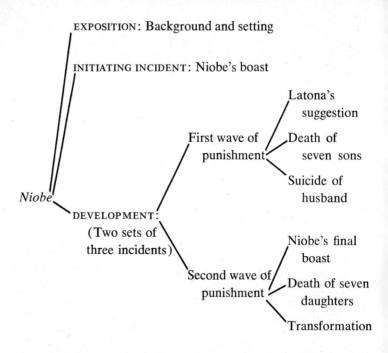

EXPOSITION: Background and setting

INITIATING INCIDENT: Niobe's boast

Niobe

DEVELOPMENT:
(Two sets of
three incidents)

First wave of punishment

Latona's suggestion

Death of seven sons

Suicide of husband

Second wave of punishment

Niobe's final boast

Death of seven daughters

Transformation

2. Compare the complex structure of these two myths with the simple structure of *Diana and Actaeon*. **3.** Work out the description of the two webs in parallels and contrasts. **4.** Compare the exposition of *Minerva and Arachne* with *Niobe*. How are they alike? How do they differ? **5.** Write a transformation myth of your own in which you account for one of the following:

the many legs of the centipede   the firefly
the knock of the woodpecker   the color of robins' eggs

Here are two myths with different story patterns. Read *Echo and Narcissus* and *Clytie*.

ECHO
AND
NARCISSUS

Echo was a beautiful nymph, fond of the woods and hills, where she devoted herself to woodland sports. She was a favourite of Diana, and attended her in the chase. But Echo had one failing; she was fond of talking, and whether in chat or argument, would have the last word. One day Juno was seeking her husband, who, she had reason to fear, was amusing himself among the nymphs. Echo by her talk contrived to detain the goddess till the nymphs made their escape. When Juno discovered it, she passed sentence upon Echo in these words: "You shall forfeit the use of that tongue with which you have cheated me, except for that one purpose you are so fond of— *reply*. You shall still have the last word, but no power to speak first."

This nymph saw Narcissus, a beautiful youth, as he pursued the chase upon the mountains. She loved him and followed his footsteps. O how she longed to address him in the softest accents, and win him to converse! But it was not in her power. She waited with impatience for him to speak first, and had her answer ready. One day the youth, being separated from his companions, shouted aloud, "Who's here?" Echo replied, "Here." Narcissus looked around, but seeing no one, called out, "Come." Echo answered, "Come." As no one came, Narcissus called again, "Why do you shun me?" Echo asked the same question. "Let us join one another," said the youth. The maid answered with all her heart in the same words, and hastened to the spot, ready to throw her arms about his neck. He started back, exclaiming, "Hands off! I would rather die than you should have me!" "Have me," said she; but it was all in vain. He left her, and she went to hide her blushes in the recesses of the woods. From that time forth she lived in caves and among mountain cliffs. Her form faded with grief, till at last all her flesh shrank away. Her bones were changed into rocks and there was nothing left of her but her voice. With that she is still ready to reply to any one who calls her, and keeps up her old habit of having the last word.

Narcissus's cruelty in this case was not the only instance. He shunned all the rest of the nymphs, as he had done poor Echo. One day a maiden who had in vain endeavoured to attract him uttered a prayer that he might some time or other feel what it was to love and meet no return of affection. The avenging goddess heard and granted the prayer.

There was a clear fountain, with water like silver, to which the shepherds never drove their flocks, nor the mountain goats resorted, nor any of the beasts of the forests; neither was it defaced with fallen leaves or branches; but the grass grew fresh around it, and the rocks sheltered it from the sun. Hither came one day the youth, fatigued with hunting, heated and thirsty. He stooped down to drink, and saw his own image in the water; he thought it was some beautiful water-spirit living in the fountain. He stood gazing with admiration at those bright eyes, those locks curled like the locks of Bacchus or Apollo, the rounded cheeks, the ivory neck, the parted lips, and the glow of health and exercise over all. He fell in love with himself. He brought his lips near to take a kiss; he plunged his arms in to embrace the beloved object. It fled at the touch, but returned again after a moment and renewed the fascination. He could not tear himself away; he lost all thought of food or rest, while he hovered over the brink of the fountain gazing upon his own image. He talked with the supposed spirit: "Why, beautiful being, do you shun me? Surely my face is not one to repel you. The nymphs love me, and you yourself look not indifferent upon me. When I stretch forth my arms you do the same; and you smile upon me and answer my beckonings with the like." His tears fell into the water and disturbed the image. As he saw it depart, he exclaimed, "Stay, I entreat you! Let me at least gaze upon you, if I may not touch you." With this, and much more of the same kind, he cherished the flame that consumed him, so that by degrees he lost his colour, his vigour, and the beauty which formerly had so charmed the nymph Echo. She kept near him, however, and when he exclaimed, "Alas! alas!" she answered him with the same words. He pined away and died; and when his shade passed the Stygian river, it leaned over the boat to catch a look of itself in the waters. The nymphs mourned for him, especially the water-nymphs; and when they smote their breasts Echo smote hers also. They prepared a funeral pile and would have burned the body, but it was nowhere to be found; but in its place a flower, purple within, and surrounded with white leaves, which bears the name and preserves the memory of Narcissus.

CLYTIE

Clytie was a water-nymph in love with Apollo, who made her no return. So she pined away, sitting all day long upon the cold ground, with her unbound tresses streaming over her shoulders. Nine days she sat and tasted neither food nor drink, her own tears and the chilly dew her only food. She gazed on the sun when he rose, and as he passed through his daily course to his setting; she saw no other object, her face turned constantly on him. At last, they say, her limbs rooted in the ground, her face became a flower, which turns on its stem so as always to face the sun throughout its daily course; for it retains to that extent the feeling of the nymph from whom it sprang. The sunflower is a favorite emblem of constancy.

1. How do these two myths differ in their story patterns? **2.** Work out the story pattern of *Echo and Narcissus*. Is the pattern simple or complex? **3.** Write a transformation myth based on *Clytie*.

Now read *Minerva and Athens* and *Latona and the Rustics*.

MINERVA AND ATHENS

Minerva, the goddess of wisdom, was the daughter of Jupiter. She was said to have leaped forth from his brain, mature, and in complete armor. She presided over the useful and ornamental arts, both those of men—such as agriculture and navigation—and those of women—spinning, weaving, and needlework. She was also a warlike divinity; but it was defensive war only that she patronized, and she had no sympathy with Mars' savage love of violence and bloodshed. Athens was her chosen seat, her own city, awarded to her as the prize of a contest with Neptune, who also aspired to it. The tale ran that in the reign of Cecrops, the first king of Athens, the two deities contended for the possession of the city. The gods decreed that it should be awarded to that one who contributed the gift most useful to mortals. Neptune gave the horse; Minerva produced the olive. The gods gave judgment that the olive was the more useful of the two, and awarded the city to the goddess; and it was named after her, Athens, her name in Greek being Athena.

LATONA
AND THE RUSTICS

In Licia there is a pond. Near it stands an ancient altar, black with the smoke of sacrifice and almost buried in the reeds. It is the altar of the goddess Latona, whose story the country people like to tell.

The royal Juno in her jealousy drove Latona from land to land, denying her any spot on earth on which to bring up her twins. Bearing in her arms the infant deities, Latona reached this land, weary with her burden and parched with thirst. By chance she saw in the valley this pond of clear water, where the country people were at work gathering willows.

The goddess approached, and kneeling on the bank would have slaked her thirst in the cool stream, but the rustics forbade her. "Why do you refuse me water?" said she; "water is free for all. Nature allows no one to claim as property the sunshine, the air, or the water. I come to take my share of the common blessing. Yet I ask it of you as a favour. I have no intention of washing my limbs in it, weary though they be, but only to quench my thirst. My mouth is so dry that I can hardly speak. A draught of water would be nectar to me; it would revive me, and I would own myself indebted to you for life itself. Let these infants move your pity, who stretch out their little arms as if to plead for me." And the children, as it happened, were stretching out their arms.

Who would not have been moved with these gentle words of the goddess? But these clowns waded into the pond and stirred up the mud with their feet, so as to make the water unfit to drink. Latona was so angry that she ceased to mind her thirst.

She no longer supplicated, but lifting up her hands to heaven she exclaimed, "May they never quit that pool, but pass their lives there!"

They now live in the water, sometimes totally submerged, then raising their heads above the surface or swimming upon it. Sometimes they come out upon the bank, but soon leap back again into the water. They still use their bass voices in railing, and though they have the water all to themselves, are not ashamed to croak in the midst of it. Their voices are harsh, their throats bloated, their mouths have become stretched by constant railing, their necks have shrunk up and disappeared, and their heads are joined to their bodies. Their backs are green, their disproportioned bellies white, and in short they are now frogs, and dwell in the slimy pond.

1. Is *Minerva and Athens* a transformation myth? Is it an explanatory myth? Explain. **2.** Even though it is short, does it have a patterning of incidents? What is the pattern? **3.** Work out the storytelling pattern of *Latona and the Rustics*. **4.** Write a similar transformation myth accounting for

> the long neck of the giraffe
> the shell of the turtle
>   the pouch of the kangaroo

For examples of a different kind of myth, read *Prometheus* and *Pandora*.

PROMETHEUS

The creation of the world is a problem naturally fitted to excite the liveliest interest of man, its inhabitant. The ancient pagans had their own way of telling the story, which is as follows:

Before earth and sea and heaven were created, all things wore one aspect, to which we give the name of Chaos—a confused and shapeless mass, nothing but dead weight, in which, however, slumbered the seeds of things. Earth, sea, and air were all mixed up together; so the earth was not solid, the sea was not fluid, and the air was not transparent. God and Nature at last interposed, and put an end to this discord, separating earth from sea, and heaven from both. The fiery part, being the lightest, sprang up, and formed the skies; the air was next in weight and place. The earth, being heavier, sank below; and the water took the lowest place, and buoyed up the earth.

Here some god—it is not known which—gave his good offices in arranging and disposing the earth. He appointed rivers and bays their places, raised mountains, scooped out valleys, distributed woods, fountains, fertile fields, and stony plains. The air being cleared, the stars began to appear, fishes took possession of the sea, birds of the air, and four-footed beasts of the land.

But a nobler animal was wanted, and Man was made. It is not known whether the creator made him of divine materials, or whether in the earth, so lately separated from heaven, there lurked still some heavenly seeds. Prometheus took some of this earth, and kneading it up with water made man in the image of the gods. He gave him an upright stature, so that while all other animals turn their faces downward, and look to the earth, he raises his to heaven, and gazes on the stars.

Prometheus was one of the Titans, a gigantic race, who inhabited the earth before the creation of man. To him and his brother Epimetheus was committed the office of making man, and providing him and all other animals with the faculties necessary for their preservation. Epimetheus undertook to do this, and Prometheus was to overlook his work, when it was done. Epimetheus accordingly proceeded to bestow upon the different animals the various gifts of courage, strength, swiftness, sagacity; wings to one, claws to another, a shelly covering to a third, etc. But when man came to be provided for, who was to be superior to all other animals, Epimetheus had been so prodigal of his resources that he had nothing left to bestow upon him. In his perplexity he resorted to his brother Prometheus, who, with the aid of Minerva, went up to heaven, and lighted his torch at the chariot of the sun, and brought down fire to man. With this gift man was more than a match for all other animals. It enabled him to make weapons wherewith to subdue them; tools with which to cultivate the earth; to warm his dwelling, so as to be comparatively independent of climate; and finally to introduce the arts and to coin money, the means of trade and commerce.

PANDORA

The story is that Jupiter made woman and sent her to Prometheus and his brother, to punish them for their presumption in stealing fire from heaven; and man, for accepting the gift. The first woman was named Pandora. She was made in heaven, every god contributing something to perfect her. Venus gave her beauty, Mercury persuasion, Apollo music, etc. Thus equipped, she was conveyed to earth, and presented to Epimetheus, who gladly accepted her, though cautioned by his brother to beware of Jupiter and his gifts. Epimetheus had in his house a jar, in which were kept certain noxious articles for which, in fitting man for his new abode, he had had no occasion. Pandora was seized with an eager curiosity to know what this jar contained; and one day she slipped off the cover and looked in. Forthwith there escaped a multitude of plagues for hapless man,—such as gout, rheumatism, and colic for his body, and envy, spite, and revenge for his mind,—and scattered themselves far and wide. Pandora hastened to replace the lid! but, alas! the whole contents of the jar had escaped, one thing only excepted, which lay at the bottom, and that was *hope.* So we see at this day, whatever evils are abroad, hope never entirely leaves us; and while we have *that,* no amount of other ills can make us completely wretched.

1. *Prometheus* and *Pandora* are creative myths. How do they differ from transformation myths? 2. Find the story *Prometheus Bound.* Write a short narrative showing that in some situation in your life you have shown either Promethean (forethought) or Epimethean (afterthought) characteristics. Be sure to establish a narrative pattern in your story. 3. After you have read *Pandora,* write a paragraph explaining the Greek theory of evil in the world. 4. Compare the Greek theory with the Bible account. 5. Jot down in list form the incidents that make up the story structure of *Prometheus.*

Now read *Apollo and Daphne* and *Venus and Adonis.*

APOLLO
AND
DAPHNE

Daphne was Apollo's first love. It was not brought about by accident, but by the malice of Cupid. Apollo saw the boy playing with his bow and arrows; and being himself elated with his recent victory over Python, he said to him, "What have you to do with warlike weapons, saucy boy? Leave them for hands worthy of them. Behold the conquest I have won by means of them over the vast serpent who stretched his poisonous body over acres of the plain! Be content with your torch, child, and kindle up your flames, as you call them, where you will, but presume not to meddle with my weapons." Venus's boy heard these words, and rejoined, "Your arrows may strike all things else, Apollo, but mine shall strike you." So saying, he took his stand on a rock of Parnassus, and drew from his quiver two arrows of different workmanship, one to excite love, the other to repel it. The former was of gold and sharp pointed, the latter blunt and tipped with lead. With the leaden shaft he struck the nymph Daphne, the daughter of the river god Peneus, and with the golden one Apollo, through the heart. Forthwith the god was seized with love for the maiden, and she abhorred the thought of loving. Her delight was in woodland sports and in the spoils of the chase. Many lovers sought her, but she spurned them all, ranging the woods, and taking no thought of Cupid nor of Hymen. Her father often said to her, "Daughter, you owe me a son-in-law; you owe me grandchildren." She, hating the thought of marriage as a crime, with her beautiful face tinged all over with blushes, threw her arms around her father's neck, and said, "Dear father, grant me this favour, that I may always remain unmarried, like Diana." He consented, but at the same time said, "Your own face will forbid it."

Apollo loved her, and longed to obtain her; and he who gives oracles to all the world was not wise enough to look into his own fortunes. He saw her hair flung loose over her shoulders, and said, "If so charming in disorder, what would it be if arranged?" He saw her eyes bright as stars; he saw her lips, and was not satisfied with only seeing them. He admired her hands and arms, naked to the shoulder, and whatever was hidden from view he imagined more beautiful still. He followed her; she fled, swifter than the wind, and delayed not a moment at his entreaties. "Stay," said he, "daughter of Peneus; I am not a foe. Do not fly me as a lamb flies the wolf, or a dove the hawk. It is for love I pursue you. You make me miserable, for fear you should fall and hurt yourself on these stones, and I should be the cause. Pray run slower, and I will follow slower. I am no clown, no rude peasant. Jupiter is my father, and I am lord of Delphos and Tenedos, and know all things, present and future. I am the god of song and the lyre. My arrows fly true to the mark; but, alas! an arrow more fatal than mine has pierced my heart! I am the god of medicine, and know the virtues of all healing plants. Alas! I suffer a malady that no balm can cure!"

The nymph continued her flight, and left his plea half uttered. And even as she fled she charmed him. The wind blew her garments, and her unbound hair streamed loose behind her. The god grew impatient to find his wooings thrown away, and, sped by Cupid, gained upon her in the race. It was like a hound pursuing a hare, with open jaws ready to seize, while the feebler animal darts forward, slipping from the very grasp. So flew the god and the virgin—he on the wings of love, and she on those of fear. The pursuer is the more rapid, however, and gains upon her, and his panting breath blows upon her hair. Her strength begins to fail, and, ready to sink, she calls upon her father, the river god: "Help me, Peneus! open the earth to enclose me, or change my form, which has brought me into this danger!" Scarcely had she spoken, when a stiffness seized all her limbs; her bosom began to be enclosed in a tender bark; her hair became leaves; her arms became branches; her foot stuck fast in the ground, as a root; her face became a tree-top, retaining nothing of its former self but its beauty. Apollo stood amazed. He touched the stem, and felt the flesh tremble under the new bark. He embraced the branches, and lavished kisses on the wood. The branches shrank from his lips. "Since you cannot be my wife," said he, "you shall assuredly be my tree. I will wear you for my crown; I will decorate you with my harp and my quiver; and when the great Roman conquerors lead up the triumphal pomp to the Capitol, you shall be woven into wreaths for their brows. And, as eternal youth is mine, you also shall be always green, and your leaf know no decay." The nymph, now changed into a laurel tree, bowed its head in grateful acknowledgment.

VENUS AND ADONIS

Venus, playing one day with her boy Cupid, wounded her bosom with one of his arrows. She pushed him away, but the wound was deeper than she thought. Before it healed she beheld Adonis, and was captivated with him. She no longer took any interest in her favourite resorts—Paphos, and Cnidos, and Amathos, rich in metals. She absented herself even from heaven, for Adonis was dearer to her than heaven. Him she followed and bore him company. She who used to love to recline in the shade, with no care but to cultivate her charms, now rambles through the woods and over the hills, dressed like the huntress Diana; and calls her dogs, and chases hares and stags, or other game that it is safe to hunt, but keeps clear of the wolves and bears, reeking with the slaughter of the herd. She charged Adonis, too, to beware of such dangerous animals.

Having given him this warning, she mounted her chariot

drawn by swans, and drove away through the air. But Adonis was too noble to heed such counsels. The dogs had roused a wild boar from his lair, and the youth threw his spear and wounded the animal with a sidelong stroke. The beast drew out the weapon with his jaws, and rushed after Adonis, who turned and ran; but the boar overtook him, and buried his tusks in his side, and stretched him dying upon the plain.

Venus, in her swan-drawn chariot, had not yet reached Cyprus, when she heard coming up through mid-air the groans of her beloved, and turned her white-winged coursers back to earth. As she drew near and saw from on high his lifeless body bathed in blood, she alighted and, bending over it, beat her breast and tore her hair. Reproaching the Fates, she said, "Yet theirs shall be but a partial triumph; memorials of my grief shall endure, and the spectacle of your death, my Adonis, and of my lamentation shall be annually renewed. Your blood shall be changed into a flower; that consolation none can envy me." Thus speaking, she sprinkled nectar on the blood; and as they mingled, bubbles rose as in a pool on which raindrops fall, and in an hour's time there sprang up a flower of bloody hue like that of the pomegranate. But it is short-lived. It is said the wind blows the blossoms open, and afterwards blows the petals away; so it is called Anemone, or Wind Flower, from the cause which assists equally in its production and its decay.

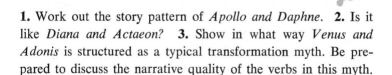

1. Work out the story pattern of *Apollo and Daphne.* **2.** Is it like *Diana and Actaeon?* **3.** Show in what way *Venus and Adonis* is structured as a typical transformation myth. Be prepared to discuss the narrative quality of the verbs in this myth.

The next myth you will read, *Cupid and Psyche,* is an allegorical myth.

CUPID AND PSYCHE

A certain king and queen had three daughters. The charms of the two elder were more than common, but the beauty of the youngest was so wonderful that the poverty of language is unable to express its due praise. The fame of her beauty was so great that strangers from neighbouring countries came in crowds to enjoy the sight, and looked on her with amazement, paying her that homage which is due only to Venus herself. In fact Venus found her altars deserted, while men turned their devotion to this young virgin. As she passed along, the people sang her praises, and strewed her way with chaplets and flowers.

This perversion of homage, due only to the immortal powers, to the exaltation of a mortal gave great offence to the real Venus. Shaking her ambrosial locks with indignation, she exclaimed, "Am I then to be eclipsed in my honours by a mortal girl?"

Thereupon she calls her winged son Cupid, mischievous enough in his own nature, and rouses and provokes him yet more by her complaints. She points out Psyche to him and says, "My dear son, punish that contumacious beauty; give thy mother a revenge as sweet as her injuries are great; infuse into the bosom of that haughty girl a passion for some low, mean, unworthy being, so that she may reap a mortification as great as her present exultation and triumph."

Cupid prepared to obey the commands of his mother. There are two fountains in Venus's garden, one of sweet waters, the other of bitter. Cupid filled two amber vases, one from each fountain, and suspending them from his quiver, hastened to the chamber of Psyche, whom he found asleep. He shed a few drops from the bitter fountain over her lips, though the sight of her almost moved him to pity; then touched her side with the point of his arrow. At the touch she awoke, and opened eyes upon Cupid (himself invisible), which so startled him that in his confusion he wounded himself with his own arrow. Heedless of his wound, his whole thought now was to repair the mischief he had done, and he poured the balmy drops of joy over all her silken ringlets.

Psyche, henceforth frowned upon by Venus, derived no benefit from all her charms. True, all eyes were cast eagerly upon her, and every mouth spoke her praises; but neither king, royal youth, nor plebeian presented himself to demand her in marriage. Her two elder sisters of moderate charms had now long been married to two royal princes; but Psyche, in her lonely apartment, deplored her solitude, sick of that beauty which, while it procured abundance of flattery, had failed to awaken love.

Her parents, afraid that they had unwittingly incurred the anger of the gods, consulted the oracle of Apollo, and received this answer: "The virgin is destined for the bride of no mortal lover. Her future husband awaits her on the top of the mountain. He is a monster whom neither gods nor men can resist."

This dreadful decree of the oracle filled all the people with dismay, and her parents abandoned themselves to grief. But Psyche said, "Why, my dear parents, do you now lament me? You should rather have grieved when the people showered upon me undeserved honours, and with one voice called me a Venus. I now perceive that I am a victim to that name. I submit. Lead me to that rock to which my unhappy fate has destined me." Accordingly, all things being prepared, the royal maid took her place in the procession, which more resembled a funeral than a nuptial pomp, and with her parents, amid the lamentations of the people, ascended the mountain, on the summit of which they left her alone, and with sorrowful hearts returned home.

While Psyche stood on the ridge of the mountain, panting with fear and with eyes full of tears, the gentle Zephyr raised her from the earth and bore her with an easy motion into a flowery dale. By degrees her mind became composed, and she laid herself down on the grassy bank to sleep. When she awoke refreshed with sleep, she looked round and beheld nearby a pleasant grove of tall and stately trees. She entered it, and in the midst discovered a fountain, sending forth clear and crystal waters, and fast by, a magnificent palace whose august front impressed the spectator that it was not the work of mortal hands, but the happy retreat of some god. Drawn by admiration and wonder, she approached the building and ventured to enter. Every object she met filled her with pleasure and amazement. Golden pillars supported the vaulted roof, and the walls were enriched with carvings and paintings representing beasts of the chase and rural scenes, adapted to delight the eye of the beholder. Proceeding onward, she perceived that besides the apartments of state there were others filled with all manner of treasures, and beautiful and precious productions of nature and art.

While her eyes were thus occupied, a voice addressed her, though she saw no one, uttering these words: "Sovereign lady, all that you see is yours. We whose voices you hear are your servants and shall obey all your commands with our utmost care and diligence. Retire, therefore, to your chamber and repose on your bed of down, and when you see fit repair to the bath. Supper awaits you in the adjoining alcove when it pleases you to take your seat there."

Psyche gave ear to the admonitions of her vocal attendants, and after repose and the refreshment of the bath, seated herself in the alcove, where a table immediately presented itself, without any visible aid from waiters or servants, and covered with the greatest delicacies of food and the most nectareous wines. Her ears too were feasted with music from invisible performers; of whom one sang, another played on the lute, and all closed in the wonderful harmony of a full chorus.

She had not yet seen her destined husband. He came only in the hours of darkness and fled before the dawn of morning, but his accents were full of love, and inspired a like passion in her. She often begged him to stay and let her behold him, but he would not consent. On the contrary he charged her to make no attempt to see him, for it was his pleasure, for the best of reasons, to keep concealed. "Why should you wish to behold me?" he said; "have you any doubt of my love? have you any wish ungratified? If you saw me, perhaps you would fear me, perhaps adore me, but all I ask of you is to love me. I would rather you would love me as an equal than adore me as a god."

This reasoning somewhat quieted Psyche for a time, and while the novelty lasted she felt quite happy. But at length the thought of her parents, left in ignorance of her fate, and of her sisters, precluded from sharing with her the delights of her situation, preyed on her mind and made her begin to feel her palace as but a splendid prison. When her husband came one night, she told him her distress, and at last drew from him an unwilling consent that her sisters should be brought to see her.

So, calling Zephyr, she acquainted him with her husband's commands, and he, promptly obedient, soon brought them across the mountain down to their sister's valley. They embraced her and she returned their caresses. "Come," said Psyche, "enter with me my house and refresh yourselves with whatever your sister has to offer." Then taking their hands she led them into her golden palace, and committed them to the care of her numerous train of attendant voices, to refresh them in her baths and at her table, and to show them all her treasures. The view of these celestial delights caused envy to enter their bosoms, at seeing their young sister possessed of such state and splendour, so much exceeding their own.

They asked her numberless questions, among others what sort of a person her husband was. Psyche replied that he was a beautiful youth, who generally spent the daytime in hunting upon the mountains. The sisters, not satisfied with this reply, soon made her confess that she had never seen him. Then they proceeded to fill her bosom with dark suspicions. "Call to mind," they said, "the Pythian oracle that declared you destined to marry a direful and tremendous monster. The inhabitants of this valley say that your husband is a terrible and monstrous serpent, who nourishes you for a while with dainties that he may by and by devour you. Take our advice. Provide yourself with a lamp and a sharp knife; put them in concealment that your husband may not discover them, and when he is sound asleep, slip out of bed, bring forth your lamp, and see for yourself whether what they say is true or not. If it is, hesitate not to cut off the monster's head, and thereby recover your liberty."

Psyche resisted these persuasions as well as she could, but they did not fail to have their effect on her mind, and when her sisters were gone, their words and her own curiosity were too strong for her to resist. So she prepared her lamp and a sharp knife, and hid them out of sight of her husband. When he had fallen into his first sleep, she silently rose and uncovering her lamp beheld not a hideous monster, but the most beautiful and charming of the gods, with his golden ringlets wandering over his snowy neck and crimson cheek, with two dewy wings on his shoulders, whiter than snow, and with shining feathers like the tender blossoms of spring. As she leaned the lamp over to have a nearer view of his face a drop of burning oil fell on the shoulder of the god, startled with which he opened his eyes and fixed them full upon her; then, without saying one word, he spread his white wings and flew out of the window. Psyche, in vain endeavouring to follow him, fell from the window to the ground. Cupid, beholding her as she lay in the dust, stopped his flight for an instant and said, "O foolish Psyche, is it thus you repay my love? After having disobeyed my mother's commands and made you my wife, will you think me a monster and cut off my head? But go; return to your sisters, whose advice you seem to think preferable to mine. I inflict no other punishment on you than to leave you for ever. Love cannot dwell with suspicion." So saying, he fled away, leaving poor Psyche prostrate on the ground, filling the place with mournful lamentations.

When she had recovered some degree of composure she looked around her, but the palace and gardens had vanished, and she found herself in the open field not far from the city where her sisters dwelt. She repaired thither and told them the whole story of her misfortunes, at which, pretending to grieve, those spiteful creatures inwardly rejoiced. "For now," said they, "he will perhaps choose one of us." With this idea, without saying a word of her intentions, each of them rose early the next morning and ascended the mountain, and having reached the top, called upon Zephyr to receive her and bear her to his lord; then leaping up, and not being sustained by Zephyr, fell down the precipice and was dashed to pieces.

Psyche meanwhile wandered day and night, without food or repose, in search of her husband. Casting her eyes on a lofty mountain having on its brow a magnificent temple, she sighed and said to herself, "Perhaps my love, my lord, inhabits there," and directed her steps thither.

She had no sooner entered than she saw heaps of corn, some in loose ears and some in sheaves, with mingled ears of barley. Scattered about, lay sickles and rakes, and all the instruments of harvest, without order, as if thrown carelessly out of the weary reapers' hands in the sultry hours of the day.

This unseemly confusion the pious Psyche put an end to, by separating and sorting everything to its proper place and kind, believing that she ought to neglect none of the gods, but endeavour by her piety to engage them all in her behalf. The holy Ceres, whose temple it was, finding her so religiously employed, thus spoke to her: "O Psyche, truly worthy of our pity, though I cannot shield you from the frowns of Venus, yet I can teach you how best to allay her displeasure. Go, then, and voluntarily surrender yourself to your lady and sovereign, and try by modesty and submission to win her forgiveness, and perhaps her favour will restore you the husband you have lost."

Psyche obeyed the commands of Ceres and took her way to the temple of Venus, endeavouring to fortify her mind and ruminating on what she should say and how best propitiate the angry goddess, feeling that the issue was doubtful and perhaps fatal.

Venus received her with angry countenance. "Most undutiful and faithless of servants," said she, "do you at last remember that you really have a mistress? Or have you rather come to see your sick husband, yet laid up of the wound given him by his loving wife? You are so ill-favoured and disagreeable that the only way you can merit your lover must be by dint of industry and diligence. I will make trial of your housewifery." Then she ordered Psyche to be led to the storehouse of her temple, where was laid up a great quantity of wheat, barley, millet, vetches, beans, and lentils prepared for food for her pigeons, and said, "Take and separate all these grains, putting all of the same kind in a parcel by themselves, and see that you get it done before evening." Then Venus departed and left her to her task.

But Psyche, in a perfect consternation at the enormous work, sat stupid and silent, without moving a finger to the inextricable heap.

While she sat despairing, Cupid stirred up the little ant, a native of the fields, to take compassion on her. The leader of the ant-hill, followed by whole hosts of his six-legged subjects, approached the heap, and with the utmost diligence taking grain by grain, they separated the pile, sorting each kind to its parcel; and when it was all done, they vanished out of sight in a moment.

Venus at the approach of twilight returned from the banquet of the gods, breathing odours and crowned with roses. Seeing the task done, she exclaimed, "This is no work of yours, wicked one, but his, whom to your own and his misfortune you have enticed." So saying, she threw her a piece of black bread for her supper and went away.

Next morning Venus ordered Psyche to be called and said to her, "Behold yonder grove which stretches along the margin of the water. There you will find sheep feeding without a shepherd, with golden-shining fleeces on their backs. Go, fetch me a sample of that precious wool gathered from every one of their fleeces."

Psyche obediently went to the riverside, prepared to do her best to execute the command. But the river god inspired the reeds with harmonious murmurs, which seemed to say, "O maiden, severely tried, tempt not the dangerous flood, nor venture among the formidable rams on the other side, for as long as they are under the influence of the rising sun, they burn with a cruel rage to destroy mortals with their sharp horns or rude teeth. But when the noontide sun has driven the cattle to the shade, and the serene spirit of the flood has lulled them to rest, you may then cross in safety, and you will find the woolly gold sticking to the bushes and the trunks of the trees."

Thus the compassionate river god gave Psyche instructions

how to accomplish her task, and by observing his directions she soon returned to Venus with her arms full of the golden fleece; but she received not the approbation of her implacable mistress, who said, "I know very well it is by none of your own doings that you have succeeded in this task, and I am not satisfied yet that you have any capacity to make yourself useful. But I have another task for you. Here, take this box and go your way to the infernal shades, and give this box to Proserpine and say, 'My mistress Venus desires you to send her a little of your beauty, for in tending her sick son she has lost some of her own.' Be not too long on your errand, for I must paint myself with it to appear at the circle of the gods and goddesses this evening."

Psyche was now satisfied that her destruction was at hand, being obliged to go with her own feet directly down to Erebus. Wherefore, to make no delay of what was not to be avoided, she goes to the top of a high tower to precipitate herself head-long, thus to descend the shortest way to the shades below. But a voice from the tower said to her, "Why, poor unlucky girl, dost thou design to put an end to thy days in so dreadful a manner? And what cowardice makes thee sink under this last danger who hast been so miraculously supported in all thy former?" Then the voice told her how by a certain cave she might reach the realms of Pluto, and how to avoid all the dangers of the road, to pass by Cerebus, the three-headed dog, and prevail on Charon, the ferryman, to take her across the black river and bring her back again. But the voice added, "When Proserpine has given you the box filled with her beauty, of all things this is chiefly to be observed by you, that you never once open or look into the box nor allow your curiosity to pry into the treasure of the beauty of the goddesses."

Psyche, encouraged by this advice, obeyed it in all things, and taking heed to her ways travelled safely to the kingdom of Pluto. She was admitted to the place of Proserpine, and without accepting the delicate seat or delicious banquet that was offered her, but contented with coarse bread for her food, she delivered her message from Venus. Presently the box was returned to her, shut and filled with the precious commodity. Then she returned the way she came, and glad was she to come out once more into the light of day.

But having got so far successfully through her dangerous task, a longing desire seized her to examine the contents of the box. "What," said she, "shall I, the carrier of this divine beauty, not take the least bit to put on my cheeks to appear to more advantage in the eyes of my beloved husband!" So she carefully opened the box, but found nothing there of any beauty at all, but an infernal and truly Stygian sleep, which being thus set free from its prison, took possession of her, and she fell down in the midst of the road, a sleepy corpse without sense or motion.

But Cupid, being now recovered from his wound, and not able longer to bear the absence of his beloved Psyche, slipping through the smallest crack of the window of his chamber which happened to be left open, flew to the spot where Psyche lay, and gathering up the sleep from her body closed it again in the box, and waked Psyche with a light touch of one of his arrows. "Again," said he, "hast thou almost perished by the same curiosity. But now perform exactly the task imposed on you by my mother, and I will take care of the rest."

Then Cupid, as swift as lightning penetrating the heights of heaven, presented himself before Jupiter with his supplication. Jupiter lent a favouring ear, and pleaded the cause of the lovers so earnestly with Venus that he won her consent. On this he sent Mercury to bring Psyche up to the heavenly assembly, and when she arrived, handing her a cup of ambrosia, he said, "Drink this, Psyche, and be immortal; nor shall Cupid ever break away from the knot in which he is tied, but these nuptials shall be perpetual."

Thus Psyche became at last united to Cupid, and in due time they had a daughter born to them whose name was Pleasure.

The myth of Cupid and Psyche is usually considered allegorical. The Greek name for a *butterfly* is Psyche, and the same word means the *soul*. There is no illustration of the immortality of the soul so striking and beautiful as the butterfly, bursting on brilliant wings from the tomb in which it has lain, after a dull, grovelling, caterpillar existence, to flutter in the blaze of day and feed on the most fragrant and delicate productions of the spring. Psyche, then, is the human soul, which is purified by sufferings and misfortunes, and is thus prepared for the enjoyment of true and pure happiness.

In works of art Psyche is represented as a maiden with the wings of a butterfly, along with Cupid, in the different situations described in the allegory.

1. Is the structure of *Cupid and Psyche* simple or complex? **2.** Explain the meaning of allegory as it is used in the comment after the myth. **3.** Is this a transformation myth? Explain.

Now read the myths *Phaëton, Midas,* and *Baucis and Philemon.*

PHAËTON

Phaëton was the son of Apollo and the nymph Clymene. One day a schoolfellow laughed at the idea of his being the son of the god, and Phaëton went in rage and shame and reported it to his mother. "If," said he, "I am indeed of heavenly birth, give me, mother, some proof of it, and establish my claim to the honour." Clymene stretched forth her hands towards the skies, and said, "I call to witness the Sun which looks down upon us, that I have told you the truth. If I speak falsely, let this be the last time I behold his light. But it needs not much labour to go and inquire for yourself; the land whence the Sun rises lies next to ours. Go and demand of him whether he will own you as a son." Phaëton heard with delight. He travelled to India, which lies directly in the regions of sunrise; and, full of hope and pride, approached the goal whence his parent begins his course.

Clymene's son advanced up the steep ascent, and entered the halls of his disputed father. He approached the paternal presence, but stopped at a distance, for the light was more than he could bear. Phoebus, arrayed in a purple vesture, sat on a throne, which glittered as with diamonds. On his right hand and his left stood the Day, the Month, and the Year, and, at regular intervals, the Hours. Spring stood with her head crowned with flowers, and Summer, with garment cast aside, and a garland formed of spears of ripened grain, and Autumn, with his feet stained with grape-juice, and icy Winter, with his hair stiffened with hoar frost. Surrounded by these attendants, the Sun, with the eye that sees everything, beheld the youth dazzled with the novelty and splendour of the scene, and inquired the purpose of his errand. The youth replied, "O light of the boundless world, Phoebus, my father,—if you permit me to use that name,—give me some proof, I beseech you, by which I may be known as yours." He ceased; and his father, laying aside the beams that shone all around his head, bade him approach, and embracing him, said, "My son, you deserve not to be disowned, and I confirm what your mother has told you. To put an end to your doubts, ask what you will, the gift shall be yours. I call to witness that dreadful lake, which I never saw, but which we gods swear by in our most solemn engagements." Phaëton immediately asked to be permitted for one day to drive the chariot of the sun. The father repented of his promise; thrice and four times he shook his radiant head in warning. "I have spoken rashly," said he; "this only request I would fain deny. I beg you to withdraw it. It is not a safe boon, nor one, my Phaëton, suited to your youth and strength. Your lot is mortal, and you ask what is beyond a mortal's power. In your ignorance you aspire to do that which not even the gods themselves may do. None but myself may drive the flaming car of day. Not even Jupiter, whose terrible right arm hurls the thunderbolts. The first part of the way is steep, and such as the horses when fresh in the morning can hardly climb; the middle is high up in the heavens, whence I myself can scarcely, without alarm, look down and behold the earth and sea stretched beneath me. The last part of the road descends rapidly, and requires most careful driving. Tethys, who is waiting to receive me, often trembles for me lest I should fall headlong. Add to all this, the heaven is all the time turning round and carrying the stars with it. I have to be perpetually on my guard lest that movement, which sweeps everything else along, should hurry me also away. Suppose I should lend you the chariot, what would you do? Could you keep your course while the sphere was revolving under you? Perhaps you think that there are forests and cities, the abodes of gods, and palaces and temples on the way. On the contrary, the road is through the midst of frightful monsters. You pass by the horns of the Bull, in front of the Archer, and near the Lion's jaws, and where the Scorpion stretches its arms in one direction and the Crab in another. Nor will you find it easy to guide those horses, with their breasts full of fire that they breathe forth from their mouths and nostrils. I can scarcely govern them myself, when they are unruly and resist the reins. Beware, my son, lest I be the donor of a fatal gift; recall your request while yet you may. Do you ask me for a proof that you are sprung from my blood? I give you a proof in my fears for you. Look at my face—I would that you could look into my breast, you would there see all a father's anxiety. Finally," he continued, "look round the world and choose whatever you will of what earth or sea contains most precious—ask it and fear no refusal. This only I pray you not to urge. It is not honour, but destruction you seek. Why do you hang round my neck and still entreat me? You shall have it if you persist—the oath is sworn and must be kept—but I beg you to choose more wisely."

He ended; but the youth rejected all admonition and held to his demand. So, having resisted as long as he could, Phoebus at last led the way to where stood the lofty chariot.

It was of gold, the gift of Vulcan; the axle was of gold, the pole and wheels of gold, the spokes of silver. Along the seat were rows of chrysolites and diamonds which reflected all around the brightness of the sun. While the daring youth gazed in admiration, the early Dawn threw open the purple doors of the east, and showed the pathway strewn with roses. The stars withdrew, marshalled by the Day-star, which last of all retired also. The father, when he saw the earth beginning to glow, and the Moon preparing to retire, ordered the Hours to harness up the horses. They obeyed, and led forth from the lofty stalls the steeds full fed with ambrosia, and attached the reins. Then the father bathed the face of his son with a powerful unguent, and made him capable of enduring the brightness of the flame. He set the rays on his head, and, with a foreboding sigh, said, "If, my son, you will in this at least heed my advice, spare the whip and hold tight the reins. They go fast enough of their own accord; the labour is to hold them in. You are not to take the straight road directly between the five circles, but turn off to the left. Keep within the limit of the middle zone, and avoid the northern and the southern alike. You will see the marks of the wheels, and they will serve to guide you. And, that the skies and the earth may each receive their due share of heat, go not too high, or you will burn the heavenly dwellings, nor too low, or you will set the earth on fire; the middle course is safest and best. And now I leave you to your chance, which I hope will plan better for you than you have done for yourself. Night is passing out of the western gates and we can delay no longer. Take the reins; but if at last your heart fails you, and you will benefit by my advice, stay where you are in safety, and suffer me to light and warm the earth." The agile youth sprang into the chariot, stood erect, and grasped the reins with delight, pouring out thanks to his reluctant parent.

Meanwhile the horses fill the air with their snortings and fiery breath, and stamp the ground impatient. Now the bars are let down, and the boundless plain of the universe lies open before them. They dart forward and cleave the opposing clouds, and outrun the morning breezes which started from the same eastern goal. The steeds soon perceived that the load they drew was lighter than usual; and as a ship without ballast is tossed hither and thither on the sea, so the chariot, without its accustomed weight, was dashed about as if empty. They rush headlong and leave the travelled road. He is alarmed, and knows not how to guide them; nor, if he knew, has he the power. Then, for the first time, the Great and Little Bear were scorched with heat, and would fain, if it were possible, have plunged into the water; and the Serpent which lies coiled up round the north pole, torpid and harmless, grew warm, and with warmth felt its rage revive. Boötes, they say, fled away, though encumbered with his plough, and all unused to rapid motion.

When hapless Phaëton looked down upon the earth, now spreading in vast extent beneath him, he grew pale and his knees shook with terror. In spite of the glare all around him, the sight of his eyes grew dim. He wished he had never touched his father's horses, never learned his parentage, never prevailed in his request. He is borne along like a vessel that flies before a tempest, when the pilot can do no more and betakes himself to his prayers. What shall he do? Much of the heavenly road is left behind, but more remains before. He turns his eyes from one direction to the other; now to the goal whence he began his course, now to the realms of sunset which he is not destined to reach. He loses his self-command, and knows not what to do,— whether to draw tight the reins or throw them loose; he forgets the names of the horses. He sees with terror the monstrous forms scattered over the surface of heaven. Here the Scorpion extended his two great arms, with his tail and crooked claws stretching over two signs of the zodiac. When the boy beheld him, reeking with poison and menacing with his fangs, his courage failed, and the reins fell from his hands. The horses, when they felt them loose on their backs, dashed headlong, and unrestrained went off into unknown regions of the sky, in among the stars, hurling the chariot over pathless places, now up in high heaven, now down almost to the earth. The moon saw with astonishment her brother's chariot running beneath her own. The clouds begin to smoke, and the mountain tops take fire; the fields are parched with heat, the plants wither, the trees with their leafy branches burn, the harvest is ablaze! But these are small things. Great cities perished, with their walls and towers; whole nations with their people were consumed to ashes! The forest-clad mountains burned, Athos and Taurus and Tmolus and Oete; Ida, once celebrated for fountains, but now all dry; the Muses' mountain

Helicon, and Haemus; Aetna, with fires within and without, and Parnassus, with his two peaks, and Rhodope, forced at last to part with his snowy crown. Her cold climate was no protection to Scythia, Caucasus burned, and Ossa and Pindus, and greater than both, Olympus; the Alps high in air, and the Apennines crowned with clouds.

Then Phaëton beheld the world on fire, and felt the heat intolerable. The air he breathed was like the air of a furnace and full of burning ashes, and the smoke was of a pitchy darkness. He dashed forward he knew not whither. Then, it is believed, the people of Aethiopia became black by the blood being forced so suddenly to the surface, and the Libyan desert was dried up to the condition in which it remains to this day. The Nymphs of the fountains, with dishevelled hair, mourned their waters, nor were the rivers safe beneath their banks. The earth cracked open, and through the chinks light broke into Tartarus, and frightened the king of shadows and his queen. The sea shrank up. Where before was water, it became a dry plain; and the mountains that lie beneath the waves lifted up their heads and became islands. The fishes sought the lowest depths, and the dolphins no longer ventured as usual to sport on the surface. Even Nereus, and his wife Doris, with the Nereids, their daughters, sought the deepest caves for refuge. Thrice Neptune essayed to raise his head above the surface, and thrice was driven back by the heat. Earth, surrounded as she was by waters, yet with head and shoulders bare, screening her face with her hand, looked up to heaven, and with a husky voice called on Jupiter:

"O ruler of the gods, if I have deserved this treatment, and it is your will that I perish with fire, why withhold your thunderbolts? Let me at least fall by your hand. Is this the reward of my fertility, of my obedient service? Is it for this that I have supplied herbage for cattle, and fruits for men, and frankincense for your altars? But if I am unworthy of regard, what has my brother Ocean done to deserve such a fate? If neither of us can excite your pity, think, I pray you, of your own heaven, and behold how both the poles are smoking which sustain your palace, which must fall if they be destroyed. Atlas faints, and scarce holds up his burden. If sea, earth, and heaven perish, we fall into ancient Chaos. Save what yet remains to us from the devouring flame. O, take thought for our deliverance in this awful moment!"

Thus spoke Earth, and overcome with heat and thirst, could say no more. Then Jupiter omnipotent, calling to witness all the gods, including him who had lent the chariot, and showing them that all was lost unless some speedy remedy were applied, mounted the lofty tower from whence he diffuses clouds over the earth, and hurls the forked lightnings. But at that time not a cloud was to be found to interpose for a screen to earth, nor was a shower remaining unexhausted. He thundered, and brandishing a lightning bolt in his right hand launched it against the charioteer, and struck him at the same moment from his seat and from existence! Phaëton, with his hair on fire, fell headlong, like a shooting star which marks the heavens with its brightness as it falls, and Eridanus, the great river, received him and cooled his burning body. The Italian Naiads built a tomb for him and inscribed these words on the stone:

> Driver of Phoebus' chariot, Phaëton,
> Struck by Jove's thunder, rests beneath this stone.
> He could not rule his father's car of fire,
> Yet was it much so nobly to aspire.

Pia Scurante Manzoni

MIDAS

Bacchus, on a certain occasion, found his old schoolmaster and foster-father, Silenus, missing. The old man had been drinking, and in that state wandered away, and was found by some peasants, who carried him to their king, Midas. Midas recognized him, and treated him hospitably, entertaining him for ten days and nights with an unceasing round of jollity. On the

eleventh day he brought Silenus back, and restored him in safety
to his pupil. Whereupon Bacchus offered Midas his choice of a
reward, whatever he might wish. He asked that whatever he
might touch should be changed into *gold*. Bacchus consented,
though sorry that he had not made a better choice. Midas went
his way, rejoicing in his new-acquired power, which he hastened
to put to the test. He could scarce believe his eyes when he
found a twig of an oak, which he plucked from the branch,
become gold in his hand. He took up a stone; it changed to gold.
He touched a sod; it did the same. He took an apple from the
tree; you would have thought he had robbed the garden of the
Hesperides. His joy knew no bounds, and as soon as he got
home, he ordered the servants to set a splendid repast on the
table. Then he found to his dismay that whether he touched
bread, it hardened in his hand; or put a morsel to his lip, it
defied his teeth. He took a glass of wine, but it flowed down his
throat like melted gold.

In consternation at the unprecedented affliction, he strove to
divest himself of his power; he hated the gift he had lately
coveted. But all in vain; starvation seemed to await him. He
raised his arms, all shining with gold, in prayer to Bacchus,
begging to be delivered from his glittering destruction. Bacchus,
merciful deity, heard and consented. "Go," said he, "to the
River Pactolus, trace the stream to its fountain-head, there
plunge your head and body in, and wash away your fault and
its punishment." He did so, and scarce had he touched the waters
before the gold-creating power passed into them, and the river
sands became changed into *gold,* as they remain to this day.

Thenceforth Midas, hating wealth and splendour, dwelt in the
country, and became a worshipper of Pan, the god of the fields.
On a certain occasion Pan had the temerity to compare his music
with that of Apollo, and to challenge the god of the lyre to a
trial of skill. The challenge was accepted, and Tmolus, the
mountain god, was chosen umpire. The senior took his seat, and
cleared away the trees from his ears to listen. At a given signal
Pan blew on his pipes, and with his rustic melody gave great satisfaction to himself and his faithful follower Midas, who happened to be present. Then Tmolus turned his head toward

the Sun god, and all his trees turned with him. Apollo rose, his brow wreathed with Parnassian laurel, while his robe of Tyrian purple swept the ground. In his left hand he held the lyre, and with his right hand struck the strings. Ravished with the harmony, Tmolus at once awarded the victory to the god of the lyre, and all but Midas acquiesced in the judgment. He dissented, and questioned the justice of the award. Apollo would not suffer such a depraved pair of ears any longer to wear the human form, but caused them to increase in length, grow hairy, within and without, and movable on their roots; in short, to be on the perfect pattern of those of an ass.

Mortified enough was King Midas at this mishap; but he consoled himself with the thought that it was possible to hide his misfortune, which he attempted to do by means of an ample turban or head-dress. But his hair-dresser of course knew the secret. He was charged not to mention it, and threatened with dire punishment if he presumed to disobey. But he found it too much for his discretion to keep such a secret; so he went out into the meadow, dug a hole in the ground, and stooping down, whispered the story, and covered it up. Before long a thick bed of reeds sprang up in the meadow, and as soon as it had gained its growth, began whispering the story, and has continued to do so, from that day to this, every time a breeze passes over the place.

Midas was king of Phrygia. He was the son of Gordius, a poor countryman, who was taken by the people and made king, in obedience to the command of the oracle, which had said that their future king should come in a wagon. While the people were deliberating, Gordius with his wife and son came driving his wagon into the public square.

Gordius, being made king, dedicated his wagon to the deity of the oracle, and tied it up in its place with a fast knot. This was the celebrated *Gordian knot,* which, in after times it was said, whoever should untie should become lord of all Asia. Many tried to untie it, but none succeeded, till Alexander the Great, in his career of conquest, came to Phrygia. He tried his skill with as ill success as others, till growing impatient he drew his sword and cut the knot. When he afterwards succeeded in subjecting all Asia to his sway, people began to think that he had complied with the terms of the oracle according to its true meaning.

BAUCIS
AND PHILEMON

On a certain hill in Phrygia stands a linden tree and an oak, enclosed by a low wall. Not far from the spot is a marsh, formerly good habitable land, but now indented with pools, the resort of fen-birds and cormorants. Once on a time Jupiter, in human shape, visited this country, and with him his son Mercury (he of the caduceus), without his wings. They presented themselves, as weary travellers, at many a door, seeking rest and shelter, but found all closed, for it was late, and the inhospitable inhabitants would not rouse themselves to open for their reception. At last a humble mansion received them, a small thatched cottage, where Baucis, a pious old dame, and her husband Philemon, united when young, had grown old together. Not ashamed of their poverty, they made it endurable by moderate desires and kind dispositions. One need not look there for master or for servant; they two were the whole household, master and servant alike. When the two heavenly guests crossed the humble threshold, and bowed their heads to pass under the low door, the old man placed a seat, on which Baucis, bustling and attentive, spread a cloth, and begged them to sit down. Then she raked out the coals from the ashes, and kindled up a fire, fed it with leaves and dry bark, and with her scanty breath blew it into a flame. She brought out of a corner split sticks and dry branches, broke them up, and placed them under the small kettle. Her husband collected some pot-herbs in the garden, and she shred them from the stalks, and prepared them for the pot. He reached down with a forked stick a flitch of bacon hanging in the chimney, cut a small piece, and put it in the pot to boil with the herbs, setting away the rest for another time. A beechen bowl was filled with warm water, that their guests might wash. While all was doing, they beguiled the time with conversation.

On the bench designed for the guests was laid a cushion stuffed with sea-weed; and a cloth, only produced on great occasions, but ancient and coarse enough, was spread over that. The old lady, with her apron on, with trembling hand set the table. One leg was shorter than the rest, but a piece of slate put under restored the level. When fixed, she rubbed the table down with some sweet-smelling herbs. Upon it she set some of chaste Minerva's olives, some cornel berries preserved in vinegar, and added radishes and cheese, with eggs lightly cooked in the ashes. All were served in earthen dishes, and an earthenware pitcher, with wooden cups, stood beside them. When all was ready, the stew, smoking hot, was set on the table. Some wine, not of the oldest, was added; and for dessert, apples and wild honey; and over and above all, friendly faces, and simple but hearty welcome.

Now while the repast proceeded, the old folks were astonished to see that the wine, as fast as it was poured out, renewed itself in the pitcher, of its own accord. Struck with terror, Baucis and Philemon recognized their heavenly guests, fell on their knees, and with clasped hands implored forgiveness for their poor entertainment. There was an old goose, which they kept as the guardian of their humble cottage; and they bethought them to make this a sacrifice in honour of their guests. But the goose, too nimble, with the aid of feet and wings, for the old folks, eluded their pursuit, and at last took shelter between the gods themselves. They forbade it to be slain; and spoke in these words: "We are gods. This inhospitable village shall pay the penalty of its impiety; you alone shall go free from the chastisement. Quit your house, and come with us to the top of yonder hill." They hastened to obey, and, staff in hand, laboured up the steep ascent. They had reached to within an arrow's flight of the top, when, turning their eyes below, they beheld all the country sunk in a lake, only their own house left standing. While they gazed with wonder at the sight, and lamented the fate of their neighbours, that old house of theirs was changed into a temple. Columns took the place of the corner posts, the thatch grew yellow and appeared a gilded roof, the floors became marble, the doors were enriched with carving and ornaments of gold. Then spoke Jupiter in benignant accents: "Excellent old man, and woman worthy of such a husband, speak, tell us your wishes; what favour have you to ask of us?" Philemon took counsel with Baucis a few moments; then declared to the gods their united wish. "We ask to be priests and guardians of this your temple; and since here we have passed our lives in love and concord, we wish that one and the same hour may take us both from life, that I may not live to see her grave, nor be laid in my own by her." Their prayer was granted. They were the keepers of the temple as long as they lived. When grown very old, as they stood one day before the steps of the sacred edifice, and were telling the story of the place, Baucis saw Philemon begin to put forth leaves, and old Philemon saw Baucis changing in like manner. And now a leafy crown had grown over their heads, while exchanging parting words, as long as they could speak. "Farewell, dear spouse," they said, together, and at the same moment the bark closed over their mouths.

1. Study the story pattern of *Phaëton*. Is *Baucis and Philemon* like it? **2.** Select the incidents that develop the story and show the importance of the verbs in them. **3.** Select five sentences which contain verbs which both indicate action and describe it. **4.** Analyze *Midas* to find if it has unity of structure. In a paragraph, give an account of your decision with logical reasons and concrete examples. **5.** Study the myth *Baucis and Philemon*. Then write an original transformation myth, in which you show how the gods reward and punish for opposite reactions to the same situation. In this way account for the difference in plumage of some birds.

Read *The Reward for Beauty,* another myth about Minerva.

THE REWARD
FOR BEAUTY

Minerva was the goddess of wisdom, but on one occasion she did a very foolish thing; she entered into competition with Juno and Venus for the prize of beauty. It happened thus: At the nuptials of Peleus and Thetis all the gods were invited with the exception of Eris, or Discord. Enraged at her exclusion, the goddess threw a golden apple among the guests, with the inscription, "For the fairest." Thereupon Juno, Venus, and Minerva each claimed the apple. Jupiter, not willing to decide in so delicate a matter, sent the goddesses to Mount Ida, where the beautiful shepherd Paris was tending his flocks, and to him was committed the decision. The goddesses accordingly appeared before him. Juno promised him power and riches, Minerva glory and renown in war, and Venus the fairest of women for his wife, each attempting to bias his decision in her own favour. Paris decided in favour of Venus and gave her the golden apple, thus making the two other goddesses his enemies. Under the protection of Venus, Paris sailed to Greece, and was hospitably received by Menelaus, king of Sparta. Now Helen, the wife of Menelaus, was the very woman whom Venus had destined for Paris, the fairest of her sex. She had been sought as a bride by numerous suitors, and before her decision was made known, they all, at the suggestion of Ulysses, one of their number, took an oath that they would defend her from all injury and avenge her cause if necessary. She chose Menelaus, and was living with him happily when Paris became their guest. Paris, aided by Venus, persuaded her to elope with him, and carried her to Troy, whence arose the famous Trojan war, the theme of the greatest poems of antiquity, those of Homer and Virgil.

1. Does *The Reward for Beauty* have a well structured story pattern? **2.** Point out the initiating incident, the events of the development, and the dénouement. **3.** Name two great epics that include this myth as part of their action.

As your final Greek myth, read *Ceyx and Halcyone*.

CEYX AND HALCYONE:
OR,
THE HALCYON BIRDS

Ceyx was king of Thessaly, where he reigned in peace, without violence or wrong. He was son of Hesperus, the Day-star, and the glow of his beauty reminded one of his father. Halcyone, the daughter of Aeolus, was his wife, and devotedly attached to him. Now Ceyx was in deep affliction for the loss of his brother, and direful prodigies following his brother's death made him feel as if the gods were hostile to him. He thought best, therefore, to make a voyage to Carlos in Ionia, to consult the oracle of Apollo. But as soon as he disclosed his intention to his wife Halcyone, a shudder ran through her frame, and her face grew deadly pale. "What fault of mine, dearest husband, has turned your affection from me? Where is that love of me that used to be uppermost in your thoughts? Have you learned to feel easy in the absence of Halcyone? Would you rather have me away?" She also endeavoured to discourage him, by describing the violence of the winds, which she had known familiarly when she lived at home in her father's house,—Aeolus being the god of the winds, and having as much as he could do to restrain them. "They rush together," said she, "with such fury that fire flashes from the conflict. But if you must go," she added, "dear husband, let me go with you, otherwise I shall suffer not only the real evils which you must encounter, but those also which my fears suggest."

These words weighed heavily on the mind of King Ceyx, and it was no less his own wish than hers to take her with him, but he could not bear to expose her to the dangers of the sea. He answered, therefore, consoling her as well as he could, and finished with these words: "I promise, by the rays of my father the Day-star, that if fate permits I will return before the moon shall have twice rounded her orb." When he had thus spoken, he ordered the vessel to be drawn out of the shiphouse, and the oars and sails to be put aboard. When Halcyone saw these preparations she shuddered, as if with a presentiment of evil. With tears and sobs she said farewell, and then fell senseless to the ground.

Ceyx would still have lingered, but now the young men grasped their oars and pulled vigorously through the waves, with long and measured strokes. Halcyone raised her streaming eyes, and saw her husband standing on the deck, waving his hand to her. She answered his signal till the vessel had receded so far that she could no longer distinguish his form from the rest. When the vessel itself could no more be seen, she strained her eyes to catch the last glimmer of the sail, till that too disappeared. Then, retiring to her chamber, she threw herself on her solitary couch.

Meanwhile they glide out of the harbour, and the breeze plays among the ropes. The seamen draw in their oars, and hoist their sails. When half or less of their course was passed, as night drew on, the sea began to whiten with swelling waves, and the east wind to blow a gale. The master gave the word to take in sail, but the storm forbade obedience, for such is the roar of the winds and waves his orders are unheard. The men, of their own accord, busy themselves to secure the oars, to strengthen the ship, to reef the sail. While they thus do what to each one seems best, the storm increases.

The vessel seems like a wild beast that rushes on the spears of the hunters. The men are stupefied with terror. The thought of parents, and kindred, and pledges left at home, comes over their minds. Ceyx thinks of Halcyone. No name but hers is on his lips, and while he yearns for her, he yet rejoices in her absence. Presently the mast is shattered by a stroke of lightning, the rudder broken, and the triumphant surge curling over looks down upon the wreck, then falls, and crushes it to fragments. Some of the seamen, stunned by the stroke, sink, and rise no more; others cling to fragments of the wreck. Ceyx, with the hand that used to grasp the sceptre, holds fast to a plank, calling for help,—alas, in vain,—upon his father and his father-in-law. But oftenest on his lips was the name of Halcyone. To her his thoughts cling. He prays that the waves may bear his body to her sight, and that it may receive burial at her hands. At length the waters overwhelm him, and he sinks. The Day-star looked dim that night. Since it could not leave the heavens, it shrouded its face with clouds.

In the meanwhile Halcyone, ignorant of all these horrors, counted the days till her husband's promised return. To all the gods she offers frequent incense, but more than all to Juno. The goddess, at length, could not bear any longer to be pleaded with for one already dead, and to have hands raised to her altars that ought rather to be offering funeral rites. So, calling Iris, she said, "Iris, my faithful messenger, go to the drowsy dwelling of Somnus, and tell him to send a vision to Halcyone in the form of Ceyx, to make known to her the event."

Iris puts on her robe of many colours, and tinging the sky with her bow, seeks the palace of the King of Sleep. Near the Cimmerian country, a mountain cave is the abode of the dull god Somnus. Here Phoebus dares not come, either rising, at midday, or setting. Clouds and shadows are exhaled from the ground, and the light glimmers faintly. The bird of dawning, with crested head, never there calls aloud to Aurora, nor watchful dog, nor more sagacious goose disturbs the silence. No wild beast, nor cattle, nor branch moved with the wind, nor sound of human conversation, breaks the stillness. Silence reigns there; but from the bottom of the rock the River Lethe flows, and by its murmur invites to sleep. Poppies grow abundantly before the door of the cave, and other herbs, from whose juices Night collects slumbers, which she scatters over the darkened earth. There is no gate to the mansion, to creak on its hinges, nor watchman;

but in the midst a couch of blackest ebony, adorned with black plumes and black curtains. There the god reclines, his limbs relaxed with sleep. Around him lie dreams, resembling all various forms, as many as the harvest bears stalks, or the forest leaves, or the seashore sand grains.

As soon as the goddess entered and brushed away the dreams that hovered around her, her brightness lit up all the cave. The god, scarce opening his eyes, and ever and anon dropping his beard upon his breast, at last shook himself free from himself, and leaning on his arm, inquired her errand,—for he knew who she was. She answered, "Somnus, gentlest of the gods, tranquillizer of minds and soother of care-worn hearts, Juno sends you her commands that you despatch a dream to Halcyone, in the city of Trachine, representing her lost husband and all the events of the wreck."

Then Somnus called one of his numerous sons,—Morpheus, —the most expert in counterfeiting forms, and in imitating the walk, the countenance, and mode of speaking, even the clothes and attitudes most characteristic of each. But he only imitates men, leaving it to another to personate birds, beasts, and serpents. Him they call Icelos; and Phantasos is a third, who turns himself into rocks, waters, woods, and other things without life. These wait upon kings and great personages in their sleeping hours, while others move among the common people. Somnus chose, from all the brothers, Morpheus, to perform the command of Iris; then laid his head on his pillow and yielded himself to grateful repose.

Morpheus flew, making no noise with his wings, and soon came to the Haemonian city, where, laying aside his wings, he assumed the form of Ceyx. Under that form, but pale like a dead man, naked, he stood before the couch of the wretched wife. His beard seemed soaked with water, and water trickled from his drowned locks. Leaning over the bed, tears streaming from his eyes, he said, "Do you recognize your Ceyx, unhappy wife, or has death too much changed my visage? Behold me, know me, your husband's shade, instead of himself. Your prayers, Halcyone, availed me nothing. I am dead. No more deceive yourself with vain hopes of my return. The stormy winds sunk my ship in the Aegean Sea, waves filled my mouth while it called aloud on you. No uncertain messenger tells you this, no vague rumour brings it to your ears. I come in person, a shipwrecked man, to tell you my fate. Arise! give me tears, give me lamentations, let me not go down to Tartarus unwept." To these words Morpheus added the voice, which seemed to be that of her husband; he seemed to pour forth genuine tears; his hands had the gestures of Ceyx.

Halcyone, weeping, groaned, and stretched out her arms in her sleep, striving to embrace his body, but grasping only the air. "Stay!" she cried; "whither do you fly? let us go together." Her own voice awakened her. Starting up, she gazed eagerly around, to see if he was still present, for the servants, alarmed by her cries, had brought a light. When she found him not, she smote her breast and rent her garments. She cares not to unbind her hair, but tears it wildly. Her nurse asks what is the cause of her grief. "Halcyone is no more," she answers, "she perished with her Ceyx. Utter not words of comfort; he is shipwrecked and dead. I have seen him; I have recognized him. I stretched out my hands to seize him and detain him. His shade vanished, but it was the true shade of my husband. Not with the accustomed features, not with the beauty that was his, but pale, naked, and with his hair wet with sea water, he appeared to wretched me. Here, in this very spot, the sad vision stood"— and she looked to find the mark of his footsteps.

It was now morning. She went to the seashore, and sought the spot where she last saw him, on his departure. Looking out over the sea, she descries an indistinct object floating in the water. At first she was in doubt what it was, but by degrees the waves bore it nearer, and it was plainly the body of a man. Though unknowing of whom, yet, as it was of some shipwrecked one, she was deeply moved, and gave it her tears, saying, "Alas! unhappy one, and unhappy, if such there be, thy wife!" Borne by the waves, it came nearer. As she more and more nearly views it, she trembles more and more. Now, now it approaches the shore. Now marks that she recognizes appear. It is her husband! Stretching out her trembling hands towards it, she exclaims, "O dearest husband, is it thus you return to me?"

There was built out from the shore a mole, constructed to break the assaults of the sea, and stem its violent ingress. She leaped upon this barrier and (it was wonderful she could do so) she flew, and striking the air with wings produced on the instant, skimmed along the surface of the water, an unhappy bird. As she flew, her throat poured forth sounds full of grief, and like the voice of one lamenting. When she touched the mute and bloodless body, she enfolded its beloved limbs with her new-formed wings, and tried to give kisses with her horny beak. Whether Ceyx felt it, or whether it was only the action of the waves, those who looked on doubted, but the body seemed to raise its head. But indeed he did feel it, and by the pitying gods both of them were changed into birds. They mate and have their young ones. For seven placid days, in winter time, Halcyone broods over her nest, which floats upon the sea. Then the way is safe to seamen. Aeolus guards the winds and keeps them from disturbing the deep. The sea is given up, for the time, to his grandchildren.

1. Is *Ceyx and Halcyone* simple or complex in story structure?
2. Work out the story pattern of this myth.

Words from Mythology

1. List modern words derived from:

Halcyone   Aurora   Lethe   Morpheus   Aeolus

2. Do some reference work in the library to identify the following:

Oedipus	Antigone	Jason
Orpheus	Pygmalion	the Minotaur
Gorgon Medusa	Atlas	Hercules
the Hydra	the Sphinx	Daedalus
Icarus	Hestia (Vesta)	Gordian knot

3. Find and list the twelve labors of Hercules.

4. Use your dictionary to explain the mythological origin of:

vulcanize	hygiene	calliope	jovial
Aeolean	panic	iridescent	atlas
aurora	saturnine	Olympic	mercurial

5. Use an unabridged dictionary to find the meaning and origin of:

centaur	halcyon	vampire	styx	phoenix
chimera	unicorn	behemoth	cockatrice	mermaid
basilisk	gorgon	nemesis	griffin	salamander
	werewolf	goblin	gargantua	

6. Look up these mythological names in your dictionary. Syllabicate each, mark the accent, and give the diacritical marks. Be ready to pronounce these words in class.

Actaeon	Python	Prometheus	Amalthea	Baucis
Minerva	Tartarus	Epimetheus	Halcyone	Midas
Arachne	Zephyr	Pandora	Daphne	Delphos
Niobe	Ceyx	Phoebus	Phaëton	Chaos
Narcissus	Latona	Parnassus	Psyche	Nereids
Clytie	Cecrops	Cimmerian	Clymene	Hermes

Read the following stories from Norse mythology, and then answer the questions.

Know stories

Creation in
Norse Mythology

According to the Eddas there was once no heaven above nor earth beneath, but only a bottomless deep, and a world of mist in which flowed a fountain. Twelve rivers issued from this fountain, and when they had flowed far from their source, they froze into ice, and one layer accumulating over another, the great deep was filled up.

Southward from the world of mist was the world of light. From this flowed a warm wind upon the ice and melted it. The vapours rose in the air and formed clouds, from which sprang Ymir, the Frost giant and his progeny, and the cow Audhumbla, whose milk afforded nourishment and food to the giant. The cow got nourishment by licking the hoar frost and salt from the ice. While she was one day licking the salt stones there appeared at first the hair of a man, on the second day the whole head, and on the third the entire form endowed with beauty, agility, and power. This new being was a god, from whom and his wife, a daughter of the giant race, sprang the three brothers Odin, Vili, and Ve. They slew the giant Ymir, and out of his body formed the earth, of his blood the seas, of his bones the mountains, of his hair the trees, of his skull the heavens, and of his brain clouds, charged with hail and snow. Of Ymir's eyebrows the gods formed Midgard (mid earth), destined to become the abode of man.

Odin then regulated the periods of day and night and the seasons by placing in the heavens the sun and moon, and appointing to them their respective courses. As soon as the sun began to shed its rays upon the earth, it caused the vegetable world to bud and sprout. Shortly after the gods had created the world they walked by the side of the sea, pleased with their new work, but found that it was still incomplete, for it was without human beings. They therefore took an ash tree and made a man out of it, and they made a woman out of an alder, and called the man Aske and the woman Embla. Odin then gave them life and soul, Vili reason and motion, and Ve bestowed upon them the senses, expressive features, and speech. Midgard was then given them as their residence, and they became the progenitors of the human race.

The mighty ash tree, Ygdrasill, was supposed to support the whole universe. It sprang from the body of Ymir, and had three immense roots, extending one into Asgard (the dwelling of the gods), the other into Jotunheim (the abode of the giants), and the third to Niffleheim (the regions of darkness and cold). By the side of each of these roots is a spring, from which it is watered. The root that extends into Asgard is carefully tended by the three Norns, goddesses, who are regarded as the dispensers of fate. They are Urdur (the past), Verdandi (the present), Skuld (the future). The spring at the Jotunheim side is Ymir's well, in which wisdom and wit lie hidden, but that of Niffleheim feeds the adder Nidhogge (darkness), which perpetually gnaws at the root. Four harts run across the branches of the tree and bite the buds; they represent the four winds. Under the tree lies Ymir, and when he tries to shake off its weight the earth quakes.

Asgard is the name of the abode of the gods, access to which is only gained by crossing the bridge Bifrost (the rainbow). Asgard consists of golden and silver palaces, the dwellings of the gods, but the most beautiful of these is Valhalla, the residence of Odin. When seated on his throne he overlooks all heaven and earth. Upon his shoulders are the ravens Hugin and Munin, who fly every day over the whole world, and on their return report to him all they have seen and heard. At his feet lie his two wolves, Geri and Freki, to whom Odin gives all the meat that is set before him, for he himself stands in no need of food. Mead is for him both food and drink. He invented the Runic characters, and it is the business of the Norns to engrave the runes of fate upon a metal shield. From Odin's name, spelt Woden, as it sometimes is, came Wednesday, the name of the fourth day of the week.

Odin is frequently called Alfdaur (All-father), but this name is sometimes used in a way that shows that the Scandinavians had an idea of a deity superior to Odin, uncreated and eternal.

Of the Joys of Valhalla

Valhalla is the great hall of Odin, wherein he feasts with his chosen heroes, all those who have fallen bravely in battle, for all who die a peaceful death are excluded. The flesh of the boar Schrimnir is served up to them, and is abundant for all. For although this boar is cooked every morning, he becomes whole again every night. For drink the heroes are supplied abundantly with mead from the she-goat Heidrum. When the heroes are not feasting they amuse themselves with fighting. Every day they ride out into the court or field and fight until they cut each other in pieces. This is their pastime; but when meal time comes they recover from their wounds and return to feast in Valhalla.

The Valkyrior

The Valkyrior are warlike virgins, mounted upon horses and armed with helmets and spears. Odin, who is desirous to collect a great many heroes in Valhalla, to be able to meet the giants in a day when the final contest must come, sends down to every battlefield to make choice of those who shall be slain. The

Valkyrior are his messengers, and their name means "Choosers of the slain." When they ride forth on their errand, their armour sheds a strange flickering light, which flashes up over the northern skies, making what men call the "Aurora Borealis," or "Northern Lights."

Of Thor
and the Other Gods

Thor, the thunderer, Odin's eldest son, is the strongest of gods and men, and possesses three very precious things. The first is a hammer, which both the Frost and the Mountain giants know to their cost, when they see it hurled against them in the air, for it has split many a skull of their fathers and kindred. When thrown, it returns to his hand of its own accord. The second rare thing he possesses is called the belt of strength. When he girds it about him his divine might is doubled. The third, also very precious, is his iron gloves, which he puts on whenever he would use his mallet efficiently. From Thor's name is derived our word Thursday.

Frey is one of the most celebrated of the gods. He presides over rain and sunshine and all the fruits of the earth. His sister Freya is the most propitious of the goddesses. She loves music, spring, and flowers, and is particularly fond of the Elves (fairies). She is very fond of love ditties, and all lovers would do well to invoke her.

Bragi is the god of poetry, and his song records the deeds of warriors. His wife, Iduna, keeps in a box the apples which the gods, when they feel old age approaching, have only to taste of to become young again.

Heimdall is the watchman of the gods, and is therefore placed on the borders of heaven to prevent the giants from forcing their way over the bridge Bifrost (the rainbow). He requires less sleep than a bird, and sees by night as well as by day a hundred miles around him. So acute is his ear that no sound escapes him, for he can even hear the grass grow and the wool on a sheep's back.

Of Loki and His Progeny

There is another deity who is described as the calumniator of the gods and the contriver of all fraud and mischief. His name is Loki. He is handsome and well made, but of a very fickle mood and most evil disposition. He is of the giant race, but forced himself into the company of the gods, and seems to take pleasure in bringing them into difficulties, and in extricating them out of the danger by his cunning, wit, and skill. Loki has three children. The first is the wolf Fenris, the second the Midgard serpent, the third Hela (Death). The gods were not ignorant that these monsters were growing up, and that they would one day bring much evil upon gods and men. So Odin deemed it advisable to send one to bring them to him. When they came he threw the serpent into that deep ocean by which the earth is surrounded. But the monster had grown to such an enormous size that holding his tail in his mouth he encircles the whole earth. Hela he cast into Niffleheim, and gave her power over nine worlds or regions, into which she distributes those who are sent to her; that is, all who die of sickness or old age. Her hall is called Elvidner. Hunger is her table, Starvation her knife, Delay her man, Slowness her maid, Precipice her threshold, Care her bed, and Burning Anguish forms the hangings of the apartments. She may easily be recognized, for her body is half flesh colour and half blue, and she has a dreadfully stern and forbidding countenance.

The wolf Fenris gave the gods a great deal of trouble before they succeeded in chaining him. He broke the strongest fetters as if they were made of cobwebs. Finally the gods sent a messenger to the mountain spirits, who made for them the chain called Gleipnir. It is fashioned of six things, viz., the noise made by the footfall of a cat, the beards of women, the roots of stones, the breath of fishes, the nerves (sensibilities) of bears, and the spittle of birds. When finished it was as smooth and soft as a silken string. But when the gods asked the wolf to suffer himself to be bound with this apparently slight ribbon, he suspected their design, fearing that it was made by enchantment. He therefore only consented to be bound with it upon condition that one of the gods put his hand in his (Fenris's) mouth as a pledge that the band was to be removed again. Tyr (the god of battles) alone had courage enough to do this. But when the wolf found that he could not break his fetters, and that the gods would not release him, he bit off Tyr's hand, and he has ever since remained one-handed.

How Thor Paid the Mountain Giant His Wages

Once on a time, when the gods were constructing their abodes and had already finished Midgard and Valhalla, a certain artificer came and offered to build them a residence so well fortified that they should be perfectly safe from the incursions of the Frost giants and the giants of the mountains. But he demanded for his reward the goddess Freya, together with the sun and moon. The gods yielded to his terms, provided he would finish the whole work himself without any one's assistance, and all within the space of one winter. But if anything remained unfinished on the first day of summer he should forfeit the recompense agreed on. On being told these terms the artificer stipulated that he should be allowed the use of his horse Svadilfari, and this by the advice of Loki was granted to him. He accordingly set to work on the first day of winter, and during the night let his horse draw stones for the building. The enormous size of the stones struck the gods with astonishment, and they saw clearly that the horse did one-half more of the toilsome work than his master. Their bargain, however, had been concluded, and confirmed by solemn oaths, for without these precautions a giant would not have thought himself safe among the gods, especially when Thor should return from an expedition he had then undertaken against the evil demons.

As the winter drew to a close, the building was far advanced, and the bulwarks were sufficiently high and massive to render the place impregnable. In short, when it wanted but three days to summer, the only part that remained to be finished was the gateway. Then sat the gods on their seats of justice and entered into consultation, inquiring of one another who among them could have advised to give Freya away, or to plunge the heavens in darkness by permitting the giant to carry away the sun and the moon.

They all agreed that no one but Loki, the author of so many evil deeds, could have given such bad counsel, and that he should be put to a cruel death if he did not contrive some way to prevent the artificer from completing his task and obtaining the stipulated recompense. They proceeded to lay hands on Loki, who in his fright promised upon oath that, let it cost him what it would, he would so manage matters that the man should lose his reward. That very night when the man went with Svadilfari for building stone, a mare suddenly ran out of a forest and began to neigh. The horse thereat broke loose and ran after the mare into the forest, which obliged the man also to run after his horse, and thus between one and another the whole night was lost, so that at dawn the work had not made the usual progress. The man, seeing that he must fail of completing his task, resumed his own gigantic stature, and the gods now clearly perceived that it was in reality a mountain giant who had come amongst them. Feeling no longer bound by their oaths, they called on Thor, who immediately ran to their assistance, and lifting up his mallet, paid the workman his wages, not with the sun and moon, and not even by sending him back to Jotunheim, for with the first blow he shattered the giant's skull to pieces and hurled him headlong into Niffleheim.

The Recovery
of the Hammer

Once upon a time it happened that Thor's hammer fell into the possession of the giant Thrym, who buried it eight fathoms deep under the rocks of Jotunheim. Thor sent Loki to negotiate with Thrym, but he could only prevail so far as to get the giant's promise to restore the weapon if Freya would consent to be his bride. Loki returned and reported the result of his mission, but the goddess of love was quite horrified at the idea of bestowing her charms on the king of the Frost giants. In this emergency Loki persuaded Thor to dress himself in Freya's clothes and accompany him to Jotunheim. Thrym received his veiled bride with due courtesy, but was greatly surprised at seeing her eat for her supper eight salmons and a full grown ox, besides other delicacies, washing the whole down with three tuns of mead. Loki, however, assured him that she had not tasted anything for eight long nights, so great was her desire to see her lover, the renowned ruler of Jotunheim. Thrym had at length the curiosity to peep under his bride's veil, but started back in affright and demanded why Freya's eyeballs glistened with fire. Loki repeated the same excuse and the giant was satisfied. He ordered the hammer to be brought in and laid on the maiden's lap. Thereupon Thor threw off his disguise, grasped his redoubted weapon, and slaughtered Thrym and all his followers.

Frey also possessed a wonderful weapon, a sword which would of itself spread a field with carnage whenever the owner desired it. Frey parted with this sword, but was less fortunate than Thor and never recovered it. It happened in this way: Frey once mounted Odin's throne, from whence one can see over the whole universe, and looking round saw far off in the giant's kingdom a beautiful maid, at the sight of whom he was struck with sudden sadness, insomuch that from that moment he could neither sleep, nor drink, nor speak. At last Skirnir, his messenger, drew his secret from him, and undertook to get him the maiden for his bride, if he would give him his sword as a reward. Frey consented and gave him the sword, and Skirnir set off on his journey and obtained the maiden's promise that within the nine nights she would come to a certain place and there wed Frey. Skirnir having reported the success of his errand, Frey exclaimed:

> "Long is one night,
>   Long are two nights,
>   But how shall I hold out three?
>   Shorter hath seemed
>   A month to me oft
>   Than of this longing time the half."

So Frey obtained Gerda, the most beautiful of all women, for his wife, but he lost his sword.

Thor's Visit to Jotunheim, The Giant's Country

One day the god Thor, with his servant Thialfi, and accompanied by Loki, set out on a journey to the giant's country. Thialfi was of all men the swiftest afoot. He bore Thor's wallet, containing their provisions. When night came on they found themselves in an immense forest, and searched on all sides for a place where they might pass the night, and at last came to a very large hall, with an entrance that took the whole breadth of one end of the building. Here they lay down to sleep, but towards midnight were alarmed by an earthquake which shook the whole edifice. Thor, rising up, called on his companions to seek with him a place of safety. On the right they found an adjoining chamber, into which the others entered, but Thor remained at the doorway with his mallet in his hand, prepared to defend himself, whatever might happen. A terrible groaning was heard during the night, and at dawn of day Thor went out and found lying near him a huge giant, who slept and snored in the way that had alarmed them so. It is said that for once Thor was afraid to use his mallet, and as the giant soon waked up, Thor contented himself wtih simply asking his name.

"My name is Skrymir," said the giant, "but I need not ask thy name, for I know that thou art the god Thor. But what has become of my glove?" Thor then perceived that what they had taken overnight for a hall was the giant's glove, and the chamber where his two companions had sought refuge was the thumb. Skrymir then proposed that they should travel in company, and Thor consenting, they sat down to eat their breakfast, and when they had done, Skrymir packed all the provisions into one wallet, threw it over his shoulder, and strode on before them, taking such tremendous strides that they were hard put to it to keep up with him. So they travelled the whole day, and at dusk Skrymir chose a place for them to pass the night in under a large oak tree. Skrymir then told them he would lie down to sleep. "But take ye the wallet," he added, "and prepare your supper."

Skrymir soon fell asleep and began to snore strongly; but when Thor tried to open the wallet, he found the giant had tied it up so tight he could not untie a single knot. At last Thor became wroth, and grasping his mallet with both hands he struck a furious blow on the giant's head. Skrymir, awakening, merely asked whether a leaf had not fallen on his head, and whether they had supped and were ready to go to sleep. Thor answered that they were just going to sleep, and so saying went and laid himself down under another tree. But sleep came not that night to Thor, and when Skrymir snored again so loud that the forest re-echoed with the noise, he arose, and grasping his mallet launched it with such force at the giant's skull that it made a deep dint in it. Skrymir, awakening, cried out, "What's the matter? Are there any birds perched on this tree? I felt some moss from the branches fall on my head. How fares it with thee, Thor?" But Thor went away hastily, saying that he had just then awoke, and that as it was only midnight, there was still time for sleep. He, however, resolved that if he had an opportunity of striking a third blow, it should settle all matters between them. A little before daybreak he perceived that Skrymir was again fast asleep, and again grasping his mallet, he dashed it with such violence that it forced its way into the giant's skull up to the handle. But Skrymir sat up, and stroking his cheek said, "An acorn fell on my head. What! Art thou awake, Thor? Methinks it is time for us to get up and dress ourselves; but you have not now a long way before you to the city called Utgard. I have heard you whispering to one another that I am not a man of small dimensions; but if you come to Utgard you will see there many men much taller than I. Wherefore I advise you, when you come there, not to make too much of yourselves, for the followers of Utgard-Loki will not brook the boasting of such little fellows as you are. You must take the road that leads eastward, mine lies northward, so we must part here."

Hereupon he threw his wallet over his shoulders and turned away from them into the forest, and Thor had no wish to stop him or to ask for any more of his company.

Thor and his companions proceeded on their way, and towards noon descried a city standing in the middle of a plain. It was so lofty that they were obliged to bend their necks quite back on their shoulders in order to see to the top of it. On arriving they entered the city, and seeing a large palace before them with the door wide open, they went in, and found a number of men of prodigious stature, sitting on benches in the hall. Going further, they came before the king, Utgard-Loki, whom they saluted with great respect. The king, regarding them with a scornful smile, said, "If I do not mistake me, that stripling yonder must be the god Thor." Then addressing himself to Thor, he said, "Perhaps thou mayest be more than thou appearest to be. What are the feats that thou and thy fellows deem yourselves skilled in, for no one is permitted to remain here who does not, in some feat or other, excel all other men?"

"The feat that I know," said Loki, "is to eat quicker than any one else, and in this I am ready to give a proof against any one here who may choose to compete with me."

"That will indeed be a feat," said Utgard-Loki, "if thou performest what thou promisest, and it shall be tried forthwith."

He then ordered one of his men who was sitting at the farther end of the bench, and whose name was Logi, to come forward and try his skill with Loki. A trough filled with meat having been set on the hall floor, Loki placed himself at one end, and Logi at the other, and each of them began to eat as fast as he could, until they met in the middle of the trough. But it was found that Loki had only eaten the flesh, while his adversary had devoured both flesh and bone, and the trough to boot. All the company therefore adjudged that Loki was vanquished.

Utgard-Loki then asked what feat the young man who accompanied Thor could perform. Thialfi answered that he would run a race with any one who might be matched against him. The king observed that skill in running was something to boast of, but if the youth would win the match he must display great agility. He then arose and went with all who were present to a plain where there was good ground for running on, and calling a young man named Hugi, bade him run a match with Thialfi. In the first course Hugi so much outstripped his competitor that he turned back and met him not far from the starting place. Then they ran a second and a third time, but Thialfi met with no better success.

Utgard-Loki then asked Thor in what feats he would choose to give proofs of that prowess for which he was so famous. Thor answered that he would try a drinking match with any one. Utgard-Loki bade his cupbearer bring the large horn which his followers were obliged to empty when they had trespassed in any way against the law of the feast. The cupbearer having presented it to Thor, Utgard-Loki said, "Whoever is a good drinker will empty that horn at a single draught, though most men make two of it, but the most puny drinker can do it in three."

Thor looked at the horn, which seemed of no extraordinary size though somewhat long; however, as he was very thirsty, he set it to his lips, and without drawing breath, pulled as long and as deeply as he could, that he might not be obliged to make a second draught of it; but when he set the horn down and looked in, he could scarcely perceive that the liquor was diminished.

After taking breath, Thor went to it again with all his might, but when he took the horn from his mouth, it seemed to him that he had drunk rather less than before, although the horn could now be carried without spilling.

"How now, Thor?" said Utgard-Loki; "thou must not spare thyself; if thou meanest to drain the horn at the third draught thou must pull deeply; and I must needs say that thou wilt not be called so mighty a man here as thou art at home if thou showest no greater prowess in other feats than methinks will be shown in this."

Thor, full of wrath, again set the horn to his lips, and did his best to empty it; but on looking in found the liquor was only a little lower, so he resolved to make no further attempt, but gave back the horn to the cupbearer.

"I now see plainly," said Utgard-Loki, "that thou art not quite so stout as we thought thee: but wilt thou try any other feat, though methinks thou art not likely to bear any prize away with thee hence."

"What new trial hast thou to propose?" said Thor.

"We have a very trifling game here," answered Utgard-Loki, "in which we exercise none but children. It consists in merely lifting my cat from the ground; nor should I have dared to mention such a feat to the great Thor if I had not already observed that thou art by no means what we took thee for."

As he finished speaking, a large grey cat sprang on the hall floor. Thor put his hand under the cat's belly and did his utmost to raise him from the floor, but the cat, bending his back, had, notwithstanding all Thor's efforts, only one of his feet lifted up, seeing which Thor made no further attempt.

"This trial has turned out," said Utgard-Loki, "just as I imagined it would. The cat is large, but Thor is little in comparison to our men."

"Little as ye call me," answered Thor, "let me see who among you will come hither now I am in wrath and wrestle with me."

"I see no one here," said Utgard-Loki, looking at the men sitting on the benches, "who would not think it beneath him to wrestle with thee; let somebody, however, call hither that old crone, my nurse Elli, and let Thor wrestle with her if he will. She has thrown to the ground many a man not less strong than this Thor is."

A toothless old woman then entered the hall, and was told by Utgard-Loki to take hold of Thor. The tale is shortly told. The more Thor tightened his hold on the crone the firmer she stood. At length after a very violent struggle Thor began to lose his footing, and was finally brought down upon one knee. Utgard-Loki then told them to desist, adding that Thor had now no occasion to ask any one else in the hall to wrestle with him, and it was also getting late; so he showed Thor and his companions to their seats, and they passed the night there in good cheer.

The next morning, at break of day, Thor and his companions dressed themselves and prepared for departure. Utgard-Loki ordered a great table to be set for them, on which there was no lack of victuals or drink. After the repast Utgard-Loki led them to the gate of the city, and on parting asked Thor how he thought his journey had turned out, and whether he had met with any men stronger than himself. Thor told him that he could not deny but that he had brought great shame on himself. "And what grieves me most," he added, "is that ye will call me a person of little worth."

"Nay," said Utgard-Loki, "it behooves me to tell thee the truth, now thou art out of the city, which so long as I live and have my way thou shalt never enter again. And, by my troth, had I known beforehand that thou hadst so much strength in thee, and wouldst have brought me so near to a great mishap, I would not have suffered thee to enter this time. Know then that I have all along deceived thee by my illusions; first in the forest, where I tied up the wallet with iron wire so that thou couldst not untie it. After this thou gavest me three blows with thy mallet; the first, though the least, would have ended my days had it fallen on me, but I slipped aside and thy blows fell on the mountain, where thou wilt find three glens, one of them remarkably deep. These are the dints made by thy mallet. I have made use of similar illusions in the contests you have had with my followers. In the first, Loki, like hunger itself, devoured all that was set before him, but Logi was in reality nothing else than Fire, and therefore consumed not only the meat, but the trough which held it. Hugi, with whom Thialfi contended in running, was Thought, and it was impossible for Thialfi to keep pace with that. When thou in thy turn didst attempt to empty the horn, thou didst perform, by my troth, a deed so marvellous that had I not seen it myself I should never have believed it. For one end of that horn reached the sea, which thou wast not aware of, but when thou comest to the shore thou wilt perceive how much the sea has sunk by thy draughts. Thou didst perform a feat no less wonderful by lifting up the cat, and to tell thee the truth, when we saw that one of his paws was off the floor, we were all of us terror-stricken, for what thou tookest for a cat was in reality the Midgard serpent that encompasseth the earth, and he was so stretched by thee that he was barely long enough to enclose it between his head and tail. Thy wrestling with Elli was also a most astonishing feat, for there was never yet a man, nor ever will be, whom Old Age, for such in fact was Elli, will not sooner or later lay low. But now, as we are going to part, let me tell thee that it will be better for both of us if thou never come near me again, for shouldst·thou do so, I shall again defend myself by other illusions, so that thou wilt only lose thy labour and get no fame from the contest with me."

On hearing these words Thor in a rage laid hold of his mallet and would have launched it at him, but Utgard-Loki had disappeared, and when Thor would have returned to the city to destroy it, he found nothing around him but a verdant plain.

The Death of Baldur

Baldur the Good, having been tormented with terrible dreams indicating that his life was in peril, told them to the assembled gods, who resolved to conjure all things to avert from him the threatened danger. Then Frigga, the wife of Odin, exacted an oath from fire and water, from iron and all other metals, from stones, trees, diseases, beasts, birds, poisons, and creeping things, that none of them would do any harm to Baldur. Odin, not satisfied with all this, and feeling alarmed for the fate of his son, determined to consult the prophetess Angerbode, a giantess, mother of Fenris, Hela, and the Midgard serpent. She was dead, and Odin was forced to seek her in Hela's dominions.

But the other gods, feeling that what Frigga had done was quite sufficient, amused themselves with using Baldur as a mark, some hurling darts at him, some stones, while others hewed at him with their swords and battle-axes; for do what they would, none of them could harm him. And this became a favourite pastime with them and was regarded as an honour shown to Baldur. But when Loki beheld the scene he was sorely vexed that Baldur was not hurt. Assuming, therefore, the shape of a woman, he went to Fensalir, the mansion of Frigga. That goddess, when she saw the pretended woman, inquired of her if she knew what the gods were doing at their meetings. She replied that they were throwing darts and stones at Baldur, without being able to hurt him. "Ay," said Frigga, "neither stones, nor sticks, nor anything else can hurt Baldur, for I have exacted an oath from all of them." "What," exclaimed the woman, "have all things sworn to spare Baldur?" "All things," replied Frigga, "except one little shrub that grows on the eastern side of Valhalla, and is called Mistletoe, and which I thought too young and feeble to crave an oath from."

As soon as Loki heard this he went away, and resuming his natural shape, cut off the mistletoe, and repaired to the place where the gods were assembled. There he found Hodur standing apart, without partaking of the sports, on account of his blindness, and going up to him, said, "Why dost thou not also throw something at Baldur?"

"Because I am blind," answered Hodur, "and see not where Baldur is, and have, moreover, nothing to throw."

"Come, then," said Loki, "do like the rest, and show honour to Baldur by throwing this twig at him, and I will direct thy arm towards the place where he stands."

Hodur then took the mistletoe, and under the guidance of Loki, darted it at Baldur, who, pierced through and through, fell down lifeless. Surely never was there witnessed, either among gods or men, a more atrocious deed than this. When Baldur fell, the gods were struck speechless with horror, and then they looked at each other and all were of one mind to lay hands on him who had done the deed, but they were obliged to delay their vengeance out of respect for the sacred place where they were assembled. They gave vent to their grief by loud lamentations. When the gods came to themselves, Frigga asked who among them wished to gain all her love and good will. "For this," said she, "shall he have who will ride to Hel and offer

Hela a ransom if she will let Baldur return to Asgard." Whereupon Hermod, surnamed the Nimble, the son of Odin, offered to undertake the journey. Odin's horse, Sleipnir, which has eight legs and can outrun the wind, was then led forth, on which Hermod mounted and galloped away on his mission. For the space of nine days and as many nights he rode through deep glens so dark that he could not discern anything, until he arrived at the river Gyoll, which he passed over on a bridge covered with glittering gold. The maiden who kept the bridge asked him his name and lineage, telling him that the day before five bands of dead persons had ridden over the bridge, and did not shake it as much as he alone. "But," she added, "thou hast not death's hue on thee; why then ridest thou here on the way to Hel?"

"I ride to Hel," answered Hermod, "to seek Baldur. Hast thou perchance seen him pass this way?"

She replied, "Baldur hath ridden over Gyoll's bridge, and yonder lieth the way he took to the abodes of death."

Hermod pursued his journey until he came to the barred gates of Hel. Here he alighted, girthed his saddle tighter, and remounting clapped both spurs to his horse, who cleared the gate by a tremendous leap without touching it. Hermod then rode on to the palace, where he found his brother Baldur occupying the most distinguished seat in the hall, and passed the night in his company. The next morning he besought Hela to let Baldur ride home with him, assuring her that nothing but lamentations were to be heard among the gods. Hela answered that it should now be tried whether Baldur was so beloved as he was said to be. "If, therefore," she added, "all things in the world, both living and lifeless, weep for him, then shall he return to life; but if any one thing speak against him or refuse to weep, he shall be kept in Hel."

Hermod then rode back to Asgard and gave an account of all he had heard and witnessed.

The gods upon this despatched messengers throughout the world to beg everything to weep in order that Baldur might be delivered from Hel. All things very willingly complied with this request, both men and every other living being, as well as earths, and stones, and trees, and metals, just as we have all seen these things weep when they are brought from a cold place into a hot one. As the messengers were returning, they found an old hag named Thaukt sitting in a cavern, and begged her to weep Baldur out of Hel. But she answered:

> "Thaukt will wail
> With dry tears
> Baldur's bale-fire.
> Let Hela keep her own."

It was strongly suspected that this hag was no other than Loki himself, who never ceased to work evil among gods and men. So Baldur was prevented from coming back to Asgard.

THE NORSE MYTH OF CREATION

1. Compare the Norse myth of creation with the Greek myth of creation (Prometheus). 2. Tell the Bible story of creation. 3. To which Greek god does Odin correspond? 4. What in Greek mythology corresponds with Valhalla? 5. Who are the Valkyrior?

OF THOR AND THE OTHER GODS AND OF LOKI AND HIS PROGENY

1. What are the three precious possessions of Thor? 2. To which day of the week does Thor give his name? 3. Who are Frey and Freya? 4. Which Greek goddess is like Freya? 5. Who is the Norse god of poetry? The Greek? 6. Who is the watchman of the gods? 7. What kind of god is Loki? 8. Who are Loki's children? 9. Of what was the chain made with which the gods chained Fenris?

HOW THOR PAID THE MOUNTAIN GIANT HIS WAGES, THE RECOVERY OF THE HAMMER, AND THOR'S VISIT TO JOTUNHEIM

1. Tell the story of how Thor paid the mountain giant his wages. 2. Work out the story structure of this myth. 3. Tell the story

about the way Frey obtained the beautiful Gerda. **4.** When Thor visits Jotunheim, he meets the giant Skrymir. Describe this meeting. **5.** What feats do the gods and the giant perform? **6.** Who is the cleverest?

THE DEATH OF BALDUR

1. How much of this account is exposition? **2.** What is the initiating incident—the event that begins the action that ends in Baldur's death? **3.** List the friends of Baldur; list his enemies. **4.** What part of this myth is explanatory? **5.** Which characters of Norse mythology did you also meet in other myths? **6.** What is the point of this story—the dénouement? Is it Baldur's death or his remaining in Hel? **7.** Does the story remind you of any story or story motifs you met in Greek mythology? **8.** Why should Loki despise Baldur? **9.** Why is all of the evil of the story centered in Loki? **10.** The man who throws the mistletoe at Loki's command is blind. Is there any significance in this? **11.** Now that you have read some of the stories contained in Norse mythology, you should be able to identify the following names:

Eddas	Elves	Asgard	Baldur	Woden
Ymir	Skrymir	Jotunheim	Alfdaur	Freya
Odin	Logi	Valhalla	Niffleheim	Loki
Vili	Mistletoe	Frey	Ve	Utgard-Loki
Valkyrior	Midgard	Heimdall	Norns	Frigga
Thor	Ygdrasil	Utgard	Skuld	Hel

12. The names of the week originate directly or indirectly from classical or Norse mythology. Find the myth that provides each name.

Sunday—Sun's day (Old English: sunnandaeg)
Monday—Moon's day (Old English: monandaeg)
Tuesday—Tiu's day (Norse)
Wednesday—Woden's day (Norse)
Thursday—Thor's day (Norse)
Friday—Freya's day (Norse)
Saturday—Saturn's day (Roman)

-a Find a Norse myth of the god Tiu. **-b** Which god of Greek mythology is Tiu like? **-c** What is another Norse name for Woden? Which god of Greek mythology is like Woden? **-d** Relate a myth of the god Thor. **-e** Which Greek goddess is like Freya? **-f** By what name is the god Saturn known in Greek mythology?

Stories that Teach—Fables

Long ago, men tried to explain in the Greek myth of creation the beginning of the world and of animal and human life. In this myth we find the seeds that later develop into the fable. Reread the myth *Prometheus,* page 125, that tells the story of creation.

MEN AGAINST ANIMALS: The myth on creation shows us that primitive men found it difficult to cope with the cunning and ferocity of animals. In early animal stories the beasts have qualities that make them a threat to men. It is thought that the beast story came from an age so far back in time that men had not as yet developed weapons that made it easy for them to subdue animals. In the old animal tales that preceded the fable, men are shown at a disadvantage in the presence of the speed of the winged creatures, the courage of the ferocious tiger, the cunning of the panther, the keen vision of the eagle.

The animal story was built around one dominant animal trait, such as keenness of sight or scent, toughness of hide, speed of foot or wing. In time, from the animal story the fable developed. The single animal trait began to stand for some quality of men, good or bad; and the animal characters were used to mock the behavior of human beings. Then the animal story was a fully developed fable.

READING AND STUDYING FABLES: The best known fables are those of Aesop. In them we find a way of telling stories, in which a story develops on two levels of meaning—one literal, the other symbolic. Every important detail on the literal level has its true meaning only on a deeper level. Animals and inanimate objects are given human characteristics. You will find when you read these fables that the events are created or selected to teach truth or to mock human beings. To make certain that the point will not be missed, the storyteller of fables repeats the moral point as a kind of proverb at the close of his story.

Read these nine fables.

The Fox and the Grapes

A hungry fox saw some ripe clusters of grapes hanging from a vine. She jumped at them, but failed to reach them. She tried every trick she knew, but still she couldn't reach them. At last she turned away in weary disappointment.

"Just as I thought. The grapes are sour!"

It is easy to scorn what we cannot have.

The Shepherd Boy and the Wolf

A shepherd boy who tended his sheep grew lonely. Thinking to have some fun and pass the time he cried out, "Wolf! Wolf!"

His neighbors rushed over to help him, but of course there was no wolf. He merely laughed at them for coming. Three times he raised a false cry of *Wolf*. Three times the neighbors came running.

At last the wolf really did come. The shepherd boy cried out in terror, "Wolf! Wolf! The wolf is killing the sheep."

No one came or paid any attention to his cries. The wolf, having nothing to fear, proceeded to destroy the entire flock.

No one believes a liar—even when he speaks the truth.

The Dog and the Shadow

It happened that a Dog had got a piece of meat and was carrying it home in his mouth to eat it in peace. Now on his way home he had to cross a plank lying across a running brook.

As he crossed, he looked down and saw his own shadow reflected in the water beneath. Thinking it was another dog with another piece of meat, he made up his mind to have that also. So he made a snap at the shadow in the water, but as he opened his mouth the piece of meat fell out, dropped into the water and was never seen more.

Beware lest you lose the substance by grasping at the shadow.

The North Wind and the Sun

The North Wind and the Sun had an argument over who was more powerful. They agreed to settle their disagreement by a contest: whoever could first take the coat off a traveler would be declared the winner.

The North Wind tried first. He blew and blew and blew with all his might, but the harder he blew, the closer the traveler wrapped his coat around him. At last the North Wind gave up. Then the Sun had a try.

He shone out in all his warmth. The traveler, feeling the warmth of his rays, began to take off one garment after another. At last, almost overcome by the heat, he took off his clothing and bathed in a stream by the roadside.

Persuasion is better than force.

The Old Man and Death

A poor old peasant, worn out with age and work, toiled along a country road. He carried a heavy load of firewood over his shoulders. As he walked painfully along toward his distant cottage, he considered his lot and began to despair. He put the burden down and sat beside it.

"What pleasure have I known since I first drew breath? From morning to night it is one round of thankless toil. My cupboards are bare; my wife is discontented; my children are disobedient! If only Death would free me from my troubles."

"Did you call me?" It was Death, the King of Terrors, standing before him. "What request did you make?"

"N-n-nothing;" stammered the old man. "Please help me get back on my shoulders the bundle of firewood I let fall."

We would often be sorry if our wishes were gratified.

The Crow and the Pitcher

A Crow, half-dead with thirst, came upon a Pitcher which had once been full of water; but when the Crow put its beak into the mouth of the Pitcher he found that only very little water was left in it, and that he could not reach far enough down to get at it. He tried, and he tried, but at last had to give up in despair. Then a thought came to him, and he took a pebble and dropped it into the Pitcher. Then he took another pebble and dropped it into the Pitcher. Then he took another pebble and dropped that into the Pitcher. Then he took another pebble and dropped that into the Pitcher. Then took another pebble and dropped that into the Pitcher. Then he took another pebble and dropped that into the Pitcher. At last, at last, he saw the water mount up near him; and after casting in a few more pebbles he was able to quench his thirst and save his life.

Little by little does the trick.

The Wolf in Sheep's Clothing

A Wolf found great difficulty in getting at the sheep owing to the vigilance of the shepherd and his dogs. But one day it found the skin of a sheep that had been flayed and thrown aside, so it put it on over its own pelt and strolled down among the sheep. The Lamb that belonged to the sheep, whose skin the Wolf was wearing, began to follow the Wolf in the Sheep's clothing; so, leading the Lamb a little apart, he soon made a meal off her, and for some time he succeeded in deceiving the sheep, and enjoying hearty meals.

Appearances are deceptive.

The Fox and the Crow

A Fox once saw a Crow fly off with a piece of cheese in its beak and settle on a branch of a tree. "That's for me, as I am a Fox," said Master Reynard, and he walked up to the foot of the tree. "Good-day, Mistress Crow," he cried. "How well you are looking to-day: how glossy your feathers; how bright your eye. I feel sure your voice must surpass that of other birds, just as your figure does; let me hear but one song from you that I may greet you as the Queen of Birds." The Crow lifted up her head and began to caw her best, but the moment she opened her mouth the piece of cheese fell to the ground, only to be snapped up by Master Fox. "That will do," said he. "That was all I wanted. In exchange for your cheese I will give you a piece of advice for the future—

Do not trust flatterers."

The Dog in the Manger

A Dog looking out for its afternoon nap jumped into the Manger of an Ox and lay there cosily upon the straw. But soon the Ox, returning from its afternoon work, came up to the Manger and wanted to eat some of the straw. The Dog in a rage, being awakened from its slumber, stood up and barked at the Ox, and whenever it came near attempted to bite it. At last the Ox had to give up the hope of getting at the straw, and went away muttering:

"Ah, people often grudge others what they cannot enjoy themselves."

1. Show how each detail in *The Dog and the Shadow* on the literal level of story finds its real meaning on the allegorical level. Does the statement of the moral help the story? Explain. 2. In your own words state the moral of each of these fables. 3. Of

the nine fables in your textbook, one personifies inanimate objects. Which fable is this? Is this more or is it less effective than animal personification? Give reasons for your answer. **4.** List some common human traits that we tend to poke fun at. Try your hand at a fable that ridicules a human trait. **5.** Find ten proverbs which could be developed into fables. State each proverb as the moral point of a fable. **6.** Does your library have Thurber's FABLES FOR OUR TIMES and MORE FABLES FOR OUR TIMES? Read several of them if they are available. **7.** Write a paragraph explaining how the myth differs from the fable in tone and in story structure. **8.** Read and study the nine fables for their structure. Then write a fable of your own. Here is a modern one written by a freshman:

The Flea

CONNIE STOLINSKI

There was a flea who was greatly enamored of his personality. To himself he shone in greatness as the sun. One day he came upon an idle Sputnik. Thinking it was only another inanimate object, the flea crawled upon the rocket and bragged about his own ability to get places. Sputnik, bored by the flea's raving, launched himself. The flea, not being able to cope with the new atmosphere, flew off into outer space. Moral: It is better to be modest than out of this world.

Other Stories that Teach—Parables

The parable is another type of folk story that teaches lessons. Like the fable, it has two levels of meaning. On one level a story is told. On the other some truth of life is taught through the story. The parable has a more fully developed story than the fable. It is not satirical, and it does not have a moral point as its conclusion.

READING AND STUDYING PARABLES: We are familiar with the beautiful parables of Christ. But how many of us know that Our Lord was teaching His disciples and the people through an old folk-type of storytelling? The parable can easily be used to teach because it has two levels of meaning. The events of the parable are selected for the moral meaning, not for the literal level of story.

In the parable there is a simple plot on the literal level of story. There are also characters. There may be setting. But these do not have much meaning in themselves. They are included only to help the story put across its allegorical meaning. The one who tells or writes a parable keeps his attention on the theme or religious meaning so completely that his characters are usually types unrelated to the action. Because the characters and the action are not closely related, the structure of a parable is linear.

To put its meaning across, the parable uses symbols. A symbol is really a person or object that stands for something else. For example, a flag is an object that stands for a country. A green light on the street stands for safety and is a go signal. A red light stands for danger and is a stop signal. In much the same way, in literature persons and things often stand for some meaning other than themselves.

The parables of Christ are beautiful stories. In them, theme, in the sense of lesson, shapes the meaning on the literal level of story to impress on the listeners the moral or religious situation which the events of the story parallel on the symbolic level of meaning.

Recall the familiar parable of *The Prodigal Son*. It is often referred to as an example of a parable that has the literary stature of a short story, because the story on the literal level of meaning is effective in itself. Actually, it is not a short story but a very good parable. It has literary excellence because it is a superb structure of its own kind, the parable.

Read *The Prodigal Son*.

THE PRODIGAL SON

LUKE 15:11–32

A certain man had two sons. And the younger of them said to his father: Father, give me the portion of substance that falleth to me. And he divided unto them his substance.

And not many days after, the younger son, gathering all together, went abroad into a far country: and there wasted his substance, living riotously. And after he had spent all, there came a mighty famine in that country: and he began to be in want. And he went and cleaved to one of the citizens of that country. And he sent him into his farm to feed swine. And he would fain have filled his belly with the husks the swine did eat: and no man gave unto him.

And returning to himself, he said: How many hired servants in my father's house abound with bread, and I here perish with hunger! I will arise and will go to my father and say to him: Father, I have sinned against heaven and before thee. I am not worthy to be called thy son: make me as one of thy hired servants.

And rising up, he came to his father. And when he was yet a great way off, his father saw him and was moved with compassion and running to him fell upon his neck and kissed him.

And the son said to him: Father, I have sinned against heaven and before thee. I am not now worthy to be called thy son.

And the father said to his servants: Bring forth quickly the first robe and put it on him: and put a ring on his hand and shoes on his feet. And bring hither the fatted calf, and kill it: and let us eat and make merry. Because this my son was dead and is come to life again, was lost and is found. And they began to be merry.

Now his elder son was in the field: and when he came and drew nigh to the house, he heard music and dancing. And he called one of the servants and asked what these things meant. And he said to him: Thy brother is come and thy father hath killed the fatted calf, because he hath received him safe.

And he was angry and would not go in. His father therefore coming out began to entreat him. And he answering, said to his father: Behold, for so many years do I serve thee and I have never transgressed thy commandment: and yet thou hast never given me a kid to make merry with my friends. But as soon as this thy son is come, who hath devoured his substance with harlots, thou hast killed for him the fatted calf.

But he said to him: Son, thou art always with me; and all I have is thine. But it was fit that we should make merry and be glad: for this thy brother was dead and is come to life again; he was lost, and is found.

Notice the story structure. The narrative falls into the familiar pattern of three, so common in well structured stories. There is a beginning that initiates the action of the story, a middle that develops the consequences of the initiating incident, and an end that follows logically from the beginning and the middle. Although the plot is well developed, it serves the theme or moral for which it exists: . . . *we are bound to make merry and rejoice, for this thy brother was dead, and has come to life; he was lost and is found.*

The action has its motivation in character. The story is not a mere commentary on the waywardness of one individual son and the goodness of one father. On the symbolic level the son becomes any human prodigal and the Father is God. The vagueness of time and place is not just the characteristic vagueness of typical folk tales. It moves into the symbolic level of meaning

where the human race and God are the actors during all the
time man lives on earth.

1. Show how the plot of *The Prodigal Son* patterns the theme.
2. Find another parable in the Bible and be prepared to tell it
in class.

Read *The Godson*.

The Godson

LEO TOLSTOY

"Ye have heard that it was said, An eye for an eye,
and a tooth for a tooth, but I say unto you,
Resist not him that is evil."—MATTHEW V. 38, 39.

"Vengeance is mine; I will repay."—ROMANS XII. 19.

A son was born to a poor peasant. He was glad, and went
to his neighbor to ask him to stand godfather to the boy. The
neighbor refused—he did not like standing godfather to a poor
man's child. The peasant asked another neighbor, but he too
refused, and after that the poor father went to every house in the
village, but found no one willing to be godfather to his son. So
he set off to another village, and on the way he met a man who
stopped and said:

"Good-day, my good man; where are you off to?"

"God has given me a child," said the peasant, "to rejoice my
eyes in youth, to comfort my old age, and to pray for my soul
after death. But I am poor, and no one in our village will stand
godfather to him, so I am now on my way to seek a godfather
for him elsewhere."

"Let me be godfather," said the stranger.

The peasant was glad, and thanked him, but added:

"And whom shall I ask to be godmother?"

"Go to the town," replied the stranger, "and, in the square, you will see a stone house with shop-windows in the front. At the entrance you will find the tradesman to whom it belongs. Ask him to let his daughter stand godmother to your child."

The peasant hesitated.

"How can I ask a rich tradesman?" said he. "He will despise me, and will not let his daughter come."

"Don't trouble about that. Go and ask. Get everything ready by to-morrow morning, and I will come to the christening."

The poor peasant returned home, and then drove to the town to find the tradesman. He had hardly taken his horse into the yard, when the tradesman himself came out.

"What do you want?" said he.

"Why, sir," said the peasant, "you see God has given me a son to rejoice my eyes in youth, to comfort my old age, and to pray for my soul after death. Be so kind as to let your daughter stand godmother to him."

"And when is the christening?" said the tradesman.

"To-morrow morning."

"Very well. Go in peace. She shall be with you at Mass to-morrow morning."

The next day the godmother came, and the godfather also, and the infant was baptized. Immediately after the christening the godfather went away. They did not know who he was and never saw him again.

II

The child grew up to be a joy to his parents. He was strong, willing to work, clever and obedient. When he was ten years old his parents sent him to school to learn to read and write. What others learnt in five years, he learnt in one, and soon there was nothing more they could teach him.

Easter came round, and the boy went to see his godmother, to give her his Easter greeting.

"Father and mother," said he when he got home again, "where does my godfather live? I should like to give him my Easter greeting, too."

And his father answered:

"We know nothing about your godfather, dear son. We often regret it ourselves. Since the day you were christened we have never seen him, nor had any news of him. We do not know where he lives, or even whether he is still alive."

The son bowed to his parents.

"Father and mother," said he, "let me go and look for my godfather. I must find him and give him my Easter greeting."

So his father and mother let him go, and the boy set off to find his godfather.

III

The boy left the house and set out along the road. He had been walking for several hours when he met a stranger who stopped him and said:

"Good-day to you, my boy. Where are you going?"

And the boy answered:

"I went to see my godmother and to give her my Easter greeting, and when I got home I asked my parents where my godfather lives, that I might go and greet him also. They told me they did not know. They said he went away as soon as I was christened, and they know nothing about him, not even if he be still alive. But I wished to see my godfather, and so I have set out to look for him."

Then the stranger said: "I am your godfather."

The boy was glad to hear this. After kissing his godfather three times for an Easter greeting, he asked him:

"Which way are you going now, godfather? If you are coming our way, please come to our house; but if you are going home, I will go with you."

"I have no time now," replied his godfather, "to come to your house. I have business in several villages, but I shall return home again to-morrow. Come and see me then."

"But how shall I find you, godfather?"

"When you leave home, go straight towards the rising sun, and you will come to a forest; going through the forest you will come to a glade. When you reach this glade sit down and rest awhile, and look around you and see what happens. On the 'further side of the forest you will find a garden, and in it a house with a golden roof. That is my home. Go up to the gate, and I will myself be there to meet you."

And having said this the godfather disappeared from his godson's sight.

IV

The boy did as his godfather had told him. He walked eastward until he reached a forest, and there he came to a glade, and in the midst of the glade he saw a pine tree to a branch of which was tied a rope supporting a heavy log of oak. Close under this log stood a wooden trough filled with honey. Hardly had the boy had time to wonder why the honey was placed there and why the log hung above it, when he heard a crackling in the wood and saw some bears approaching: a she-bear, followed by a yearling and three tiny cubs. The she-bear, sniffing the air, went straight to the trough, the cubs following her. She thrust her muzzle into the honey, and called the cubs to do the same. They scampered up and began to eat. As they did so, the log, which the she-bear had moved aside with her head, swung away a little and, returning, gave the cubs a push. Seeing this the she-bear shoved the log away with her paw. It swung further out and returned more forcibly, striking one cub on the back and another on the head. The cubs ran away howling with pain, and the mother, with a growl, caught the log in her fore paws and, raising it above her head, flung it away. The log flew high in the air, and the yearling, rushing to the trough, pushed his muzzle into the honey and began to suck noisily. The others also drew near, but they had not reached the trough when the log, flying back, struck the yearling on the head and killed him. The mother growled louder than before and seizing the log, flung it from her with all her might. It flew higher than the branch it was tied to; so high that the rope slackened; and the she-bear returned to the trough, and the little cubs after her. The log flew higher and higher, then stopped, and began to fall. The nearer it came the faster it swung, and at last, at full speed, it crashed down on her head. The she-bear rolled over, her legs jerked, and she died. The cubs ran away into the forest.

V

The boy watched all this in surprise, and then continued his way. Leaving the forest, he came upon a large garden in the midst of which stood a lofty palace with a golden roof. At the gate stood his godfather, smiling. He welcomed his godson, and led him through the gateway into the garden. The boy had never dreamed of such beauty and delight as surrounded him in that place.

Then his godfather led him into the palace, which was even more beautiful inside than out. The godfather showed the boy through all the rooms: each brighter and finer than the other, but at last they came to one door that was sealed up.

"You see this door," said he. "It is not locked, but only sealed. It can be opened, but I forbid you to open it. You may live here, and go where you please, and enjoy all the delights of the place. My only command is—do not open that door! But should you ever do so, remember what you saw in the forest."

Having said this the godfather went away. The godson remained in the palace, and life there was so bright and joyful that he thought he had only been there three hours when he had really lived there thirty years. When thirty years had gone by the godson happened to be passing the sealed door one day, and he wondered why his godfather had forbidden him to enter that room.

"I'll just look in and see what is there," thought he, and he gave the door a push. The seals gave way, the door opened, and the godson entering saw a hall more lofty and beautiful than all the others, and in the midst of it a throne. He wandered about the hall for a while, and then mounted the steps and seated himself upon the throne. As he sat there he noticed a sceptre leaning against the throne, and took it in his hand. Hardly had he done so when the four walls of the hall suddenly disappeared. The godson looked around, and saw the whole world, and all that men were doing in it. He looked in front, and saw the sea with ships sailing on it. He looked to the right, and saw where strange heathen people lived. He looked to the left, and saw where men who were Christians, but not Russians, lived. He looked round, and on the fourth side, he saw Russian people, like himself.

"I will look," said he, "and see what is happening at home, and whether the harvest is good."

He looked towards his father's fields and saw the sheaves standing in shocks. He began counting them to see whether there was much corn, when he noticed a peasant driving in a cart. It was night, and the godson thought it was his father coming to cart the corn by night. But as he looked he recognized Vasíli Kudryashóv, the thief, driving into the field and beginning to load the sheaves on to his cart. This made the godson angry and he called out:

"Father, the sheaves are being stolen from our field!"

His father, who was out with the horses in the night-pasture, woke up.

"I dreamt the sheaves were being stolen," said he. "I will just ride down and see."

So he got on a horse and rode out to the field. Finding Vasíli there, he called together other peasants to help him, and Vasíli was beaten, bound, and taken to prison.

Then the godson looked at the town, where his godmother lived. He saw that she was now married to a tradesman. She lay asleep, and her husband rose and went to his mistress. The godson shouted to her:

"Get up, get up, your husband has taken to evil ways."

The godmother jumped up and dressed, and finding out where her husband was, she shamed and beat his mistress, and drove him away.

Then the godson looked for his mother, and saw her lying asleep in her cottage. And a thief crept into the cottage and began to break open the chest in which she kept her things. The mother awoke and screamed, and the robber, seizing an axe, swung it over his head to kill her.

The godson could not refrain from hurling the sceptre at the robber. It struck him upon the temple, and killed him on the spot.

As soon as the godson had killed the robber, the walls closed and the hall became just as it had been before.

Then the door opened and the godfather entered, and coming up to his godson he took him by the hand and led him down from the throne.

"You have not obeyed my command," said he. "You did one wrong thing when you opened the forbidden door; another, when you mounted the throne and took my sceptre into your hands; and you have now done a third wrong, which has much increased the evil in the world. Had you sat here an hour longer, you would have ruined half mankind."

Then the godfather led his godson back to the throne, and took the sceptre in his hand; and again the walls fell asunder and all things became visible. And the godfather said:

"See what you have done to your father. Vasíli has now been a year in prison, and has come out having learnt every kind of wickedness, and has become quite incorrigible. See, he has stolen two of your father's horses, and he is now setting fire to his barn. All this you have brought upon your father."

The godson saw his father's barn breaking into flames, but his godfather shut off the sight from him, and told him to look another way.

"Here is your godmother's husband," he said. "It is a year since he left his wife, and now he goes after other women. His former mistress has sunk to still lower depths. Sorrow has driven his wife to drink. That's what you have done to your godmother."

The godfather shut off this also, and showed the godson his father's house. There he saw his mother weeping for her sins, repenting, and saying:

"It would have been better had the robber killed me that night. I should not have sinned so heavily."

"That," said the godfather, "is what you have done to your mother."

He shut this off also, and pointed downwards; and the godson saw two wardens holding the robber in front of a prisonhouse.

And the godfather said:

"This man had murdered ten men. He should have expiated his sins himself, but by killing him you have taken his sins on yourself. Now you must answer for all his sins. That is what you have done to yourself. The she-bear pushed the log aside once, and disturbed her cubs; she pushed it again, and killed her yearling; she pushed it a third time, and was killed herself. You have done the same. Now I give you thirty years to go into the world and atone for the robber's sins. If you do not atone for them, you will have to take his place."

"How am I to atone for his sins?" asked the godson.

And the godfather answered:

"When you have rid the world of as much evil as you have brought into it, you will have atoned both for your own sins and for those of the robber."

"How can I destroy evil in the world?" the godson asked.

"Go out," replied the godfather, "and walk straight towards the rising sun. After a time you will come to a field with some men in it. Notice what they are doing, and teach them what you know. Then go on and note what you see. On the fourth day you will come to a forest. In the midst of the forest is a cell, and in the cell lives a hermit. Tell him all that has happened. He will teach you what to do. When you have done all he tells you, you will have atoned for your own and the robber's sins."

And, having said this, the godfather led his godson out of the gate.

VII

The godson went his way, and as he went he thought:

"How am I to destroy evil in the world? Evil is destroyed by banishing evil men, keeping them in prison, or putting them to death. How then am I to destroy evil without taking the sins of others upon myself?"

The godson pondered over it for a long time, but could come to no conclusion. He went on until he came to a field where corn was growing thick and good and ready for the reapers. The godson saw that a little calf had got in among the corn. Some men who were at hand saw it, and mounting their horses they chased it backwards and forwards through the corn. Each time the calf was about to come out of the corn, some one rode up and the calf got frightened and turned back again, and they all galloped after it, trampling down the corn. On the road stood a woman crying.

"They will chase my calf to death," she said.

And the godson said to the peasants:

"What are you doing? Come out of the cornfield, all of you, and let the woman call her calf."

The men did so; and the woman came to the edge of the cornfield and called to the calf. "Come along, browny, come along," said she. The calf pricked up its ears, listened awhile, and then ran towards the woman of its own accord, and hid its head in her skirts, almost knocking her over. The men were glad, the woman was glad, and so was the little calf.

The godson went on, and he thought:

"Now I see that evil spreads evil. The more people try to drive away evil, the more the evil grows. Evil, it seems, cannot be destroyed by evil; but in what way it can be destroyed, I do not know. The calf obeyed its mistress and so all went well; but if it had not obeyed her, how could we have got it out of the field?"

The godson pondered again, but came to no conclusion, and continued his way.

VIII

He went on until he came to a village. At the furthest end he stopped and asked leave to stay the night. The woman of the house was there alone, house-cleaning, and she let him in. The godson entered, and taking his seat upon the brick oven he watched what the woman was doing. He saw her finish scrubbing the room and begin scrubbing the table. Having done this, she began wiping the table with a dirty cloth. She wiped it from side to side—but it did not come clean. The soiled cloth left streaks of dirt. Then she wiped it the other way. The first streaks disappeared, but others came in their place. Then she wiped it from one end to the other, but again the same thing happened.

The soiled cloth messed the table; when one streak was wiped off another was left on. The godson watched for a while in silence, and then said:

"What are you doing, mistress?"

"Don't you see I'm cleaning up for the holiday. Only I can't manage this table, it won't come clean. I'm quite tired out."

"You should rinse your cloth," said the godson, "before you wipe the table with it."

The woman did so, and soon had the table clean.

"Thank you for telling me," said she.

In the morning he took leave of the woman and went on his way. After walking a good while, he came to the edge of a forest. There he saw some peasants who were making wheel-rims of bent wood. Coming nearer, the godson saw that the men were going round and round, but could not bend the wood.

He stood and looked on, and noticed that the block, to which the piece of wood was fastened, was not fixed, but as the men moved round it went round too. Then the godson said:

"What are you doing, friends?"

"Why, don't you see, we are making wheel-rims. We have twice steamed the wood, and are quite tired out, but the wood will not bend."

"You should fix the block, friends," said the godson, "or else it goes round when you do."

The peasants took his advice and fixed the block, and then the work went on merrily.

The godson spent the night with them, and then went on. He walked all day and all night, and just before dawn he came upon some drovers encamped for the night, and lay down beside them. He saw that they had got all their cattle settled, and were trying to light a fire. They had taken dry twigs and lighted them, but before the twigs had time to burn up, they smothered them with damp brushwood. The brushwood hissed, and the fire smouldered and went out. Then the drovers brought more dry wood, lit it, and again put on the brushwood—and again the fire went out. They struggled with it for a long time, but could not get the fire to burn. Then the godson said:

"Do not be in such a hurry to put on the brushwood. Let the

dry wood burn up properly before you put any on. When the fire is well alight you can put on as much as you please."

The drovers followed his advice. They let the fire burn up fiercely before adding the brushwood, which then flared up so that they soon had a roaring fire.

The godson remained with them for a while and then continued his way. He went on, wondering what the three things he had seen might mean; but he could not fathom them.

IX

The godson walked the whole of that day, and in the evening came to another forest. There he found a hermit's cell, at which he knocked.

"Who is there?" asked a voice from within.

"A great sinner," replied the godson. "I must atone for another's sins as well as for my own."

The hermit hearing this came out.

"What sins are those that you have to bear for another?"

The godson told him everything: about his godfather; about the she-bear with the cubs; about the throne in the sealed room; about the commands his godfather had given him, as well as about the peasants he had seen trampling down the corn, and the calf that ran out when its mistress called it.

"I have seen that one cannot destroy evil by evil," said he, "but I cannot understand how it is to be destroyed. Teach me how it can be done."

"Tell me," replied the hermit, "what else you have seen on your way."

The godson told him about the woman washing the table, and the men making wheel-rims, and the drovers lighting their fire.

The hermit listened to it all, and then went back to his cell and brought out an old jagged axe.

"Come with me," said he.

When they had gone some way, the hermit pointed to a tree.

"Cut it down," he said.

The godson felled the tree.

"Now chop it into three," said the hermit.

The godson chopped the tree into three pieces. Then the hermit went back to his cell, and brought out some blazing sticks.

"Burn those three logs," said he.

So the godson made a fire, and burnt the three logs till only three charred stumps remained.

"Now plant them half in the ground, like this."

The godson did so.

"You see that river at the foot of the hill. Bring water from there in your mouth, and water these stumps. Water this stump, as you taught the woman: this one, as you taught the wheel-wrights: and this one, as you taught the drovers. When all three have taken root and from these charred stumps apple-trees have sprung, you will know how to destroy evil in men, and will have atoned for all your sins."

Having said this, the hermit returned to his cell. The godson pondered for a long time, but could not understand what the hermit meant. Nevertheless he set to work to do as he had been told.

X

The godson went down to the river, filled his mouth with water, and returning, emptied it on to one of the charred stumps. This he did again and again, and watered all three stumps. When he was hungry and quite tired out, he went to the cell to ask the old hermit for some food. He opened the door, and there upon a bench he saw the old man lying dead. The godson looked round for food, and he found some dried bread, and ate a little of it. Then he took a spade and set to work to dig the hermit's grave. During the night he carried water and watered the stumps, and in the day he dug the grave. He had hardly finished the grave, and was about to bury the corpse, when some people from the village came, bringing food for the old man.

The people heard that the old hermit was dead, and that he had given the godson his blessing and left him in his place. So they buried the old man, gave the bread they had brought to the godson, and promising to bring him some more, they went away.

The godson remained in the old man's place. There he lived, eating the food people brought him, and doing as he had been told: carrying water from the river in his mouth and watering the charred stumps.

He lived thus for a year and many people visited him. His fame spread abroad, as a holy man who lived in the forest and brought water from the bottom of a hill in his mouth to water charred stumps for the salvation of his soul. People flocked to see him. Rich merchants drove up bringing him presents, but he kept only the barest necessaries for himself and gave the rest away to the poor.

And so the godson lived: carrying water in his mouth and watering the stumps half the day, and resting and receiving people the other half. And he began to think that this was the way he had been told to live in order to destroy evil and atone for his sins.

He spent two years in this manner, not omitting for a single day to water the stumps. But still not one of them sprouted.

One day, as he sat in his cell, he heard a man ride past, singing as he went. The godson came out to see what sort of a man it was. He saw a strong young fellow, well dressed, and mounted on a handsome, well-saddled horse.

The godson stopped him, and asked him who he was, and where he was going.

"I am a robber," the man answered, drawing rein. "I ride about the highways killing people, and the more I kill, the merrier are the songs I sing."

The godson was horror-struck, and thought:

"How can the evil be destroyed in such a man as this? It is easy to speak to those who come to me of their own accord and confess their sins. But this one boasts of the evil he does."

So he said nothing and turned away, thinking: "What am I to do now? This robber may take to riding about here, and he will frighten away the people. They will leave off coming to me. It will be a loss to them, and I shall not know how to live."

So the godson turned back and said to the robber:

"People come to me here, not to boast of their sins, but to repent and to pray for forgiveness. Repent of your sins, if you fear God; but if there is no repentance in your heart, then go away and never come here again. Do not trouble me, and do not frighten people away from me. If you do not hearken, God will punish you."

The robber laughed:

"I am not afraid of God, and I will not listen to you. You are not my master," said he. "You live by your piety, and I by my robbery. We all must live. You may teach the old women who come to you, but you have nothing to teach me. And because you have reminded me of God, I will kill two more men to-morrow. I would kill you, but I do not want to soil my hands just now. See that in future you keep out of my way!"

Having uttered this threat, the robber rode away. He did not come again, and the godson lived in peace, as before, for eight more years.

XI

One night the godson watered his stumps, and, after returning to his cell, he sat down to rest, and watched the footpath, wondering if some one would soon come. But no one came at all that day. He sat alone till evening, feeling lonely and dull, and he thought about his past life. He remembered how the robber had reproached him for living by his piety; and he reflected on his way of life. "I am not living as the hermit commanded me to," thought he. "The hermit laid a penance upon me, and I have made both a living and fame out of it; and have been so tempted by it, that now I feel dull when people do not come to me; and when they do come, I only rejoice because they praise my holiness. That is not how one should live. I have been led astray by love of praise. I have not atoned for my past sins, but have added fresh ones. I will go to another part of the forest where people will not find me; and I will live so as to atone for my old sins and commit no fresh ones."

Having come to this conclusion the godson filled a bag with dried bread and, taking a spade, left the cell and started for a ravine he knew of in a lonely spot, where he could dig himself a cave and hide from the people.

As he was going along with his bag and his spade he saw

the robber riding toward him. The godson was frightened and started to run away, but the robber overtook him.

"Where are you going?" asked the robber.

The godson told him he wished to get away from the people and live somewhere where no one would come to him. This surprised the robber.

"What will you live on, if people do not come to see you?" asked he.

The godson had not even thought of this, but the robber's question reminded him that food would be necessary.

"On what God pleases to give me," he replied.

The robber said nothing, and rode away.

"Why did I not say anything to him about his way of life?" thought the godson. "He might repent now. To-day he seems in a gentler mood, and has not threatened to kill me." And he shouted to the robber:

"You have still to repent of your sins. You cannot escape from God."

The robber turned his horse, and drawing a knife from his girdle threatened the godson with it. The latter was alarmed, and ran away further into the forest.

The robber did not follow him, but only shouted:

"Twice I have let you off, old man, but next time you come in my way I will kill you!"

Having said this, he rode away. In the evening when the godson went to water his stumps—one of them was sprouting! A little apple-tree was growing out of it.

XII

After hiding himself from everybody, the godson lived all alone. When his supply of bread was exhausted, he thought: "Now I must go and look for some roots to eat." He had not gone far, however, before he saw a bag of dried bread hanging on a branch. He took it down, and as long as it lasted he lived upon that.

When he had eaten it all, he found another bagful on the same branch. So he lived on, his only trouble being his fear of the robber. Whenever he heard the robber passing, he hid, thinking:

"He may kill me before I have had time to atone for my sins."

In this way he lived for ten more years. The one apple-tree continued to grow, but the other two stumps remained exactly as they were.

One morning the godson rose early and went to his work. By the time he had thoroughly moistened the ground round the stumps, he was tired out and sat down to rest. As he sat there he thought to himself:

"I have sinned, and have become afraid of death. It may be God's will that I should redeem my sins by death."

Hardly had this thought crossed his mind when he heard the robber riding up, swearing at something. When the godson heard this, he thought:

"No evil and no good can befall me from any one but from God."

And he went to meet the robber. He saw the robber was not alone, but behind him on the saddle sat another man, gagged, and bound hand and foot. The man was doing nothing, but the robber was abusing him violently. The godson went up and stood in front of the horse.

"Where are you taking this man?" he asked.

"Into the forest," replied the robber. "He is a merchant's son, and will not tell me where his father's money is hidden. I am going to flog him till he tells me."

And the robber spurred on his horse, but the godson caught hold of his bridle, and would not let him pass.

"Let this man go!" he said.

The robber grew angry, and raised his arm to strike.

"Would you like a taste of what I am going to give this man? Have I not promised to kill you? Let go!"

The godson was not afraid.

"You shall not go," said he. "I do not fear you. I fear no one but God, and He wills that I should not let you pass. Set this man free!"

The robber frowned, and snatching out his knife, cut the

ropes with which the merchant's son was bound, and set him free.

"Get away, both of you," he said, "and beware how you cross my path again."

The merchant's son jumped down and ran away. The robber was about to ride on, but the godson stopped him again, and again spoke to him about giving up his evil life. The robber heard him to the end in silence, and then rode away without a word.

The next morning the godson went to water his stumps and lo! the second stump was sprouting. A second young apple-tree had begun to grow.

XIII

Another ten years had gone by. The godson was sitting quietly one day, desiring nothing, fearing nothing, and with a heart full of joy.

"What blessings God showers on men!" thought he. "Yet how needlessly they torment themselves. What prevents them from living happily?"

And remembering all the evil in men and the troubles they bring upon themselves, his heart filled with pity.

"It is wrong of me to live as I do," he said to himself. "I must go and teach others what I have myself learnt."

Hardly had he thought this, when he heard the robber approaching. He let him pass, thinking:

"It is no good talking to him, he will not understand."

That was his first thought, but he changed his mind and went out into the road. He saw that the robber was gloomy, and was riding with downcast eyes. The godson looked at him, pitied him, and running up to him laid his hand upon his knee.

"Brother, dear," said he, "have some pity on your own soul! In you lives the spirit of God. You suffer, and torment others, and lay up more and more suffering for the future. Yet God loves you and has prepared such blessings for you. Do not ruin yourself utterly. Change your life!"

The robber frowned and turned away.

"Leave me alone!" said he.

But the godson held the robber still faster, and began to weep.

Then the robber lifted his eyes and looked at the godson. He looked at him for a long time, and alighting from his horse, fell on his knees at the godson's feet.

"You have overcome me, old man," said he. "For twenty years I have resisted you, but now you have conquered me. Do what you will with me, for I have no more power over myself. When you first tried to persuade me, it only angered me more. Only when you hid yourself from men did I begin to consider your words, for I saw then that you asked nothing of them for yourself. Since that day I have brought food for you, hanging it upon the tree."

Then the godson remembered that the woman got her table clean only after she had rinsed her cloth. In the same way, it was only when he ceased caring about himself, and cleansed his own heart, that he was able to cleanse the hearts of others.

The robber went on.

"When I saw that you did not fear death, my heart turned."

Then the godson remembered that the wheelwrights could not bend the rims until they had fixed their block. So, not till he had cast away the fear of death and made his life fast in God, could he subdue this man's unruly heart.

"But my heart did not quite melt," continued the robber, "until you pitied me and wept for me."

The godson, full of joy, led the robber to the place where the stumps were. And when they got there, they saw that from the third stump an apple-tree had begun to sprout. And the godson remembered that the drovers had not been able to light the damp wood until the fire had burnt up well. So it was only when his own heart burnt warmly, that another's heart had been kindled by it.

And the godson was full of joy that he had at last atoned for his sins.

He told all this to the robber, and died. The robber buried him, and lived as the godson had commanded him, teaching to others what the godson had taught him.

1. Notice how many uses of patterning with *three's* there are in *The Godson*. List them. **2.** Why does the author not give names to the characters? **3.** Write six related sentences explaining the symbolic meaning. **4.** What makes this story a parable?

Read *How Much Land Does a Man Need?*

HOW MUCH LAND
DOES A MAN NEED?

LEO TOLSTOY
TRANSLATED BY LOUISE AND AYLMER MAUDE

An elder sister came to visit her younger sister in the country. The elder was married to a tradesman in town, the younger to a peasant in the village. As the sisters sat over their tea talking, the elder began to boast of the advantages of town life: saying how comfortably they lived there, how well they dressed, what fine clothes her children wore, what good things they ate and drank, and how she went to the theater, promenades, and entertainments.

The younger sister was piqued, and in turn disparaged the life of a tradesman, and stood up for that of a peasant.

"I would not change my way of life for yours," she said. "We may live roughly, but at least we are free from anxiety. You live in better style than we do, but though you often earn more than you need, you are very likely to lose all you have. You know the proverb, 'Loss and gain are brothers twain.' It often happens that people who are wealthy one day are begging their bread the next. Our way is safer. Though a peasant's life is not a fat one, it is a long one. We shall never grow rich, but we shall always have enough to eat."

The elder sister said sneeringly:

"Enough? Yes, if you like to share with the pigs and the calves! What do you know of elegance or manners! However much your good man may slave, you will die as you are living —on a dung-heap—and your children the same."

"Well, what of that?" replied the younger. "Of course our work is rough and coarse. But, on the other hand, it is sure, and we need not bow to anyone. But you, in your towns, are surrounded by temptations; today all may be right, but tomorrow the Evil One may tempt your husband with cards, wine, or women, and all will go to ruin. Don't such things happen often enough?"

Pahom, the master of the house, was lying on the top of the stove and he listened to the women's chatter.

"It is perfectly true," thought he. "Busy as we are from childhood tilling mother earth, we peasants have no time to let any nonsense settle in our heads. Our only trouble is that we haven't land enough. If I had plenty of land, I shouldn't fear the Devil himself!"

The women finished their tea, chatted a while about dress, and then cleared away the tea things and lay down to sleep.

But the Devil had been sitting behind the stove, and had heard all that was said. He was pleased that the peasant's wife had led her husband into boasting, and that he had said that if he had plenty of land he would not fear the Devil himself.

"All right," thought the Devil. "We will have a tussle. I'll give you land enough; and by means of that land I will get you into my power."

Close to the village there lived a lady, a small landowner who had an estate of about three hundred acres. She had always lived on good terms with the peasants until she engaged as her steward an old soldier, who took to burdening the people with fines. However careful Pahom tried to be, it happened again and again that now a horse of his got among the lady's oats, now a cow strayed into her garden, now his calves found their way into her meadows—and he always had to pay a fine.

Pahom paid up, but grumbled, and going home in a temper, was rough with his family. All through that summer, Pahom had much trouble because of this steward, and he was even glad when winter came and the cattle had to be stabled. Though he grudged the fodder when they could no longer graze on the pasture land, at least he was free from anxiety about them.

In the winter the news got about that the lady was going to sell her land and that the keeper of the inn on the highroad was bargaining for it. When the peasants heard this they were very much alarmed.

"Well," thought they, "if the innkeeper gets the land, he will worry us with fines worse than the lady's steward. We all depend on that estate."

So the peasants went on behalf of their commune, and asked the lady not to sell the land to the innkeeper, offering her a better price for it themselves. The lady agreed to let them have it. Then the peasants tried to arrange for the commune to buy the whole estate, so that it might be held by them all in common. They met twice to discuss it, but could not settle the matter; the Evil One sowed discord among them and they could not agree. So they decided to buy the land individually, each according to his means; and the lady agreed to this plan as she had to the other.

Presently Pahom heard that a neighbor of his was buying fifty acres, and that the lady had consented to accept one half in cash and to wait a year for the other half. Pahom felt envious.

"Look at that," thought he, "the land is all being sold, and I shall get none of it." So he spoke to his wife.

"Other people are buying," said he, "and we must also buy twenty acres or so. Life is becoming impossible. That steward is simply crushing us with his fines."

So they put their heads together and considered how they could manage to buy it. They had one hundred roubles laid by. They sold a colt and one half of their bees, hired out one of their sons as a laborer and took his wages in advance; borrowed the rest from a brother-in-law, and so scraped together half the purchase money.

Having done this, Pahom chose out a farm of forty acres, some of it wooded, and went to the lady to bargain for it. They came to an agreement, and he shook hands with her upon it and paid her a deposit in advance. Then they went to town and signed the deeds; he paying half the price down, and undertaking to pay the remainder within two years.

So now Pahom had land of his own. He borrowed seed, and sowed it on the land he had bought. The harvest was a good one, and within a year he had managed to pay off his debts both to the lady and to his brother-in-law. So he became a landowner, plowing and sowing his own land, making hay on his own land, cutting his own trees, and feeding his cattle on his own pasture. When he went out to plow his fields, or to look at his growing corn, or at his grass meadows, his heart would fill with joy. The grass that grew and the flowers that bloomed there seemed to him unlike any that grew elsewhere. Formerly, when he had passed by that land, it had appeared the same as any other land, but now it seemed quite different.

So Pahom was well contented, and everything would have been right if the neighboring peasants would only not have trespassed on his cornfields and meadows. He appealed to them most civilly, but they still went on: now the communal herdsmen would let the village cows stray into his meadows, then horses from the night pasture would get among his corn. Pahom turned them out again and again, and forgave their owners, and for a long time he forbore to prosecute anyone. But at last he lost patience and complained to the District Court. He knew it was the peasants' want of land, and no evil intent on their part, that caused the trouble, but he thought:

"I cannot go on overlooking it or they will destroy all I have. They must be taught a lesson."

So he had them up, gave them one lesson, and then another, and two or three of the peasants were fined. After a time Pahom's neighbors began to bear him a grudge for this, and would now and then let their cattle onto his land on purpose. One peasant even got into Paham's wood at night and cut down five young lime trees for their bark. Pahom passing through the wood one day noticed something white. He came nearer and saw the stripped trunks lying on the ground, and close by stood the stumps where the trees had been. Pahom was furious.

"If he had only cut one here and there it would have been bad enough," thought Pahom, "but the rascal has actually cut down a whole clump. If I could only find out who did this, I would pay him out."

He racked his brains as to who it could be. Finally he decided: "It must be Semyon—no one else could have done it." So he went to Semyon's homestead to have a look round, but he found nothing, and only had an angry scene. However, he now felt more certain than ever that Semyon had done it, and he lodged a complaint. Semyon was summoned. The case was tried, and retried, and at the end of it all Semyon was acquitted, there being no evidence against him. Pahom felt still more aggrieved, and let his anger loose upon the elder and the judges.

"You let thieves grease your palms," said he. "If you were honest folk yourselves you would not let a thief go free."

So Pahom quarreled with the judges and with his neighbors. Threats to burn his buildings began to be uttered. So though Pahom had more land, his place in the commune was much worse than before.

About this time a rumor got about that many people were moving to new parts.

"There's no need for me to leave my land," thought Pahom. "But some of the others might leave our village and then there would be more room for us. I would take over their land myself and make my estate a bit bigger. I could then live more at ease. As it is, I am still too cramped to be comfortable."

One day Pahom was sitting at home when a peasant, passing through the village, happened to call in. He was allowed to stay the night, and supper was given him. Pahom had a talk with this peasant and asked him where he came from. The stranger answered that he came from beyond the Volga, where he had been working. One word led to another, and the man went on to say that many people were settling in those parts. He told how some people from his village had settled there. They had joined the commune, and had had twenty-five acres per man granted them. The land was so good, he said, that the rye sown on it grew as high as a horse, and so thick that five cuts of a sickle made a sheaf. One peasant, he said, had brought nothing with him but his bare hands, and now he had six horses and two cows of his own.

Pahom's heart kindled with desire. He thought:

"Why should I suffer in this narrow hole, if one can live so well elsewhere? I will sell my land and my homestead here, and with the money I will start afresh over there and get everything new. In this crowded place one is always having trouble. But I must first go and find out all about it myself.

Towards summer he got ready and started. He went down the Volga on a steamer to Samara, then walked another three hundred miles on foot, and at last reached the place. It was just as the stranger had said. The peasants had plenty of land: every man had twenty-five acres of communal land given him for his use, and anyone who had money could buy, besides, at a rouble an acre as much good freehold land as he wanted.

Having found out all he wished to know, Pahom returned home as autumn came on, and began selling off his belongings. He sold his land at a profit, sold his homestead and all his cattle, and withdrew from membership of the commune. He only waited till the spring, and then started with his family for the new settlement.

As soon as Pahom and his family reached their new abode, he applied for admission into the commune of a large village. He stood treat to the elders and obtained the necessary documents. Five shares of communal land were given him for his own and his sons' use: that is to say—one hundred and twenty-five acres (not all together, but in different fields) besides the use of the communal pasture. Pahom put up the buildings he needed, and bought cattle. Of the communal land alone he had three times as much as at his former home, and the land was good cornland. He was ten times better off than he had been. He had plenty of arable land and pasturage, and could keep as many head of cattle as he liked.

At first, in the bustle of building and settling down, Pahom was pleased with it all, but when he got used to it he began to think that even here he had not enough land. The first year, he sowed wheat on his share of the communal land and had a good crop. He wanted to go on sowing wheat, but had not enough communal land for the purpose, and what he had already used was not available; for in those parts wheat is only sown on virgin soil or on fallow land. It is sown for one or two years, and then the land lies fallow till it is again overgrown with prairie grass. There were many who wanted such land and there was not enough for all; so that people quarreled about it. Those who were better off wanted it for growing wheat, and those who were poor wanted it to let to dealers, so that they might raise money to pay their taxes. Pahom wanted to sow more wheat, so he rented land from a dealer for a year. He sowed much wheat and had a fine crop, but the land was too far from the village—the wheat had to be carted more than ten miles. After a time Pahom noticed that some peasant-dealers were living on separate farms and were growing wealthy; and he thought:

"If I were to buy some freehold land and have a homestead on it, it would be a different thing altogether. Then it would all be nice and compact."

The question of buying freehold land recurred to him again and again.

He went on in the same way for three years, renting land and sowing wheat. The seasons turned out well and the crops were good, so that he began to lay money by. He might have gone on living contentedly, but he grew tired of having to rent other people's land every year, and having to scramble for it. Wherever there was good land to be had, the peasants would rush for it and it was taken up at once, so that unless you were sharp about it you got none. It happened in the third year that he and a dealer together rented a piece of pasture land from some peasants; and they had already plowed it up, when there was some dispute and the peasants went to law about it, and things fell out so that the labor was all lost.

"If it were my own land," thought Pahom, "I should be independent, and there would not be all this unpleasantness."

So Pahom began looking out for land which he could buy; and he came across a peasant who had bought thirteen hundred acres, but having got into difficulties was willing to sell again cheap. Pahom bargained and haggled with him, and at last they settled the price at fifteen hundred roubles, part in cash and part to be paid later. They had all but clinched the matter when a passing dealer happened to stop at Pahom's one day to get feed for his horses. He drank tea with Pahom and they had a talk. The dealer said that he was just returning from the land of the Bashkirs, far away, where he had bought thirteen thousand acres of land, all for a thousand roubles. Pahom questioned him further, and the tradesman said:

"All one need do is to make friends with the chiefs. I gave away about one hundred roubles' worth of silk robes and carpets, besides a case of tea, and I gave wine to those who would drink it; and I got the land for less than a kopeck an acre." And he showed Pahom the title deeds, saying:

"The land lies near a river, and the whole prairie is virgin soil."

Pahom plied him with questions, and the tradesman said:

"There is more land there than you could cover if you walked a year, and it all belongs to the Bashkirs. They are as simple as sheep, and land can be got almost for nothing."

"There now," thought Pahom, "with my one thousand roubles, why should I get only thirteen hundred acres, and saddle myself with a debt besides? If I take it out there, I can get more than ten times as much for the money."

Pahom inquired how to get to the place, and as soon as the tradesman had left him, he prepared to go there himself. He left his wife to look after the homestead, and started on his journey, taking his man with him. They stopped at a town on their way and bought a case of tea, some wine, and other presents, as the tradesman had advised. On and on they went until they had gone more than three hundred miles, and on the seventh day they came to a place where the Bashkirs had pitched their tents. It was all just as the tradesman had said. The people lived on the steppes, by a river, in felt-covered tents. They neither tilled the ground nor ate bread. Their cattle and horses grazed iɴ herds on the steppe. The colts were tethered behind the tents, and the mares were driven to them twice a day. The mares were milked, and from the milk kumiss was made. It was the women who prepared kumiss, and they also made cheese. As far as the men were concerned, drinking kumiss and eating mutton, and playing on their pipes, was all they cared about. They were all stout and merry, and all the summer long they never thought of doing any work. They were quite ignorant, and knew no Russian, but were good-natured enough.

As soon as they saw Pahom, they came out of their tents and gathered round their visitor. An interpreter was found, and Pahom told them he had come about some land. The Bashkirs seemed very glad; they took Pahom and led him into one of the best tents, where they made him sit on some down cushions placed on a carpet, while they sat round him. They gave him some tea and kumiss, and had a sheep killed, and gave him mutton to eat. Pahom took presents out of his cart and distributed them among the Bashkirs, and divided the tea amongst them. The Bashkirs were delighted. They talked a great deal among themselves, and then told the interpreter to translate.

"They wish to tell you," said the interpreter, "that they like you, and that it is our custom to do all we can to please a guest and repay him for his gifts. You have given us presents, now tell us which of the things we possess please you best, that we may present them to you."

"What pleases me best here," answered Pahom, "is your land. Our land is crowded and the soil is exhausted; but you have plenty of land and it is good land. I never saw the like of it."

The interpreter translated. The Bashkirs talked among themselves for a while. Pahom could not understand what they were saying, but saw that they were much amused and that they shouted and laughed. Then they were silent and looked at Pahom while the interpreter said:

"They wish me to tell you that in return for your presents they will gladly give you as much land as you want. You have only to point it out with your hand and it is yours."

The Bashkirs talked again for a while and began to dispute.

Pahom asked what they were disputing about, and the interpreter told him that some of them thought they ought to ask their Chief about the land and not act in his absence, while others thought there was no need to wait for his return.

While the Bashkirs were disputing, a man in a large fox-fur cap appeared on the scene. They all became silent and rose to their feet. The interpreter said, "This is our Chief himself."

Pahom immediately fetched the best dressing gown and five pounds of tea, and offered these to the Chief. The Chief accepted them, and seated himself in the place of honor. The Bashkirs at once began telling him something. The Chief listened for a while, then made a sign with his head for them to be silent, and addressing himself to Pahom, said in Russian:

"Well, let it be so. Choose whatever piece of land you like; we have plenty of it."

"How can I take as much as I like?" thought Pahom. "I must get a deed to make it secure, or else they may say, 'It is yours,' and afterwards may take it away again."

"Thank you for your kind words," he said aloud. "You have much land, and I only want a little. But I should like to be sure which bit is mine. Could it not be measured and made over to me? Life and death are in God's hands. You good people give it to me, but your children might wish to take it away again."

"You are quite right," said the Chief. "We will make it over to you."

"I heard that a dealer had been here," continued Pahom, "and that you gave him a little land, too, and signed title deeds to that effect. I should like to have it done in the same way."

The Chief understood.

"Yes," replied he, "that can be done quite easily. We have a scribe, and we will go to town with you and have the deed properly sealed."

"And what will be the price?" asked Pahom.

"Our price is always the same: one thousand roubles a day."

Pahom did not understand.

"A day? What measure is that? How many acres would that be?"

"We do not know how to reckon it out," said the Chief. "We sell it by the day. As much as you can go round on your feet in a day is yours, and the price is one thousand roubles a day."

Pahom was surprised.

"But in a day you can get round a large tract of land," he said.

The Chief laughed.

"It will all be yours" said he "But there is one condition: If you don't return on the same day to the spot whence you started, your money is lost."

"But how am I to mark the way that I have gone?"

"Why, we shall go to any spot you like, and stay there. You must start from that spot and make your round, taking a spade with you. Wherever you think necessary, make a mark. At every turning, dig a hole and pile up the turf; then afterwards we will go round with a plow from hole to hole. You may make as large a circuit as you please, but before the sun sets you must return to the place you started from. All the land you cover will be yours."

Pahom was delighted. It was decided to start early next morning. They talked awhile, and after drinking some more kumiss and eating some more mutton, they had tea again, and then the night came on. They gave Pahom a feather bed to sleep on, and the Bashkirs dispersed for the night, promising to assemble the next morning at daybreak and ride out before sunrise to the appointed spot.

Pahom lay on the feather bed, but could not sleep. He kept thinking about the land.

"What a large tract I will mark off!" thought he. "I can easily do thirty-five miles in a day. The days are long now, and within a circuit of thirty-five miles what a lot of land there will be! I will sell the poorer land, or let it to peasants, but I'll pick out the best and farm it. I will buy two ox teams, and hire two more laborers. About a hundred and fifty acres shall be plowland, and I will pasture cattle on the rest."

Pahom lay awake all night, and dozed off only just before dawn. Hardly were his eyes closed when he had a dream. He thought he was lying in that same tent and heard somebody chuckling outside. He wondered who it could be, and rose and went out, and he saw the Bashkir Chief sitting in front of the tent holding his sides and rolling about with laughter. Going nearer to the Chief, Pahom asked: "What are you laughing at?" But he saw that it was no longer the Chief, but the dealer who had recently stopped at his house and had told him about the land. Just as Pahom was going to ask, "Have you been here long?" he saw that it was not the dealer, but the peasant who had come up from the Volga, long ago, to Pahom's old home. Then he saw that it was not the peasant either, but the Devil himself with hoofs and horns, sitting there and chuckling, and before him lay a man barefoot, prostrate on the ground, with only trousers and shirt on. And Pahom dreamt that he looked more attentively to see what sort of a man it was that was lying there, and he saw that the man was dead, and that it was himself! He awoke horror-struck.

"What things one does dream," thought he.

Looking round he saw through the open door that the dawn was breaking. "It's time to wake them up," thought he. "We ought to be starting."

He got up, roused his man (who was sleeping in his cart), bade him harness; and went to call the Bashkirs.

"It's time to go to the steppe to measure the land," he said.

The Bashkirs rose and assembled, and the Chief came too. Then they began drinking kumiss again, and offered Pahom some tea, but he would not wait.

"If we are to go, let us go. It is high time," said he.

The Bashkirs got ready and they all started: some mounted on horses, and some in carts. Pahom drove in his own small cart with his servant and took a spade with him. When they reached the steppe, the morning red was beginning to kindle. They ascended a hillock (called by the Bashkirs a *shikhan*) and dismounting from their carts and their horses, gathered in one spot. The Chief came up to Pahom and stretching out his arm towards the plain:

"See," said he, "all this, as far as your eye can reach, is ours. You may have any part of it you like."

Pahom's eyes glistened: it was all virgin soil, as flat as the palm of your hand, as black as the seed of a poppy, and in the hollows different kinds of grasses grew breast-high.

The Chief took off his fox-fur cap, placed it on the ground and said:

"This will be the mark. Start from here, and return here again. All the land you go round shall be yours."

Pahom took out his money and put it on the cap. Then he took off his outer coat, remaining in his sleeveless undercoat. He unfastened his girdle and tied it tight below his stomach, put a little bag of bread into the breast of his coat, and tying a flask of water to his girdle, he drew up the tops of his boots, took the spade from the man, and stood ready to start. He considered for some moments which way he had better go—it was tempting everywhere.

"No matter," he concluded, "I will go towards the rising sun."

He turned his face to the east, stretched himself, and waited for the sun to appear above the rim.

"I must lose no time," he thought, "and it is easier walking while it is still cool."

The sun's rays had hardly flashed above the horizon, before Pahom, carrying the spade over his shoulder, went down into the steppe.

Pahom started walking neither slowly nor quickly. After having gone a thousand yards he stopped, dug a hole, and placed pieces of turf one on another to make it more visible. Then he went on; and now that he had walked off his stiffness he quickened his pace. After a while he dug another hole.

Pahom looked back. The hillock could be distinctly seen in the sunlight, with the people on it, and the glittering tires of the cart wheels. At a rough guess Pahom concluded that he had walked three miles. It was growing warmer; he took off his undercoat, flung it across his shoulder, and went on again. It had grown quite warm now; he looked at the sun, it was time to think of breakfast.

"The first shift is done, but there are four in a day, and it is too soon yet to turn. But I will just take off my boots," said he to himself.

He sat down, took off his boots, stuck them into his girdle, and went on. It was easy walking now.

"I will go on for another three miles," thought he, "and then turn to the left. This spot is so fine, that it would be a pity to lose it. The further one goes, the better the land seems."

He went straight on for a while, and when he looked round, the hillock was scarcely visible and the people on it looked like black ants, and he could just see something glistening there in the sun.

"Ah," thought Pahom, "I have gone far enough in this direction, it is time to turn. Besides I am in a regular sweat, and very thirsty."

He stopped, dug a large hole, and heaped up pieces of turf. Next he untied his flask, had a drink, and then turned sharply to the left. He went on and on; the grass was high, and it was very hot.

Pahom began to grow tired: he looked at the sun and saw that it was noon.

"Well," he thought, "I must have a rest."

He sat down, and ate some bread and drank some water; but he did not lie down, thinking that if he did he might fall asleep. After sitting a little while, he went on again. At first he walked easily: the food had strengthened him; but it had become terribly hot and he felt sleepy, still he went on, thinking: "An hour to suffer, a lifetime to live."

He went a long way in this direction also, and was about to turn to the left again, when he perceived a damp hollow: "It would be a pity to leave that out," he thought. "Flax would do well there." So he went on past the hollow, and dug a hole on the other side of it before he turned the corner. Pahom looked towards the hillock. The heat made the air hazy: it seemed to be quivering, and through the haze the people on the hillock could scarcely be seen.

"Ah!" thought Pahom, "I have made the sides too long; I must make this one shorter." And he went along the third side, stepping faster. He looked at the sun: it was nearly halfway to the horizon, and he had not yet done two miles of the third side of the square. He was still ten miles from the goal.

"No," he thought, "though it will make my land lopsided, I must hurry back in a straight line now. I might go too far, and as it is I have a great deal of land."

So Pahom hurriedly dug a hole, and turned straight towards the hillock.

Pahom went straight towards the hillock, but he now walked with difficulty. He was done up with the heat, his bare feet were cut and bruised, and his legs began to fail. He longed to rest, but it was impossible if he meant to get back before sunset. The sun waits for no man, and it was sinking lower and lower.

"Oh, dear," he thought, "if only I have not blundered trying for too much! What if I am too late?"

He looked towards the hillock and at the sun. He was still far from his goal, and the sun was already near the rim.

Pahom walked on and on; it was very hard walking but he went quicker and quicker. He pressed on, but was still far from the place. He began running, threw away his coat, his boots, his flask, and his cap, and kept only the spade which he used as a support.

"What shall I do," he thought again, "I have grasped too much and ruined the whole affair. I can't get there before the sun sets."

And this fear made him still more breathless. Pahom went on running; his soaking shirt and trousers stuck to him and his mouth was parched. His breast was working like a blacksmith's bellows, his heart was beating like a hammer, and his legs were giving way as if they did not belong to him. Pahom was seized with terror lest he should die of the strain.

Though afraid of death, he could not stop. "After having run all that way they will call me a fool if I stop now," thought he. And he ran on and on, and drew near and heard the Bashkirs yelling and shouting to him, and their cries inflamed his heart still more. He gathered his last strength and ran on.

The sun was close to the rim, and cloaked in mist looked large, and red as blood. Now, yes now, it was about to set! The sun was quite low, but he was also quite near his aim. Pahom could already see the people on the hillock waving their arms to hurry him up. He could see the fox-fur cap on the ground and the money on it, and the Chief sitting on the ground holding his sides. And Pahom remembered his dream.

"There is plenty of land," thought he, "but will God let me live on it? I have lost my life, I have lost my life! I shall never reach that spot!"

Pahom looked at the sun, which had reached the earth: one side of it had already disappeared. With all his remaining strength he rushed on, bending his body forward so that his legs could hardly follow fast enough to keep him from falling. Just as he reached the hillock it suddenly grew dark. He looked up— the sun had already set! He gave a cry: "All my labor has been in vain." thought he, and was about to stop, but he heard the Bashkirs still shouting, and remembered that though to him, from below, the sun seemed to have set, they on the hillock could still see it. He took a long breath and ran up the hillock. It was still light there. He reached the top and saw the cap. Before it sat the Chief laughing and holding his sides. Again Pahom remembered his dream, and he uttered a cry: his legs gave way beneath him, he fell forward and reached the cap with his hands.

"Ah, that's a fine fellow!" exclaimed the Chief. "He has gained much land!"

Pahom's servant came running up and tried to raise him, but he saw that blood was flowing from his mouth. Pahom was dead!

The Bashkirs clicked their tongues to show their pity.

His servant picked up the spade and dug a grave long enough for Pahom to lie in, and buried him in it. Six feet from his head to his heels was all he needed.

1. Tell the story of this parable on the literal level. 2. State the theme that is taught on the symbolic level. 3. Is there any patterning with *three's* in this parable? 4. In what way is this parable like a fable? 5. In what way is it like *The Godson*?

Stories that Explain Life—Folk Tales and Fairy Tales

Much of the literature you can close your eyes and remember belongs to the broad and rich class called folk tales. Myths, fables, parables, legends, tall tales, and fairy tales—*Pandora, Rip Van Winkle, Rumpelstiltskin, Three Billy Goats Gruff, Hansel and Gretel*—you know them and have known them for a long time. And so has the human race. Folk tales belong not only to your childhood but to the childhood of mankind.

Some folk tales, often included in books of fairy tales, are not really fairy tales but belong to a class of their own. These are not myths, legends, parables, fables, fairy tales, or tall tales but a special kind of story that originates from the folk. They are stories which, like *Peter Klaus*, treat the folk motifs and themes realistically, never straying far from the wholesome peasants who tell them. They are set in a real world of farm and fields where a man knows what he is about. And when good fortune comes, it comes as a stranger and leaves that way. *Jack and the Beanstalk* belongs to this kind of folk tale. So does *Dick Whittington*.

Read the fairy tale *Peter Klaus*.

PETER KLAUS

FROM A TALE BY OTMAR, TRANSLATED BY THOMAS ROSCOE

In the village of Sittendorf at the foot of a mountain lived Peter Klaus, a goatherd who was in the habit of pasturing his flock upon the near-by Kyffhausen Hills. Toward evening he generally let them browse upon a green plot surrounded by an old ruined wall, from which he could take a muster of his whole flock.

During one period he observed that one of his prettiest goats usually disappeared soon after its arrival at this spot and did not join the fold again until late in the evening. He watched her again and again, and at last found that she slipped through a gap into a passage which widened into a cavern. When he entered the cavern, he found the goat busy picking up oats that fell through some crevices above. He looked up, shook his head at this odd shower, and at first could find no explanation for it.

At length he heard over his head the neighing and stamping of horses; he listened, and concluded that the oats must have fallen through a manger where horses were being fed. The poor goatherd was sadly at a loss to know what horses were doing in that uninhabited part of the mountain, but so it was, for a groom soon made his appearance and, without saying a word, beckoned him to follow.

Peter obeyed and followed him up some steps which led into an open courtyard surrounded by old walls. Next to this was a still more spacious ravine, surrounded by rocky heights and overhung with trees and shrubs which admitted only a kind of twilight. Peter continued on and came at last to a smoothshaven green, where twelve ancient knights, none of whom spoke a word, were engaged in playing ninepins. His guide now beckoned to Peter to pick up the ninepins and then went his way.

At first, trembling in every limb, Peter did not venture to disobey, but after a time he began to cast stolen glances at the players, and saw at once that their long beards and slashed doublets belonged to a fashion long past. By degrees his looks grew bolder, and, noting among other things a tankard near him filled with wine whose aroma was excellent, he took a draught. It seemed to give him renewed life; and whenever he began to feel tired, he applied with fresh ardor to the tankard. Finally the wine overpowered him, and he fell fast asleep.

When he opened his eyes again, he found himself on the grassy plot once more, in the same old spot where he was in the habit of feeding his goats. He rubbed his eyes and looked round but could see neither dog nor flock. This surprised him, but he was even more surprised at the long rank grass that grew about him, and at trees and bushes which he had never before seen.

He shook his head and walked a little farther, looking for the old sheep path and the hillocks and road where he used daily to drive his flock; but he could find no trace of them. Yet he saw the village just before him. He hastened down the hill to inquire after his flock.

All the, people whom he met going into the village were strangers to him, and all were strangely dressed and spoke in a way different from that of his old neighbors. When he asked about his goats, these people only stared at him and fixed their eyes upon his chin. He put his hand unconsciously to his mouth, and to his great surprise found that he had grown a beard at least a foot long.

He now began to think that both he and all the world around him were in a dream; and yet he knew the mountain he had just come down was the Kyffhausen. And there were the cottages with their gardens and grassy plots, much as he had left them. Besides, when he asked the lads who had collected round him what place it was, they answered that it was Sittendorf.

Still shaking his head, he went farther into the village to look for his own house. He found it, but greatly altered, and for the worse: a strange goatherd in an old tattered frock lay before the door, and near him lay Peter's old dog, which only growled and showed its teeth when Peter tried to call him. He went through the entrance which had once had a door, but all within was empty and deserted. He staggered out of the house like a drunken man, and called for his wife and children again and again by name; but no one listened and no one gave answer.

Soon, however, a crowd of women and children gathered round the stranger with the long hoary beard and asked him what it was he wanted. Peter thought it was such a strange kind of thing to stand before his own house and inquire for his own wife and children, as well as about himself, that, evading these questions he asked for an old neighbor, Kurt Steffen, the blacksmith. Most of the spectators only stared at him blankly, till an old woman at last said, "Why he has been in Sachsenburg these twelve years."

"Where then is Valentine Meier, the tailor?" Peter asked the bystanders.

"The Lord rest his soul!" cried another old woman leaning upon her crutch. "He has been lying more than these fifteen years in a house he will never leave."

Then Peter recognized in these women two who had been young neighbors of his. They seemed to have grown old with incredible suddenness, but he had little inclination to inquire further.

At this moment there appeared, making her way through the crowd of spectators, a sprightly young woman with a year-old baby in her arms and with a girl of about four holding her hand. All three bore a striking resemblance to the wife he was seeking.

"What are your names?" he cried out in surprise.

"Mine is Maria," the woman said.

"And your father's?" continued Peter.

"God rest his soul! Peter Klaus, to be sure. It is now twenty years since we were all looking for him day and night upon the Kyffhausen—after his flock came home without him. I was then," continued the woman, "only seven years old."

The goatherd could no longer contain himself. "I am Peter Klaus," he cried, "Peter and no other." And he took his daughter's child and kissed it. The spectators were struck dumb with astonishment, until first one and then another began to see, "Yes, indeed, that is Peter Klaus! Welcome, good neighbor, after twenty years' absence, welcome home."

1. Notice that this story is told as if it really happened. How does the author make the story seem real? **2.** Where did the groom take Peter? **3.** How long was Peter asleep? **4.** Work out the story pattern of this folk tale. **5.** Use your dictionary for these words:

muster	*evading*	*sprightly*
ravine	*incredible*	*ninepins*

6. Keep the motif of this folk tale in mind when later you read the legend *Rip Van Winkle*.

Good fortune and magic are right at home in the romantic fairy tale. Reality shines with the splendor of spells and the mysterious other world where people come and go in the fairy tale. These stories of knights and castles come from the simple people too, but they are filled with the idealized life the peasants yearn for when they look across the fields to the courtyard of the castle, where the prince and the princess are getting ready to ride. The charm of courtesy, the color and sound of pageantry are captured in these stories for listeners who know that only through magic can such things come about.

One of the most interesting characteristics of these tales is the recurring motif. Character, situation, theme appear in many stories from different times and countries. These characters, situations, and themes are called motifs. Among the common motifs are underworld journeys, quests, challenges, the selling of one's soul, the shrewish wife reformed, the simple outwitting the wise. These motifs recur because they come from human experience. Whether a man rides a donkey or drives a car, when he tells a good story it comes from experiences that are common to mankind.

The structure of the special kind of folk tale and the fairy tale is simple: a brief exposition, often just the formula *Once upon a time* or *Long ago in a faraway land;* an initiating incident that begins the action; and the development of the line of action to the point of the story. Often the development is structured in a pattern of *three's*—three quests, three tests, three riddles. The end is always a satisfying one, for in folk and fairy tales most people *live happily ever after.*

Read *The Sleeping Beauty in the Wood.*

The Sleeping Beauty
in the Wood

Once upon a time there was a king and a queen who were very sorry that they had no children—so sorry that it cannot be told.

At last, however, the Queen had a daughter. There was a very fine christening; and the Princess had for her godmothers all the fairies they could find in the whole kingdom (there were seven of them), so that every one of them might confer a gift upon her, as was the custom of fairies in those days. By this means the Princess had all the perfections imaginable.

After the christening was over, the company returned to the King's palace, where was prepared a great feast for the fairies. There was placed before every one of them a magnificent cover with a case of massive gold, wherein were a spoon, and a knife and fork, all of pure gold set with diamonds and rubies. But as they were all sitting down at table they saw a very old fairy come into the hall. She had not been invited, because for more than fifty years she had not been out of a certain tower, and she was believed to be either dead or enchanted.

The King ordered her a cover, but he could not give her a case of gold as the others had, because seven only had been made for the seven fairies. The old fairy fancied she was slighted, and muttered threats between her teeth. One of the young fairies who sat near heard her, and, judging that she might give the little Princess some unlucky gift, hid herself behind the curtains as soon as they left the table. She hoped that she might speak last and undo as much as she could the evil which the old fairy might do.

In the meanwhile all the fairies began to give their gifts to the Princess. The youngest gave her for her gift that she should be the most beautiful person in the world; the next, that she should have the wit of an angel; the third, that she should be able to do everything she did gracefully; the fourth, that she should dance perfectly; the fifth, that she should sing like a nightingale; and the sixth, that she should play all kinds of musical instruments to the fullest perfection.

The old fairy's turn coming next, her head shaking more with spite than with age, she said that the Princess should pierce her hand with a spindle and die of the wound. This terrible gift made the whole company tremble, and everybody fell a-crying.

At this very instant the young fairy came from behind the curtains and said these words in a loud voice:—

"Assure yourselves, O King and Queen, that your daughter shall not die of this disaster. It is true, I have no power to undo entirely what my elder has done. The Princess shall indeed pierce her hand with a spindle; but, instead of dying, she shall only fall into a deep sleep, which shall last a hundred years, at the end of which a king's son shall come and awake her."

The King, to avoid the misfortune foretold by the old fairy, issued orders forbidding any one, on pain of death, to spin with a distaff and spindle, or to have a spindle in his house. About fifteen or sixteen years after, the King and Queen being absent at one of their country villas, the young Princess was one day running up and down the palace; she went from room to room, and at last she came into a little garret on the top of the tower, where a good old woman, alone, was spinning with her spindle. This good woman had never heard of the King's orders against spindles.

"What are you doing there, my good woman?" said the Princess.

"I am spinning, my pretty child," said the old woman, who did not know who the Princess was.

"Ha!" said the Princess, "this is very pretty; how do you do it? Give it to me. Let me see if I can do it."

She had no sooner taken it into her hand than, either because she was too quick and heedless, or because the decree of the fairy had so ordained, it ran into her hand, and she fell down in a swoon.

The good old woman, not knowing what to do, cried out for help. People came in from every quarter; they threw water upon the face of the Princess, unlaced her, struck her on the palms of her hands, and rubbed her temples with cologne water; but nothing would bring her to herself.

Then the King, who had returned and heard the cry, remembered what the fairies had foretold. He knew very well that this must come to pass, since the fairies had foretold it, and he caused the Princess to be carried into the finest room in his palace, and to be laid upon a bed all embroidered with gold and silver. One would have taken her for a little angel, she was so beautiful; for her swooning had not dimmed the brightness of her complexion: her cheeks were carnation, and her lips coral. It is true her eyes were shut, but she was heard to breathe softly, which satisfied those who were gathered about her that she was not dead.

The King gave orders that they should let her sleep quietly till the time came for her to awake. The good fairy who had saved her life by condemning her to sleep a hundred years was in the kingdom of Matakin, twelve thousand leagues off, when this accident befell the Princess; but she was instantly informed of it by a little dwarf, who had seven-leagued boots, that is, boots with which he could stride over seven leagues of ground at once. The fairy started off at once, and arrived, about an hour later, in a fiery chariot drawn by dragons.

The King handed her out of the chariot, and she approved everything he had done; but as she had very great foresight, she thought that when the Princess should awake she might not know what to do with herself, if she was all alone in this old palace. This was what she did: she touched with her wand everything in the palace (except the King and Queen),—governesses, maids of honor, ladies of the bedchamber, gentlemen, officers, stewards, cooks, undercooks, kitchen maids, guards with their porters, pages, and footmen; she likewise touched all the horses which were in the stables, the cart horses, the hunters and the saddle horses, the grooms, the great dogs in the outward court, and little Mopsey, too, the Princess's spaniel, which was lying on the bed.

As soon as she touched them they all fell asleep, not to awake again until their mistress did, that they might be ready to wait upon her when she wanted them. The very spits at the fire, as full as they could hold of partridges and pheasants, fell asleep, and the fire itself as well. All this was done in a moment. Fairies are not long in doing their work.

And now the King and Queen, having kissed their dear child without waking her, went out of the palace and sent forth orders that nobody should come near it.

These orders were not necessary; for in a quarter of an hour's time there grew up all round about the park such a vast number of trees, great and small, bushes and brambles, twining one within another, that neither man nor beast could pass through; so that nothing could be seen but the very top of the towers of the palace; and that, too, only from afar off. Every one knew that this also was the work of the fairy in order that while the Princess slept she should have nothing to fear from curious people.

After a hundred years the son of the King then reigning, who was of another family from that of the sleeping Princess, was a-hunting on that side of the country, and he asked what those towers were which he saw in the middle of a great thick wood. Every one answered according as they had heard. Some said that it was an old haunted castle, others that all the witches of the country held their midnight revels there, but the common opinion was that it was an ogre's dwelling, and that he carried to it all the little children he could catch, so as to eat them up at his leisure, without any one being able to follow him, for he alone had the power to make his way through the wood.

The Prince did not know what to believe, and presently a very aged countryman spake to him thus:—

"May it please your royal Highness, more than fifty years since I heard from my father that there was then in this castle the most beautiful princess that was ever seen; that she must sleep there a hundred years, and that she should be waked by a king's son, for whom she was reserved."

The young Prince on hearing this was all on fire. He thought, without weighing the matter, that he could put an end to this rare adventure; and, pushed on by love and the desire of glory, resolved at once to look into it.

As soon as he began to get near to the wood, all the great trees and bushes and brambles gave way of themselves to let him pass through. He walked up to the castle which he saw at the end of a large avenue; and you can imagine he was a good deal surprised when he saw none of his people following him, because the trees closed again as soon as he had passed through them. However, he did not cease from continuing his way; a young prince in search of glory is ever valiant.

He came into a spacious outer court, and what he saw was enough to freeze him with horror. A frightful silence reigned over all; the image of death was everywhere, and there was nothing to be seen but what seemed to be the outstretched bodies of dead men and animals. He, however, very well knew, by the ruby faces and pimpled noses of the porters, that they were only asleep; and their goblets, wherein still remained some drops of wine, showed plainly that they had fallen asleep while drinking their wine.

He then crossed a court paved with marble, went up the stairs, and came into the guard chamber, where guards were standing in their ranks, with their muskets upon their shoulders, and snoring with all their might. He went through several rooms full of gentlemen and ladies, some standing and others sitting, but all were asleep. He came into a gilded chamber, where he saw upon a bed, the curtains of which were all open, the most beautiful sight ever beheld—a princess who appeared to be about fifteen or sixteen years of age, and whose bright and resplendent beauty had something divine in it. He approached with trembling and admiration, and fell down upon his knees before her.

Then, as the end of the enchantment was come, the Princess awoke, and looking on him with eyes more tender than could have been expected at first sight, said:—

"Is it you, my Prince? You have waited a long while."

The Prince, charmed with these words, and much more with

the manner in which they were spoken, knew not how to show his joy and gratitude; he assured her that he loved her better than he did himself. Their discourse was not very connected, but they were the better pleased, for where there is much love there is little eloquence. He was more at a loss than she, and we need not wonder at it; she had had time to think of what to say to him; for it is evident (though history says nothing of it) that the good fairy, during so long a sleep, had given her very pleasant dreams. In short, they talked together for four hours, and then they said not half they had to say.

In the meanwhile all the palace had woke up with the Princess; every one thought upon his own business, and as they were not in love, they were ready to die of hunger. The lady of honor, being as sharp set as the other folks, grew very impatient, and told the Princess aloud that the meal was served. The Prince helped the Princess to rise. She was entirely and very magnificently dressed; but his royal Highness took care not to tell her that she was dressed like his great-grandmother, and had a high collar. She looked not a bit the less charming and beautiful for all that.

They went into the great mirrored hall, where they supped, and were served by the officers of the Princess's household. The violins and hautboys played old tunes, but they were excellent, though they had not been played for a hundred years; and after supper, without losing any time, the lord almoner married them in the chapel of the castle. They had but very little sleep— the Princess scarcely needed any; and the Prince left her next morning to return into the city, where his father was greatly troubled about him.

The Prince told him that he lost his way in the forest as he was hunting, and that he had slept in the cottage of a charcoal-burner, who gave him cheese and brown bread.

The King, his father, who was a good man, believed him; but his mother could not be persuaded that it was true; and seeing that he went almost every day a-hunting, and that he always had some excuse ready for so doing, though he had been out three or four nights together, she began to suspect that he was married; for he lived thus with the Princess above two whole years, during which they had two children, the elder, a daughter, was named Dawn, and the younger, a son, they called Day, because he was a great deal handsomer than his sister.

The Queen spoke several times to her son, to learn after what manner he was passing his time, and told him that in this he ought in duty to satisfy her. But he never dared to trust her with his secret; he feared her, though he loved her, for she was of the race of the Ogres, and the King married her for her vast riches alone. It was even whispered about the Court that she had Ogreish inclinations, and that, whenever she saw little children passing by, she had all the difficulty in the world to prevent herself from falling upon them. And so the Prince would never tell her one word.

But when the King was dead, which happened about two years afterward, and he saw himself lord and master, he openly declared his marriage; and he went in great state to conduct his Queen to the palace. They made a magnificent entry into the capital city, she riding between her two children.

Soon after, the King made war on Emperor Cantalabutte, his neighbor. He left the government of the kingdom to the Queen, his mother, and earnestly commended his wife and children to her care. He was obliged to carry on the war all the summer, and as soon as he left, the Queen-mother sent her daughter-in-law and her children to a country house among the woods, that she might with the more ease gratify her horrible longing. Some few days afterward she went thither herself, and said to her head cook:—

"I intend to eat little Dawn for my dinner to-morrow."

"O! madam!" cried the head cook.

"I will have it so," replied the Queen (and this she spoke in the tone of an Ogress who had a strong desire to eat fresh meat), "and will eat her with a sharp sauce."

The poor man, knowing very well that he must not play tricks with Ogresses, took his great knife and went up into little Dawn's chamber. She was then nearly four years old, and came up to him, jumping and laughing, to put her arms round his neck, and ask him for some sugar-candy. Upon which he began to weep, the great knife fell out of his hand, and he went into the back yard and killed a little lamb, and dressed it with such good sauce that his mistress assured him she had never eaten anything so good in her life. He had at the same time taken up little Dawn and carried her to his wife, to conceal her in his lodging at the end of the courtyard.

Eight days afterwards the wicked Queen said to the chief cook, "I will sup upon little Day."

He answered not a word, being resolved to cheat her again as he had done before. He went to find little Day, and saw him with a foil in his hand, with which he was fencing with a great monkey: the child was then only three years of age. He took him up in his arms and carried him to his wife, that she might conceal him in her chamber along with his sister, and instead of little Day he served up a young and very tender kid, which the Ogress found to be wonderfully good.

All had gone well up to now; but one evening this wicked Queen said to her chief cook:—

"I will eat the Queen with the same sauce I had with her children."

Now the poor chief cook was in despair and could not imagine how to deceive her again. The young Queen was over twenty years old, not reckoning the hundred years she had been asleep; and how to find something to take her place greatly puzzled him. He then decided, to save his own life, to cut the Queen's throat; and going up into her chamber, with intent to do it at once, he put himself into as great fury as he possibly could, and came into the young Queen's room with his dagger in his hand. He would not, however, deceive her, but told her, with a great deal of respect, the orders he had received from the Queen-mother.

"Do it; do it," she said, stretching out her neck. "Carry out your orders, and then I shall go and see my children, my poor children, whom I loved so much and so tenderly."

For she thought them dead, since they had been taken away without her knowledge.

"No, no, madam," cried the poor chief cook, all in tears; "you shall not die, and you shall see your children again at once. But then you must go home with me to my lodgings, where I have concealed them, and I will deceive the Queen once more, by giving her a young hind in your stead."

Upon this he forthwith conducted her to his room, where, leaving her to embrace her children, and cry along with them, he went and dressed a young hind, which the Queen had for her supper, and devoured with as much appetite as if it had been the young Queen. She was now well satisfied with her cruel deeds, and she invented a story to tell the King on his return, of how the Queen his wife and her two children had been devoured by mad wolves.

One evening, as she was, according to her custom, rambling round about the courts and yards of the palace to see if she could smell any fresh meat, she heard, in a room on the ground floor, little Day crying, for his mamma was going to whip him, because he had been naughty; and she heard, at the same time, little Dawn begging mercy for her brother.

The Ogress knew the voice of the Queen and her children at once, and being furious at having been thus deceived, she gave orders (in a most horrible voice which made everybody tremble) that, next morning by break of day, they should bring into the middle of the great court a large tub filled with toads, vipers, snakes, and all sorts of serpents, in order to have the Queen and her children, the chief cook, his wife and maid, thrown into it, all of whom were to be brought thither with their hands tied behind them.

They were brought out accordingly, and the executioners were just going to throw them into the tub, when the King, who was not so soon expected, entered the court on horseback and asked, with the utmost astonishment, what was the meaning of that horrible spectacle.

No one dared to tell him, when the Ogress, all enraged to see what had happened, threw herself head foremost into the tub, and was instantly devoured by the ugly creatures she had ordered to be thrown into it to kill the others. The King was of course very sorry, for she was his mother; but he soon comforted himself with his beautiful wife and his pretty children.

1. Why do we say this fairy tale is romantic? **2.** Compare this tale with *Cinderella*. **3.** Contrast it with *The Emperor's New Clothes*. **4.** Work out the storytelling pattern of this fairy tale. **5.** Does the author use the pattern of three?

Read *The Iron Stove*.

THE IRON STOVE

Once upon a time when wishes came true there was a king's son who was enchanted by an old witch, so that he was obliged to sit in a large iron stove in a wood. There he lived for many years, and no one could free him. At last a king's daughter came into the wood; she had lost her way and could not find her father's kingdom again. She had been wandering round and round for nine days, and she came at last to the iron stove. A voice came from within and asked her: "Where do you come from and where do you want to go?" She answered: "I have lost my way to my father's kingdom, and I shall never get home again." Then the voice from the iron stove said: "I will help you to find your home again, and that in a very short time, if you will promise to do what I ask you. I am a greater prince than you are a princess, and I will marry you." Then she grew frightened and thought: "What can a young lassie do with an iron stove?" But as she wanted very much to go home to her father, she promised to do what he wished. He said: "You must come again, and bring a knife with you to scrape a hole in the iron."

Then he gave her some one for a guide, who walked near her and said nothing, but he brought her in two hours to her house. There was great joy in the castle when the Princess came back, and the old King fell on her neck and kissed her. But she was very much troubled and said: "Dear father, listen to what has befallen me. I should never have come home again out of the great wildwood if I had not come to an iron stove, and I have had to promise that I will go back to free him and marry him!" The old King was so frightened that he nearly fainted, for she was his only daughter. So they consulted together and determined that the miller's daughter, who was very beautiful, should take her place. They took her there, gave her a knife, and said she must scrape at the iron stove. She scraped for twenty-four hours, but did not make the least impression. When the day broke a voice called from the iron stove: "It seems to me that it is day outside." Then she answered: "It seems so to me; I think I hear my father's mill rattling."

"So you are a miller's daughter! Then go away at once and tell the King's daughter to come."

Then she went away and told the old King that the thing inside the iron stove would not have her, but wanted the Princess. The old King was frightened, and his daughter wept. But they had a swineherd's daughter who was even more beautiful than the miller's daughter, and they gave her a piece of gold to go to the iron stove instead of the Princess. Then she was taken there and made to scrape for twenty-four hours, but she could make no impression. As soon as the day broke the voice from the stove called out: "It seems to be daylight outside." Then she answered: "It seems so to me, too; I think I hear my father blowing his horn." "So you are a swineherd's daughter! Go away at once and let the King's daughter come. And say to her that what I foretell shall come to pass, and if she does not come everything in the kingdom shall fall into ruin, and not one stone shall be left upon another." When the Princess heard this she began to cry, but it was no good; she had to keep her word. She took leave of her father, put a knife in her belt, and went to the iron stove in the wood. As soon as she reached it she began to scrape and the iron gave way, and before two hours had passed she had made a little hole. Then she peeped in and saw such a beautiful youth all shining with gold and precious stones that she fell in love with him on the spot. So she scraped away harder than ever, and made the hole so large that he could get out. Then he said: "You are mine and I am thine; you are my bride and have set me free!" He wanted to take her with him to his kingdom, but she begged him just to let her go once more to her father; and the Prince let her go, but told her not to say more than three words to her father, then to come back again. So she went home, but, alas! she said more than three words; and immediately the iron stove vanished and went away over a mountain of glass and sharp swords. But the Prince was free and was no longer shut up in it. Then she said good-by to her father, and took a little money with her and went again into the great wood to look for the iron stove; but she could not find it. She sought it for nine days, and then her hunger became so great that she did not know how she could live any longer. And when it was evening she climbed a little tree and wished that the night would not come, because she was afraid of the wild beasts. When midnight came she saw afar off a little light and thought: "Ah, if only I could reach that!" Then she got down from the tree and went toward the light. She came to a little old house with a great deal of grass growing around, and stood in front of a little heap of wood. She thought, "Alas! what am I coming to?" and peeped through the window; but she saw nothing inside except big and little toads and a table beautifully spread with roast meats and wine, and all the dishes and drinking cups were of silver, so she took heart and knocked. Then a fat toad called out:

> "Little green toad with leg like crook,
> Open wide the door, and look
> Who it was the latch that shook."

And a little toad came forward and let her in. When she entered they all bade her welcome and made her sit down. They asked her how she came there and what she wanted. Then she told everything that had happened to her, and how, because she had exceeded her permission only to speak three words, the stove had disappeared with the Prince; and how she had searched a very long time, and must wander over mountain and valley till she found him.

Then the old toad said:

"Little green toad whose leg doth twist,
Go to the corner of which you wist,
And bring to me the large old kist."

And the little toad went and brought out a great chest. Then they gave her food and drink and led her to a beautifully made bed of silk and samite, on which she lay down and slept soundly. When the day dawned she arose, and the old toad gave her three things out of the huge chest to take with her. She would have need of them, for she had to cross a high glass mountain, three cutting swords, and a great lake. When she had passed these she would find her lover again. So she was given three large needles, a plow wheel, and three nuts, which she was to take great care of. She set out with these things, and when she came to the glass mountain which was so slippery, she stuck the three needles behind her feet and then in front, and so got over it, and when she was on the other side put them carefully away.

Then she reached the three cutting swords and got on her plow wheel and rolled over them. At last she came to a great lake, and, when she had crossed that, arrived at a beautiful castle. She went in and gave herself out as a servant, a poor maid who would gladly be engaged. But she knew that the Prince whom she had freed from the iron stove in the great wood was in the castle. So she was taken on as a kitchen maid for very small wages. Now, the Prince was about to marry another princess, for he thought she was dead long ago.

In the evening, when she had washed up and was ready, she felt in her pocket and found the three nuts which the old toad had given her. She cracked one and was going to eat the kernel, when behold! there was a beautiful royal dress inside it. When the bride heard of this she came and begged for the dress and wanted to buy it, saying that it was not a dress for a serving maid. Then she said she would not sell it unless she was granted one favor—namely, to sleep by the Prince's door. The bride granted her this, because the dress was so beautiful and she had so few like it. When it was evening she said to her bridegroom: "That stupid maid wants to sleep by your door."

"If you are contented, I am," he said. But she gave him a glass of wine in which she had poured a sleeping draught. Then they both went to their room, but he slept so soundly that she could not wake him. The maid wept all night long and said: "I freed you in the wildwood out of the iron stove. I have sought you and have crossed a glassy mountain, three sharp swords, and a great lake before I found you, and will you not hear me now?" The servants outside heard how she cried the whole night, and they told their master in the morning.

When she had washed up the next evening she bit the second nut, and there was a still more beautiful dress inside. When the bride saw it she wanted to buy it also. But the maid did not want money and asked that she should sleep again by the Prince's door. The bride, however, gave him a sleeping draught, and he slept so soundly that he heard nothing. But the kitchen maid wept the whole night long and said: "I have freed you in a wood and from an iron stove; I sought you and have crossed a glassy mountain, three sharp swords, and a great lake to find you, and now you will not hear me!" The servants outside heard how she cried the whole night, and in the morning they told their master. And when she had washed up on the third night she bit the third nut, and there was a still more beautiful dress inside that was made of pure gold. When the bride saw it she wanted to have it, but the maid would only give it her on condition that she should sleep for the third time by the Prince's door. But the Prince took care not to drink the sleeping draught. When she began to weep and to say, "Dearest sweetheart, I freed you in the horrible wildwood and from an iron stove," he jumped up and said: "Thou art right. Thou art mine and I am thine." Though it was still night, he got into a carriage with her, and they took the false bride's clothes away, so that she could not follow them. When they came to the great lake they rowed across, and when they reached the three sharp swords they sat on the plow wheel, and on the glassy mountain they stuck the three needles in. So they arrived at last at the little old house, but when they stepped inside it turned into a large castle. The toads were all freed and were beautiful king's children running about for joy. There they were married, and they remained in the castle, which was much larger than that of the Princess's father. But because the old man did not like being left alone they went and fetched him. So they had two kingdoms and lived in great wealth.

> "A mouse has run,
> My story's done."

1. Chart the action line of *The Iron Stove*. **2.** Does action depend on character? **3.** Discover the patterns of three. **4.** Compare the quest cycle of this story with the quest cycle of *Psyche*.

COLLECTORS OF FAIRY TALES AND FOLK TALES: If you have to thank anyone for keeping the folk tales and fairy tales alive, you may turn to the Grimm brothers and to Charles Perrault. The Grimm brothers collected the folk tales of Germany. These two scholars went from village to village listening and recording the tales told by grandmothers and grandfathers around the kitchen fire. They never thought that these tales, which they called *Märchen* or *household* tales, would become popular with children all over the world.

In France, Charles Perrault collected folk and fairy tales. He also wrote his own fairy tales. Among these are two of the loveliest fairy tales—*Cinderella* and *The Sleeping Beauty in the Wood*.

There is another man who shares honors with the Grimm brothers and Charles Perrault. The children of Denmark know him as *our storyteller*. You know him as Hans Christian Andersen. Reading his tales, you will make a discovery. There is the romantic tale, and yet there is something more. Some of his tales seem to be making fun of someone or something. *The Emperor's New Clothes* is amusing for that reason. Everyone laughs at one man's vanity and all men's stupidity. You will find too that some of his tales do not end happily. At first it is a shock, but then you remember that Andersen did not merely record the tales of the folk as he heard them. He revised and in some cases wrote his own tales on folk motifs.

Read Andersen's *The Constant Tin-Soldier.*

THE CONSTANT TIN-SOLDIER

There were once five-and-twenty Tin-soldiers, all brothers, for they had all been made out of one old tin-spoon. They carried muskets in their arms, and held themselves very upright, and their uniforms were red and blue—very gay indeed. The first word that they heard in this world, when the lid was taken off the box wherein they lay, was, "Tin-soldiers!" It was a little boy who made this exclamation, clapping his hands at the same time. They had been given to him because it was his birth-day, and he now set them out on the table. The soldiers resembled each other to a hair; one only was rather different from the rest; he had but one leg, for he had been made last, when there was not quite tin enough left; however, he stood as firmly upon his one leg as the others did upon their two. And this identical Tin-soldier it is whose fortunes seem to us worthy of record.

On the table where the Tin-soldiers were set out were several other playthings, but the most charming of them all was a pretty pasteboard castle. Through its little windows one could look into the rooms. In front of the castle stood some tiny trees, clustering round a little mirror intended to represent a lake, and waxen swans swam in the lake, and were reflected on its surface. All this was very pretty; but prettiest of all was a little damsel standing in the open doorway of the castle. She, too, was cut out of pasteboard; but she had on a frock of the clearest muslin, a little sky-blue riband was flung across her shoulders like a scarf, and in the midst of this scarf was set a bright gold wing. The little lady stretched out both her arms, for she was a dancer, and raised one of her legs so high in the air that the Tin-soldier could not find it, and fancied that she had, like him, only one leg.

"That would be just the wife for me," thought he; "but, then, she is of rather too high rank, she lives in a castle. I have only a box; besides, there are all our five-and-twenty men in it, it is no place for her! However, there will be no harm in my making acquaintance with her." And so he stationed himself behind a snuff box that stood on the table; from this place he had a full view of the delicate little lady, who still remained standing on one leg, yet without losing her balance.

When evening came, all the other Tin-soldiers were put away into the box, and the people of the house went to bed. The play-things now began to play in their turn; they pretended to visit, to fight battles, and give balls. The Tin-soldiers rattled in the box, for they wanted to play too, but the lid would not come off. The nut-crackers cut capers, and the slate-pencil played at commerce on the slate; there was such a racket that the canary-bird waked up, and began to talk too; but he always talked in verse. The only two who did not move from their places were the Tin-soldier and the little dancer; she constantly remained in her graceful position, standing on the point of her foot, with outstretched arms; and as for him, he stood just as firmly on his one leg, never for one moment turning his eyes away from her.

Twelve o'clock struck—crash! open sprang the lid of the snuff-box; but there was no snuff inside it; no, out jumped a little black Conjuror; in fact, it was a Jack-in-the-box.

"Tin-soldier!" said the Conjuror, "wilt thou keep thine eyes to thyself?"

But the Tin-soldier pretended not to hear.

"Well, only wait till to-morrow!" quoth the Conjuror.

When the morrow had come, and the children were out of bed, the Tin-soldier was placed on the window-ledge, and, whether the Conjuror or the wind occasioned it, all at once the window flew open, and out fell the Tin-soldier, head foremost, from the third story to the ground. A dreadful fall was that! his one leg turned over and over in the air, and at last he rested, poised on his soldier's cap, with his bayonet between the paving-stones.

The maid-servant and the little boy immediately came down to look for him; but although they were nearly trod on him, they could not see him. If the Tin-soldier had but called out, "Here I am!" they might easily have found him; but he thought it would not be becoming for him to cry out, as he was in uniform.

It now began to rain; every drop fell heavier than the last; there was a regular shower. When it was over, two boys came by.

"Look," said one, "here is a Tin-soldier! he shall have a sail for once in his life."

So they made a boat out of an old newspaper, put the Tin-soldier into it, and away he sailed down the gutter, both the boys running along by the side and clapping their hands. The paper-boat rocked to and fro, and every now and then veered round so quickly that the Tin-soldier became quite giddy; still he moved not a muscle, looked straight before him, and held his bayonet tightly clasped.

All at once the boat sailed under a long gutter-board; he found it as dark here as at home in his own box.

"Where shall I get to next?" thought he; "yes, to be sure, it is all that Conjuror's doing! Ah, if the little maiden were but sailing with me in the boat, I would not care for its being twice as dark!"

Just then a great Water-Rat, that lived under the gutter-board, darted out.

"Have you a passport?" asked the Rat. "Where is your passport?"

But the Tin-soldier was silent, and held his weapon with a still firmer grasp. The boat sailed on, and the Rat followed. Oh! how furiously he showed his teeth, and cried out to sticks and straws, "Stop him, stop him! he has not paid the toll! he has not shown his passport!" But the stream grew stronger and stronger. The Tin-soldier could already catch a glimpse of the bright day-light before the boat came from under the tunnel, but at the same time he heard a roaring noise, at which the boldest heart might well have trembled. Only fancy! where the tunnel ended, the water of the gutter fell perpendicularly into a great canal; this was as dangerous for the Tin-soldier as sailing down a mighty waterfall would be for us.

He was now so close that he could no longer stand upright; the boat darted forwards, the poor Tin-soldier held himself as stiff and immovable as possible, no one could accuse him of having even blinked. The boat spun round and round, three, nay, four times, and was filled with water to the brim; it must sink. The Tin-soldier stood up to his neck in water, deeper and deeper sank the boat, softer and softer grew the paper; the water went over the soldier's head; he thought of the pretty little dancer, whom he should never see again, and these words rang in his ears:—

> "Wild adventure, mortal danger
> Be thy portion, valiant stranger!"

The paper now tore asunder, the Tin-soldier fell through the rent; but in the same moment he was swallowed up by a large fish.

Oh, how dark it was! worse even than under the gutter-board, and so narrow too!—but the Tin-soldier's resolution was as constant as ever; there he lay, at full length, shouldering his arms.

The fish turned and twisted about, and made the strangest movements! at last he became quite still; a flash of lightning, as it were, darted through him. The daylight shone brightly, and someone exclaimed, "Tin-soldier!" The fish had been caught, taken to the market, sold, and brought home into the kitchen, where the servant-girl was cutting him up with a large knife. She seized the Tin-soldier by the middle with two of her fingers, and took him into the parlour, where every one was eager to see the wonderful man who had travelled in the maw of a fish;—however, our little warrior was by no means proud. They set him on the table, and there—no, how could anything so extraordinary happen in this world!—the Tin-soldier was in the very same room in which he had been before; he saw the same children, the same playthings stood on the table, among them the beautiful castle with the pretty little dancing maiden, who was still standing upon one leg, whilst she held the other high in the air; she, too, was constant. It quite affected the Tin-soldier; he could have found it in his heart to weep tin-tears, but such weakness would have been unbecoming in a soldier. He looked at her, and she looked at him, but neither spoke a word.

And now one of the little boys took the Soldier and threw him without ceremony into the stove. He did not give any reason for so doing, but, no doubt, the Conjuror in the snuff box must have had a hand in it.

The Tin-soldier now stood in a blaze of red light; he felt extremely hot; whether this heat was the result of the actual fire, or of the flames of love within him, he knew not. He had entirely lost his color; whether this change had happened during his travels, or were the effect of strong emotion, I know not. He looked upon the little damsel, she looked upon him, and he felt that he was melting; but, constant as ever, he still stood shouldering his arms. A door opened, the wind seized the Dancer, and, like a sylph, she flew straightway into the stove, to the Tin-soldier; they both flamed up into a blaze—and were gone! The Soldier was melted to a hard lump, and when the maid took the ashes out the next day, she found his remains in the shape of a little tin-heart: of the Dancer there remained only the gold wing, and that was burnt black as a coal.

1. Pick out two things in this story that keep it in the realm of fantasy. 2. How does it differ from the other fairy tales you have read? 3. Does the fact that the main characters do not live happily ever after make it less a fairy tale? 4. Show what the fairy tale has in common with the fable. 5. Choose some interesting incident. Reshape it with magic and convert it into a patterned fairy tale. It may be in the manner of a romantic fairy tale or it may be a ridiculing fairy tale. 6. Listen to the Hans Christian Andersen records with Danny Kaye. Note especially this version of *The Emperor's New Clothes*. Does it retain the clever ridiculing of human nature that you find in

Andersen's original or is it just fun? Listen carefully to *The Ugly Duckling*. Work out the story pattern.

Stories that Once Were True—Legends

Legends are stories told over and over as if they really were true. There may have been some small core of truth in these stories when they were first told, but with each retelling they seem to have moved farther away from it. The time came when they were not historical at all. Then they were legends.

There are legends among all people. The Greeks and Trojans have legends of their heroes like Hector and Achilles. The Anglo-Saxons have legends of Beowulf; the Britons, of Arthur and his knights. The Christian Middle Ages have their legendary lives of saints, like the story of St. Christopher, which you will read here.

One of the many legends that show Arthur as a great man is the account of his miraculous sword.

HOW ARTHUR GETS HIS SWORD
FROM THE LADY OF THE LAKE

So Arthur and Merlin rode till they came to a lake, the which was a fair water and broad, and in the midst of the lake Arthur was ware of an arm clothed in white samite, that held a fair sword in that hand.

Lo! said Merlin, yonder is that sword. With that they saw a damsel going upon the lake.

What damsel is that? said Arthur.

That is the Lady of the Lake, said Merlin; and within that lake is a rock, and therein is as fair a place as any on earth, and richly beseen; and this damsel will come to you anon, and then speak ye fair to her that she will give you that sword. Anon withal came the damsel unto Arthur, and saluted him, and he her again.

Damsel, said Arthur, what sword is that, that yonder the arm holdeth above the water? I would it were mine, for I have no sword.

Sir Arthur, king, said the damsel, that sword is mine, and if ye will give me a gift when I ask it you, ye shall have it.

By my faith, said Arthur, I will give you what gift ye will ask.

Well! said the damsel, go ye into yonder barge, and row yourself to the sword, and take it and the scabbard with you, and I will ask my gift when I see my time. So Sir Arthur and Merlin alighted and tied their horses to two trees, and so they went into the ship, and when they came to the sword that the hand held, Sir Arthur took it up by the handles, and took it with him, and the arm and the hand went under the water. And so they came unto the land and rode forth.

Then Sir Arthur looked on the sword, and liked it passing well.

Whether liketh you better, said Merlin, the sword or the scabbard?

Me liketh better the sword, said Arthur.

Ye are more unwise, said Merlin, for the scabbard is worth ten of the sword, for whiles ye have the scabbard upon you, ye shall never lose no blood, be ye never so sore wounded; therefore keep well the scabbard always with you. So they came unto Carleon, whereof his knights were passing glad. And when they heard of his adventures, they marveled that he would jeopard his person so, alone. But all men of worship said it was merry to be under such a chieftain, that would put his person in adventure as other poor knights did.

1. Have you read the other legend of Excalibur, in which Arthur draws the sword from a stone? Find this legend and tell

it to the class. **2.** What heroic qualities does this legend give Arthur? **3.** Who is Merlin? Find some information on him in the library. **4.** Is there a mixture of the natural and the supernatural in this legend? Give some examples of this kind of mixing. **5.** Is this a well structured story with an initiating incident, development, and point? Show how the incidents shape the story. **6.** Why do we call this story a legend?

Some stories of saints are what we call apocryphal; that is, they do not have any real historical basis. *The Legend of Saint Christopher, Breaker of Men* is this kind of saint's life.

The Legend
of St. Christopher,
Breaker of Men

C. C. MARTINDALE, S.J.

It was while Cratylus was at school that he got his nickname, Breaker of Men. This was not because he was a bully, or brutal, or hurt for the pleasure of hurting. No doubt he had his fights, a good many of them; and always conquered in the sense that he was never frightened however big his enemy might be, and never gave in simply because he was hard hit. (And to tell the truth it was not long before everyone was quite content to do without fighting Cratylus.) But it was because the old schoolmaster had traveled a little, and was ready to teach Greek, even, to those whose parents would let them learn; and the ILIAD so fascinated Cratylus that Homer became the fashion.

How Cratylus adored Achilles! Achilles the man-breaker, the lion-souled! He could see him distinctly in imagination, upon the famous day when, raging at the death of Patroclus, the hero came out from his tent, armorless, just as he was, glorious like a sun. He could picture him standing there, settling himself, legs well apart, back hollow, hand to mouth, and then shouting! . . . And, at that shout, the despicable Trojans scuttling like so many wretched hares! He looked a young Achilles himself that day, though his hair was dark, not yellow, as he stood reading out the Homer; his boy's white cloak, wrapped over his shirt, could not hide how splendidly he was built, how easily and firmly he stood: as he unrolled and rolled the papyrus, you could see the muscles running clearly up and down his arm. The class saw it, and kicked applause with their heels against the benches. "Rhexénor! Rhexénor!" they murmured; "Breaker of Men!"

The old schoolmaster sighed. He was a Christian; and so, in name at least, was Cratylus. But father and mother were dead; and grandmother and schoolmaster and ignorant parish priest had no slightest influence over him. No doubt he had heard of God and Christ and devil; but life was so full of splendid and vigorous things to do, of pleasant things to look at and listen to, that he never troubled his head about what you could neither see nor hear. Not that he practised evil: sheer life and its opportunities of successful effort were quite enough for him.

People were inclined to wonder, at first, why Cratylus apprenticed himself to the larger of the two village smithies, instead of going soldiering at once, as he always said he meant to do. Possibly it was because he felt he was not wholly king here yet —in this little Armenian hamlet that must first be subdued before he went for larger fields. And certainly he succeeded: he became, as was inevitable, unlimitedly popular on account of his strength, his immense good humor, and his good looks. He succeeded, too, in another way. Not only in athletics and in the smithy, nothing could conquer him, but *people* too seemed to become useless when he was there; he could afford to neglect them; they could just pack up and go. Folks guessed this when the smaller smithy was closed. There was no call in the village for two smiths, when Cratylus worked for one of them. And the poor old craftsman, grown gray in Zandruanda, had, quite inevitably, to seek new trade elsewhere. Cratylus was sorry; but could he help it? Was he to work badly for a poorer workman's sake? Clearly not. The Breaker of Men became truer to his name: he set definitely before himself these two principles—"I will only serve a master who is stronger than myself"; and, "I will serve no one whom I shall see afraid." Given this resolve, his days in Zandruanda were numbered: for as to strength, in the whole countryside none equalled him: as to fear, he saw, one day, his master panic-stricken.

It was when the great bull broke loose, and plunged bellowing down the narrow street, scattering the inhabitants like sheep. The smith, too, took to his heels; but Cratylus, as the bull thundered towards him, was aware only of a sudden sheet of flame, which seemed to flood his thighs and sides and neck, and of the uncontrollable impulse which flung him at the brute, and which drove his hands at its horns. He twisted its huge head suddenly down and sideways, forcing the beast's body of its own tremendous impetus to hurtle forward, snapping the spine. The bull died with a roar, and over it stood Cratylus, laughing. It was unbelievable; a feat of giants, of Titans! The story grew; details were added, or modified; it became a myth. The bull, people told, had been colossal in size and weight; had snorted fire; had had hoofs of iron; Cratylus with one blow had felled him; or had swung him aloft like a puppy and dashed him to the ground. But to the hero of all this, one only fact stood out. The smith had fled; his master was a coward. "I have had enough of this," said Cratylus. "Next chance I get, I go."

That very evening the chance came.

A battalion of soldiers marched through the village, at their head a Roman centurion. For a helmet-buckle to be mended, they made for the forge; and there, framed in the doorway, limbs crimson in the firelight, stood Cratylus, swinging his great hammer. In the strong glow, the splendid muscles of chest and shoulders and rhythmically swinging arms and planted legs showed indomitable.

"Gods! what a man for the War-god!" shouted the centurion. "Will you come with us, lad? Will you join us?"

For answer, Cratylus flung down his hammer.

"I've done with *that!*" said he.

And so that was the end of his boyhood and life at Zandru-anda; for in spite of his old grandmother's prayers, he left next day with the centurion. "Stay with me, dear lad," the old woman had asked, "and take care of me. There are only a very few months left. Else I shall be all alone. I have no one at all but you."

"Cheer up, old mother," he had cried. "Abroad I shall get gold in quantities, and you shall have it, and instead of this hut you shall have a stone house, and live like a queen for the rest of your days. If I stay here what can I do for you?"

Suddenly the air of Zandruanda had seemed to have grown suffocating; village life was flat—meaningless—in fact, no life at all. How had he stood it for so long?

"I shall die in this home, my darling," said the old woman. "But go, if go you must; and Jesus be your strength."

With a laugh and a parting cheer Cratylus rode off, helmeted and sworded already; all Armenia, with its mountains, lay before him, and the mysterious East beyond; or Thessaly, perhaps, where Achilles came from; and eternal Rome, even, where the Emperor lived!

He rode off; and it was incredible how few of the inhabitants, who all of them turned out to wave their hero a farewell, were really sorry that he went.

Only, in her poor plaster cabin, the old woman who loved him wept bitterly; and while she wept, and afterwards, prayed earnestly for Cratylus.

> And make me feel it was my sin,
> As though no other sin there were,
> That was to Him who bore the world
> A load that He could scarcely bear.

During the next few years Cratylus traveled far, seeing many lands, serving many masters, all of whom, one after the other, proved weaker than himself, or showed themselves to be afraid. Then Cratylus would leave them, feeling himself humiliated by their weakness; and in this way very soon there was no country nor prince for whom he had not a certain contempt; love for his own home (if it had ever really existed) had died out, long ago, when with such fatal ease he had made himself its lord. He passed through that home, however, when he set out at last on his eastward journey. Rome he had seen, and had scorned that degenerate Empire. Of what use to him were its high posts, which money bought,—which were mere soft sinecures for the idle noble who should win them? Thessaly, rich plain ringed with high mountains, had long ago forgotten Achilles, and even its famous breed of horses was effete. So he set his face towards the East: who knew what fate awaited him in Bactria, in Sogdiana, or India itself? And, as he crossed Armenia, he passed through Zandruanda. It was long before he even recognized its neighborhood, so shrunken had it all become to his man's eyes; so decrepit, unpopulated, seemed the village. It was his birthplace, a flatterer reminded him. Making an effort, he recalled those old boyhood days. How had he existed, he asked himself, in that cramped life? Wondering thus, he forgot to look for the forge; and he could not identify the cottage where his old grandmother had lived three lonely months, upon the neighbors' alms, after his departure. Indeed, he wholly forgot her too, and forgot to ask to see her grave. Nor, indeed, could he have seen it (had he found a guide who could remember where it was), so overgrown was it with nettles.

During these twenty years his strength had increased, at first, and had then grown set; his body had become hard and rugged, and its beauty diminished. The expression of his face changed only towards anger or contempt, sometimes to disgust, when the stale days of reaction after some marked triumph had to be lived through. He had had enough triumphs now to find the sweetness gone even from them; but tasteless indeed were the hours when no effort was being made, no hard enterprise pursued. The old popularity was long ago departed. He loved no one, and was hated by many, whom, in his serenely unconscious power, he had trampled out of existence. His life had been more than once attempted, but he had always broken his man.

At last, on the furthest limit of the mysterious East, he thought he had found his heart's desire. The King there lived in a high fortress, all of a piece, it seemed, with the naked jumble of iron-colored crags on which it stood, so sheer did the precipice sweep upward into walls, so tiny the windows which pierced square-topped towers rising abruptly like the broken peaks of that high mountain. Only from the north could the fortress be approached; and the winding causeway was throughout commanded by smooth, black bastions and guarded battlements. On east and south and west an immense view stretched, range upon range of mountains, jagged as the teeth of saws, fainter and fainter, one behind the other, down to the horizon.

Cratylus became the King's right-hand man; winning all but the supreme power, which was vigorously guarded by the tyrant. In his square, stone room (at the top of a corner tower, and absolutely bare save for a pile of fleeces for a bed, a large stone pitcher of water, and racks of armor) Cratylus thought out the plans which should reduce into an even more absolute obedience the vast kingdom; and wholly without ruth or pity did the King have them carried out. On embassies, Cratylus could cow the haughtiest of foreign princes into submission. His rule seemed like the very mountains, made of iron and stone.

And yet this, too, had its finishing.

With an almost unreasoning severity, as it seemed, the King waged war against the complicated witchcrafts and magic rites which he knew existed among his people. Even to that far country Christianity had, in perverted forms, penetrated; and Devil-worship and hideous travesties of the sacrament were mingled with the abominable practices of ancient pagan superstitions.

One evening the King and Cratylus and some half-dozen men-at-arms were at supper in the great hall. Through the high row of westward windows the setting sun flamed in, making great red-hot squares of light on the wall opposite and leaving the high vault dark. Only over the King an oil lamp spluttered, and in the middle of the hall stood a high brazier. Suddenly the door crashed open. A body of soldiers, evidently guarding a prisoner in their midst, burst in; they rushed up to the dais, dragging the wretched creature with them, and a storm of execration arose. At last it could be seen that they held in their grasp a very old woman. She was a magician, they cried. Only yesterday, on being refused alms by a poor woman with a baby at her breast, she had taken the child in her arms and dandled it, and kissed it, and that very night it had fallen into convulsions, and today it was dead. They had brought her to the King: let him punish her—make an example of her!

Furious at being defied by an old woman, the King demanded nothing more. The old crone remained silent, but he would ask no questions, seek no defense.

"To the brazier with her!" he shouted. "Let us see whether she will like the kiss of coal! Let us see whether she, too, has blood that fire can drink!"

Silence for a moment, and then the sudden crackle of burning flesh, as a red coal, held in tongs, was pressed upon the old woman's lips. And then a shriek; and then, from that flayed mouth, a stream of blasphemy.

"Curse you," she screamed; "the devil curse you—may the devil curse you! He that has made of the world a pestilence, curse you body and soul, flesh and brain and soul for the hurt you are doing me. . . ."

And as she shrieked on the devil she shriveled suddenly and fell. The frame of the very old cannot resist much agony; and as the soldiers, with iron pincers, put coal after coal to her, she died.

They carried her away, and there was silence again.

The King sat, bent completely double, his face on his knees, his hands clasping his head. But his fingers, Cratylus saw, glistened with sweat, and his hair was matted.

Cratylus leaned over him.

"Gods!" he cried. "Has she bewitched you too? Are you dying? Lift your face."

The King lifted a face pale and full of shadows. His eyes moved restlessly with a hunted look, and his lips could not stay still.

Cratylus knew that look. It was terror.

"Are you afraid?" he asked, incredulous.

"Of the devil!" said the King. "She cursed me by the devil! It has been the terror of my life. O, have mercy upon me! The whole world is his, and she his favorite. . . . What will the devil do to me?"

Without a word Cratylus left the hall, and the King sank completely to the floor, where he lay shuddering violently and sobbing.

Alone in his tower-chamber, Cratylus cursed his fate. Another failure, or futile triumph! Another coward! Another of these mighty potentates trembling and aghast when *he* stayed wholly fearless. How he despised them all, these high monarchs of the earth, of whom he had just seen the highest fall to tears and sweat at the curse of an old woman! He looked out over the sea of tumbled mountains and valleys, all gloom and glow alternately beneath a sky still red-hot with sunset, but darkening rapidly. The immense outlook lashed his despondency. Oh to meet the One who could really rule all that! Who should fear nothing in it—know no law but his own sovereign will! how Cratylus would fall down and adore him! And the kingdoms of the world and the glory of them rolled out into a great vision before him, there in the conflagration of the sunset so soon to sink to ashes. To meet with their real master! to serve him, whomsoever he might be, even were he that devil at thought of whom the King had trembled.

The sun dipped, and the last mountain blackened. An extraordinary silence grew rapidly, and suddenly Cratylus was aware of the silence. Not a sound within the castle, or in its courts; not a noise of dog that barked, nor even the whirr of beetle's wing or bat's; nor even the sigh of the wind. He sat there numbed, and the silence grew in the darkness, all round him, and within him.

Then, in the black and horrible stillness, he knew distinctly that he was not alone. There was a presence in the room, close to him. Though it had now grown absolutely dark, surer was he than if his eyes had seen it, that a dreadful thing was there; a *person,* someone who was as vividly aware of him as he was of his awful visitor, whose will was compelling his own, and forcing him to submission. It made him fall on his knees; it made him listen as if for words, and be ready for an extraordinary conversation. But a bewilderingly contradictory impression mingled with all this: he felt that this appalling Force would prove to be—could he really grasp it, get at its essence—something weak. And for a moment he actually saw it, in the dense gloom, a white and sickly face, smiling with foolish lips into his eyes. An impression of utter corruption came upon him; the extreme of loathsomeness, a very filth of rottenness, was here: and yet it had its fascination; it commanded him; he felt, as he crouched, face on the stones, as if his whole self was streaming out of his keeping into it; and, as he gave himself, through and through, over and over, into its power, he knew for certain *that this was the devil, the Prince of Evil whom he had accepted for his master;* and he felt on his cheek as it were a sickening kiss, and in the very roots of his heart a heavy chain that bound him, for all time, to sin. He then consented.

The next few years in the life of Cratylus were too horrible for us to speak much of. He did not leave the King, as of course he had resolved on doing; yet it was not as the King's servant that he remained. For the supreme authority which, in the old days, had remained in the monarch's hands, now passed over, in all but the barest theory, to Cratylus. For never before had strength, both of body and of will-power, seemed so extraordinary in the Armenian; though this was not really wonderful, since so tightly was he bound to his new master that all that master's power and will seemed to have passed into him, and what the devil willed, Cratylus could do, nay *must* do. And the panic which the King had always felt for the Evil one, he now felt in regard to Cratylus, so completely did he identify (and rightly) master and man.

And so for hideous sin and crime there never had been such a time as that. Never so many unjust wars that drenched the country in the blood of the fallen and the tears of the survivors. Never such oppression of the poor, bringing sweat and sickness and starvation to the people, and sleepless nights to the rich who lived in agonies of fear concerning the gold they had got, and agonies of greed for gains still to be extorted. Never such false judgments in the courts, widow and orphan perishing before unjust judges. Never such mad and brutal pleasures, drunkenness and sin rotting men's brains and limbs after they had drugged the soul to death. And in this matter of souls was it that Cratylus seemed another man, and did truly devil's work. Hitherto he had been content to quell men's bodies; to break into an external obedience the men and women who resisted him. Of interior submission he had recked not at all. Now it was the whole man, body and soul, that he longed to smash; soul above all, since it was there that Christian faith, especially, established citadels which his terrorizing had failed to carry. Grind men's bodies as he would to powder, there had been impregnable fortresses of patience, and forgiveness, and purity left intact. Now by most loathsome trickeries and cajoleries (since he made use of arts to which he never, before, would have stooped) no less than by sheer cruelties he sought his ends, and never rested till everywhere he had lit the fires of fury and vengeance in the hearts of young men; crushed maidens under shame more dreadful than any death; driven the aged to despair. Hell's kingdom filled fast.

And all this while there kept growing within him a double mood. He hated more and more the abominable master whom he served, and whom he felt always at his side, prompting, suggesting, congratulating. He loathed that master, and he loathed himself, feeling himself the slave, not merely the servant, of that tyrant-force.

And yet that it was master, and himself a slave, he never doubted for a moment. In fact he saw, with horror, that in no way could he ever break, even should he wish it, from that slavery. But to wish to break away was just what he could not do: "He is too strong for me," he said in despair. "The Devil is my master for always; I shall go on doing his work for always. *It is too strong for me: I cannot help myself.*"

- And so at the time of his greatest worldly strength, Cratylus felt himself most weak; when most powerful for evil, he was most a slave; everywhere he did devil's work; everywhere *it was too strong for him.*

And yet the devil was not strongest of all.

There was a hermit who lived some leagues away beside a river, and, by holding up his lantern at night, showed the ford to travelers. Cratylus would make an end of that; nothing of good was too trivial for him to prevent; nothing too high for him to fear. So that lantern, he determined, should be extinguished; that little act of charity suppressed. And as for the old saint himself, might not he too be conquered, his high virtue spoiled?

He set out for the river, which he could see winding in the valley, suddenly broad after sprouting from the mountains through a chasm only a few feet wide. He mused on how he should approach the hermit, and as he mused, a shrinking made itself felt within him, a reluctance to go at all. He wrestled against it, and dragged his feet along the path, exhausted more and more every moment, struggling as in a nightmare.

Suddenly he realized that it was the masterful presence that was near him; that was tugging at him to come back . . . must he not obey? And then once more he was conscious, not only of its power but of that bewildering *weakness* he had guessed at before. And now—could it be?—it was cowering, shuddering backwards because of *fear!* Cratylus set his teeth. He would go forward. He planted his feet and bowed his body towards the hermit's hut, only a yard or two away, now. The huge power, like great arms about his waist, strained at him, tearing him backwards. Never had he experienced so vigorous a wrestle. Whence came his power to resist?

Suddenly the hermit appeared at the door, holding up a large wooden Cross.

The hermit advanced a step.

"Back, Satan!" he said. "In this sign I conquer."

Abruptly, as though a chain had snapped, Cratylus was loosed. He fell violently forward at the foot of the Cross, his head striking a stone. He remained for a space unconscious.

When he revived he was lying on a pile of ferns, and the hermit was bathing his forehead.

Thoroughly ashamed of this position, Cratylus sat up, but fell back dizzy.

"What has happened?" said he.

"You are a free man," answered the hermit. "Your master left you."

Cratylus began to remember.

"He was afraid of the Cross," went on the other. "He was not so strong as the Cross."

Cratylus recalled everything—the years of slavery, the sudden snapping of the chain, the Cross high over him as he fell.

"Henceforward," said he in a strong voice, "I will be the servant of the Cross."

Later, as his dazedness passed away, he began to make his plans.

"I will fight, father," he began. "I am strong. I will fight the King, and upset his wicked judges, and break the prisons, and rebuild all I have destroyed."

The hermit laughed quietly.

"All that may come," said he. "You have other work to do first."

Cratylus had a troubled recollection that pious Christians prayed and fasted and scourged themselves even. . . .

"Must I pray, father?" he asked.

"You shall pray in good time," said the old man, still smiling. "For the present, work; and I will pray."

"Tell me what to do, father," said the Breaker of Men, "and I will do it."

"It is not hard," said the other. "You will live with me, and you shall carry on your shoulders all travelers who wish to cross the ford. That shall be your work."

And Cratylus labored long at this simple task, making himself servant of the wayfarers who came to the river. It was a strange career, full of humiliations wholly unexpected—as when those whom of old he had commanded, or evicted from their homes, or in any other way oppressed, now came to speak insolently to him, and jeer at him, or kick him as he carried them. For the rumor had spread that Cratylus had gone crazed; that the blow on his head had made a fool of him; and in proportion as he had been hated, so was he now contemned. Even this was not so painful to him as the terror shown by many—women especially and children—who did not understand the change. They could realize nothing but that here was their persecutor of yore—what cruelty, subtle and refined, was he not planning that he was fain to carry them over rivers? What diabolical craft was this? And they fled from him.

Cratylus in time ceased to wax furious at the insults, though never to suffer at the fear the women and children showed when they saw him. Only in both cases he repeated to himself, "For Thee, Crucified," and went on with his labor. That was his only prayer. He still felt bewildered, not least by the strangeness of his appointed task. He knew nothing of Christ, but did what he was told was His work, and gradually his heart was changed.

In the idle spaces when no travelers passed, he would watch the hermit praying, and thus became familiar with long passages of the psalms and of the Church's liturgy; at other times he explored the mountains, which fell, just there, in an immense black precipice, sheer to the plain where the river flowed. The water itself he tracked, once, into its ravine. This chasm was thought to be a gate to hell, and the country folk never dared to approach it. Cratylus, who was determined now to fear not even the devil, waded against the mighty current into the very heart of the mountain, and there, clambering over boulders, he could see in the dim light which filtered from the tiny strip of sky, far above, that the water gushed out, in tremendous force, from beneath the base of a kind of rock funnel in which the fissure terminated. This huge volume of water, forced upwards, it was clear, by some subterranean stream, welled up at first silent and black like sliding ebony; then, flinging itself against the narrow walls of the chasm, it foamed, booming through the echoing rocks, until it suddenly spread itself out over the pebbly ford.

In the spring the work was made infinitely harder by the melting snows and sudden storms, which sent the river up in great floods. One night Cratylus, having labored all day against the swollen current, was heavily asleep in the hut when he felt himself shaken briskly by the shoulder. He looked up and saw at his side the hermit, with a strangely glad look upon his face.

"Up," said the hermit, "you are being called."

Cratylus could not believe it. An appalling storm was raging, with thunder and wind and torrential rain. The ford would be impassable, and who could be abroad on such a night?

"Up," repeated the old man, a little sternly, "to the work!"

Cratylus arose and quitted the house. The wind tore the door from his hand and crashed it shut behind him. The very footpath leading down to the river had become a rivulet of rain. Over the shingly ford the river escaped, hissing and rushing with a curiously shrill sound; but in the chasm, as it flung itself violently from side to side in the blackness, it sent up the most terrible bellowing, even louder than the thunder.

In spite of thunder, though, and stream, Cratylus heard a wailing voice, inexpressibly sad and fearful, calling for help.

"Carry me across!" it cried. "Help me! Fetch me across."

There was a sudden sheet of dazzling lightning in which every detail of the further bank showed clear in black and white. And on it stood a little boy, very thin and weak looking; he was dressed only in a shirt, and his hair and linen were streaming with the rain. And his hands were clasped tight to his breast as he stooped a little and cried to be fetched across.

Cratylus, without waiting to wonder at this extraordinary spectacle, plunged into the river and was soon at the other side.

"Right!" shouted Cratylus. "Where are you?"

In the next flash he saw the little boy. He was still standing by the brink of the water, soaked and shivering, but silent now.

"Right!" cried Cratylus again, shocked at the boy's thinness. "We shall be across in no time, and there's a fire waiting for you. Up with you! Arms round my neck tight; don't be afraid of hurting me. Good."

The boy, with astonishing agility, climbed on to the strong man's shoulder and sat there with one hand round his neck. He was so light that Cratylus scarcely knew when he was up.

"Now for it," he said. "Sit tight."

And he turned and went down into the stream.

The storm had not ceased, and the flood, flung violently forward from the bellowing chasm, swept even higher than before about his knees; the cold of the rain, after the warm hut, seemed to freeze his blood. Almost at once he stumbled, and only saved himself from slipping back by bending double over his huge staff. To raise himself required effort; his knees grew weak, and his shoulders bowed beneath the impact of the wind, of the weight of which he had now grown all too sensible. For as he drew himself once more upright he seemed crushed; a tremendous strain made itself felt all through him as he went forward, step by painful step. And though the storm howled in the ravine, and the waters roared and hissed loud as ever, all that suddenly seemed to be happening at an immense distance; within himself he was immediately conscious only of grinding exhaustion and intolerable fatigue. Then, in that silence of his soul he seemed to be aware of all the whole world. The storm and river and ravine had grown so unimportant, because he seemed to feel at one and the same time, all the masses of all the mountains of that land, ponderous piles of rock, titanic boulders beating against the sky—all the huge oceans that swung terrifically against its coasts, and against the coasts of all the lands he had ever traveled through—and in a moment he had, as it were, a vision of the whole gigantic Earth, the overwhelming globe of seas and islands and continents, and all looming down on him, all posed upon his shoulders. And more than that: infinite tracts of clouds swathed that hugeness; and through these clouds other huge worlds swung round or hung, infinitely vast, and all to be held by him. For, unless he supported it, what should prevent its ruin? On whom else did it depend, all that universe of matter and of motion? Not on that Enemy whom he had served! He was the destroyer, the universal antagonist! Not on the paltry race of humans, so pitiably weak, whom he himself had crushed and broken like gnats! Satan hated that universe; men were mere phantoms in it. It rested on *his* shoulders; could *he* uphold it? And he saw himself, stronger than his fellow men, no doubt; yet, compared to that sum of all things now massed upon him, he too was weak like a ghost or dream. What was the world to do? What could *he* do? "O God Almighty," he panted, "have mercy on me."

He moved a few steps easily. Then a second time the terrific weight pressed down on his shoulders, and he moved through the water, crouching almost double. And this time an added horror broke him. For in the vast globe of all the universe he saw that there was *sin*. The pitiable race of human people, of which he was one—(he saw that, now; he was just one of many, equally responsible, unprivileged—nay, more responsible in that he was stronger than his fellows, though certainly not greater just because of that)—this weak race rose up, and in the face of the Power which kept them and their whole world in being, declared for their own will and supremacy. Cratylus stood in a sudden panic. Surely the Power, in scorn of all that insolence, would let go of the world; would simply let the universe, with the miserable revolutionaries in it, roll back into the nothingness whence it originally had come? And he seemed to feel the world left more and more to himself to bear; felt, too, more and more his own incredible dependence on that great Power; realized what had been *his* share in that appalling arrogance and revolt. "O God, most Merciful," he gasped, "be merciful to me, a sinner."

The bank was in sight already, but even as he pressed forward to cross the remaining water, there came down upon his bowed shoulders a new and wholly unconquerable load. Raised upon that sinful world, which he was struggling to carry, was a Cross, and on the Cross was lifted all the sin and all the sorrow of that world from its beginning to its distant end. It was all summed up in that hanging figure, and Cratylus felt it. And with it the pressure of the infinite Love which had brought the Son of God so to take upon himself that sin, and by that sorrow to atone for it. And beneath the triple burden of his new humility and repentance and love, Cratylus at last fell forward, crying as he fell, "I cannot bear it; Jesus, Thou knowest that I love Thee; save me, or I perish."

Cratylus fell, but found that his hands struck the further bank, and he was safe. The little boy slipped from his shoulder, and held out his hand. Cratylus took it, and stepped on to dry land, and looked into the Child's eyes. He knelt down, still looking, and then bowed till his face touched the ground. He had watched the wonderful change come over the Child's form and features, and, though he had never seen Him before, knew Him.

"I am Jesus," said the Child. "I am He through whom all the world was made and is preserved. In carrying Me, you carried the whole world. And I am He who, in My own body, carried your sins and all the sins of the world; and of their weight I suffered you to feel as it were the shadow. And now you know that it is I who carry you, and ever have carried, and ever shall."

"Lord," said Cratylus, speaking like a little child, "how was it, long ago, that I did not perish; that you did not, for my service of Satan and my oppression of your elect, long ago condemn me?"

"Because," answered the Child, "there never has been the time when you were not being rescued by the prayers of those whom you persecuted; of the very weak, like your old grandmother in the village; of your old schoolmaster; of all whom you strove to break; they were too strong for you; and in the end My heart obeyed them, and I have saved you."

"Lord," said the Breaker of Men, "may I be your servant?"

"You shall be my friend," answered Jesus; "and your new name shall be Christopher; for you have carried Christ on your shoulder, and henceforward you shall always carry Him in your heart."

When the hermit came down to the river at sunrise, he found Christopher still kneeling, and the glorious light, now that the storm was over, made a halo all about him.

1. Before Christopher served God, what was his name? **2.** What does Cratylus mean? **3.** What are the characteristics of Cratylus? **4.** Why does Cratylus like Achilles? **5.** Do you know what part Achilles had in the Trojan War? **6.** Who was Patroclus? **7.** In how many ways is Cratylus a breaker of men? List them. **8.** What is the turning point of the story? **9.** In what ways is this a very well-structured story? **10.** Why is this story called a legend? **11.** Why is it also called an apocryphal saint's life? **12.** Use your dictionary for this vocabulary:

despicable	forge	contempt	embassies	superstition
causeway	brazier	travesties		magician
potentates	cajoleries	bewitched	bewildering	vengeance

The Devil and Tom Walker is an example of a New England legend in which men deal with preternatural beings.

THE DEVIL AND TOM WALKER

WASHINGTON IRVING

A few miles from Boston in Massachusetts, there is a deep inlet, winding several miles into the interior of the country from Charles Bay, and terminating in a thickly wooded swamp or morass. On one side of this inlet is a beautiful dark grove; on the opposite side the land rises abruptly from the water's edge into a high ridge, on which grow a few scattered oaks of great age and immense size.

Under one of these gigantic trees, according to old stories, there was a great amount of treasure buried by Kidd the pirate. The inlet allowed a facility to bring the money in a boat secretly and at night to the very foot of the hill; the elevation of the place permitted a good lookout to be kept that no one was at hand; while the remarkable trees formed good landmarks by which the place might easily be found again. The old stories add, moreover, that the devil presided at the hiding of the money, and took it under his guardianship; but this, it is well known, he always does with buried treasure, particularly when it has been ill-gotten. Be that as it may, Kidd never returned to recover his wealth, being shortly after seized at Boston, sent out to England, and there hanged for a pirate.

About the year 1727, just at the time that earthquakes were prevalent in New England, and shook many tall sinners down upon their knees, there lived near this place a meager, miserly fellow, of the name of Tom Walker. He had a wife as miserly as himself; they were so miserly that they even conspired to cheat each other. Whatever the woman could lay hands on, she hid away; a hen could not cackle but she was on the alert to secure the new-laid egg. Her husband was continually prying about to detect her secret hoards, and many and fierce were the conflicts that took place about what ought to have been common property.

They lived in a forlorn looking house that stood alone, and had an air of starvation. A few straggling savin trees, emblems of sterlity, grew near it; no smoke ever curled from its chimney; no traveler stopped at its door. A miserable horse, whose ribs were as articulate as the bars of a gridiron, stalked about a field, where a thin carpet of moss, scarcely covering the ragged beds of pudding stone, tantalized and balked his hunger; and sometimes he would lean his head over the fence, look piteously at the passerby, and seem to petition deliverance from this land of famine.

The house and its inmates had altogether a bad name. Tom's wife was a tall termagant, fierce of temper, loud of tongue, and strong of arm. Her voice was often heard in wordy warfare with her husband; and his face sometimes showed signs that their conflicts were not confined to words. No one ventured, however, to interfere between them. The lonely wayfarer shrunk within himself at the horrid clamor and clapper-clawing, eyed the den of discord askance; and hurried on his way, rejoicing, if a bachelor, in his celibacy.

One day that Tom Walker had been to a distant part of the neighborhood, he took what he considered a short cut homeward, through the swamp. Like most short cuts, it was an ill-chosen route. The swamp was thickly grown with great gloomy pines and hemlocks, some of them ninety feet high, which made it dark at noonday and a retreat for all the owls of the neighborhood. It was full of pits and quagmires, partly covered with weeds and mosses, where the green surface often betrayed the traveler into a gulf of black, smothering mud; there were also dark and stagnant pools, the abodes of the tadpole, the bullfrog, and the water snake, where the trunks of pines and hemlocks lay half-drowned, half-rotting, looking like alligators sleeping in the mire.

Tom had long been picking his way cautiously through this treacherous forest, stepping from tuft to tuft of rushes and roots, which afforded precarious footholds among deep sloughs; or pacing carefully, like a cat, along the prostrate trunks of trees, startled now and then by the sudden screaming of the bittern, or the quacking of wild duck rising on the wing from some solitary pool. At length he arrived at a firm piece of ground, which ran out like a peninsula into the deep bosom of the swamp. It had been one of the strongholds of the Indians during their wars with the first colonists. Here they had thrown up a kind of fort, which they had looked upon as almost impregnable, and had used as a place of refuge for their squaws and children. Nothing remained of the old Indian fort but a few embankments, gradually sinking to the level of the surrounding earth and already overgrown in part by oaks and other forest trees, the foliage of which formed a contrast to the dark pines and hemlocks of the swamp.

It was late in the dusk of evening when Tom Walker reached the old fort, and he paused there awhile to rest himself. Anyone but he would have felt unwilling to linger in this lonely, melancholy place, for the common people had a bad opinion of it, from the stories handed down from the time of the Indian wars, when it was asserted that the savages held incantations here and made sacrifices to the evil spirit.

Tom Walker, however, was not a man to be troubled with any fears of the kind. He reposed himself for some time on the trunk of a fallen hemlock, listening to the boding cry of the tree toad, and delving with his walking staff into a mound of black mold at his feet. As he turned up the soil unconsciously, his staff struck against something hard. He raked it out of the vegetable mold, and lo! a cloven skull, with an Indian tomahawk buried deep in it, lay before him. The rust on the weapon showed the time that had elapsed since this deathblow had been given. It was a dreary memento of the fierce struggle that had taken place in this last foothold of the Indian warriors. "Humph!" said Tom Walker as he gave it a kick to shake the dirt from it.

"Let that skull alone!" said a gruff voice. Tom lifted up his eyes and beheld a great black man seated directly opposite him, on the stump of a tree. He was exceedingly surprised, having neither heard nor seen anyone approach; and he was still more perplexed on observing, as well as the gathering gloom would permit, that the stranger was neither Negro nor Indian. It is true he was dressed in a rude half-Indian garb, and had a red belt or sash swathed round his body; but his face was neither black nor copper color, but swarthy and dingy, and begrimed with soot, as if he had been accustomed to toil among fires and forges. He had a shock of coarse black hair that stood out from his head in all directions, and bore an ax on his shoulder.

He scowled for a moment at Tom with a pair of great red eyes.

"What are you doing on my grounds?" said the black man, with a hoarse, growling voice.

"Your grounds!" said Tom, with a sneer, "no more your grounds than mine; they belong to Deacon Peabody."

"Deacon Peabody be damned," said the stranger, "as I flatter myself he will be, if he does not look more to his own sins and less to those of his neighbors. Look yonder, and see how Deacon Peabody is faring."

Tom looked in the direction that the stranger pointed and beheld one of the great trees, fair and flourishing without, but rotten at the core, and saw that it had been nearly hewn through, so that the first high wind was likely to blow it down. On the bark of the tree was scored the name of Deacon Peabody, an eminent man who had waxed wealthy by driving shrewd bargains with the Indians. He now looked around, and found most of the tall trees marked with the name of some great man of the colony, and all more or less scored by the ax. The one on which he had been seated, and which had evidently just been hewn down, bore the name of Crowninshield; and he recollected a mighty rich man of that name, who made a vulgar display of wealth, which it was whispered he had acquired by buccaneering.

"He's just ready for burning!" said the black man, with a growl of triumph. "You see I am likely to have a good stock of firewood for winter."

"But what right have you," said Tom, "to cut down Deacon Peabody's timber?"

"The right of a prior claim," said the other. "This woodland belonged to me long before one of your white-faced race put foot upon the soil."

"And pray, who are you, if I may be so bold?" said Tom.

"Oh, I go by various names. I am the wild huntsman in some countries; the black miner in others. In this neighborhood I am known by the name of the black woodsman. I am he to whom the red men consecrated this spot, and in honor of whom they now and then roasted a white man, by way of sweet-smelling sacrifice. Since the red men have been exterminated by you white savages, I amuse myself by presiding at the persecutions of Quakers and Anabaptists, I am the great patron and prompter of slave dealers, and the grand master of the Salem witches."

"The upshot of all which is, that, if I mistake not," said Tom, sturdily, "you are he commonly called Old Scratch."

"The same, at your service!" replied the black man, with a half-civil nod.

Such was the opening of this interview, according to the old story; though it has almost too familiar an air to be credited. One would think that to meet with such a singular personage, in this wild, lonely place, would have shaken any man's nerves; but Tom was a hard-minded fellow, not easily daunted, and he had lived so long with a termagant wife that he did not even fear the devil.

It is said that after this commencement they had a long and earnest conversation together, as Tom returned homeward. The black man told him of great sums of money buried by Kidd the pirate, under the oak trees on the high ridge, not far from the morass. All these were under his command, and protected by his power, so that none could find them but such as propitiated his favor. These he offered to place within Tom Walker's reach, having conceived an especial kindness for him; but they were to be had only on certain conditions. What these conditions were may be easily surmised, though Tom never disclosed them publicly. They must have been very hard, for he required time to think of them, and he was not a man to stick at trifles when money was in view.

When they had reached the edge of the swamp, the stranger paused. "What proof have I that all you have been telling me is true?" said Tom. "There's my signature," said the black man, pressing his finger on Tom's forehead. So saying, he turned off among the thickest of the swamp, and seemed, as Tom said, to go down, down, down, into the earth, until he totally disappeared.

When Tom reached home, he found the black print of a finger burned, as it were, into his forehead, which nothing could obliterate.

The first news his wife had to tell him was the sudden death of Absalom Crowninshield, the rich buccaneer. It was announced in the papers with the usual flourish that "A great man had fallen in Israel."

Tom recollected the tree which his black friend had just hewn down and which was ready for burning. "Let the freebooter roast," said Tom; "who cares!" He now felt convinced that all he had heard and seen was no illusion.

He was not prone to let his wife into his confidence; but as this was an uneasy secret, he willingly shared it with her. All her avarice was awakened at the mention of hidden gold, and she urged her husband to comply with the black man's terms, and secure what would make them wealthy for life. However Tom might have felt disposed to sell himself to the devil, he was determined not to do so to oblige his wife; so he flatly refused, out of the mere spirit of contradiction. Many were the quarrels they had on the subject; but the more she talked, the more resolute was Tom not to be damned to please her.

At length she determined to drive the bargain on her own account, and if she succeeded, to keep all the gain to herself. Being of the same fearless temper as her husband, she set off for the old Indian fort toward the close of a summer's day. She was many hours absent. When she came back, she was reserved and sullen in her replies. She spoke something of a black man, whom she met about twilight hewing at the root of a tall tree. He was sulky, however, and would not come to terms; she was to go again with a propitiatory offering, but what it was she forbore to say.

The next evening she set off again for the swamp, with her apron heavily laden. Tom waited and waited for her, but in vain; midnight came, but she did not make her appearance; morning, noon, night returned, but still she did not come. Tom now grew uneasy for her safety, especially as he found she had carried off in her apron the silver teapot and spoons, and every portable article of value. Another night elapsed, another morning came; but no wife. In a word, she was never heard of more.

What was her real fate nobody knows, in consequence of so many pretending to know. It is one of those facts which have become confounded by a variety of historians. Some asserted that she lost her way among the tangled mazes of the swamp, and sank into some pit or slough; others, more uncharitable, hinted that she had eloped with the household booty, and made off to some other province; while others surmised that the tempter had decoyed her into a dismal quagmire, on the top of which her hat was found lying. In confirmation of this, it was said a great black man, with an ax on his shoulder, was seen late that very evening coming out of the swamp, carrying a bundle tied in a check apron, with an air of surly triumph.

The most current and probable story, however, observes that Tom Walker grew so anxious about the fate of his wife and his property that he set out at length to seek them both at the Indian fort. During a long summer's afternoon he searched about the gloomy place, but no wife was to be seen. He called her name repeatedly, but she was nowhere to be heard. The bittern alone responded to his voice, as he flew screaming by; or the bullfrog croaked dolefully from a neighboring pool. At length, it is said, just in the brown hour of twilight, when the owls began to hoot, and the bats to flit about, his attention was attracted by the clamor of carrion crows hovering about a cypress tree. He looked up and beheld a bundle tied in a check apron and hanging in the branches of the tree, with a great vulture perched hard by, as if keeping watch upon it. He leaped with joy; for he recognized his wife's apron and supposed it to contain the household valuables.

"Let us get hold of the property," said he consolingly to himself, "and we will endeavor to do without the woman."

As he scrambled up the tree, the vulture spread its wide wings and sailed off screaming into the deep shadows of the forest. Tom seized the check apron, but, woeful sight! found nothing but a heart and liver tied up in it!

Such, according to this most authentic old story, was all that was to be found of Tom's wife. She had probably attempted to deal with the black man as she had been accustomed to deal with her husband; but though a female scold is generally considered a match for the devil, yet in this instance she appears to have had the worst of it. She must have died game, however; for it is said Tom noticed many prints of cloven feet deeply stamped upon the tree, and found handfuls of hair that looked as if they had been plucked from the coarse black shock of the woodsman. Tom knew his wife's prowess by experience. He shrugged his shoulders as he looked at the signs of a fierce clapper-clawing. "Egad," said he to himself, "Old Scratch must have had a tough time of it!"

Tom consoled himself for the loss of his property with the loss of his wife, for he was a man of fortitude. He even felt something like gratitude toward the black woodsman, who, he considered, had done him a kindness. He sought, therefore, to cultivate a further acquaintance with him, but for some time without success; the old black-legs played shy, for whatever people may think, he is not always to be had for the calling for; he knows how to play his cards when he is pretty sure of his game.

At length, it is said, when delay had whetted Tom's eagerness to the quick, and prepared him to agree to anything rather than not gain the promised treasure, he met the black man one evening in his usual woodsman's dress, with his ax on his shoulder, sauntering along the swamp and humming a tune. He affected to receive Tom's advances with great indifference, made brief replies, and went on humming his tune.

By degrees, however, Tom brought him to business, and they began to haggle about the terms on which the former was to have the pirate's treasure. There was one condition which need not be mentioned, being generally understood in all cases where the devil grants favors; but there were others about which, though of less importance, he was inflexibly obstinate. He insisted that the money found through his means should be employed in his service. He proposed, therefore, that Tom should employ it in the black traffic; that is to say, that he should fit out a slave ship. This, however, Tom resolutely refused; he was bad enough in all conscience, but the devil himself could not tempt him to turn slave trader.

Finding Tom so squeamish on this point, he did not insist upon it, but proposed, instead, that he should turn usurer, the devil being extremely anxious for the increase of usurers, looking upon them as his peculiar people.

To this no objections were made, for it was just to Tom's taste.

"You shall open a broker's shop in Boston next month," said the black man.

"I'll do it tomorrow, if you wish," said Tom Walker.

"You shall lend money at two per cent a month."

"Egad, I'll charge four!" replied Tom Walker.

"You shall extort bonds, foreclose mortgages, drive the merchants to bankruptcy—"

"I'll drive them to the devil," cried Tom Walker.

"You are the usurer for my money!" said black-legs with delight. "When will you want the rhino?"

"This very night."

"Done!" said the devil.

"Done!" said Tom Walker. So they shook hands and struck a bargain.

A few days' time saw Tom Walker seated behind his desk in a counting house in Boston.

His reputation for a ready-moneyed man, who would lend money out for a good consideration, soon spread abroad. Everybody remembers the time of Governor Belcher, when money was particularly scarce. It was a time of paper credit. The country had been deluged with government bills, the famous Land Bank had been established; there had been a rage for speculating; the people had run mad with schemes for new settlements, for building cities in the wilderness; land jobbers went about with maps of grants, and townships, and El Dorados, lying nobody knew where, but which everybody was ready to purchase. In a word, the great speculating fever which breaks out every now and then in the country had raged to an alarming degree, and everybody was dreaming of making sudden fortunes from nothing. As usual the fever had subsided; the dream had gone off, and the imaginary fortunes with it; the patients were left in doleful plight, and the whole country resounded with the consequent cry of "hard times."

At this propitious time of public distress did Tom Walker set up as usurer in Boston. His door was soon thronged by customers. The needy and adventurous, the gambling speculator, the dreaming land jobber, the thriftless tradesman, the merchant with cracked credit—in short, everyone driven to raise money by desperate means and desperate sacrifices hurried to Tom Walker.

Thus Tom was the universal friend of the needy, and acted like a "friend in need"; that is to say, he always exacted good pay and good security. In proportion to the distress of the applicant was the hardness of his terms. He accumulated bonds and mortgages; gradually squeezed his customers closer and closer; and sent them at length, dry as a sponge, from his door.

In this way he made money hand over hand; became a rich and mighty man, and exalted his cocked hat upon 'Change. He built himself, as usual, a vast house, out of ostentation; but left the greater part of it unfinished and unfurnished, out of parsimony. He even set up a carriage in the fullness of his vainglory, though he nearly starved the horses which drew it; and as the ungreased wheels groaned and screeched on the axletrees, you would have thought you heard the souls of the poor debtors he was squeezing.

As Tom waxed old, however, he grew thoughtful. Having secured the good things of this world, he began to feel anxious about those of the next. He thought with regret on the bargain he had made with his black friend, and set his wits to work to cheat him out of the conditions. He became, therefore, all of a sudden, a violent churchgoer. He prayed loudly and strenuously, as if heaven were to be taken by force of lungs. Indeed, one might always tell when he had sinned most during the week by the clamor of his Sunday devotion. The quiet Christians who had been modestly and steadfastly traveling Zionward, were struck with self-reproach at seeing themselves so suddenly outstripped in their career by this new-made convert. Tom was as rigid in religious as in money matters; he was a stern supervisor and censurer of his neighbors, and seemed to think every sin entered up to their account became a credit on his own side of the page. He even talked of the expediency of reviving the persecution of Quakers and Anabaptists. In a word, Tom's zeal became as notorious as his riches.

Still, in spite of all this strenuous attention to forms, Tom had a lurking dread that the devil, after all, would have his due. That he might not be taken unawares, therefore, it is said he always carried a small Bible in his coat pocket. He had also a great folio Bible on his counting-house desk, and would frequently be found reading it when people called on business; on such occasions he would lay his green spectacles in the book, to mark the place, while he turned round to drive some usurious bargain.

Some say that Tom grew a little crack-brained in his old days, and that, fancying his end approaching, he had his horse new shod, saddled and bridled, and buried with his feet uppermost; because he supposed that at the last day the world would be turned upside down in which case he should find his horse standing ready for mounting, and he was determined at the worst to give his old friend a run for it. This, however, is probably a mere old wives' fable. If he really did take such a precaution, it was totally superfluous; at least so says the authentic old legend, which closes his story in the following manner.

One hot summer afternoon in the dog days, just as a terrible black thundergust was coming up, Tom sat in his counting house in his white cap and India-silk morning gown. He was on the point of foreclosing a mortgage, by which he would complete the ruin of an unlucky land speculator for whom he had professed the greatest friendship. The poor land jobber begged him to grant a few months' indulgence. Tom had grown testy and irritated, and refused another day.

"My family will be ruined and brought upon the parish," said the land jobber.

"Charity begins at home," replied Tom; "I must take care of myself in these hard times."

"You have made much money out of me," said the jobber.

Tom lost his patience and his piety. "The devil take me," said he, "if I have made a farthing!"

Just then there were three loud knocks at the street door. He stepped out to see who was there. A black man was holding a black horse, which neighed and stamped and tossed its head with impatience.

"Tom, you're come for," said the black fellow, gruffly. Tom shrank back, but too late. He had left his little Bible at the bottom of his coat pocket, and his big Bible on the desk buried under the mortgage he was about to foreclose; never was sinner taken more unawares. The black man whisked him like a child into the saddle, gave the horse the lash, and away he galloped, with Tom on his back, in the midst of the thunderstorm. The clerks stuck their pens behind their ears, and stared after him from the windows. Away went Tom Walker, dashing down the streets, his white cap bobbing up and down, his morning gown fluttering in the wind, and his steed striking fire out of the pavement at every bound. When the clerks turned to look for the black man, he had disappeared.

Tom Walker never returned to foreclose the mortgage. A countryman, who lived on the border of the swamp, reported that in the height of the thundergust he had heard a great clattering of hoofs and a howling along the road, and running to the window caught sight of a figure, such as I have described, on a horse that galloped like mad across the fields, over the hills, and down into the black hemlock swamp toward the old Indian fort; and that shortly after, a thunderbolt falling in that direction seemed to set the whole forest in a blaze.

The good people of Boston shook their heads and shrugged their shoulders, but had been so much accustomed to witches and goblins and tricks of the devil in all kinds of shapes, from the first settlement of the colony, that they were not so much horror-struck as might have been expected. Trustees were appointed to take charge of Tom's effects. There was nothing, however, to administer upon. On searching his coffers, all his bonds and mortgages were found reduced to cinders. In place of gold and silver, his iron chest was filled with chips and shavings; two skeletons lay in his stable instead of his half-starved horses, and the very next day his great house took fire and burned to the ground.

Such was the end of Tom Walker and his ill-gotten wealth. Let all griping money brokers lay this story to heart. The truth of it is not to be doubted. The very hole under the oak trees whence he dug Kidd's money is to be seen to this day; and the neighboring swamp and the old Indian fort are often haunted on stormy nights by a figure on horseback, in morning gown and white cap, which is doubtless the troubled spirit of the usurer. In fact, the story has resolved itself into a proverb, and is the origin of that popular saying, so prevalent throughout New England, of "The Devil and Tom Walker."

1. Find out who Captain Kidd is. 2. In what way are Tom Walker and his wife like Captain Kidd and Absalom Crowninshield? 3. Does the character of Tom Walker cause the action of this story? 4. What characteristics of legend does the story have? 5. What sign does Tom have to prove that he really met Old Scratch? 6. What is the meaning of the check apron tied to a tree? 7. Is this legend like a parable in any way? Explain. 8. How does the author relate the legend to New England? 9. Use your dictionary for these words.

articulate	termagant	askance	quagmire	gridiron
tantalize	precarious	stagnant		sloughs
memento	propritiatory	buccaneering	forebore	daunted
user	squeamish	inflexibly		foreclose

Now read a legend of New York, *Rip Van Winkle*.

Rip Van Winkle

WASHINGTON IRVING

By Woden, God of Saxons,
From whence comes Wensday, that is Wodensday,
Truth is a thing that ever I will keep
Unto thylke day in which I creep into
My sepulcher.

CARTWRIGHT

Whoever has made a voyage up the Hudson must remember the Kaatskill Mountains. They are a dismembered branch of the great Appalachian family, and are seen away to the west of the river, swelling up to a noble height, and lording it over the surrounding country. Every change of season, every change of weather, indeed, every hour of the day, produces some change in the magical hues and shapes of these mountains, and they are regarded by all the good wives, far and near, as perfect barometers. When the weather is fair and settled, they are clothed in blue and purple, and print their bold outlines on the clear evening sky; but sometimes, when the rest of the landscape is cloudless, they will gather a hood of gray vapors about their summits, which, in the last rays of the setting sun, will glow and light up like a crown of glory.

At the foot of these fairy mountains, the voyager may have descried the light smoke curling up from a village, whose shingle-roofs gleam among the trees just where the blue tints of the upland melt away into the fresh green of the nearer landscape. It is a little village of great antiquity, having been founded by some of the Dutch colonists in the early times of the province, just about the beginning of the government of the good Peter Stuyvesant, (may he rest in peace!) and there were some of the houses of the original settlers standing within a few years, built of small yellow bricks brought from Holland, having latticed windows and gable fronts, surmounted with weathercocks.

In that same village, and in one of these very houses (which, to tell the precise truth, was sadly time-worn and weather-beaten) there lived many years since, while the country was yet a province of Great Britain, a simple good-natured fellow, of the name of Rip Van Winkle. He was a descendant of the Van Winkles who figured so gallantly in the chivalrous days of Peter Stuyvesant, and accompanied him to the siege of Fort Christina. He inherited, however, but little of the martial char-acter of his ancestors. I have observed that he was a simple, good-natured man; he was, moreover, a kind neighbor, and an obedient, hen-pecked husband. Indeed, to the latter circumstance might be owing that meekness of spirit which gained him such universal popularity; for those men are most apt to be obse-quious and conciliating abroad, who are under the discipline of shrews at home. Their tempers, doubtless, are rendered pliant and malleable in the fiery furnace of domestic tribula-tion; and a curtain lecture is worth all the sermons in the world for teaching the virtues of patience and long-suffering. A terma-gant wife may, therefore, in some respects be considered a tolerable blessing; and if so, Rip Van Winkle was thrice blessed.

Certain it is, that he was a great favorite among all the good wives of the village, who, as usual with the amiable sex, took his part in all family squabbles, and never failed, whenever they talked those matters over in their evening gossipings, to lay all the blame on Dame Van Winkle. The children of the village, too, would shout with joy whenever he approached. He assisted at their sports, made their playthings, taught them to fly kites and shoot marbles, and told them long stories of ghosts, witches, and Indians. Whenever he went dodging about the village, he was surrounded by a troop of them, hanging on his skirts, clam-bering on his back, and playing a thousand tricks on him with impunity; and not a dog would bark at him throughout the neighborhood.

The great error in Rip's composition was an insuperable aversion to all kinds of profitable labor. It could not be from the want of assiduity or perseverance; for he would sit on a wet rock, with a rod as long and heavy as a Tartar's lance, and fish all day without a murmur, even though he should not be encouraged by a single nibble. He would carry a fowling-piece on his shoulder for hours together, trudging through woods and swamps, and up hill and down dale, to shoot a few squirrels or wild pigeons. He would never refuse to assist a neighbor, even in the roughest toil, and was a foremost man at all country frolics for husking Indian corn, or building stone-fences; the women of the village, too, used to employ him to run their errands, and to do such little odd jobs as their less obliging husbands would not do for them. In a word, Rip was ready to attend to anybody's business but his own; but as to doing family duty, and keeping his farm in order, he found it impossible.

In fact, he declared it was of no use to work on his farm; it was the most pestilent little piece of ground in the whole country; everything about it went wrong, and would go wrong, in spite of him. His fences were continually falling to pieces; his cow would either go astray or get among the cabbages; weeds were sure to grow quicker in his fields than anywhere else; the rain always made a point of setting in just as he had some outdoor work to do; so that though his patrimonial estate had dwindled away under his management, acre by acre, until there was little more left than a mere patch of Indian corn and potatoes, yet it was the worst conditioned farm in the neighborhood.

His children, too, were as ragged and wild as if they belonged to nobody. His son Rip, an urchin begotten in his own likeness, promised to inherit the habits, with the old clothes, of his father. He was generally seen trooping like a colt at his mother's heels, equipped in a pair of his father's castoff galligaskins, which he had much ado to hold up with one hand, as a fine lady does her train in bad weather.

Rip Van Winkle, however, was one of those happy mortals, of foolish, well-oiled dispositions, who take the world easy, eat white bread or brown, whichever can be got with least thought or trouble, and would rather starve on a penny than work for a pound. If left to himself, he would have whistled life away in perfect contentment; but his wife kept continually dinning in his ears about his idleness, his carelessness, and the ruin he was bringing on his family. Morning, noon, and night, her tongue was incessantly going, and everything he said or did was sure to produce a torrent of household eloquence. Rip had but one way of replying to all lectures of the kind, and that, by frequent use, had grown into a habit. He shrugged his shoulders, shook his head, cast up his eyes, but said nothing. This, however, always provoked a fresh volley from his wife; so that he was fain to draw off his forces, and take to the outside of the house—the only side which, in truth, belongs to a hen-pecked husband.

Rip's sole domestic adherent was his dog Wolf, who was as much henpecked as his master; for Dame Van Winkle regarded them as companions in idleness, and even looked upon Wolf with an evil eye, as the cause of his master's going so often astray. True it is, in all points of spirit befitting an honorable dog, he was as courageous an animal as ever scoured the woods —but what courage can withstand the ever-during and all-besetting terrors of a woman's tongue? The moment Wolf entered the house his crest fell, his tail drooped to the ground, or curled between his legs, he sneaked about with a gallows air, casting many a sidelong glance at Dame Van Winkle, and at the least flourish of a broomstick or ladle, he would fly to the door with yelping precipitation.

Times grew worse and worse with Rip Van Winkle as years of matrimony rolled on; a tart temper never mellows with age, and a sharp tongue is the only edged tool that grows keener with constant use. For a long while he used to console himself, when driven from home, by frequenting a kind of perpetual club of the sages, philosophers, and other idle personages of the village, which held its sessions on a bench before a small inn, designated by a rubicund portrait of His Majesty George the Third. Here they used to sit in the shade through a long lazy summer's day, talking listlessly over village gossip, or telling endless sleepy stories about nothing. But it would have been worth any statesman's money to have overheard the profound discussions that sometimes took place, when by chance a newspaper fell into their hands from some passing traveler. How solemnly they would listen to the contents, as drawled out by Derrick Van Brummel, the schoolmaster, a dapper learned little man, who was not to be daunted by the most gigantic word in the dictionary; and how sagely they would deliberate upon public events some months after they had taken place.

The opinions of this junto were completely controlled by Nicholas Vedder, a patriarch of the village, and landlord of the inn, at the door of which he took his seat from morning till night, just moving sufficiently to avoid the sun and keep in the shade of a large tree; so that the neighbors could tell the hour by his movements as accurately as by a sun-dial. It is true he was rarely heard to speak, but smoked his pipe incessantly. His adherents, however (for every great man has his adherents) perfectly understood him, and knew how to gather his opinions. When anything that was read or related displeased him, he was observed to smoke his pipe vehemently, and to send forth short, frequent, and angry puffs; but when pleased, he would inhale the smoke slowly and tranquilly, and emit it in light and placid clouds; and sometimes, taking the pipe from his mouth, and letting the fragrant vapor curl about his nose, would gravely nod his head in token of perfect approbation.

From even this stronghold the unlucky Rip was at length routed by his termagant wife, who would suddenly break in upon the tranquillity of the assemblage and call the members all to naught; nor was that august personage, Nicholas Vedder himself, sacred from the daring tongue of this terrible virago, who charged him outright with encouraging her husband in habits of idleness.

Poor Rip was at last reduced almost to despair; and his only alternative, to escape from the labor of the farm and clamor of his wife, was to take gun in hand and stroll away into the woods. Here he would sometimes seat himself at the foot of a tree, and share the contents of his wallet with Wolf, with whom he sympathized as a fellow-sufferer in persecution. "Poor Wolf," he would say, "thy mistress leads thee a dog's life of it; but never mind, my lad, whilst I live thou shalt never want a friend to stand by thee!" Wolf would wag his tail, look wistfully in his master's face, and if dogs can feel pity I verily believe he reciprocated the sentiment with all his heart.

In a long ramble of the kind on a fine autumnal day, Rip had unconsciously scrambled to one of the highest parts of the Kaatskill Mountains. He was after his favorite sport of squirrel shooting, and the still solitudes had echoed and re-echoed with the reports of his gun. Panting and fatigued, he threw himself, late in the afternoon, on a green knoll, covered with mountain herbage, that crowned the brow of a precipice. From an opening between the trees he could overlook all the lower country for many a mile of rich woodland. He saw at a distance the lordly Hudson, far, far below him, moving on its silent but majestic course, with the reflection of a purple cloud, or the sail of a lagging bark, here and there sleeping on its glassy bosom, and at last losing itself in the blue highlands.

On the other side he looked down into a deep mountain glen, wild, lonely, and shagged, the bottom filled with fragments from the impending cliffs, and scarcely lighted by the reflected rays of the setting sun. For some time Rip lay musing on this scene; evening was gradually advancing; the mountains began to throw their long blue shadows over the valleys; he saw that it would be dark long before he could reach the village, and he heaved a heavy sigh when he thought of encountering the terrors of Dame Van Winkle.

As he was about to descend, he heard a voice from a distance, hallooing, "Rip Van Winkle! Rip Van Winkle!" He looked round, but could see nothing but a crow winging its solitary flight across the mountain. He thought his fancy must have deceived him, and turned again to descend, when he heard the same cry ring through the still evening air: "Rip Van Winkle! Rip Van Winkle!" At the same time Wolf bristled up his back, and giving a low growl, skulked to his master's side, looking fearfully down into the glen. Rip now felt a vague apprehension stealing over him; he looked anxiously in the same direction, and perceived a strange figure slowly toiling up the rocks, and bending under the weight of something he carried on his back. He was surprised to see any human being in this lonely and unfrequented place; but supposing it to be someone of the neighborhood in need of his assistance, he hastened down to yield it.

On nearer approach he was still more surprised at the singularity of the stranger's appearance. He was a short, square-built old fellow, with thick bushy hair, and a grizzled beard. His dress was of the antique Dutch fashion—a cloth jerkin strapped round the waist—several pair of breeches, the outer one of ampe volume, decorated with rows of buttons down the sides, and bunches at the knees. He bore on his shoulder a stout keg, that seemed full of liquor, and made signs for Rip to approach and assist him with the load. Though rather shy and distrustful of this new acquaintance, Rip complied with his usual alacrity; and mutually relieving one another, they clambered up a narrow gully, apparently the dry bed of a mountain torrent. As they ascended, Rip every now and then heard long rolling peals, like distant thunder, that seemed to issue out of a deep ravine, or rather cleft between lofty rocks, toward which their rugged path conducted. He paused for an instant, but supposing it to be the muttering of one of those transient thunder-showers which often take place in mountain heights, he proceeded. Passing through the ravine, they came to a hollow, like a small amphitheater, surrounded by perpendicular precipices, over the brinks of which impending trees shot their branches, so that you only caught glimpses of the azure sky and the bright evening cloud. During the whole time Rip and his companion had labored on in silence; for though the former marveled greatly what could be the object of carrying a keg of liquor up this wild mountain, yet there was something strange and incomprehensible about the unknown, that inspired awe and checked familiarity.

On entering the amphitheater, new objects of wonder presented themselves. On a level spot in the center was a company of odd-looking personages playing at ninepins. They were dressed in a quaint outlandish fashion; some wore short doublets, others jerkins, with long knives in their belts, and most of them had enormous breeches of similar style with that of the guide's. Their visages, too, were peculiar: one had a large beard, broad face, and small piggish eyes; the face of another seemed to consist entirely of nose, and was surmounted by a white sugar-loaf hat, set off with a little red cock's tail. They all had beards, of various shapes and colors. There was one who seemed to be the commander. He was a stout old gentleman, with a weather-beaten countenance; he wore a laced doublet, broad belt and hanger, high-crowned hat and feather, red stockings, and high-heeled shoes, with roses in them. The whole group reminded Rip of the figures in an old Flemish painting in the parlor of Dominie Van Shaick, the village parson, and which had been brought over from Holland at the time of the settlement.

What seemed particularly odd to Rip was, that though these folks were evidently amusing themselves, yet they maintained the gravest faces, the most mysterious silence, and were, withal, the most melancholy party of pleasure he had ever witnessed. Nothing interrupted the stillness of the scene but the noise of the balls, which, whenever they were rolled, echoed along the mountains like rumbling peals of thunder.

As Rip and his companion approached them, they suddenly desisted from their play, and stared at him with such fixed, statue-like gaze, and such strange, uncouth, lack-luster countenances, that his heart turned within him, and his knees smote together. His companion now emptied the contents of the keg into large flagons, and made signs to him to wait upon the company. He obeyed with fear and trembling; they quaffed the liquor in profound silence, and then returned to their game.

By degrees Rip's awe and apprehension subsided. He even ventured, when no eye was fixed upon him, to taste the beverage, which he found had much of the flavor of excellent Hollands. He was naturally a thirsty soul, and was soon tempted to repeat the draught. One taste provoked another; and he reiterated his visits to the flagon so often that at length his senses were overpowered, his eyes swam in his head, his head gradually declined, and he fell into a deep sleep.

On waking, he found himself on the green knoll whence he had first seen the old man of the glen. He rubbed his eyes—it was a bright, sunny morning. The birds were hopping and twittering among the bushes, and the eagle was wheeling aloft, and breasting the pure mountain breeze. "Surely," thought Rip, "I have not slept here all night." He recalled the occurrences before he fell asleep. The strange man with a keg of liquor—the mountain ravine—the wild retreat among the rocks—the woe-begone party at ninepins—the flagon—"Oh! that flagon! that wicked flagon!" thought Rip—"what excuse shall I make to Dame Van Winkle?"

He looked round for his gun, but in place of the clean, well-oiled fowling-piece, he found an old firelock lying by him, the barrel incrusted with rust, the lock falling off, and the stock worm-eaten. He now suspected that the grave roisterers of the mountain had put a trick upon him, and, having dosed him with liquor, had robbed him of his gun. Wolf, too, had disappeared, but he might have strayed away after a squirrel or partridge. He whistled after him, and shouted his name, but all in vain; the echoes repeated his whistle and shout, but no dog was to be seen.

He determined to revisit the scene of the last evening's gambol, and if he met with any of the party, to demand his dog and gun. As he rose to walk, he found himself stiff in the joints, and wanting in his usual activity. "These mountain beds do not agree with me," thought Rip, "and if this frolic should lay me up with a fit of rheumatism, I shall have a blessed time with Dame Van Winkle." With some difficulty he got down into the glen: he found the gully up which he and his companion had ascended the preceding evening; but to his astonishment a mountain stream was now foaming down it, leaping from rock to rock, and filling the glen with babbling murmurs. He, however, made shift to scramble up its sides, working his toilsome way through thickets of birch, sassafras, and witch-hazel, and sometimes tripped up or entangled by the wild grapevines that twisted their coils or tendrils from tree to tree, and spread a kind of network in his path.

At length he reached to where the ravine had opened through the cliffs to the ampitheater; but no traces of such opening remained. The rocks presented a high, impenetrable wall, over which the torrent came tumbling in a sheet of feathery foam, and fell into a broad, deep basin, black from the shadows of the surrounding forest. Here, then, poor Rip was brought to a stand. He again called and whistled after his dog; he was only answered by the cawing of a flock of idle crows, sporting high in air about a dry tree that overhung a sunny precipice; and who, secure in their elevation, seemed to look down and scoff at the poor man's perplexities. What was to be done? The morning was passing away, and Rip felt famished for want of his breakfast. He grieved to give up his dog and gun; he dreaded to meet his wife; but it would not do to starve among the mountains. He shook his head, shouldered the rusty firelock, and, with a heart full of trouble and anxiety, turned his steps homeward.

As he approached the village he met a number of people, but none whom he knew, which somewhat surprised him, for he had thought himself acquainted with everyone in the country round. Their dress, too, was of a different fashion from that to which he was accustomed. They all stared at him with equal marks of surprise, and whenever they cast their eyes upon him, invariably stroked their chins. The constant recurrence of this gesture induced Rip, involuntarily, to do the same; when, to his astonishment, he found his beard had grown a foot long!

He had now entered the skirts of the village. A troop of strange children ran at his heels, hooting after him, and pointing at his gray beard. The dogs, too, not one of which he recognized for an old acquaintance, barked at him as he passed. The very village was altered; it was larger and more populous. There were rows of houses which he had never seen before, and those which had been his familiar haunts had disappeared. Strange names were over the doors—strange faces at the windows—everything was strange. His mind now misgave him; he began to doubt whether both he and the world around him were not bewitched. Surely this was his native village, which he had left but the day before. There stood the Kaatskill Mountains—there ran the silver Hudson at a distance—there was every hill and dale precisely as it had always been—Rip was sorely perplexed—"That flagon last night," thought he, "has addled my poor head sadly!"

It was with some difficulty that he found the way to his own house, which he approached with silent awe, expecting every moment to hear the shrill voice of Dame Van Winkle. He found the house gone to decay—the roof fallen in, the windows shattered, and the doors off the hinges. A half-starved dog that looked like Wolf was skulking about it. Rip called him by name, but the cur snarled, showed his teeth, and passed on. This was an unkind cut indeed—"My very dog," sighed poor Rip, "has forgotten me!"

He entered the house, which, to tell the truth, Dame Van Winkle had always kept in neat order. It was empty, forlorn, and apparently abandoned. This desolateness overcame all his connubial fears—he called loudly for his wife and children—the lonely chambers rang for a moment with his voice, and then all again was silence.

He now hurried forth, and hastened to his old resort, the village inn—but it, too, was gone. A large, rickety wooden building stood in its place, with great gaping windows, some of them broken and mended with old hats and petticoats, and over the door was painted, "The Union Hotel, by Jonathan Doolittle." Instead of the great tree that used to shelter the quiet little Dutch inn of yore, there now was reared a tall naked pole, with something on the top that looked like a red night-cap, and from it was fluttering a flag, on which was a singular assemblage of stars and stripes—all this was strange and incomprehensible. He recognized on the sign, however, the ruby face of King George, under which he had smoked so many a peaceful pipe; but even this was singularly metamorphosed. The red coat was changed for one of blue and buff, a sword was held in the hand instead of a scepter, the head was decorated with a cocked hat, and underneath was painted in large characters, GENERAL WASHINGTON.

There was, as usual, a crowd of folk about the door, but none that Rip recollected. The very character of the people seemed changed. There was a busy, bustling, disputatious tone about it, instead of the accustomed phlegm and drowsy tranquillity. He looked in vain for the sage Nicholas Vedder, with his broad face, double chin, and fair long pipe, uttering clouds of tobacco smoke instead of idle speeches; or Van Bummel, the schoolmaster, doling forth the contents of an ancient newspaper. In place of these, a lean, bilious-looking fellow with his pockets full of hand bills, was haranguing vehemently about rights of citizens—elections—members of Congress—liberty—Bunker's Hill—heroes of seventy-six—and other words, which were a perfect Babylonish jargon to the bewildered Van Winkle.

The appearance of Rip, with his long grizzled beard, his rusty fowling-piece, his uncouth dress, and an army of women and children at his heels, soon attracted the attention of the tavern politicians. They crowded round him, eyeing him from head to foot with great curiosity. The orator bustled up to him, and, drawing him partly aside, inquired "on which side he voted?" Rip stared in vacant stupidity. Another short but busy little fellow pulled him by the arm, and, rising on tiptoe, inquired in his ear, "whether he was Federal or Democrat?" Rip was equally at a loss to comprehend the question; when a knowing, self-important old gentleman, in a sharp cocked hat, made his way through the crowd, putting them to the right and left with his elbows as he passed, and planting himself before Van Winkle, with one arm akimbo, the other resting on his cane, his keen eyes and sharp hat penetrating, as it were, into his very soul, demanded in an austere tone, "what brought him to the election with a gun on his shoulder, and a mob at his heels, and whether he meant to breed a riot in the village?"—"Alas! gentlemen," cried Rip, somewhat dismayed, "I am a poor quiet man, a native of the place, and a loyal subject of the King, God bless him!"

Here a general shout burst from the bystanders—"A Tory! a Tory! a spy! a refugee! hustle him! away with him!" It was with great difficulty that the self-important man in the cocked hat restored order; and, having assumed a tenfold austerity of brow, demanded again of the unknown culprit what he came there for, and whom he was seeking? The poor man humbly assured him that he meant no harm, but merely came there in search of some of his neighbors, who used to keep about the tavern.

"Well—who are they?—name them."

Rip bethought himself a moment, and inquired, "Where's Nicholas Vedder?"

There was a silence for a little while, when an old man replied, in a thin, piping voice, "Nicholas Vedder why, he is dead and gone these eighteen years! There was a wooden tombstone in the churchyard that used to tell all about him, but that's rotten and gone too."

"Where's Brom Dutcher?"

"Oh, he went off to the army in the beginning of the war; some say he was killed at the storming of Stony Point—others say he was drowned in a squall at the foot of Antony's Nose. I don't know—he never came back again."

"Where's Van Bummel, the schoolmaster?"

"He went off to the wars too, was a great militia general, and is now in Congress."

Rip's heart died away at hearing of these sad changes in his home and friends, and finding himself thus alone in the world. Every answer puzzled him too, by treating of such enormous lapses of time, and of matters which he could not understand: war—Congress—Stony Point; he had no courage to ask after any more friends, but cried out in despair, "Does nobody here know Rip Van Winkle?"

"Oh, Rip Van Winkle!" exclaimed two or three. "Oh, to be sure! that's Rip Van Winkle yonder, leaning against the tree."

Rip looked, and beheld a precise counterpart of himself, as he went up the mountain: apparently as lazy, and certainly as ragged. The poor fellow was now completely confounded. He doubted his own identity, and whether he was himself or another man. In the midst of his bewilderment, the man in the cocked hat demanded who he was, and what was his name?

"God knows," exclaimed he, at his wit's end; "I'm not myself —I'm somebody else—that's me yonder—no—that's somebody else got into my shoes—I was myself last night, but I fell asleep on the mountain, and they've changed my gun, and every thing's changed, and I'm changed, and I can't tell what's my name, or who I am!"

The bystanders began now to look at each other, nod, wink significantly, and tap their fingers against their foreheads. There was a whisper, also, about securing the gun, and keeping the old fellow from doing mischief, at the very suggestion of which the self-important man in the cocked hat retired with some precipitation. At this critical moment a fresh, comely woman pressed through the throng to get a peep at the gray-bearded man. She had a chubby child in her arms, which, frightened at his looks, began to cry. "Hush, Rip," cried she, "hush, you little fool; the old man won't hurt you." The name of the child, the air of the mother, the tone of her voice, all awakened a train of recollections in his mind. "What is your name, my good woman?" asked he.

"Judith Gardenier."

"And your father's name?"

"Ah, poor man, Rip Van Winkle was his name, but it's twenty years since he went away from home with his gun, and never has been heard of since—his dog came home without him; but whether he shot himself, or was carried away by the Indians, nobody can tell. I was then but a little girl."

Rip had but one question more to ask; but he put it with a faltering voice:—

"Where's your mother?"

"Oh, she too had died but a short time since; she broke a bood-vessel in a fit of passion at a New England peddler."

There was a drop of comfort, at least, in this intelligence. The honest man could contain himself no longer. He caught his daughter and her child in his arms. "I am your father!" cried he—"Young Rip Van Winkle once—old Rip Van Winkle now! —Does nobody know poor Rip Van Winkle?"

All stood amazed, until an old woman, tottering out from among the crowd, put her hand to her brow, and peering under it in his face for a moment, exclaimed, "Sure enough! it is Rip Van Winkle—it is himself! Welcome home again, old neighbor —Why, where have you been these twenty long years?"

Rip's story was soon told, for the whole twenty years had been to him but as one night. The neighbors stared when they heard it; some were seen to wink at each other, and put their tongues in their cheeks; and the self-important man in the cocked hat, who, when the alarm was over, had returned to the field, screwed down the corners of his mouth, and shook his head—upon which there was a general shaking of the head throughout the assemblage.

It was determined, however, to take the opinion of old Peter Vanderdonk, who was seen slowly advancing up the road. He was a descendant of the historian of that name, who wrote one of the earliest accounts of the province. Peter was the most ancient inhabitant of the village, and well versed in all the wonderful events and traditions of the neighborhood. He recollected Rip at once, and corroborated his story in the most satisfactory manner. He assured the company that it was a fact, handed down from his ancestor the historian, that the Kaatskill Mountains had always been haunted by strange beings. That it was affirmed that the great Hendrick Hudson, the first discoverer of the river and country, kept a kind of vigil there every twenty years, with his crew of the *Half-moon;* being permitted in this way to revisit the scenes of his enterprise, and keep a guardian eye upon the river and the great city called by his name. That his father had once seen them in their old Dutch dresses playing at ninepins in a hollow of the mountain; and that he himself had heard, one summer afternoon, the sound of their bowling, like distant peals of thunder.

To make a long story short, the company broke up, and returned to the more important concerns of the election. Rip's daughter took him home to live with her; and she had a snug well-furnished house, and a stout cheery farmer for a husband, whom Rip recollected for one of the urchins that used to climb upon his back. As to Rip's son and heir, who was the ditto of himself, seen leaning against the tree, he was employed to work on the farm, but evinced an hereditary disposition to attend to anything else but his business.

Rip now resumed his old walks and habits; he soon found many of his former cronies, though all rather the worse for the wear and tear of time; and preferred making friends among the rising generation, with whom he soon grew into great favor.

Having nothing to do at home, and being arrived at that happy age when a man can be idle with impunity, he took his place once more on the bench at the inn door, and was reverenced as one of the patriarchs of the village, and a chronicler of the old times "before the war." It was some time before he could get into the regular track of gossip, or be made to comprehend the strange events that had taken place during his long torpor. How that there had been a revolutionary war—that the country had thrown off the yoke of old England—and that, instead of being a subject of His Majesty George the Third, he was now a free citizen of the United States. Rip, in fact, was no politician; the changes of states and empires made but little impression on him; but there was one species of despotism under which he had long groaned, and that was—petticoat government. Happily that was at an end; he had got his neck out of the yoke of matrimony, and could go in and out whenever he pleased, without dreading the tyranny of Dame Van Winkle. Whenever her name was mentioned, however, he shook his head, shrugged his shoulders, and cast up his eyes; which might pass either for an expression of resignation to his fate, or joy at his deliverance.

He used to tell his story to every stranger that arrived at Mr. Doolittle's hotel. He was observed, at first, to vary on some points every time he told it, which was, doubtless, owing to his having so recently awaked. It at last settled down precisely to the tale I have related, and not a man, woman or child in the neighborhood but knew it by heart. Some always pretended to doubt the reality of it, and insisted that Rip had been out of his head, and that this was one point on which he always remained flighty. The old Dutch inhabitants, however, almost universally gave it full credit. Even to this day they never hear a thunderstorm of a summer afternoon about the Kaatskills, but they say Hendrick Hudson and his crew are at their game of ninepins; and it is a common wish of all hen-pecked husbands in the neighborhood, when life hangs heavy on their hands, that they might have a quieting draught out of Rip Van Winkle's flagon.

1. In what locality of the United States did this legend originate? **2.** Look up some information on Peter Stuyvesant and New York. **3.** Does the story give both time and place in the setting? What are they? **4.** What characteristics make Rip a

likeable person but a poor husband? **5.** Why does Dame Win-
kle dislike Wolf? **6.** What does she mean by the evil eye? **7.**
Describe the queer beings Rip shares a keg of liquor with in
the mountains. **8.** What are the characteristics of legend in
Rip Van Winkle? **9.** How does Irving relate this legend to New
England? **10.** What differences are there between this legend
and *The Devil and Tom Walker*? **11.** Reread the folk tale
Peter Klaus. Find all the similarities between it and *Rip Van
Winkle*. **12.** Use your dictionary for these words:

barometer	*antiquity*	*frequenter*	*incessantly*
galligaskins	*reciprocate*	*impending*	*apprehension*
skulk	*transient*	*incomprehensible*	*amphitheater*

Stories of Hyperbole—Tall Tales

Some people look on the tall tale as just another kind of
fish story. That is not correct. The tall tale, like all folk tales,
has its own storytelling method. It is not merely a ridiculous
exaggeration. Some of its qualities are like those of myth, some
like those of legend. Like myth, it gives an imaginative explanation for lakes and rivers, mountains and canyons, and other
features of the earth. Like legend, it shapes a story around a
person by having him do unusual feats.

The hero of the tall tale, like the legendary hero, can travel
faster and farther than other men; he can eat more; he can
endure greater hardships. He can also perform feats that ordinary men could not even imagine.

To give his story unity, the teller of tall tales uses hyperbole.
In other words, he uses exaggeration. Some tall tales are told
about wholly imaginary main characters, like Paul Bunyan and
Pecos Bill. Others are about real people who, in time, became
legendary figures in a locality, like Davy Crockett and Daniel
Webster.

Read *Crockett's Morning Hunt*.

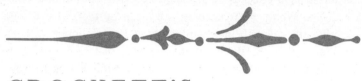

CROCKETT'S
MORNING HUNT

One January morning it was so all-screwen-up cold that the forest trees war so stiff they couldn't shake, and the very daybreak froze fast as it war tryin' to dawn. The tinderbox in my cabin would no more ketch fire than a sunk raft at the bottom o' the sea. Seein' that daylight war so far behind time, I thought creation war in a fair way for freezin' fast.

"So," thinks I, "I must strike a leetle fire from my fingers, light my pipe, travel out a few leagues, and see about it."

Then I brought my knuckles together like two thunderclouds, but the sparks froze up afore I could begin to collect 'em—so out I walked, and endeavored to keep myself unfriz by goin' at a hop, step, and jump gait, and whistlin' the tune of "Fire in the Mountains!" as I went along in three-double-quick time. Well, arter I had walked about twenty-five miles up the peak o' Daybreak Hill, I soon discovered what war the matter. The airth had actually friz fast in her axis, and couldn't turn round; the sun had got jammed between two cakes o' ice under the wheels, an' thar he had bin shinin' and workin' to get loose, till he friz in his cold sweat.

"C-r-e-a-t-i-o-n!" thought I, "this are the toughest sort o' suspension—somethin' must be done, or human creation is done for."

It war then so antediluvian and premature cold that my upper and lower teeth an' tongue war all collapsed together as tight as a friz oyster. I took a fresh twenty-pound bear off o' my back that I'd picked up on the road, an' beat the animal agin the ice till the hot ile began to walk out on him at all sides. I then took an' held him over the airth's axes, an' squeezed him till I thaw'd 'em loose, poured about a ton on it over the sun's face, give the airth's cogwheel one kick backward till I got the sun loose, whistled "Push along, keep movin'!", an' in about fifteen seconds the airth gin a grunt and begun movin'—the sun walked up beautiful, salutin' me with sich a wind o' gratitude that it made me sneeze. I lit my pipe by the blaze o' his topknot, shouldered my bear, an' walked home, introducin' the people to fresh daylight with a piece of sunrise in my pocket, with which I cooked my bear steaks, an' enjoyed one o' the best breakfasts I had tasted for some time. If I didn't, jist wake some mornin' and go with me to the office o' sunrise!

1. To what extent is this story of Davy Crockett a legend? **2.** What characteristics of the tall tale does it have? **3.** Look up some information on the real Davy Crockett. **4.** To what extent does the tall tale catch any of Crockett's actual qualities?

You have discovered how Davy Crockett became a legendary hero and then the hero of a tall tale. In the same way Daniel Webster became a legendary hero in New England. In the story *The Devil and Daniel Webster* you will find him the hero of a tall tale.

The Devil
and Daniel Webster

STEPHEN VINCENT BENÉT

It's a story they tell in the border country, where Massachusetts joins Vermont and New Hampshire.

Yes, Dan'l Webster's dead—or, at least, they buried him.
But every time there's a thunderstorm around Marshfield, they
say you can hear his rolling voice in the hollows of the sky.
And they say that if you go to his grave and speak loud and
clear, "Dan'l Webster—Dan'l Webster!" the ground'll begin to
shiver and the trees begin to shake. And after a while you'll
hear a deep voice saying, "Neighbor, how stands the Union?"
Then you better answer the Union stands as she stood, rock
bottom and copper sheathed, one and indivisible, or he's liable
to rear right out of the ground. At least, that's what I was told
when I was a youngster.

You see, for a while, he was the biggest man in the country.
He never got to be President, but he was the biggest man.
There were thousands that trusted in him right next to God
Almighty, and they told stories about him and all the things
that belonged to him that were like stories of patriarchs and
such. They said, when he stood up to speak, stars and stripes
came right out of the sky, and once he spoke against a river
and made it sink into the ground. They said, when he walked
the woods with his fishing rod, Killall, the trout would jump
out of the streams right into his pockets, for they knew it was
no use putting up a fight against him; and, when he argued a
case, he could turn the harps of the blessed and the shaking of

the earth underground. That was the kind of man he was, and his big farm up at Marshfield was suitable to him. The chickens he raised were all white meat down through the drumsticks; the cows were tended like children, and the big ram he called Goliath had horns with a curl like a morning-glory vine and could butt through an iron door. But Dan'l wasn't one of your gentlemen farmers; he knew all the ways of the land, and he'd be up by candlelight to see that the chores got done. A man with a mouth like a mastiff, a brow like a mountain and eyes like burning anthracite—that was Dan'l Webster in his prime. And the biggest case he argued never got written down in the books, for he argued it against the devil, nip and tuck and no holds barred. And this is the way I used to hear it told.

There was a man named Jabez Stone, lived at Cross Corners, New Hampshire. He wasn't a bad man to start with, but he was an unlucky man. If he planted corn, he got borers; if he planted potatoes, he got blight. He had good-enough land, but it didn't prosper him; he had a decent wife, and children, but the more children he had, the less there was to feed them. If stones cropped up in his neighbor's field, boulders boiled up in his; if he had a horse with the spavins, he'd trade it for one with the staggers and give something extra. There's some folks bound to be like that, apparently. But one day Jabez Stone got sick of the whole business.

He'd been plowing that morning and he'd just broke the plowshare on a rock that he could have sworn hadn't been there yesterday. And, as he stood looking at the plowshare, the off horse began to cough—that ropy kind of cough that means sickness and horse doctors. There were two children down with the measles, his wife was ailing, and he had a whitlow on his thumb. It was about the last straw for Jabez Stone. "I vow," he said, and he looked around him kind of desperate, "I vow it's enough to make a man want to sell his soul to the devil! And I would, too, for two cents!"

Then he felt a kind of queerness come over him at having said what he'd said; though, naturally, being a New Hampshireman, he wouldn't take it back. But, all the same, when it got to be evening and, as far as he could see, no notice had been taken, he felt relieved in his mind, for he was a religious man. But notice is always taken, sooner or later, just like the Good Book says. And, sure enough, next day, about supper-time, a soft-spoken, dark-dressed stranger drove up in a handsome buggy and asked for Jabez Stone.

Well, Jabez told his family it was a lawyer, come to see him about a legacy. But he knew who it was. He didn't like the looks of the stranger, nor the way he smiled with his teeth. They were white teeth, and plentiful—some say they were filed to a point, but I wouldn't vouch for that. And he didn't like it when the dog took one look at the stranger and ran away howling, with his tail between his legs. But having passed his word, more or less, he stuck to it, and they went out behind the barn and made their bargain. Jabez Stone had to prick his finger to sign, and the stranger lent him a silver pin. The wound healed clean, but it left a little white scar.

After that, all of a sudden, things began to pick up and prosper for Jabez Stone. His cows got fat and his horses sleek; his crops were the envy of the neighborhood, and lightning might strike all over the valley, but it wouldn't strike his barn. Pretty soon he was one of the prosperous people of the county; there began to be talk of running him for the state senate. All in all, you might say the Stone family was as happy and contented as cats in a dairy. And so they were, except for Jabez Stone.

He'd been contented enough the first few years. It's a great thing when bad luck turns; it drives most other things out of your head. True, every now and then, especially in rainy weather, the little white scar on his finger gave him a twinge. And once a year, punctual as clockwork, the stranger with the handsome buggy would come driving by. But the sixth year the stranger lighted, and, after that, his peace was over for Jabez Stone.

The stranger came up through the lower field, switching his boots with a cane—they were handsome black boots, but Jabez Stone never liked the look of them, particularly the toes. And, after he'd passed the time of day, he said, "Well, Mr. Stone, you're a hummer! It's a very pretty property you've got here, Mr. Stone."

"Well, some might favor it and others might not," said Jabez Stone, for he was a New Hampshireman.

"Oh, no need to decry your industry!" said the stranger, very easy, showing his teeth in a smile. "After all, we know what's been done, and it's been according to contract and specifications. So when—ahem—the mortgage falls due next year, you shouldn't have any regrets."

"Speaking of that mortgage, mister," said Jabez Stone, and he looked around for help to the earth and the sky, "I'm beginning to have one or two doubts about it."

"Doubts?" said the stranger not quite so pleasantly.

"Why, yes," said Jabez Stone. "This being the U. S. A. and me always having been a religious man." He cleared his throat and got bolder. "Yes, sir," he said, "I'm beginning to have considerable doubts as to that mortgage holding in court."

"There's courts and courts," said the stranger, clicking his teeth. "Still, we might as well have a look at the original document." And he hauled out a big black pocketbook, full of papers. "Sherwin, Slater, Stevens, Stone," he muttered. " 'I, Jabez Stone, for a term of seven years—' Oh, it's quite in order, I think."

But Jabez Stone wasn't listening, for he saw something else flutter out of the black pocketbook. It was something that looked like a moth, but it wasn't a moth. And as Jabez Stone stared at it, it seemed to speak to him in a small sort of piping voice, terrible small and thin, but terrible human. "Neighbor Stone!" it squeaked. "Neighbor Stone! Help me! For God's sake, help me!"

But before Jabez Stone could stir hand or foot, the stranger whipped out a big bandanna handkerchief, caught the creature in it, just like a butterfly, and started tying up the ends of the bandanna.

"Sorry for the interruption," he said. "As I was saying—" But Jabez Stone was shaking all over like a scared horse.

"That's Miser Stevens' voice!" he said in a croak. "And you've got him in your handkerchief!"

The stranger looked a little embarrassed.

"Yes, I really should have transferred him to the collecting box," he said with a simper, "but there were some rather unusual specimens there and I didn't want them crowded. Well, well, these little contretemps will occur."

"I don't know what you mean by contertan," said Jabez Stone, "but that was Miser Stevens' voice! And he ain't dead! You can't tell me he is! He was just as spry and mean as a woodchuck Tuesday!"

"In the midst of life . . ." said the stranger, kind of pious. "Listen!" Then a bell began to toll in the valley and Jabez Stone listened, with the sweat running down his face. For he knew it was tolled for Miser Stevens and that he was dead.

"These long-standing accounts," said the stranger with a sigh; "one really hates to close them. But business is business."

He still had the bandanna in his hand, and Jabez Stone felt sick as he saw the cloth struggle and flutter.

"Are they all as small as that?" he asked hoarsely.

"Small?" said the stranger. "Oh, I see what you mean. Why, they vary." He measured Jabez Stone with his eyes, and his teeth showed. "Don't worry, Mr. Stone," he said. "You'll go with a very good grade. I wouldn't trust you outside the collecting box. Now, a man like Dan'l Webster, of course—well, we'd have to build a special box for him, and even at that, I imagine the wing spread would astonish you. He'd certainly be a prize. I wish we could see our way clear to him. But, in your case, as I was saying—"

"Put that handkerchief away!" said Jabez Stone, and he began to beg and to pray. But the best he could get at the end was a three years extension, with conditions.

But till you make a bargain like that, you've got no idea of how fast four years can run. By the last months of those years Jabez Stone's known all over the state and there's talk of running him for governor—and it's dust and ashes in his mouth. For every day, when he gets up, he thinks, "There's one more night gone," and every night, when he lies down, he thinks of the black pocketbook and the soul of Miser Stevens, and it makes him sick at heart. Till, finally, he can't bear it any longer, and, in the last days of the last year, he hitches up his horse and drives off to seek Dan'l Webster. For Dan'l was born in New Hampshire, only a few miles from Cross Corners, and it's well known that he has a particular soft spot for old neighbors.

It was early in the morning when he got to Marshfield, but Dan'l was up already, talking Latin to the farm hands and wrestling with the ram, Goliath, and trying out a new trotter and working up speeches to make against John C. Calhoun. But when he heard a New Hampshireman had come to see him, he dropped everything else he was doing, for that was Dan'l's way. He gave Jabez Stone a breakfast that five men couldn't eat, went into the living history of every man and woman in Cross Corners, and finally asked him how he could serve him.

Jabez Stone allowed that it was a kind of mortgage case.

"Well, I haven't pleaded a mortgage case in a long time, and I don't generally plead now, except before the Supreme Court," said Dan'l, "but if I can, I'll help you."

"Then I've got hope for the first time in ten years," said Jabez Stone and told him the details.

Dan'l walked up and down as he listened, hands behind his back, now and then asking a question, now and then plunging his eyes at the floor, as if they'd bore through it like gimlets. When Jabez Stone had finished, Dan'l puffed out his cheeks and blew. Then he turned to Jabez Stone and a smile broke out over his face like the sunrise over Monadnock.

"You've certainly given yourself the devil's own row to hoe, Neighbor Stone," he said, "but I'll take your case."

"You'll take it?" said Jabez Stone, hardly daring to believe.

"Yes," said Dan'l Webster. "I've got about seventy-five other things to do and the Missouri Compromise to straighten out, but I'll take your case. For if two New Hampshiremen aren't a match for the devil, we might as well give the country back to the Indians."

Then he shook Jabez Stone by the hand and said, "Did you come down here in a hurry?"

"Well, I admit I made time," said Jabez Stone.

"You'll go back faster," said Dan'l Webster, and he told 'em to hitch up Constitution and Constellation to the carriage. They were matched grays with one white forefoot, and they stepped like greased lightning.

Well, I won't describe how excited and pleased the whole Stone family was to have the great Dan'l Webster for a guest, when they finally got there. Jabez Stone had lost his hat on the way, blown off when they overtook a wind, but he didn't take much account of that. But after supper he sent the family off to bed, for he had most particular business with Mr. Webster. Mrs. Stone wanted them to sit in the front parlor, but Dan'l Webster knew front parlors and said he preferred the kitchen. So it was there they sat, waiting for the stranger, with a jug on the table between them and a bright fire on the hearth— the stranger being scheduled to show up on the stroke of midnight, according to specification.

Well, most men wouldn't have asked for better company than Dan'l Webster and a jug. But with every tick of the clock Jabez Stone got sadder and sadder. His eyes roved round, and though he sampled the jug you could see he couldn't taste it. Finally, on the stroke of 11:30 he reached over and grabbed Dan'l Webster by the arm.

"Mr. Webster, Mr. Webster!" he said, and his voice was shaking with fear and a desperate courage. "For God's sake, Mr. Webster, harness your horses and get away from this place while you can!"

"You've brought me a long way, neighbor, to tell me you don't like my company," said Dan'l Webster, quite peaceable, pulling at the jug.

"Miserable wretch that I am!" groaned Jabez Stone. "I've brought you a devilish way, and now I see my folly. Let him take me if he wills. I don't hanker after it, I must say, but I can stand it. But you're the Union's stay and New Hampshire's pride! He mustn't get you, Mr. Webster! He mustn't get you!"

Dan'l Webster looked at the distracted man, all gray and shaking in the firelight, and laid a hand on his shoulder.

"I'm obliged to you, Neighbor Stone," he said gently. "It's kindly thought of. But there's a jug on the table and a case in hand. And I never left a jug or a case half finished in my life."

And just at that moment there was a sharp rap on the door.

"Ah," said Dan'l Webster very coolly, "I thought your clock was a trifle slow, Neighbor Stone." He stepped to the door and opened it. "Come in!" he said.

The stranger came in—very dark and tall he looked in the

firelight. He was carrying a box under his arm—a black japanned box with little air holes in the lid. At the sight of the box Jabez Stone gave a low cry and shrank into a corner of the room.

"Mr. Webster, I presume," said the stranger, very polite, but with his eyes glowing like a fox's deep in the woods.

"Attorney of record for Jabez Stone," said Dan'l Webster, but his eyes were glowing too. "Might I ask your name?"

"I've gone by a good many," said the stranger carelessly. "Perhaps Scratch will do for the evening. I'm often called that in these regions."

Then he sat down at the table and poured himself a drink from the jug. The liquor was cold in the jug, but it came steaming into the glass.

"And now," said the stranger, smiling and showing his teeth, "I shall call upon you, as a law-abiding citizen, to assist me in taking possession of my property."

Well, with that the argument began—and it went hot and heavy. At first Jabez Stone had a flicker of hope, but when he saw Dan'l Webster being forced back at point after point, he just sat scrunched in his corner, with his eyes on that japanned box. For there wasn't any doubt as to the deed or the signature —that was the worst of it. Dan'l Webster twisted and turned and thumped his fist on the table, but he couldn't get away from that. He offered to compromise the case; the stranger wouldn't hear of it. He pointed out the property had increased in value, and state senators ought to be worth more; the stranger stuck to the letter of the law. He was a great lawyer, Dan'l Webster, but we know who's the King of Lawyers, as the Good Book tells us, and it seemed as if, for the first time, Dan'l Webster had met his match.

Finally, the stranger yawned a little. "Your spirited efforts on behalf of your client do you credit, Mr. Webster," he said, "but if you have no more arguments to adduce, I'm rather pressed for time . . ." and Jabez Stone shuddered.

Dan'l Webster's brow looked as dark as a thundercloud.

"Pressed or not, you shall not have this man!" he thundered. "Mr. Stone is an American citizen, and no American citizen may be forced into the service of a foreign prince. We fought England for that in '12 and we'll fight all hell for it again!"

"Foreign," said the stranger. "And who calls me a foreigner?"

"Well, I never heard of the dev—of your claiming American citizenship," said Dan'l Webster with surprise.

"And who with better right?" said the stranger with one of his terrible smiles. "When the first wrong was done to the first Indian, I was there. When the first slaver put out for the Congo, I stood on her deck. Am I not in your books and stories and beliefs, from the first settlements on? Am I not spoken of still in every church in New England? 'Tis true the North claims me for Southerner and the South for a Northerner, but I am neither. I am merely an honest American like yourself—and of the best descent—for, to tell the truth, Mr. Webster, though I don't like to boast of it, my name is older in this country than yours."

"Aha!" said Dan'l Webster with the veins standing out in his forehead. "Then I stand on the Constitution! I demand a trial for my client!"

"The case is hardly one for an ordinary court," said the stranger, his eyes flickering. "And, indeed, the lateness of the hour—"

"Let it be any court you choose, so it is an American judge and an American jury!" said Dan'l Webster in his pride. "Let it be the quick or the dead; I'll abide the issue!"

"You have said it," said the stranger, and pointed his finger at the door. And with that, and all of a sudden, there was a rushing of wind outside and a noise of footsteps. They came, clear and distinct, through the night. And yet they were not like the footsteps of living men.

"In God's name, who comes by so late?" cried Jabez Stone in an ague of fear.

"The jury Mr. Webster demands," said the stranger, sipping at his boiling glass. "You must pardon the rough appearance of one or two; they will have come a long way."

And with that the fire burned blue and the door blew open and twelve men entered, one by one.

If Jabez Stone had been sick with terror before, he was blind with terror now. For there was Walter Butler, the loyalist, who spread fire and horror through the Mohawk Valley in the times of the Revolution; and there was Simon Girty, the renegade, who saw white men burned at the stake and whooped with the Indians to see them burn. His eyes were green, like a catamount's, and the stains on his hunting shirt did not come from the blood of the deer. King Philip was there, wild and proud as he had been in life, with the great gash in his head that gave him his death wound, and cruel Governor Dale, who broke men on the wheel. There was Morton of Merry Mount, who so vexed the Plymouth Colony, with his flushed, loose, handsome face and his hate of the godly. There was Teach, the bloody pirate, with his black beard curling on his breast. The Reverend John Smeet, with his strangler's hands and his Geneva gown, walked as daintily as he had to the gallows. The red print of the rope was still around his neck, but he carried a perfumed handkerchief in one hand. One and all, they came into the room with the fires of hell still upon them, and the stranger named their names and their deeds as they came, 'till the tale of twelve was told. Yet the stranger had told the truth—they had all played a part in America.

"Are you satisfied with the jury, Mr. Webster?" said the stranger mockingly, when they had taken their places.

The sweat stood upon Dan'l Webster's brow, but his voice was clear.

"Quite satisfied," he said. "Though I miss General Arnold from the company."

"Benedict Arnold is engaged upon other business," said the stranger with a glower. "Ah, you asked for justice, I believe."

He pointed his finger once more, and a tall man, soberly clad in Puritan garb, with the burning gaze of the fanatic, stalked into the room and took his judge's place.

"Judge Hathorne is a jurist of experience," said the stranger. "He presided at certain witch trials once held in Salem. There were others who repented of the business later, but not he."

"Repent of such notable wonders and undertakings?" said the stern old justice. "Nay, hang them—hang them all!" And he muttered to himself in a way that struck ice into the soul of Jabez Stone.

Then the trial began, and, as you might expect, it didn't look anyways good for the defense. And Jabez Stone didn't make much of a witness in his own behalf. He took one look at Simon Girty and screeched, and they had to put him back in his corner in a kind of swoon.

It didn't halt the trial though; the trial went on, as trials do. Dan'l Webster had faced some hard juries and hanging judges in his time, but this was the hardest he'd ever faced, and he knew it. They sat there with a kind of glitter in their eyes, and the stranger's smooth voice went on and on. Every time he'd raise an objection, it'd be "Objection sustained," but whenever Dan'l objected, it'd be "Objection denied." Well, you couldn't expect fair play from a fellow like this Mr. Scratch.

It got to Dan'l in the end, and he began to heat, like iron in the forge. When he got up to speak he was going to flay that stranger with every trick known to the law, and the judge and jury too. He didn't care if it was contempt of court or what would happen to him for it. He didn't care any more what happened to Jabez Stone. He just got madder and madder, thinking of what he'd say. And yet, curiously enough, the more he thought about it, the less he was able to arrange his speech in his mind.

Till, finally, it was time for him to get up on his feet, and he did so, all ready to bust out with lightnings and denunciations. But before he started he looked over the judge and jury for a moment, such being his custom. And he noticed the glittter in their eyes was twice as strong as before, and they all leaned forward. Like hounds just before they get the fox, they looked, and the blue mist of evil in the room thickened as he watched them. Then he saw what he'd been about to do, and he wiped his forehead, as a man might who's just escaped falling into a pit in the dark.

For it was him they'd come for, not only Jabez Stone. He read it in the glitter of their eyes and in the way the stranger hid his mouth with one hand. And if he fought them with their own weapons, he'd fall into their power; he knew that, though he couldn't have told you how. It was his own anger and horror that burned in their eyes; and he'd have to wipe that out or the case was lost. He stood there for a moment, his black eyes burning like anthracite. And then he began to speak.

He started off in a low voice, though you could hear every word. They say he could call on the harps of the blessed when he chose. And this was just as simple and easy as a man could talk. But he didn't start out by condemning or reviling. He was talking about the things that make a country a country and a man a man.

And he began with the simple things that everybody's known and felt—the freshness of a fine morning when you're young, and the taste of food when you're hungry, and the new day that's every day when you're a child. He took them up and he turned them in his hands. They were good things for any man. But without freedom they sickened. And when he talked of those enslaved, and of the sorrows of slavery, his voice got like a big bell. He talked of the early days of America and the men who had made those days. It wasn't a spread-eagle speech, but he made you see it. He admitted all the wrong that had ever been done. But he showed how, out of the wrong and the right, the suffering and the starvations, something new had come. And everybody had played a part in it, even the traitors.

Then he turned to Jabez Stone and showed him as he was— an ordinary man who'd had hard luck and wanted to change it. And, because he'd wanted to change it, now he was going to be punished for all eternity. And yet there was good in Jabez Stone, and he showed that good. He was hard and mean, in some ways, but he was a man. There was sadness in being a man, but it was a proud thing too. And he showed what the pride of it was till you couldn't help feeling it. Yes, even in hell, if a man was a man, you'd know it. And he wasn't pleading for any one person any more, though his voice rang like an organ. He was telling the story and the failures and the endless journey of mankind. They got tricked and trapped and bamboozled, but it was a great journey. And no demon that was ever foaled could know the inwardness of it—it took a man to do that.

The fire began to die on the hearth and the wind before morning to blow. The light was getting gray in the room when Dan'l Webster finished. And his words came back at the end to New

Hampshire ground, and the one spot of land that each man loves and clings to. He painted a picture of that, and to each one of that jury he spoke of things long forgotten. For his voice could search a heart, and that was his gift and his strength. And to one his voice was like the forest and its secrecy, and to another like the sea and the storms of the sea; and one heard the cry of his lost nation in it, and another saw a little harmless scene he hadn't remembered for years. But each saw something. And when Dan'l Webster finished he didn't know whether or not he'd saved Jabez Stone. But he knew he'd done a miracle. For the glitter was gone from the eyes of judge and jury, and, for the moment, they were men again, and knew they were men.

"The defense rests," said Dan'l Webster, and stood there like a mountain. His ears were still ringing with his speech, and he didn't hear anything else till he heard Judge Hathorne say, "The jury will retire to consider its verdict."

Walter Butler rose in his place and his face had a dark, gay pride on it.

"The jury has considered its verdict," he said, and looked the stranger full in the eye. "We find for the defendant, Jabez Stone."

With that, the smile left the stranger's face, but Walter Butler did not flinch.

"Perhaps 'tis not strictly in accordance with the evidence," said he, "but even the damned may salute the eloquence of Mr. Webster."

With that, the long crow of a rooster split the gray morning sky, and judge and jury were gone from the room like a puff of smoke and as if they had never been there. The stranger returned to Dan'l Webster, smiling wryly.

"Major Butler was always a bold man," he said. "I had not thought him quite so bold. Nevertheless, my congratulations, as between two gentlemen."

"I'll have that paper first, if you please," said Dan'l Webster, and he took it and tore it into four pieces. It was queerly warm to the touch. "And now," he said, "I'll have you!" and his hand came down like a bear trap on the stranger's arm. For he knew that once you bested anybody like Mr. Scratch in a fair fight, his power on you was gone. And he could see that Mr. Scratch knew it too.

The stranger twisted and wriggled, but he couldn't get out of that grip. "Come, come, Mr. Webster," he said, smiling palely. "This sort of thing is ridic—ouch!—is ridiculous. If you're worried about the costs of the case, naturally, I'd be glad to pay—"

"And so you shall!" said Dan'l Webster, shaking him till his teeth rattled. "For you'll sit right down at that table and draw up a document, promising never to bother Jabez Stone nor his heirs or assigns nor any other New Hampshireman till doomsday! For any hades we want to raise in this state, we can raise ourselves, without assistance from strangers."

"Ouch!" said the stranger. "Ouch! Well, they never did run very big to the barrel, but—ouch!—I agree!"

So he sat down and drew up the document. But Dan'l Webster kept his hand on his coat collar all the time.

"And now may I go?" said the stranger, quite humble, when Dan'l 'd seen the document's in proper and legal form.

"Go?" said Dan'l, giving him another shake. "I'm still trying to figure out what I'll do with you. For you've settled the costs of the case, but you haven't settled with me. I think I'll take you back to Marshfield," he said, kind of reflec-tive. "I've got a ram there named Goliath that can butt through an iron door. I'd kind of like to turn you loose on his field and see what he'd do."

Well, with that the stranger began to beg and to plead. And he begged and he pled so humble that finally Dan'l, who was naturally kindhearted, agreed to let him go. The stranger seemed terrible grateful for that and said, just to show they were friends, he'd tell Dan'l's fortune before leaving. So Dan'l agreed to that, though he didn't take much stock in fortune tellers ordinarily. But, naturally, the stranger was a little different.

Well, he pried and peered at the lines in Dan'l's hands. And he told him one thing and another that was quite remarkable. But they were all in the past.

"Yes, all that's true, and it happened," said Dan'l Webster. "But what's to come in the future?"

The stranger grinned, kind of happily, and shook his head.

"The future's not as you think it," he said. "It's dark. You have a great ambition, Mr. Webster."

"I have," said Dan'l firmly, for everybody knew he wanted to be President.

"It seems almost within your grasp," said the stranger, "but you will not attain it. Lesser men will be made President and you will be passed over."

"And, if I am, I'll still be Daniel Webster," said Dan'l. "Say on."

"You have two strong sons," said the stranger, shaking his head. "You look to found a line. But each will die in war and neither reach greatness."

"Live or die, they are still my sons," said Dan'l Webster. "Say on."

"You have made great speeches," said the stranger. "You will make more."

"Ah," said Dan'l Webster.

"But the last great speech you make will turn many of your own against you," said the stranger. "They will call you Ichabod; they will call you by other names. Even in New England some will say you have turned your coat and sold your country, and their voices will be loud against you till you die."

"So it is an honest speech, it does not matter what men say," said Dan'l Webster. Then he looked at the stranger and their glances locked.

"One question," he said, "I have fought for the Union all my life. Will I see that fight won against those who would tear it apart?"

"Not while you live," said the stranger grimly, "but it will be won. And after you are dead, there are thousands who will fight your cause, because of words that you spoke."

"Why, then, you long-barrelled, slab-sided, lantern-jawed, fortune-telling note shaver," said Dan'l Webster with a great roar of laughter, "be off with you to your own place before I put my mark on you! For, by the thirteen original colonies, I'd go to the Pit itself to save the Union!"

And with that he drew back his foot for a kick that would

have stunned a horse. It was only the tip of his shoe that caught the stranger, but he went flying out of the door with his collect-ing box under his arm.

"And now," said Dan'l Webster, seeing Jabez Stone begin-ning to rouse from his swoon, "let's see what's left in the jug, for it's dry work talking all night. I hope there's pie for breakfast, Neighbor Stone."

But they say that whenever the devil comes near Marshfield, even now, he gives it a wide berth. And he hasn't been seen in the state of New Hampshire from that day to this. I'm not talking about Massachusetts or Vermont.

1. Explain what we mean by calling Daniel Webster a legendary hero. 2. In what way is this tall tale like the legend *The Devil and Tom Walker*? 3. In what way is it different? 4. Show specifically how the author uses hyperbole. 5. What character-istics of *The Devil and Daniel Webster* are like *Crockett's Morning Hunt*? 6. Use your dictionary for:

renegade	*patriarch*	*anthracite*	*twinge*	*decry*
spavins	*legacy*	*japanned*	*adduce*	*flickering*

Most tall tales belong to a particular region. *Crockett's Morning Hunt* belongs to the American frontier. *The Devil and Daniel Webster* belongs to New England. The tall tale hero Pecos Bill breathes the air of Texas that makes even the coyotes grow into huge beasts.

Pecos Bill
and the Willful Coyote

WILLIAM C. WHITE

As Bill got older and his wind wasn't so good any more, he had to give up chasing coyotes, that is, until Baby came along.

I was with him the night he ran into Baby and I'll never forget it. We were riding along forty miles south of El Paso on as nice a night as I ever saw. The stars were out and it was bright. There was even a piece of moon. That was what made it so funny. We were riding along and Bill was singing,

Beat the drums lowly and play your fifes slowly,
Play the dead march as you drag me along.
Take me to the graveyard and lay a sod o'er me.
For I'm a poor cowboy and I know I done wrong.

Pecos Bill always sang that song when he was feeling extra happy.

All of a sudden he says, "That's funny!"

"What's funny?"

"There, on that ridge, that thunderstorm coming up."

I looked and saw a black cloud coming up all right but the stars and the moon were still shining.

"Never saw a thunderstorm on a starbright night," Bill said. "I'd call that almost a first-class miracle."

Something flashed on the ridge and Bill said, "It's lightning all right." We rode on faster. Bill stopped sudden. "That's funny!"

"What's funny?"

"Did you hear any thunder after that lightning?"

"Nope." I said that because I didn't hear any thunder and we were close enough to the storm to hear it if there was any thunder. "Nope, I didn't hear any."

"Look! Lightning again and no thunder!" Bill shook his head. "I believe in miracles but only one at a time. A thunderstorm so close with lightning and no thunder, that's almost a first-class miracle."

We rode closer and suddenly we heard a sound. I guess you'd call it laughter but it was a child's laughter and a woman's laughter and a waterfall's laughter, mixed with a horse's neigh and the noise of a tin can full of pebbles, and the roar of a lot of cowboys howling at a joke. It sounded like "Hayheehaw! Haiharhoo! Hearhoiheh!" and ended with "Huh, huh, huh!" delicate, like a sceptical baby.

"A laughing thunderstorm," Bill said angry, "would be a third miracle. Hell, that's a coyote and the lightning is his eyes flashing!"

The black cloud raised a head and we could see right enough it was a coyote and the biggest one I ever saw and no one ever saw a bigger one. It was easy to tell it was a female because she walked dainty. She was so big she'd have to lie on her side and bend her neck out of shape to nibble at sagebrush. She must have heard us for the next thing she came at us, just like a thunderstorm that got up on its heels and began chasing you. She went by in such a rush, the air around was chilly for the next half hour. Bill didn't have a chance to draw his gun and fire. All he said was "Oh, Baby!"

That's how Baby got her name!

"Baby!" Bill repeated.

Somewhere, off in the distance, in the next county or maybe over in New Mexico we heard the "Hayheehaw" and so on and then the final "Huh, huh, huh!"

Bill was awful thoughtful for a while. "I'm going to hunt that baby and get her if it's the last thing I do. Baby! There's a coyote's coyote!"

Me and Bill hunted Baby all that year and all the next and the year after that and the year after that, too. Maybe there were even more years but those are all I remember. It was a long time.

Hunting Baby wasn't hard. She was always obliging and willing to hang around and be hunted. We chased her over most of Texas. When we couldn't find her on dark nights she'd let out that laugh of hers, particularly the "Huh, huh, huh" part, and off we'd go. Other times her eyes would flash in the distance and there we'd go again. Sometimes that fooled us—more than fifty times we saw flashes like that and went off hell for leather and found that what we were chasing on the horizon was really a thunderstorm or a twister. Of course, when it thundered, then we knew it wasn't Baby. Half the times Baby'd have been lying low, watching us make fools of ourselves. As we turned back soaking wet we'd hear her "Huh, huh, huh!" off in the other direction. Other times we could get on her trail by waiting till she went to a water hole. She had a thirst like a desert and could drink a hole dry with the noise of a rusty pump. Some nights when we thought we'd lost her, her tracks would help us. They were always deep round holes and you couldn't miss 'em. It's getting off my story but it was those tracks that helped develop West Texas—they were so deep they caught a lot of rain water and held it through dry spells and the grass grew thick around 'em. A lot of cattlemen today still use those tracks for water holes.

It wasn't hunting Baby that was tough, it was bagging her. In five years Pecos Bill must have had a thousand shots at her, from all distances from a hundred feet to a mile, and he shot at her with lead and iron and silver and a couple of times with a shot gun full of scrap iron. Nothing took any effect. Sometimes the stuff we fired hit Baby's sides and bounced back at us. Once we had to hide under a *mesquite* thicket for an hour while it rained railroad scrap all around us. As a six-inch piece of steel rail hit Bill on the neck he said, "We just won't try that one again. It's like being hunted by a coyote and shot at."

Other times when Baby was feeling frisky she didn't bother to bounce bullets back at us. She just timed the shot so that as it came to her she leaped up in the air and the bullets went right under her. Then she'd land with a smack you could hear a long way off and sometimes the earth would crack under her. Half the *arroyos,* those little canyons, in West Texas is from where

Baby landed after those jumps. She'd have probably started up a couple of earthquakes in any country not so tough as West Texas.

"That Baby!" Bill would say after missing her once again. He sounded awful proud. "She's just willful! Plumb willful!"

I guess it got to be a game with Baby because no matter what we tried to do, her laugh never changed or got angry or snarly. Some nights when Bill didn't feel like going out after her, Baby'd hang around and there was a kind of disappointment in her laugh, like a kid you promised ice cream for supper he didn't get.

I know it got to be a game with Bill and I never saw him so happy. Of course, from time to time we'd take a job to get enough money to try out some new scheme Bill had thought up for getting Baby. That was all he did think about, night after night. He figured out all kinds of baits and snares and devices but none of 'em worked. He figured out every kind of trap. After Baby picked up one of 'em and heaved it in the air with her hind foot and it landed on Bill and me and kept us pinned down for five days, we gave up traps. Even that didn't make Bill sore. He laughed and shook his head. "That Baby! She's smart." That was the way he was talking about her. Sometimes when he saw Baby running in the moonlight he'd say, "Look at the way that moonlight shines her gray fur! I bet you never saw anything prettier." And when she'd run fast Bill'd say, "I bet that's the fastest animule there is!" The way he'd talk, you might have thought Bill was raising a child to show off at the State Fair.

One idea Bill had almost did get Baby. The idea was to chase her into the middle of Randall County, which we did, and then to run barbed wire right around the boundaries of the county, which we did. We used all the barbed wire in West Texas doing it and we strung it right. When we got done, stringing it over trees and poles and houses, I never saw such a mess of barbed wire. There wasn't a hole in it big enough for a rattlesnake to crawl through and we ran it so high that not even Baby could jump over it. There we had Baby penned up right and all we had to do now was to wait until she got too weak to move.

That wouldn't take too long because we'd been having a drought and the water holes were as dry as sun-bleached bones. And Baby was always thirsty.

We must have waited outside that barbed wire a couple of weeks and all the time Bill kept saying, "We got her this time all right, we got her! She won't be willful no more!" And Bill would jump around excited like a colt in a loco patch. "When man matches his intelligence with animules," Bill would say, "man must win. That's natchural!" Every night we heard Baby crying inside there behind the wire like she was trying to find a way out and getting madder and madder. The more she cried the more Bill grinned and yelled, "We got her this time!"

Then one night when we were watching there was a new sound behind the wire, a soft "Plop, plop, plop!"

"What's that mean?" Bill asked nervous. "Sounds like she was throwing mud pies." Then he guessed it. "Baby's digging, that's what it is. She's trying to dig her way out and she's throwing up dirt!" He looked half proud as he said, "I knew she'd figure out something to do." He looked half mad as he said, "That won't get her nowhere. We'll surround the fence and when her head shows we'll wallop her."

So Bill called out all the people from Potter, Armstrong, Swisher, and Deaf Smith counties, the ones around Randall. They were glad to stand watch because they're always glad to take a crack at anyone or anything coming from Randall County.

Three days and three nights we waited and the "Plop, plop, plop" continued but it got fainter and fainter as Baby dug deeper. "This time we got her sure," Bill said. He patrolled the fence day and night with a paddle made from a wagon tongue.

About midnight we heard a new kind of noise. It began as a hiss and turned into a roar and the earth shook and half the people around the fence ran like hell. The roar got louder and right then I felt rain in my face. It felt like rain, it was wet, but when I got some on my hand it had a funny smell.

In the midst of the loud roaring we heard a funny noise. It was "Hayheehaw," and the rest of it and then "Huh, huh, huh!" It sounded awful frightened, but it wasn't coming from back of the fence, it was coming from somewhere behind us.

"That's Baby!" Bill started to jump. "And she's out, she's gotten out!" I never saw a man so mad but he wasn't so mad he couldn't say, "She's that smart, that Baby."

It was beginning to rain even harder. "How'd she get out?"

"Blew out," Bill said. "That's not rain, it's oil. It's got the same smell as the stuff I used to rub on my stiff joints. She dug to hit a pocket and a gusher blew her out."

Way off in the distance, running like a breeze toward Mexico, we heard Baby. "That scared her," Bill said rueful. "She ought to know I didn't mean to have it happen like that. She's scared. She won't come back."

Her laugh was awful faint. "She must be over the Rio Grande by now."

Bill nodded. "I didn't think she'd take it like that." He sounded all choked up and he went to his horse and rode off like mad toward Amarillo.

It took me four days to find him. When I caught up with him he was in Amarillo at the Unweaned Calf bar. He wasn't alone, either. Somewhere he'd picked up a girl whose name was Kankakee Katie. I ain't much for women myself— I never learned how to tell a good one from a bad one and I've never been sure there's any real difference. Katie was a big blonde and from the way she was lapping up *pulque,* a pretty fair forager. She was comforting Bill and that was what mattered. I heard he'd been crying for three days when he got to town. Now he sat gloomy like and all he'd say was "Baby!"

"Who's this Baby you're muling over?" Katie asked him.

He just shook his head.

"I never heard a man make as much fuss over me," Katie said like it annoyed her.

Bill just says "Baby," dreamy like.

"It's awful bad manners," Katie said, "to keep grieving over one lady when you're in the company of another."

"Baby was no lady," Bill said.

"What was she, a hell cat?"

Bill shook his head. "A coyote!"

"That's no way to talk about her," Katie said, like she had to defend her sex. "What was she, blond or brunet?"

"Gray," Bill said, "gray like early morning. Baby!"

Katie lapped up some more *pulque*. "I think you're loco but I tell you, I could go for a man who'd say 'Katie' the way you say 'Baby.'"

Bill reached for the bottle and began to cry at the same time and when he cries it's like the first freshets coming down an *arroyo* in spring.

"Katie," I said, "he's really upset about a coyote." I told her about Baby and how Bill was afraid she was gone for good.

"He's grieving like that over a four-footed long-haired howling animal?" I didn't know whether Katie was going to laugh or upset the table. She didn't do either. She began to cry. "I never thought I'd meet such a tender-hearted person in all my life. Bill reminds me of my mother—she was tender-hearted like that, too." And she cried as hard as Bill.

Bill blinked and smiled at me. "Pete, here's what I need— sympathy and a chance to forget Baby." As he pounded his fist on the table, the walls of the Unweaned Calf shook and the barkeep looked scared. "Katie, if you'll have me, I'm yours. How's for marrying me and lighting out and we'll get a little ranch and raise cattle?"

Katie didn't know whether she was being kidded or not. Then she hit the table with her fist and the walls shook even harder and down to the floor dropped a little guy who was standing at the bar but not holding on tight. "Pardner," Katie said. "I heard about marriage and I always wanted to try it. It's a deal!" She stopped crying and dried her eyes on her shirtwaist sleeve. "We'll get a ranch house and we'll paper the walls with the pages of a mail-order catalogue and make everything snug." Then she looked worried. "Nope, it's only a dream."

Bill's face got black. "When I make a promise it's a promise."

Katie shook her head. "What about Baby? I know men better than anything in the world except maybe women. Sooner or later you'll get the old hankering to go after Baby and then not even a good woman's love or a forty-foot fence could hold you."

"I told you I was through with Baby," Bill roared and he made such a noise the little guy at the bar hit the floor again.

"A man's a man and a woman's a fool for forgetting it,"

Katie said, almost ready to cry again. "I just can't risk having my heart broken over a coyote." She finished off the bottle of *pulque*. "Nope, we'll stay friends, Bill, and I'll be a sister to you."

"I'll be consternated!" Bill yelled. "I believe you're jealous of Baby!"

"A lady has a right to her feelings, such as she feels," Katie said, wiping her eyes on her shirtwaist sleeve. "I'll tell you what to do, Bill. I ain't going to have no coyote come between us. You bring me Baby's hide and I'll marry you."

Bill just sat back in his chair.

"Besides, it'd be convenient to have," Katie said. "If Baby's as big as you say we could use the hide for a parlor rug and have some lap over in the dining room and what's left we could stuff chinks with."

"I can't do that," Bill said promptly. "I've been trying for years with no luck."

"You don't sound like you even wanted to get it," Katie said with a pout.

"Sure I want to get it, but how?"

"You talk like you're glad a coyote's smarter than Pecos Bill."

"That's enough." Bill banged the table and half the bottles on the bar fell down. "It's a bargain. I'll get it."

"Right now?"

"Right now!"

"Then I'll go off and hunt up a wedding dress and some shoes," Katie said. "You bring the hide back here and we'll have the hottest wedding there ever was in Amarillo." She headed for the door, like a barn being carried off in a spring flood.

Bill didn't say anything for quite a while. He picked up the *pulque* bottle and found it was empty. He asked, "Got any ideas, Pete?"

"About Katie?" I shook my head.

"About getting Baby. I can't let the little woman down."

He stood up and started to the bar. "Let's have a drink and start thinking."

When Bill asked the barkeep for *pulque* the barkeep shook

his head. "You finished the last bottle. I haven't got a drop."

"Then gimme whiskey."

"On top of *pulque?*" The barkeep looked astonished and the little man beside the bar fell to the floor and lay there.

"What's wrong with that?" Bill asked, getting hot.

"You mix my drinks like that, they'll take the hide off you." But the barkeep poured out whiskey. "However, it's your hide."

Bill swung around like he was boiling mad. "What did you say?"

"I said if you mix my drinks they'll take the hide off you—!"

"Yeep!" Bill brought a fist down on the bar and cracked the top plank. "We got it!" He slugged down the whiskey. "We got it!"

I thought he was crazy. "Got what?"

He pounded me on the back and I bounced toward the front door. "Hurry out, Pete, and get two big water tanks!"

Well, I came back to the bar with the tanks and when I got there Bill had every bottle off the shelves and he was opening them so fast the popping of corks sounded like gunfire. From somewhere he had got fifty gallons of *pulque* and that went into the tanks first. Then he poured in all the whiskey in the place.

He was awful enthusiastic. "We'll mix up a drink for Baby that'll take her hide off sure. There's been a drought in this Dust Bowl and we'll pick up a good dry water hole, fill it up with this mixture, and see what Baby does."

In the tanks went twenty gallons of rum, three cases of Bourbon, seven bottles of gin, and a bottle of soda water. The barkeep came up from the cellar with another armful of bottles. One of them had a funny shape.

"What's that?" Bill asked.

"Something called 'Cream dess Violets.' A salesman give it to me."

"Put it in!"

"Here's Liquor dess Peaches."

"Put it in!"

In went cherry brandy, a bottle of bitters, and a gallon of Dago red. Bill didn't look satisfied. "Got anything else in bottles?"

The barkeep who was baldheaded handed over a flask of hair tonic.

Bill stuck his finger in the soup and licked it. "Tastes pretty nearly right. What else you got?"

The barkeep offered a bottle of ketchup and that went in.

Again Bill sampled the results. "Almost right. Got anything else in a bottle?"

"Some perfume called Eau d'Amour I was saving for my wife."

"Put it in!"

Bill stuck his finger in once more. "That's perfect! It ought to take the hide off a cactus!"

Three teams of horses and ten men and the biggest dray in the county drew the tanks out to the water hole that Bill had decided to use. He had to hope the odor would attract Baby, wherever she was. The mixture from one tank went into the hole with a splash and the odor it gave off knocked seven men to the ground. I felt a little dizzy myself but Bill was too excited to notice anything. Twenty-one lizards who lived around that hole ran to it, took one small drink, and twenty of them lay on their backs with their toes turned up. The twenty-first just vanished in a small explosion.

After the men revived they started to move the second tank to the hole but Bill stopped them. "Hold it! Baby may not come here before this stuff dries up and we'd better save the other tank for another night. We never could mix this drink again the same way."

With the hole half filled we drove off a piece and waited. We waited a long while and we tried to keep Bill quiet but he was pretty nervous. Most of the time he said, "I hope she comes." Sometimes he said, "This is a dirty trick to play on Baby!" Even from a mile away the water hole smelled like an old barroom on Sunday morning. Bill walked up and down saying, "I wonder where Baby is, I wonder what Katie's doing, I wonder if Baby is coming, I wonder if Katie is getting ready," until he sounded all mixed up, as if he was expecting Katie to turn up at the water hole while Baby got ready for a wedding.

Every so often there would be little explosions at the water hole and Bill said, "That must be jack rabbits coming in for a drink! Boy, if only Baby'd come."

Then we heard a funny noise off in the distance, the noise of a rush of a big wind. Bill knew what it was and he yelled, "It's Baby! She's sniffing!" A minute later, over the horizon, came the black shadow that was Baby, running full speed. She came so fast that she had to stop herself at the water hole by braking with her front feet and threw up a sandstorm that blacked out El Paso three days later. We were too excited to pay any attention.

We saw the shadow stand by the hole and we watched Baby lower her head. We heard one more sniff, like a tornado taking a deep breath, and then there was an explosion and a roar that knocked us flat. Bill stood up first. "That got her!" He began -jumping. "That got her!" And he started to the hole with all of us running like mad.

Bill beat us all there and when we caught up to him he said, "I'm consternated! Look at this!" There lay Baby's hide, thick, gray, tangled and matted, but there was nothing of Baby inside it. Bill didn't know what to do or think. He just stood scratching his head. "I didn't think it would work as good as that." He shook his head. "Well, I got her at last!" His voice sounded funny. Then he said, "Load as much of the hide as you can on the wagon and drag the rest. We'll get back and see Katie."

We put a lot of the hide on the wagon and it was piled up like a hayrick. On the way back to town Bill remembered the unused tank of the mixture. "I'm going to bottle and sell it," he said. "It'll be a wonderful thing for knocking off warts and freckles."

We pulled up in front of the Unweaned Calf and Bill yelled, "Hey, Katie!" He was feeling pretty good again. "Hey, Katie, come out and see what I got!"

A flock of barflies rushed out but no Katie, and Bill began to grumble. "Look at the trouble you go to, just for a woman and then she's off primping herself and too busy to come look." He decided to wait for her and invited everyone in for a drink. By this time fifty guys were going up and down the street boasting how they caught the coyote by putting whiskey on her tail.

The barkeep had renewed his stock from somewhere and Bill ordered drinks all around. After twenty minutes he began to yell, "Hey, Katie!"

The barkeep gave him a funny look. "You mean that blonde you were talking to yesterday?"

"Yeah, what about her?"·

"Last night a cowhand comes in with a couple hundred dollars and said he was going up to San Antone. Katie said she always wanted to see San Antone so she goes with him. They left about midnight!"

Well, Bill stowed the hide and the tank of mixture away in a shed and he said, "Let's get out of this country, Pete." We went over to New Mexico for a time, punching cattle, but it wasn't the same Bill. He was thoughtful and silent and he never sang any more. He never talked about Baby, either. Then we drifted back to El Paso again and got a job at the One Legged M Ranch. Bill worked hard but his heart wasn't in his work. At night he used to leave our shack and go out and sit somewheres by himself and he got sore if I offered to go along. When he did talk, he was pretty gloomy. "I'm getting old," he'd say. "I think we ought to go out to Californy for our last days. That's where rich Texans and poor Texicans go before they die. They sit in the sun, I heard, and eat oranges."

Once he said, "I done wrong killing Baby. I shouldn'ta done it. I was so happy when she was around to chase, I didn't know how happy I was."

I couldn't get him interested in roping or riding or liquor or shooting. As for women, when the sister of the owner of the One Legged M came for a visit Bill ran off and hid in the hills for a week.

He came back with a funny look on his face and he wouldn't talk. But that night he said, "Come along with me."

We walked a mile from the ranch buildings. Bill said mysteriously, "Hear anything?"

All I heard was a lot of crickets and maybe a lizard in the grass. I asked, "Where?"

"Over there, back of that hill."

I listened again and I heard a horse neighing. "I don't hear nothing special."

Bill wasn't even listening to me. He was grinning like a kid. "I can hear her, coming nearer." He shook his head. "She sounds mighty lonesome tonight, mighty lonesome." He repeated, "So lonesome, that 'Huh, huh, huh!' "

I knew who he was talking about. I just chewed on a piece of grass and said nothing.

"You sure you don't hear nothing?" Bill asked.

"I got a cold." I tried to hide what I was thinking about Bill. "I don't hear nothing so good."

The next day I found Bill in the bunkhouse packing his kit. "I'm going back to Amarillo," he said and he wouldn't explain why. "I just got an idea, that's all."

He did explain on the way back. "Baby's still hanging around waiting for me, Pete. I know it." He glared at me. "You think I'm crazy."

I shook my head mighty quick. "Different people hear different things."

"The reason we can't see her is because she has no hide," Bill said like he'd thought it out. "Did you ever see a coyote without a hide?"

"Nope, I never did."

"No one ever did and that proves it. If a coyote's going to be seen he just has to have a hide!"

We rode on quite a spell and I didn't have a word to say.

Then Bill said, "When we get to Amarillo, I'm going after Baby."

I almost fell off my horse and it wasn't the horse's fault. "How will you do that?"

Bill didn't say. We came into town and he went to the shed where he stored all the stuff after he got Baby's hide. It was still there but except to pat it once, he wasn't interested in it. He went right to the tank of mixture and pounded it.

It sounded as empty as a dry well.

"It's gone and I can't even mix it again," Bill said, and he sounded heartbroken. "I figured that maybe if I drank some of it, it'd put me in the same shape as Baby. Then I could have gone after her."

I just shook my head. I couldn't say a word.

Bill began to fuss around the tank. With the top off he lowered himself inside. Then I heard him yell, "Get a cup, Pete! There's just a little bit left here."

I got him a cup and he fished up one cupful and even for that he had to scrape bottom. When he came from the tank he was grinning from earlobe to earlobe. I was pretty worried but I figured he knew what he was doing.

"You going to drink this now?"

"No, sir," Bill said with a lot of pride. "I'm going to drink it fit and proper." And with that he began to sing

> Oh, I'm wild and woolly
> And full of fleas,
> Ain't never been curried
> Below the knees

I tried to argue with him all the way to the Unweaned Calf but his mind was made up. He just kept singing. He told the barkeep, "This time I brought my own liquor."

The barkeep looked suspicious. "How about a chaser?"

"I hope I'll never need a chaser," Bill said, with a pleasant laugh. He looked around the room and saw about twenty people. "Come on, folks, gather round and I'll show you something you can tell your grandchildren." He raised the cup but I was feeling too bad to watch close.

Before he tastes it he sings

> Take me to the graveyard and lay a sod o'er me,
> For I'm a poor cowboy and I know I done wrong!

When I heard that I knew he was extra happy again.

"Pete!" he said to me. "You've been a good friend. When you find someone like Baby, don't treat her bad!"

Then he takes a good long swig from the cup.

There's a sort of flash and explosion, not loud but gentle like and when I look up, Bill's gone. Completely gone and not a sign of him! Then, and the men who were in the Unweaned Calf at that moment will swear to it, drunk or sober, we heard a gentle fluttering sound. Down from the ceiling like falling leaves came the clothes Bill had been wearing, his shirt, his hat, his pants, his boots, and the hand-carved belt he was so proud of. For a second they stood by themselves, just as if Bill was inside 'em, then they collapsed to the floor.

And that was the end of Pecos Bill, as far as anyone knew.

I hung around town for a couple of days but I was awful lonesome so I went back to my job at the One Legged M, feeling like a lost calf. I worked extra hard by day so I'd be good and tired at nights but even then I couldn't sleep.

One night I got up and walked out to where Bill and me used to sit. I was there in the quiet and I just couldn't forget Bill. The only noise I heard was a couple of lizards in the grass.

Now, I ain't going to swear to this because I never heard it again but as I was sitting there that night a wind came up sudden and it got real cold. The grass began to move or I thought it did. And right behind me I heard "Hayheehaw!" and so on and then "Huh, huh, huh!" Maybe it could have been the wind in the trees but there weren't any trees and anyway, where did that sudden wind come from? A minute later I swear I heard Bill's voice, as happy as a little child, laughing, "That Baby! She's just willful!" It sounded as if he was chasing along behind, doing what he liked to do most in all this world.

But I couldn't see a thing.

I would even think that I had dreamed it except that the next morning Bert Simmons who owns the One Legged M called us outside and we followed him behind the barn. The ground there used to be as level and smooth as a piece of harness strap but this morning there was a brand new *arroyo,* fifty feet deep and running for a quarter mile, just like a big crack in the earth. It was the sort of crack we used to see when Bill and me shot and Baby jumped in the air to duck and then landed hard.

Well, I'm sure that wasn't the finish of the whole thing although I never again heard a sound like Baby or saw any traces. But I've been reading in the newspapers about those California earthquakes and I remember what Bill used to say about wanting to finish his days in California. No one knows what causes those earthquakes, I hear, but I got my own ideas ever since I heard that California was a sort of soft place, nowhere near as tough as West Texas and a whole lot more brittle.

1. *Pecos Bill and the Willful Coyote* develops in a series of episodes. List them. 2. Arrange the events in sequence. Is there a logical sequence? 3. Does the *I* narrator help unify the events? 4. Does the *I* narrator add any credibility? 5. How is this story related to a locality? 6. What characteristics make *Pecos Bill and the Willful Coyote* a typical tall tale?

Paul Bunyan is the legendary hero of the lumberjacks of the northern woods. Hundreds of tales center about him. Here are two typical Paul Bunyan tall tales.

AN AMERICAN HERCULES

· JAMES STEVENS

Paul Bunyan, the mythical hero of the lumberjacks, is the supreme figure of American folklore. Paul was a Herculean logger who combed his beard with a young pine tree; who skidded his timber with Babe the Blue Ox, a creature so vast that he measured forty-two ax handles and a plug of chewing tobacco between the horns; who operated a camp cookhouse where the flapjack griddle was greased by twenty-four Arabs—imported from the Sahara Desert because they could stand the heat—skating to and fro with slabs of bacon strapped to their feet; who tamed the Mississippi when it was young and wild by building river corrals and driving the river through their gates (the Great Lakes remain as evidence of this feat); who ruled the American country in the period when it was only a timber-land. This epoch, according to the best authorities, began with the Winter of the Blue Snow and ended with the Spring the Rain Came Up from China.

Here, indeed, is a full-bodied myth. The Paul Bunyan stories have been told in American logging camps since 1840. They are unquestionably of Canadian origin. There was a Paul Bunyan who won fame in the Papineau Rebellion of 1837. There is no evidence that the beginnings of the stories are beyond him. The other materials and characters of the myth were developed out of the magic of bunkhouse nights; when the workday in the woods, or on the iced road, or on the drive, was done; when the camp men, isolated from all life but that of the woods, had no other outlet for their fancies than the creation of romances about their own life.

Thus Paul Bunyan; Babe the Blue Ox; Johnny Inkslinger, the timekeeper who figured with a fountain pen fed by hose lines from twenty-four barrels of ink; Hels Helson, the Big Swede and bull of the woods, who muddied the Missouri River forever with one spring bath; and many smaller characters—such as Hot Biscuit Slim, the cook; Shanty Boy, the bard; and Big Ole, the blacksmith—have been celebrated in logging camps from Bangor, Maine, to Portland, Oregon. The tall tale, the "whopper," is not confined, of course, to the lumber camps. It appears with the earliest accounts of the Appalachian pi-oneers. It is forever present in the best writings of Mark Twain. Other mythical heroes have won a certain fame, such as Tony Beaver of the Virginia mountains and Pecos Bill, the South-western *vaquero* who once straddled a cyclone and rode it to a finish. But the myth of Paul Bunyan stands alone, possessing, as it does, its own time, place, and people.

The stories are told in this manner:

Supper is over in the logging camp, and the after-supper period of smoking and quiet is also done. A murmur of talk about the day's work rises from the gang around the heating stove. There is a strong smell of steaming wool from the drying lines. Blue pipe smoke drifts through the mellow light of the Rochester burners. A gust of frosty air blows in whenever the bunkhouse door is opened. Some logger ventures the opinion that this will be the hardest winter this part of the country has ever known. Weather talk runs on until someone states solemnly that "the weather ain't what she used to be. Gettin' old now, the weather is. Take the Year of the Two Winters, in Paul Bunyan's time. Yes, sir. Then. That year two winters come all at once.—"

Then there is a contest to see who can tell the tallest tale about cold weather in the day of Paul Bunyan.

Or it is a summer night, and the loggers are circling a smudge fire outside the bunkhouse. Mosquitoes swarm up from the swamp below camp. So mosquito stories are in order. Any man is free to invent new Paul Bunyan yarns himself, or he can repeat the stories heard from other bards. Occasionally some bard is so inspired that his creation is never forgotten, and becomes a permanent addition to the Paul Bunyan myth. Such is the story of the mammoth mosquitoes and their amazing experiences with Bum and Bill, Paul Bunyan's battling bees.

Here is the story.

It was in the Year of the Dry Summer that Paul Bunyan's loggers first encountered mosquitoes. That was the season Paul Bunyan invented thunder. Day after day, week after week, month after month, the great hero-leader of the loggers toiled through experiments with all the sounds he could imagine. Just as cows, pigs, dogs, hens, and ducks could be called, so could clouds be called, thought Paul Bunyan. Seventeen thousand various kinds of calls the great logger tried that summer before he hit on the sound of thunder. Then his labors were rewarded. Paul Bunyan had not thundered once before a stray cloud rolled up from the west. He thundered on, and by midnight so many clouds had gathered that the Dry Summer ended in a downpour that was a deluge instead of a rain. Ever since that parched season the weather has used the thunder which Paul Bunyan invented for it.

But Paul Bunyan had other troubles during this wretched summer. Time and again he had to quit his important labor of trying out sounds that would call up clouds, and attend to small bothers, plagues, and worries. The most troublesome of all these troubles was the invasion of mosquitoes.

The mammoth mosquitoes came from the Tall Wolf country. There the tribe had experienced a devastating famine. For the larger it grew, the smaller became the tribe of tall wolves, the mammoth mosquitoes' natural prey. Eventually the last tall wolf was gone, and only a small company of female mosquitoes was left from the once vast and powerful insect tribe. These females were forced by hunger into migration. They were ready to fall and perish from exhaustion when they reached Paul Bunyan's loggers, who, stripped to the waist, were at work even on this, the hottest of the Dry Summer's days.

Paul Bunyan was afar from his loggers at the moment, pondering deeply on the problem of calling up the clouds. He failed to notice when the ring of axes and the drone of saws were hushed. Not until agonizing yells arose from his loggers did the hero-leader realize that a new trouble had come to camp. Then he saw that his men were struggling for their lives all through the timber five miles away. Two strides and one leap, and Paul Bunyan was on the scene of battle.

Many of his loggers were already white and faint from loss of blood, and the others were hacking desperately with their axes at the dodging, diving mosquitoes. Two of the mammoth winged females were sprawled lifelessly over some pine logs. Others had paused in the fight to bind up their split bills. The battle raged on.

Paul Bunyan was so stirred with wrath at the sight that he unloosed a yell of astonishment and anger. The loggers, of course, were all lifted off their feet and then hurled to the ground by the force of that cyclonic voice; and the mammoth mosquitoes instantly took advantage of this and plunged on the loggers with bloodthirsty hums. Each one held down seven or more men at once and prepared to feast.

For a moment Paul Bunyan was in a panic. He thought of smashing the mosquitoes with smacks of his hand but that would have crushed the loggers underneath. With a mighty effort, the great logger collected his wits. He had to think fast, and he did. Paul Bunyan was that kind of man. And at once he acted.

What he did was to call for Babe the Blue Ox, whose ears were so far from his muzzle that he couldn't hear himself snort. As he approached, Babe saw what was needed for the emergency. He did not wait for orders. Without even a glance at Paul, the Blue Ox did a squads rightabout, halted, straightened out his tail, and began to flirt the mosquitoes off the prone loggers with swishes of his huge tail brush. In one minute every frustrated mosquito was humming angrily in the air and the saved loggers were galloping for the protection of the bunkhouses. There they remained. All night the ravenous mammoth mosquitoes maintained a deafening and ominous hum over the bunkhouses. Paul Bunyan listened. He figured and planned, the ideas for sounds to call clouds forgotten for the moment. At dawn Paul Bunyan had a satisfying idea. He called for Johnny Inkslinger, his timekeeper and man of science.

"Johnny," said Paul, "you need a vacation."

"Yes, sir, Mr. Bunyan," said Johnny, but not very enthusiastically; for if there was anything he hated it was to leave his figures, his grand fountain pen and ink barrels.

"A vacation," Paul Bunyan repeated firmly. "So a vacation you shall take. A hunting vacation, Johnny. I'm going to send you bee hunting."

"Mr. Bunyan," said Johnny Inkslinger, "I am a good hunter and I like to hunt. Why, once I found a moose who had died of old age, found his moldering bones, I did, and I tracked him to his birthplace. How's that for hunting, Mr. Bunyan?" said Johnny proudly. But then he looked doubtful. "I don't know about hunting bees, though, Mr. Bunyan."

"You must not only hunt bees, Johnny. You must trap 'em and tame 'em."

"Now, Mr. Bunyan, that's asking a lot," protested Johnny Inkslinger. "I never did claim to be a bee trapper, or a bee tamer, either. Why pick on me, Mr. Bunyan?"

"Don't question orders, Johnny," said Paul Bunyan, kindly but sternly. "You pack up now for a vacation in the Mastodonic

Clover country. Once there, hunt, trap, and tame the two fightingest, savagest, irritablest, cantankerousest bees you can find. Then trot 'em home to camp."

"Trot 'em, Mr. Bunyan?"

"Trot 'em, Johnny. Trot the bees."

"Yes, sir," said Johnny; and with a will, for he was sentimental about obeying orders.

When Johnny Inkslinger was sent by Paul Bunyan to do anything, he did it. So he wasn't a day in the Mastodonic Clover country until he had hunted down, trapped, and tamed—as nearly as two such fighting, savage, irritable, and cantankerous bees could be tamed—the two famous battling bees, Bum and Bill. Johnny tamed the two bees so that they allowed him to chain their wings to their bodies. They also trusted him with their stingers, which he put in his knapsack. Then Johnny Inkslinger put calked boots on the bees' hind feet, trotted them out of the clover country, trotted them on over hill and dale, trotted them all the way to camp, just as Paul Bunyan had ordered.

Paul Bunyan had a great hive ready for the two warriors. When their wings were unchained, Bum and Bill took off their calked boots, stretched their legs, ate a hearty meal of lump sugar, and turned in for a refreshing sleep. The next morning they buzzed for their stingers at sunup and showed in other ways that they were eager for battle. Paul Bunyan himself led them to the woods, for Johnny Inkslinger insisted on getting back to his figures at once.

Logging had been continued under the tail of Babe the Blue Ox. For three days he had been swishing the ravenous mammoth mosquitoes away from the loggers. He was so tail-weary that he welcomed Bum and Bill, the battling bees, with a joyful moo that shivered the timber for miles. The bees answered with buzzes of rage, and it required all of Paul Bunyan's bee-taming art to convince the fighting bees that Babe was a friend and not the enemy. Bum and Bill were still buzzing suspicion when they sighted the actual foe. Then, with a battle cry that sounded like the rasping roar of a band saw, Bum and Bill lit out in a beeline and charged in an irresistible attack. In seventeen seconds the bodies of seventeen mammoth mosquitoes crashed down into the timber, shattering scores of great pines into splinters. A thunderous hum of fear sounded from the survivors. They flew off in a panic. Pursued and pursuers vanished in the haze of the Dry Summer, which smothered the forest. Soon the hums of fear and the buzzes of rage were only faint murmurs among the far trees. Paul Bunyan's teeth shone through his beard in a smile of triumph.

"Yay, Babe!" he commanded the Blue Ox.

The logging went on.

Paul Bunyan brushed his hands and praised the saints that this mosquito trouble had been so easily ended. Then he returned to his great task of trying out sounds which would call up clouds. The labor engrossed the great logger to such a degree that the mosquito invasion vanished from his thoughts. He also forgot the two big battling bees who had driven the invaders from the logging camp. But Johnny Inkslinger did not forget. Often he raised his head from his books and held his fountain pen poised in the air, while the hose lines from the ink barrels gushed an inky flood to the office floor. This Johnny Inkslinger did not notice in such moments, for he was remembering his grand success as a bee hunter, a bee trapper, and a bee tamer. It was one of the proudest memories of his life.

And often Johnny Inkslinger wondered what had become of the bees he had tamed, what had happened to the female mammoth mosquitoes Bum and Bill had driven from the camp. Weeks had passed, and still there was not a hum from the mosquitoes or a buzz from the bees.

Then, during such a moment of wondering and remembering, Johnny Inkslinger heard a sound from the distance that was nothing but a buzz-hum. He ran out of the office and peered into the heat haze. A small, dark cloud seemed to be moving toward the camp. Johnny watched and waited. The cloud grew larger. As it approached the loggers in the woods, Johnny saw that the cloud was a vast swarm of giant insects. They hovered over the loggers for an instant, then dived without circling. And again agonizing yells rolled up from the timber and smote Paul Bunyan's ears.

"What's happened down there?" Paul Bunyan shouted.

"The mosquitoes have come back!" said Johnny Inkslinger.

"It's a new kind, then," said Paul Bunyan, coming on the run and calling Babe the Blue Ox. "Look at 'em. They're bees!"

"They're mosquitoes," said Johnny. "Look at their bills!"

"But look at their stingers!"

"Sure enough," said Johnny Inkslinger, almost dumb with astonishment. "Why—why—Mr. Bunyan—they—"

"Look at 'em!" yelled Paul Bunyan. "Why, they got bills in front and stingers behind, and they're getting the loggers going and coming! You know what's happened? Those two bees have married the mosquitoes, that's what! And these are the offspring! Bills in front and stingers behind! Yay, Babe!"

And on Paul galloped with Babe the Blue Ox, who soon got his tail brush to working and let the loggers escape to the bunkhouses. But these mammoth insects which were half mosquito and half bee wouldn't be denied. They attacked the bunkhouses. One would stick his bill under one side of a shake on a bunkhouse roof, and his stinger under the other side; and then he would flap his wings until he had ripped off the shake; and the loggers would have to stand guard with pike poles and peavies to keep the savage insects from coming at them through the ripped roofs. Paul Bunyan saw that he needed to act quick. So he spent another night in figuring and planning. And, just as usual, he had a grand idea at daylight. He called for Johnny Inkslinger.

"Johnny," said Paul Bunyan, "we are going to carry sugar."

"Yes, Mr. Bunyan."

"We are going to throw some rafts together, Johnny, and then we are going to load the rafts with all the sugar in camp. After that we are going to rope the rafts together and have Babe the Blue Ox tow the whole raft fleet out into the middle of Lake Michigan."

Johnny Inkslinger never batted an eye. He knew the great logger too well to think that any of his ideas were foolish. So Johnny went to work without a word; and by noon the rafts were built, loaded, and roped together. Paul hitched Babe to the head raft of the fleet.

"Yay, Babe," he commanded.

And the Blue Ox bowed his neck, lumbered off, and straight to the center of Lake Michigan he towed the raft-loads of sugar. Johnny Inkslinger stayed on shore. He watched and waited. Soon he saw all the mosquito-bees flying out over the lake after the rafts. Then Johnny Inkslinger realized what Paul Bunyan was up to.

"Oh, ain't he got a brain, though?" said Johnny Inkslinger worshipfully. "Oh, but ain't Paul Bunyan got a brain?"

And a brain Paul Bunyan certainly had. For he had figured that the bee blood in the hybrid insects would send them after the sugar. And he had figured that their mosquito blood would make them fill their stomachs till they were stuffed. And Paul Bunyan knew the weight of sugar. . . .

Sure enough, the mosquito-bees glutted themselves on sugar till they could hardly fly. Then Paul Bunyan started Babe on a run for the shore. The stuffed insects tried to follow. But lower and lower they flew; and soon, with anguished buzz-hums, they all sank into the waters of the great lake; and that was the last of them.

The camp of Paul Bunyan was never again troubled by mammoth mosquitoes, or by mammoth mosquito-bees, either. Bum and Bill at last returned to camp, and gave every appearance of being ashamed of themselves. Paul Bunyan did not reproach them, but gave them a home in a furnished hive; and thereafter Bum and Bill occupied themselves solely with making honey for the loggers' flapjacks. Their fighting days were done.

History does not state the fate of the female mammoth mosquitoes. Some authorities advance the idea that they flew to Asia. They point to the elephant to prove their contention. The elephant, they assert, is descended from the mammoth mosquito of Paul Bunyan's time. Other authorities ridicule this idea, asserting that the elephant is too small to be a descendant of the mammoth mosquito.

All such ideas and contentions are guesswork, however. And guesswork has no place in the history of Paul Bunyan.

The Black Duck Dinner

JAMES STEVENS

Hot Biscuit Slim leaned against the toe of the hero's boot and wept.

"That means I must rustle deer and bear," said Paul Bunyan patiently. "Well, bear meat and venison will make a royal feast when they have passed through your kettles and ovens. Light the fires; go ahead with your plans. You may yet make history tomorrow!"

He turned away, and Hot Biscuit Slim watched him worshipfully until he was a dim figure on distant hills.

"The best friend me an' my pap ever had," he said. "I'd do anything for a boss like that. I'll learn to remember meat, by doggy, I will!"

Rumors of the marvelous dinner that was being planned reached the bunkhouses, and the loggers indulged in greedy imagining of the promised delights. The day went slowly: the sun seemed to labor down the western sky. Before it sank soft clouds obscured its light, bringing showers and early shadows.

At the approach of darkness Paul Bunyan began his return march to the camp. He was vastly disappointed by the meager results of his hunt. Although he had gone as far as the Turtle River country, he had snared but two deer and three small bears. These only filled a corner of one pocket of his mackinaw, and they would provide but a mere shred of meat apiece for his men. Paul Bunyan did not feel that he had done his best; he was not one to rest on feeble consolations. As he journeyed on he was devising other means to carry out his plans for a memorable and stupendous feast. And ere he was within an hour of the camp the Big Swede was unconsciously outlining the solution of the problem for him,

The Big Swede went to the stable some time after supper to see that Babe was at ease for the night. The clouds were thinning now, and when he opened the stable door soft light poured in on the Blue Ox, making lustrous spots and streaks on his sleek sides. He turned his head, his bulging blue eyes shining with gentleness and good-will, and his tongue covered the foreman's face in a luscious caress.

"Har noo," remonstrated the Big Swede.

As he solemnly wiped his drenched face he sniffed the fragrance of Babe's breath and stared with a feeling of envy at the clean, glowing hair. When he had finished his inspection and left the stable, it was evident that he was wrestling with some laborious problem. His whole face was tense with a terrific frown; his memory groped among the shadows of some distant happening; he scratched his sides vigorously and breathed deeply of the air, sweet with the odors of washed earth. The purity of the spring weather, the fresh cleanliness it gave the world, and the aroma and sleekness of the Blue Ox, had brought the Big Swede to face his own sore need of a washing. He dreaded it as an ordeal, an exceptional and hazardous undertaking, and for that reason he wished that he might accomplish it immediately. He wandered aimlessly on, tormented by an unaccustomed conflict of the soul and the flesh, and at last he came to the edge of a cliff. He stared in surprise at the appearance of a lake below. He could not remember so large a body of water near the camp. But the Big Swede had no room for more than one emotion at a time, and a violent resolve now smothered his surprise.

"Yah, aye do him noo," he muttered.

He disrobed swiftly and ran to a rock that jutted from the cliff. Swinging his fists he leaped twice into the air; the second time he flung himself outward in a magnificent dive, his body made a great curve, and then, head first, he plunged downward. But there was no tumultuous surge and splash of waters as a climax of this splendid dive. Instead, the Big Swede's head struck white canvas with a dull, rending impact. For he had mistaken Paul Bunyan's tarpaulin for a lake! The force of his plunge drove him through the canvas and half-buried him in the soft earth underneath. His arms were imprisoned, but his legs waved wildly, and his muffled bellows shook the earth. A prowling logger saw what seemed to be shining marble columns dancing in the moonlight and felt the ground trembling under his feet.

"It can't be," he thought bravely.

Just then the Big Swede made another heroic effort to yell for help, and the logger was shaken from his feet. He jumped up and ran to Johnny Inkslinger with an alarming tale of dancing ghosts that shook the earth. The timekeeper, after sharpening twenty-seven lead pencils to use in case it was necessary to make a report on the spot, started with his medicine case for the place where the logger had directed him. When nearly there he remembered that he had failed to bring his ten-gallon carboy of alcohol, which, next to Epsom salts, he considered the most important medicine in his chest. He ran back for it, and by the time he finally reached the Big Swede, that unfortunate's bellows had diminished to groans, and his legs waved with less and less gusto. After thoroughly examining and measuring the legs, Johnny deemed the proof positive that they belonged to the Big Swede. Then he got busy with paper and pencil and figured for half an hour. "According to the strictest mathematical calculations," he announced, "the Big Swede cannot continue to exist in his present interred, or, to be exact, half-interred condition: consequently he must be extricated. I have considered all known means by which this may be accomplished, I have figured, proved, and compared results, and I have arrived at a scientific conclusion. I direct that the Blue Ox and a cable be brought here at once."

When the loggers had obeyed this command, Johnny made a half-hitch with the cable around the Big Swede's legs, which were waving very feebly now, and in two seconds, amid a monstrous upheaval of dirt and a further rending of the canvas, the Big Swede was dragged out. For a few moments he spat mud like a river dredge; then the timekeeper proffered him the ten-gallon carboy of alcohol. It was drained at a gulp, and then, with aid from Johnny Inkslinger, he was able to stagger to the camp office. When Paul Bunyan reached the camp, the Big Swede was lying on his bunk, bundled in bandages from head to foot. Johnny Inkslinger was still busily attending him; bottles of medicine, boxes of pills, a keg of Epsom salts, rolls of bandages, and surgical implements were heaped about the room. The timekeeper gave a detailed account of what had happened, and then Paul Bunyan questioned the victim, who answered briefly, "Aye yoomped, an' aye yoomped, an'—*yeeminy!*"

Johnny Inkslinger gave his chief a voluminous report of the Big Swede's fractures, sprains and contusions.

"He is also suffering from melancholia because he is still unwashed," said Johnny. "But I think I'll restore him. I've dosed him with all my medicines and smeared him with all my salves. I'd have manipulated his spine, but, confound him, he strained his back, and he threatens violence when I touch it. But I have many formulae and systems. He shall live."

"Surely," said Paul Bunyan. "A man is the hardest thing to kill there is."

Knowing that the Big Swede's wounds were nothing in comparison with the ones which he had received in the Dakota battle, Paul Bunyan worried no more about his foreman. He stepped from the camp office, plucked up a young pine and brushed his beard, thinking again of his unrealized plan. He remembered the wordless dejection of Hot Biscuit Slim on receiving the scanty supply of deer and bear meat. He determined that the Sunday dinner should yet be as he had planned it, otherwise it would be a bad augury for great achievements in his new enterprise. He thrust the tree into his shirt pocket and walked slowly towards his outdoor headquarters, pondering various schemes that came to mind.

When he reached the white sheet of water he was astonished by its deceptive appearance. It had a silvery glitter in the moonlight, for its surface still held the moisture of the showers. Small wonder, thought Paul Bunyan, that the Big Swede had dived into it; never was a lake more temptingly beautiful or seemingly more deep. He was gazing at the torn canvas and the huge cavity made in the ground by the Big Swede, when he heard a great chorus of shrill and doleful voices in the sky. He looked up and saw an enormous host of black ducks in swerving flight. They had lost their way in the low-hanging clouds at dusk, and now they were seeking a resting place.

Here, thought Paul Bunyan, is a noble offering of chance. Was a black duck more acute than the Big Swede, that the bright, moist canvas would not deceive him also? And once deceived, would not the ensuing dive be fatal? Wasn't a black duck's neck of more delicate structure than the Big Swede's, and wouldn't it surely break when it struck the tarpaulin? This variety of black duck grew as big as a buzzard, and here they were so numerous that clouds of them darkened the moon. Now to deceive them. Paul Bunyan could mimic the voices of all the birds of the air and all the beasts of the fields and woods, save only that of the Blue Ox, who always replied with a jocular wink when his master attempted to simulate his mellow moo. In his moments of humor Paul Bunyan declared that he could mimic fish, and one Sunday when he imitated a mother whale bawling for her calf the loggers roared with merriment for seventeen hours, and were only sobered then by exhaustion. His voice had such power that he could not counterfeit the cry of a single small creature, but only the united cries of flocks and droves. So he now mimicked perfectly the chorus that rang mournfully in the sky, and at the same time he grasped the edge of the tarpaulin and fluttered it gently.

The effect was marvelous. Now indeed was the canvas a perfect imitation of water. Had you been standing by the sole of Paul Bunyan's boot and seen the gentle flutter you would have been sure that you were watching a breeze make pleasant ripples on the surface of a lake. Ere long the black ducks were enchanted by the sight and sound, and Paul Bunyan heard a violent rush of air above him as of a hurricane sweeping a forest. A vast dark cloud seemed to plunge out of the sky. Another instant and the canvas was black with feathered forms. Paul Bunyan grasped the four corners of the tarpaulin, swung the bundle over his shoulder and strode home to the cookhouse. Hot Biscuit Slim was called forth, and when he saw the mountainous pile of black ducks that filled the kitchen yard he became hysterical with delight. He called out the assistant cooks, the flunkies and dishwashers, and, led by Cream Puff Fatty, the baker, the white-clad underlings streamed for eleven minutes from the kitchen door. The chief cook then made them a short but inspiring speech and fired them with his own fierce purpose to make culinary history.

Paul Bunyan listened for a moment, and then sought repose, with peace in his benevolent heart.

All night fires roared in the ranges as preparations went on for the great dinner. The elevators brought a load of vegetables every minute from the deep bins, potatoes were pared and washed, kettles and roasting pans were made ready, the sauces and dressings were devised. The black ducks were scalded, plucked, and cleaned by the Preparations Department, and by morning the cranemen were bringing them by the hundreds to the Finishing Department, where the kettles and pans were waiting for them.

Most of the loggers stayed in their bunks this morning, and those who did come to breakfast ate sparingly, saving their appetites. Time passed quietly in the camp. The loggers washed and mended their clothes and greased their boots, but they did not worry themselves with bed-making. The other Sunday morning chores finished, they stretched out on their unmade bunks and smoked. They were silent and preoccupied, but now and again a breeze blowing from the direction of the cookhouse would cause them to sigh. What enchantment was in the air, so redolent with the aroma of roasting duck and stewing cabbages, so sharply sweet with the fragrance of hot ginger and cinnamon from the bakery where Cream Puff Fatty fashioned his creations! A logger who was shaving would take a deep breath of this incense, and the blood would trickle unnoticed from a slash in his cheek; another in his bunk would let his pipe slip from his hand and enjoy ardent inhalations, blissfully unaware of his burning shirt; yet another, engaged in greasing his boots, would halt his task and sit in motionless beatitude, his head thrown back, his eyes closed, quite unconscious of the grease that poured from a tilted can into a prized boot.

At half past eleven the hungriest of the loggers began to

mass before the cookhouse door, and as the minutes passed the throng swiftly increased. At five minutes to noon all the bunk-houses were empty and the furthest fringe of the crowd was far up Onion River valley. The ground shook under a restless tramping, and the faces of the loggers were glowing and eager as they hearkened to the clatter and rumble inside the cookhouse, as four-horse teams hauled in loads of salt, pepper, and sugar for the shakers and bowls. Then the loggers began to stamp and shout as they heard the flunkies, led by the Galloping Kid on his white horse, rushing the platters and bowls of food to the tables. Tantalizing smells wafted forth from the steaming dishes. The loggers grew more restless and eager; they surged to and fro in a tidal movement; jests and glad oaths made a joyous clamor over the throng. This was softened into a universal sigh as the doors swung open and Hot Biscuit Slim, in spotless cap and apron, appeared wearing the impressive mien of a con-quering general. He lifted an iron bar with a majestic gesture, paused for dramatic effect amid a breathless hush, and then struck a resounding note from the steel triangle that hung from the wall. At the sound a heaving torrent of men began to pour through the doors in a rush that was like the roaring plunge of water when the gate of a dam is lifted. The chief cook continued to pound out clanging rhythms until the last impatient logger was inside.

Then Hot Biscuit Slim re-entered the cookhouse. He was reminded of a forested plain veiled in thin fog as he surveyed the assemblage of darkly clad figures, wreathed with white and fra-grant blooms of steam. His impression was made the more vivid when the loggers plunged their spoons into the deep bowls of oyster soup, for the ensuing sounds seemed like the soughing of wind in the woods. The chief cook marched to the kitchen with dignity and pride, glancing to right and left at the tables that held his masterwork. He asked for no praise or acclaim; the ecstasy that now transfigured the plainest face was a sufficient light of glory for him.

The soup bowls pushed aside, the loggers began to fill their plates, which were of such circumference that even a long-armed man could hardly reach across one. The black ducks, of course, received first attention. And great as the plates were, by the time one was heaped with a brown fried drumstick, a ladle of duck dumplings, several large fragments of duck fricasee, a slab of duck baked gumbo style, a rich portion of stewed duck, and a mound of crisp brown dressing, all immersed in golden duck gravy, a formidable space was covered. Yet there was room for tender leaves of odorous cabbage beaded and streaked with creamy sauce; for mashed potatoes which seemed like fluffs of snow beside the darkness of duck and gravy; for brittle and savory potato cakes, marvelously right as to texture and thickness; for stewed tomatoes of a sultry ruddiness, pungent and ticklish with mysterious spices; for a hot cob of corn as long as a man's forearm, golden with sirupy kernels as big as buns; for fat and juicy baked beans, plump peas, sunny applesauce and buttered lettuce, not to mention various condiments. Squares of cornbread and hot biscuits were buttered and leaned against the plate; a potbellied coffee-pot was tilted over a gaping cup, into which it gushed an aromatic beverage of drowsy charm; a kingly pleasure was prepared. More than one logger swooned with delight this day when his plate was filled and, red-faced, hot-eyed, wet-lipped, he bent over it to taste the first magnificent mouthful.

In the kitchen the chief cook, the baker and their helpers watched and listened. At first the volume of sounds that filled the vast room was like the roar and crash of an avalanche, as dishes were rattled and banged about. Then the duck bones crackled like the limbs of falling trees. At last came a steady sound of eating, a sound of seventy threshing machines devouring bundles of wheat. It persisted far beyond the usual length of time, and Hot Biscuit Slim brought out his field glasses and surveyed the tables. The loggers were still bent tensely over their plates, and their elbows rose and fell with an energetic movement as they scooped up the food with undiminished vigor.

"Still eatin' duck," marveled Hot Biscuit Slim.

"They won't be more'n able to *smell* my cream puffs," said the baker enviously.

The loggers ate on. They had now spent twice their usual length of time at the table. Each plate was in a dark shadow from the tall rows of slick black duck bones and heaps of corn cobs. But—

"Still eatin' duck," reported Hot Biscuit Slim.

That no one might see his grief Cream Puff Fatty moved to a dark corner. He was now certain that none of the loggers could have room for his pastries. They ate on. They had now spent three times their usual length of time at the table. The baker was sweating and weeping; he was soaked with despair. Then, suddenly:

"They're eatin' cream puffs!" cried Hot Biscuit Slim.

Cream Puff Fatty could not believe it, but a thrill of hope urged him to see for himself. True enough, the loggers were tackling the pastries at last. On each plate cream puffs the size of squashes lay in golden mounds. As the spoons struck them their creamy contents oozed forth from breaks and crevices. Stimulated by their rich flavor, the loggers ate on with renewed gusto. They had now stayed four times as long as usual at the table. Other enchantments still kept them in their seats: lemon pies with airy frostings, yellow pumpkin pies strewn with brown spice specks, cherry pies with cracks in their flaky crusts through which the red fruit winked, custard pies with russet freckles on their golden faces, fat apple pies all odorous with cinnamon, cool, snowy cream pies, peach cobblers, chocolate puddings, glittering cakes of many colors, slabs of gingerbread, sugar-powdered jelly rolls, doughnuts as large around as saucers and as thick through as cups, and so soft and toothsome that a morsel from one melted on the tongue like cream. So endearing were the flavors of these pastries that the loggers consumed them all.

Cream Puff Fatty and Hot Biscuit Slim solemnly shook hands. There was glory enough for both of them.

At last there were no sounds at the tables save those of heavy breathing. The loggers arose in a body and moved sluggishly and wordlessly from the cookhouse. They labored over the ground towards the bunkhouses as wearily as though they had just finished a day of deadening toil. Soon Onion River valley resounded with their snores and groans. . . .

At supper time, when Hot Biscuit Slim rang the gong, Cream

Puff Fatty stood by his side. This was to be the supreme test of their achievement. For five minutes the chief cook beat the triangle, and then a solitary logger appeared in the door of a bunkhouse. He stared at them dully for a moment and then staggered back into the darkness. This was indeed a triumph! Great as other feasts in the cookhouse had been, never before had *all* the loggers been unable to appear for supper. This was a historic day. Cream Puff Fatty and Hot Biscuit Slim embraced and mingled rapturous tears. It was their high moment. They would not have traded it for all the glory that was Greece and the grandeur that was Rome. . . . They had intimations of immortality. . . .

For five weeks the loggers lay in a delicious torpor, and then Johnny Inkslinger brought them from their bunks. By this time the Big Swede had recovered from his injuries, and Paul Bunyan waited no longer to move his camp. The buildings, which rested on skids, were chained and cabled together, and the Blue Ox hauled them over the hills to the new job.

Nothing marred the beauty of that summer; stirring breezes blew all the days over the loggers as they felled the Leaning Pine trees in perfect lines on the grassy slopes. The Blue Ox waxed fat with the ease of his labor. Weeks passed without the Big Swede's having a serious accident. Dust gathered on Johnny Inkslinger's medicine case. Hot Biscuit Slim never once failed to remember meat. And a record number of logs were piled above the rollways. Paul Bunyan planned a great drive with prideful confidence that it would be the glorious climax of a historic season. But here fortune deserted him, for, after driving the logs for nine days, and seeing an exact repetition of scenery three times, he had Johnny Inkslinger survey the placid river. The river was round; it flowed in a perfect circle; and Paul Bunyan had driven the logs three times over the same course!

Nothing daunted, he thereupon determined to saw the logs and transport the lumber overland, and he erected his famed sawmill, which was nineteen stories high, with each bandsaw and each circular saw running through all the floors. A description of the original machines and devices used in this mill would fill the pages of a mail order catalogue. It is needless to say that it operated perfectly. The only great difficulty Paul Bunyan had to overcome originated from the smokestacks. He was compelled to equip them with hinges and drawbridge machinery so that they could be lowered to let the clouds go by.

1. Explain the reference to Paul Bunyan as an American Hercules. **2.** What does Paul Bunyan have to do with the Great Lakes? **3.** How does Paul Bunyan get rid of the mosquitoes? **4.** List the characteristics of the Blue Ox. **5.** Explain all the uses of hyperbole in *An American Hercules*. **6.** Who is Hot Biscuit Slim? **7.** Explain the use of hyperbole in *The Black Duck Dinner*. **8.** Show all the characteristics of the tall tale in *The Black Duck Dinner*. **9.** Compare the Paul Bunyan stories with *The Devil and Daniel Webster*. **10.** Write a tall tale of your own, paying attention to patterning with hyperbole.

Read these student tall tales for inspiration.

THAT'S OUR BOY!

A TALL TALE FROM ATOP A TALL STOOL

JOYCE NOWAK

Yeah, I know all about Ruth an' Williams an' Spahn an' the rest . . . but the greatest of all ya never even heard about, I betcha. He was a real windmill of a man, up on that mound, boy! Ya couldn't beat him atall, he was that good. Yeah, that's the whole trouble—he was too good to be true, too good for the game. All the holes in baseball rules, he found 'em, and they didn't know what to do with him, 'cause he was the most ridic'-lous pitcher you'd ever wanta see and they didn't know if he was just bein' funny or *really lookin'* for them loopholes.

"For instance, like he had the most ridic'lous delivery you'd ever wanta see. You wouldn't know it was a fast ball comin' 'til ya seen them arms an' legs goin' all directions and never knowin' which limb was doin' the pitchin'. . . . An' the fancy curve balls? While he stood there tippy-toe, like a Bali dancer not wantin' ta wrinkle his kimona, the ball is havin' itself a hotfoot all over the plate. I'm tellin' ya!

"An' like I say, they couldn't tell if he was just bein' funny or awful, awful cagey, 'cause his face never told nothin' either. 'Cept that he was a concentrator. Boy, the way he skrinched his long chin and nose up to meet the lida his cap ya knew *something* was workin' up there for sure; and ya never needed to wonder if he could see outa the skrinch—no sir!

"Like for instance there was this time (he was relief-pitchin' for the National League champs b'fore they was the third time) —there was the time this heavy hitter was botherin' 'im. The guy already had a homer, a double, was lookin' just too cool about it, an' besides was hoppin' outa the box to fuss 'im up a bit. Well, that nose, chin, and cap-lid clamped together like the Pearly Gates on a sold sinner, an' he threw out all th' other gimmicks an' just stood there hunched, pawin' the mound like a scrawny broncho on end. The hitter danced up to the plate, ponked his bat on it, and without another practise swing, raised his bat slow and easy-like to 'is shoulder, grinnin' all the while. Well that did it for our boy: he tossed the ball in th' air like he was gonna serve at tennis, an' in a split-second, all arms an' legs goin', shot in a fast curve that just flicked the lid of the hitter's cap, spinnin' it 'round an' around an' around. That batter weren't smilin' no more, you betcha! But we—we was laughin' fit to bust at the sighta Mr. Big Hitter cut down to size; the umpire just turned blue and shook a good fist at our boy. (It just missed him, too!) Not that he was scared, no sir! He knew alla time where he was puttin' it!

"Could he hit? Could he *hit?* Man, he *had* that ball, comin' an' goin'! I told ya he had the eye, and strong?—why, once he come up to the plate, an', watchin' ta knock the dust offa his shoes, hit their sides with the leaded bat. Knocked the spikes clean off an' hoppin' down the infield, he did, an' didn't think nothin' of it but ta call time ta lace up another pair! We had a short organ interlude, meanwhile.

"Series? Nah, never even got a chance ta play a series. They wouldn't let 'im. He won the N. L. Pennant, tho', for his team's third try, pinch-hittin' again, acourse. Pitched pretty reg'lar mosta that big game, an' the game was his 8-7 if he could get just one more guy out. Trouble was, the guy was a reliable old vet and just about due. Well, it seems our boy wanted it over with little more to-do: he pulled two more balls from hind pockets (an' on him full pockets was never noticed) an' b'fore an ump could drop a jaw, spun in three perfect pitches on just one throw! Swish, swish, swish, went the vet, eyeballs poppin', and the game was over! Well, it wasn't over that fast 'cause the plate ump wasn't movin' to call it—or them; he was watcha-call *trans*fixed. He was, leastways, until both managers come boundin' out ta the plate an' a dozen or so players joined the bar-b-que. Our boy just hitched up his pants and waited. What they was sayin' at the plate, well, what it *amounted* to was; I s'pose: 'He cain't do that, it ain't in the book!' 'Well, the book don't come right out an' *say* he cain't; an' besides, they was all three right over that there patch!' An' they was still goin' at it when our boy just up an' walked to the dugout with nobody on field noticin' atall.

"Well, that little one fixed him, for sure. Fact is, that little one almost fixed it so we didn't have a World Series atall that year! Th' Commissioner finally said O.K., his team could play if only they'd leave our boy home. How 'bout that?

"Meanwhile some crusadin' sports writer writes him up as a menace to baseball, an' all that, an' even the Concessionnaire's Union is down his neck 'cause when he pitches the fans cain't keep their mouths closed long enough to be interested in hot dogs an' 'cause the fans hadta be sure they was seein' what they was seein' (if ya know what I mean)—so they just came and watched the game. Now he was a menace to big business, even!

"Well, that did it—he was finished in the Majors, an' all b'cause he was just too good! An' isn't it a cryin' shame, I'm tellin' ya! His name? Funny, cain't seem to remember. . . ."

A Man and a Moose

A MODERN TALL TALE

IRENE ZIMMERMAN

Saw my cousin Katie the other day. Her and her man just come back from the fall carnival up in Muskee, where he was on exhibit. Ta hear Katie talk, the people there got quite a bang outa the way cousin Wilbert kin twist the caps offa pop bottles just like they was screwed on.

Well, anyway, it sure was good ta see Cousin Katie again. Her Junior was oney 'bout two weeks old last time I bin 'round. This time he was settin' up aready all by hisself. Guess he'll take after his ma.

Ya know, it's funny ta think of Cousin Katie bein' married. Nobody 'round here ever thought she'd fall fer a man. Finally found out, though, how it happened. That's what I went the other day again fer—neighbors bin houndin' me fer a hull year 'n' a half now (that's as long as they was married) ta git Katie ta spill her story.

It all come out easy-like. We started talkin' 'bout that there moose head she got hangin' over her kitchen stove. I asked her where she got it from. She smiled kinda shy-like (I got suspicious right there cause that ain't like Cousin Katie) and then she said it was her weddin' present from Cousin Wilbert—that's her man. You see, Cousin Katie was always the type that swore up 'n' down she weren't ever gonna git married ta nobody. That made all the young fellows run after her like crazy, 'cause they felt safe that she wouldn't rope them in all of a sudden, I s'pose. Well, Cousin Wilbert, I guess, run after her a little more harder than usual. Anyway he fell perty bad, and finally he broke the news ta her that he was gonna marry her. "Man, yer offa your rocker," she said ta him; "I won't marry ya till ya bring me a moose head that you wrung off a moose all by yerself."

Well, that jest 'bout floored Cousin Wilbert, I guess. Everybody 'round here felt sorry fer him, 'cause we knowed he's the soft-heartedest guy this side of the Pacific Ocean. Why his ma told me oncet that he couldn't even stand to let anybody 'round the house swat a fly. Finally when they got so bad even he couldn't stand 'em anymore, he collected 'em all in jars and turned 'em loose in a screened-in contraption he made fer the purpose.

Well, anyway, Cousin Wilbert he looked perty jaded after Cousin Katie turned him down. After 'bout a week he up and left town. We heard he went ta Yellowston Park 'n' got hisself a job as park service man. All of us thought that was sure right down his alley, 'cause there there ain't no shootin' er killin' of animals allowed and them park men have ta see to it that the law is obeyed and that the birds and animals are kept fed 'n' happy.

We didn't hear nothin' 'bout Wilbert fer puttner six months. Then all of a sudden he was back in town, and next thing we knowed he 'n' Cousin Katie had their bans called off in Church. We jist couldn't understand it, but now Katie finally spilled the beans.

Seems like Wilbert was perty happy at his job out in Yellowston caring fer them animals. During his off-hours he usta go ta a certain swampy area where he would jist sit and watch all the birds and animals that come by. Oncet he found a coupla quails what had their wings broken. He taped 'em up and started feedin' 'em twice a day, regular-like; and by the time their wings was healed, they'd hatched young 'uns. 'Course, with Wilbert's pettin' 'em everyday, them quail got real tame-like, and that area got ta be a reglar quail refuge. Musta ben 'bout 300 of 'em round there after coupla months.

One day when Wilbert come ta see his quail, the whole swamp was quiet. He suspicioned sumthin' immediately, 'cause them quail allays usta come out ta meet him. He looked all over the place, and finally went over ta where the quail had their nests under some scrubs and grass that grew 'bout five feet high. Lo 'n' behold when he got there he saw two big horns stickin' out of the top of the bushes. It was a moose and it'd squashed all of them quail's eggs till there weren't no stuffing in 'em anymore. When Wilbert saw whatut happened, I guess he sorta lost his head. He was so mad at that there moose fer stickin' his nose inta other animals' business, that, before he knowed it, he had jist plain taken that big moose by the horns and wrung his head off.

When Cousin Wilbert come back to his senses, he was holdin' this moose head in his hands. That really sobered him up, 'cause he never knowed afore that he had sech a temper. He decided that fer the safety of the animals he'd better give up his job in the park. Weren't till then that he remembered Cousin Katie's words about a moose head. He'd tried his darnedest ta fergit about her, I guess, thinkin' that he jest didn't have a chance wid her nohow. But then when he realized that he had this moose head ta give her, all his old feeling come back jest like that.

Cousin Katie told me that she wasn't serious 'bout that moose head in the first place—that had been jest her way of saying "no" friendly-like. But when she saw Wilbert at her back door on his knees holding up this moose head, she didn't have the heart ta turn him down again. She didn't seem exter unhappy 'bout the whole deal either, ta tell the truth on it.

Well, that's the story. I didn't stick 'round there much longer after Cousin Katie finished it—wanted to git home ta tell the neighbors. I kissed Junior on my way outa the door. He was settin' on the floor, playin' wid a iron rod he'd broken off his crib. He was twistin' off little pieces of it. I think he was chewin' one, now that I mention it. Guess maybe he takes after his old man.

SUMMING UP

I. Identify these terms:

—A

folklore	transformation myth
folk tale	story pattern
myth	narration
aesthetic myth	legend
explanatory myth	hero story

—B

beast story	tall tale
fable	allegory
parable	satire
saint's legend	symbol
fairy tale	motif

—C

initiating incident	characterization
development	conclusion
point of story	hyperbole
dénouement	characters
episode	exposition

II. Identify these classical mythological names:

—A

Zeus (Jove, Jupiter)	Ares (Mars)
Vulcan	Phoebus Apollo
Poseidon (Neptune)	Aphrodite (Venus)
Pluto (Hades)	Eros (Cupid)
Hera (Juno)	Athena (Minerva)

—B

Hermes (Mercury)	Actaeon
Demeter (Ceres)	Arachne
Persephone (Proserpine)	Niobe
Dionysus (Bacchus)	Heracles (Hercules)
Artemis (Diana)	Clytie

—C

Echo	Psyche
Narcissus	Phaëton
Latona	Ceÿx
Prometheus	Halcyone
Epimetheus	Python

—D

Titáns	Parnassus
Cimmerian	Zephyr
Cronus (Saturn)	Tartarus
Odysseus (Ulysses)	Pythian
Hestia (Vesta)	Cecrops

—E

Baucis	Aurora
Philemon	Lethe
Clymene	Gorgon Medusa
Aeolus	Adonis
Morpheus	Daphne

—F

Satyrs	The Muses
Pan	Iris
Nemesis	The Graces
The Furies	The Hydra
The Fates	The Sphinx

—G

Gordian knot	Pygmalion
Icarus	Orpheus
Daedalus	Jason
Atlas	Oedipus
The Minotaur	Antigone

III. Identify these terms from Norse mythology:

—A

Eddas	Midgard
Ymir	Ygdrasil
Odin	Asgard
Vili	Jotunheim
Ve	Niffleheim

—B

Norns	Thor
Skuld	Frey
Valkyrior	Freya
Valhalla	Elves
Woden	Heimdall

—C

Loki	Baldur
Skrymir	Frigga
Utgard	Mistletoe
Utgard-Loki	Alfdaur
Logi	Hel

IV. Knowledge of each mythological figure:

Who?	Correct pronunciation
What?	Correct spelling
Why?	

V. Knowledge of each short prose tale:

Kind	Story
Characteristics	Characters

THE GOLDEN ECHO

UNIT 3

The Bard and His Lyre

THE LONG NARRATIVE

The Bard and His Lyre

THE LONG NARRATIVE

The Blind Storyteller

Hundreds of years ago, in fact as far into the mists of time as nine hundred years before the birth of Christ, a blind storyteller unslung his lyre and sang for his enthralled listeners two great narrative poems. For the legends and myths and heroes that found life anew in his two great epics, the ILIAD and the ODYSSEY, the blind Homer reached back into the heroic age, to a time when the Trojan War had already mellowed to legend. With the skill of a great storyteller and the creative power of a gifted poet, into his gorgeous tapestry of words he wove men of old with their battles and arms and deeds of heroism. Through the voice of Homer, the legends and myths that had been kept alive in the oral tradition of hundreds of years found new and vibrant existence in the great sung stories of these two epics.

Only a great poet who is, at the same time, a great storyteller could give to the epic the power to hold his listeners' interest through thousands of lines of poetry. For the epic is a very long poem that tells a story made up of many incidents that had existence in legend and myth before the poet storyteller used them in his great work.

The epic, above all else, is a well made story. It has what we call organic structure; that is, it is built around a single main line of action. All the myths and legends that become part of the living texture of the new story poem must find their meaning caught into this one main line of action. This unity of action is evident in both the ILIAD and the ODYSSEY of Homer.

In the ILIAD Achilles' discontent and its consequences make up the single main line of action. The hero brings grief to himself, death to his friend, and the prolongation of the war. To this action all the incidents of the epic, whether they concern the gods or men, are related in some way. The story of the Trojan War is just the background for the action of Achilles. That is why the greater part of the war does not enter into the epic at all. The story covers only the last fifty days of the tenth year of the war. The descriptions of battles do not have historical purpose. They are the means the poet uses to portray men hurtled into disaster and death by clashing passions.

In the ODYSSEY the episodes have a cause-effect relationship that develops the main action: Odysseus' return from the Trojan War to his home and his restoration of order there. The story of the Trojan War is much more remote to the background of this work than it is to the ILIAD. The immediate background is the ten years of Odysseus' wandering before he reaches his home. But these ten years are telescoped, and the ODYSSEY relates only the last six weeks of the journey, while other events are brought in within the last few days.

Both of the epics of Homer fulfill the requirement that an epic be of sufficient length. These two works are fully and beautifully developed, the ILIAD structured in 15,693 lines; the ODYSSEY, in 12,160 lines.

Like all narrative poems, the epic is objective; that is, the author does not intrude into the story. In the ILIAD and the ODYSSEY, Homer says nothing in his own voice. Even his beautiful similes, which are the poet's means in a narrative poem of giving his own interpretation and point of view, are handled in such a way that they illustrate or illuminate the story, but are never mere insertions by the poet or ornaments he devises.

In these two fine epics, Homer shows the concern for form that marks the artist. This is seen in the use of the heroic measure, which is the verse form considered acceptable for the epic in Homer's day. It is seen in the careful shaping of meaning around one single line of action. It is seen in the classical restraint evident in descriptions of bloody scenes and in the striking handling of language. And it is seen in the masterful treatment of character and in the relationship between character and action.

We must keep in mind that the ILIAD and the ODYSSEY are

narrative poems, that the stories are told through the word music of verse. In the book you will use to study these beautiful epics, the stories are retold in prose. You will meet the heroes of old, see them in battle, listen to their conversations, watch them rise to heights of heroism that match that of the gods. But you will follow the action in the language of prose, not of poetry. When you have learned the meaning of these epic stories and enjoyed their beauty and movement in simple prose, you will want to read the great epics again in the beautiful language of poetry in which Homer composed them.

The Medieval Romances

To shape his great epics, the ILIAD and the ODYSSEY, Homer gathered the myths and legends of ancient paganism which had accumulated over the centuries as the folklore of the oral tradition. In much the same way, the tales and legends of the Christian Middle Ages about brave knights and beautiful ladies were, in times, gathered into the long narrative called the romance.

The most famous of medieval romances tells the story of King Arthur and his great knights of the Round Table. Over the years hundreds of short tales telling of the brave deeds of Arthur and Lancelot and Gareth and Galahad and all the rest were told and retold. These were shaped by Thomas Malory into a long continuous romance called the MORTE D'Arthur.

In your reading of a few of the stories that make up this great romance, you will meet the noble King Arthur, the great Sir Lancelot, the valiant Sir Gareth, and the good Sir Galahad. These are only a few of the knights of this long romance, but they are very important ones. Perhaps, sometime, you will enjoy reading the entire MORTE D'ARTHUR.

SUMMING UP

I. Identify these terms:

—A

epic	conflict
episode	characterization
action	complication
character	causality
setting	exposition

—B

foreshadowing	preternatural being
suspense	simile
plot	epic simile
myth	metaphor
mythology	legend

—C

folk epic	explanatory myth
art epic	soothsayer
legend	setting
hero tale	oracle
tripod	lyre
omen	

—D

joust	siege
chivalry	feudal
grail	adventure
tourney	herald
knight	hero

II. Identify these names:

—A

Homer	Paris
Trojans	Iris
King Priam	Helen of Sparta
Queen Hecuba	Menelaus
Mount Ida	Agamemnon
Achilles	

—B

Odysseus	Patroclus
Ajax	Thetis
Hector	Diomedes
Pandarus	Apple of Discord
Nestor	Bard
Scop	Minstrel

—C

Andromache	Briseis
Scaean Gates	Laocoön
Athena	Tiresias
Hera	Myrmidons
Juno	Cassandra

THE ODYSSEY

—A

Odysseus	Cyclops
Ilium	Nymphs
Ismarus	Aeolus
Penelope	Circe
Ithaca	

—B

Tantalus	Calypso
Sisyphus	Telemachus
Sirens	Laertes
Scylla	Nausicaä
Charybdis	Polyphemus

—C

Persephone   Ethiopians
Mentor   Cathay
Cimmerians

THE MORTE D'ARTHUR

—A

Sir Thomas Malory   Sir Bedivere
Uther Pendragon   King Arthur
Queen Igraine   Sir Ector
Merlin   Sir Kay
King Uriens   King Lot

—B

Gawaine   Guinevere
Gareth   Camelot
Morgan le Fay   Sir Accolon
Modred   Avalon
Excalibur

III. Know:

—A The ILIAD, the ODYSSEY, and the MORTE D'ARTHUR
as story structures.

—B The interrelationship of character and action in the
ILIAD, the ODYSSEY, and the MORTE D'ARTHUR.

Songs of Twilight

THE SHORT VERSE NARRATIVE

Songs of Twilight

THE SHORT VERSE NARRATIVE

Narrative Poetry

Narrative poetry is story and it is song. Its stories are gathered from the camp fires of the world's battlefields, from the huts of peasants, from the strongholds of medieval castles, from all the market places and palaces and hovels where human beings gather to share the meaning of life. Whether sung by minstrels in the great hall of a nobleman, told by villagers around the green of a summer evening, or handed on by fathers to their children around the cottage hearth, stories that hold listeners spellbound have qualities in common. They follow the ascents and declines of plot and of breath-taking suspense. All the devices of good narration belong to them. These may be used clumsily, but they are at least present in their simple beginnings.

The music that meets story in narrative poetry needs no accounting for. The emotional tension of story itself is always ready to break into song. When stories come to us from the oral tradition, it is difficult to know which were sung and which were told. It is of the offspring of the earliest oral tradition of the myths and legends and fables and parables that we are speaking when we discuss narrative poetry here. We are interested in those stories which, in medieval times, borrowed the storytelling patterns of the old folk tales and made new stories set to music. These sung stories are ballads or metrical tales.

THE PATTERN OF STORY IN NARRATIVE POETRY: In your study of folk tales you looked at the structure of narration. You discovered that a well told folk story has a threefold plan: an initiating incident, a development, and a point or conclusion. Before the first incident there is often a short expository section, sometimes a single sentence which gives either character identification or setting. Then one incident, the initiating one, starts a series of events that make up the development. These move forward to the last incident, which serves as the point of the story or conclusion. When there is variation in any of the three parts, new story patterns arise.

All folk tales share this basic narrative structure. But one folk type differs from another folk type in some distinct way. The myth follows the simple patterns of narration. The parable and fable are allegories and develop on two levels of meaning, the literal and the symbolic. The fairy tale may have one set of characters or it may have two. It may have only human beings engaged in unusual adventures, or it may have human beings and fairy creatures complicating its action. In structure, the action of a fairy tale is not caused by character. The beginning of the tale forms a brief background to the main action which starts abruptly and works forward quickly to the end.

Because of the natural division of narration into three parts, a well-structured story is built on the pattern of three. But because three was a number with special significance for primitive as well as medieval people, the pattern of three functions often and intricately in folk tales beyond the needs of simple story forms.

STORY AND SONG: It was not until the narrative structures of story were in time combined with the patterns of verse, or word music, that the sung stories called ballads and metrical tales came into existence. They are a combination of story and verse. In them two patterns meet: a pattern of a well told story and a pattern of word music in verse. The method followed in telling the story is the story pattern or structure. The various sound devices of poetry provide the word music—rhythm, rhyme, assonance, onomatopoeia, and alliteration. Before you begin reading narrative poems, you will learn to enjoy all of these devices of word music. Now you need only remember that these two, the structure of story and the pattern of verse, make the unity of a narrative poem. They have the help of word patterning in figures of speech: the concrete detail of the simple image, the simile, the metaphor, and personification. You will learn how these and other figures of speech serve the poet as he shapes his poem.

Reading, Writing, and Discussion of Narrative Poems

NARRATIVE STRUCTURE IN POETRY—THE FAIRY TALE

1. You have read and studied the story pattern of fairy tales. Read the fairy tale, *The Three Billy Goats Gruff,* and work out its story pattern.

THE THREE
BILLY GOATS GRUFF

Once upon a time there were three billy goats. They had a fine large field near the river to live in and all the grass they could eat.

But one day they stood and looked across the stream. The grass on the other side looked juicy and green. The littlest billy goat said, "Let's go across the river to eat some of that fine grass."

The middle-sized billy goat said, "Yes, let's."

But the biggest billy goat with the deep loud voice said, "Oh, no! The troll of the bridge will eat us."

In the end the littlest billy goat and the middle-sized billy goat won the argument, and soon they went to the other side of the river. They didn't know it, but they were walking right over the troll's roof.

"Who's walking over my roof?" a horrid voice croaked.

The littlest billy goat squeaked, "It is I, Little Billy Goat Gruff. I came to eat some grass in the meadow."

"Oh, no," said the troll. "I am the one who will eat and it is you I will eat."

"Please," said the littlest billy goat. "Don't eat me. My brother, the middle-sized goat, is fatter than I am."

"You are a skinny one," said the troll. And he let the littlest billy goat go to the meadow to eat.

Then the middle-sized billy goat heard the horrid voice croaking, "Who's that walking over my roof?"

"It is I, Middle Billy Goat Gruff. I want to eat some tender grass in the meadow."

"Oh, no," said the troll. "I'm coming up to eat you."

The middle-sized billy goat was scared as could be. He trembled as the troll began to come toward him.

"Don't eat me," he said. "My brother is fatter; wait for him."

The troll said, "You are a skinny one"; and he let the billy goat go to the meadow.

When the biggest billy goat saw his two brothers calmly munching grass across the river, he forgot all his warnings about the troll and made a dash for the bridge. Just as he reached it, he saw the big green hairy troll with long fingernails crawling up the railway. The troll lunged at the biggest billy goat to swallow him in one huge bite.

But Big Billy Goat Gruff was a match for the troll. He put his head down, snorted, and butted the troll right into the river.

That was the end of the troll.

After that the three billy goats enjoyed the fine tender grass whenever they were hungry.

2. Now read and study the following version of *Three Billy Goats Gruff* to discover what happens when the fairy tale is made into a poem.

Three
Billy
Goats
Gruff

Three Billy Goats Gruff on a warm summer day
Were tired of grass that had dried into hay.
　　Ho, hum, Billy.

While over the river so deep and serene
Was a meadow of grass, a beautiful green.
　　Yum, yum, Billy.

"Oh no!" warned the biggest in deep solemn notes,
"The troll of the bridge has a taste for young goats."
    Yum, yum, Billy.

Half hearing the warning he turned on his hoof
And trip-tropped to breakfast across the troll's roof.
    Run, run, Billy.

"Who's that a-trip-troppin' o'er my poor achin' head?
Speak up there! Don't mutter!" a horrid voice said.
    Come, come, Billy.

"It is I, Little Billy Goat Gruff, come to eat
Of the grass in the meadow so tender and sweet."
    Yum, yum, Billy.

"Oh, no," said the troll, "you're as wrong as can be.
I'll come up and eat *you;* I'm hungry, you see."
    Come, come, Billy.

The little goat froze in terror and fright
And gazed mesmerized as the troll came in sight.
    Beware, Billy.

Then finding his voice he bleated with vim,
"The second one's fatter; why not wait for *him*?"
    Take care, Billy.

"You *are* sort of skinny and raw-boned, I note,
And I think you're a poor excuse for a goat."
    There, there, Billy.

That's all that was needed. With a flick of his horn
He hurried to breakfast that sunshiny morn.
    Yum, yum, Billy.

The second goat, seeing the first at his feed,
Remarked to the third, "I too will succeed."
    Yum, yum, Billy.

"Oh, no," warned the biggest in deep solemn notes.
"The troll of the bridge has a taste for young goats."
    Ho, hum, Billy.

Half hearing the warning, he turned on his hoof
And trip-tropped to breakfast across the troll's roof.
    Yum, yum, Billy.

"Who's that a-trip-troppin' o'er my poor achin' head?
Speak up there! Don't mutter!" a horrid voice said.
    Come, come, Billy.

"It is I, Middle Billy Goat Gruff, come to eat
Of the grass in the meadow that's tender and sweet."
    Yum, yum, Billy.

"Oh, no," said the troll, "you're wrong as can be.
I'll come up and eat *you;* I'm hungry, you see."
    Come, come, Billy.

The second goat trembled and panted with fear
As the hairy green troll crept steadily near.
    Beware, Billy.

Then finding his voice he bleated with vim,
"The third one is fatter; why not wait for *him*?"
    Take care, Billy.

"You are sort of skinny and raw-boned, I note,
In fact you're a poor excuse for a goat!"
    There, there, Billy.

That's all that he needed. With a toss of his horn
He hurried to breakfast that sunshiny morn.
    Yum, yum, Billy.

Big Billy Goat saw with a stab of chagrin
The other two eating, not waiting for him.
    By gum, Billy.

Forgetting his warning in deep solemn notes
Of trolls with fancy for meat of young goats,
    Yum, yum, Billy.

He picked up the dust with fast-flying hoof
And trip-tropped in thunder across the board roof.
    Run, run, Billy.

"Who's that a-trip-troppin' o'er my poor achin' head?
The noise that you're makin' would waken the dead."
    Run, run, Billy.

"It is I, Biggest Billy Goat Gruff, come to eat
Of the grass in the meadow that's tender and sweet."
    Yum, yum, Billy.

"Oh, no," said the troll, "you're wrong as can be.
I'm coming to eat *you*. I've been waiting, you see."
    Come, come, Billy.

"Very well, come along," Big Billy Goat cried,
As he shook his long horns with masculine pride.
    Ho, hum, Billy.

The hairy green troll with long fingernails
Crawled up to the bridge and over the rails,
    Beware, Billy.

And looked upon Billy with gourmet's delight
Already tasting his very first bite.
    Take care, Billy.

With a bleat and a snort and a horrible crash,
Billy butted the troll to the river . . . ker-splash!
    Some fun, Billy.

Without waiting to watch how the bubbles would form,
He trip-tropped to breakfast that sunshiny morn.
    Ho, hum, Billy.

S.
HUBERT

1. When you studied the long narrative, you read the Arthurian romance *The Quest of the Holy Grail,* on page 204. Reread it. Be prepared to tell the story and show its story pattern. **2.** Now read this poem, *The Holy Grail,* to experience how the story-telling pattern of the romance combines with the word music of verse. Notice how the narrative is tightened by the use of verse.

The Holy Grail

Before the time when Galahad was born
A hermit came on Pentecost to say
Siege Perilous was soon to bear a knight
Who would be true and win the Holy Grail.
Then Lancelot, fair flower of knighthood, rode
Into another country on a quest
Of new adventure till he came upon
A tower rising fair and tall above
A town whose people wailing met him at
The gate and bade him free their lady from
Her hell-hot room. He strode into the tower;
The bolts flew back; the locks became undone.
The lady freed, he bravely plunged his sword
Into the untombed fire-spitting snake.
The great King Pelles came and bade the knight
Right welcome to his court. Anon,
A damsel came who bore within her hands
A chalice made of gold. The King knelt down
And likewise all his men and Lancelot.
It was the Holy Grail that they adored.
Then came Elaine, the daughter of the King,
Most beautiful and wise, the one to bear
The son of Lancelot, Sir Galahad.

Full fifteen years rolled by. At Camelot
King Arthur's knights were gathered round to keep
The Pentecostal vigil and renew
Their vows. A message came to Lancelot

To come into a nearby woods to learn
How to fulfill an ancient prophecy.
He left, and met a child not quite fifteen
Who at his own request became a knight
At Lancelot's hand. They both withdrew,
And Lancelot returned to Camelot
Where marvelous things were coming into time.
Gold words appeared upon Siege Perilous
That this would be the day it would be filled.
Close to the river bank nearby, a sword
Was stuck into a piece of floating rock.
And here were letters, too, that said, "No man
But he who is the greatest knight can wrench
Me free and bear me at his side." The king
Bade Lancelot with his hand release
The prisoned sword and claim it to be his.
This knight refused and no knight else could budge
It from the rock. And then came Galahad
And took his place upon Siege Perilous
Whose golden letters now had changed to read
His name. He likewise drew the sword from out
The floating stone; whereat he proved himself
By jousting at the king's own tournament.
And when they came again into their seats
There entered in the hall the Holy Grail
All draped in white samite so none could see,
And all the knights assembled made a vow
To undertake a quest to find the Grail.

Now Galahad was yet without a shield,
But he rode forth and in four days he came
Unto an abbey where was held a shield
Meant only for the world's most worthy knight.
So Galahad must claim it as his own.
A scarlet cross blazed on this snow-white shield,
A cross made with his kinsman's royal blood.
So Galahad rode on to seek the Grail,
And many rare adventures did he find

And conquered all. He was indeed of all
Great knights the wisest and of all most pure.
For many months he lived with Lancelot,
And when he went again all on his own
The vision of the Grail eluded him.
But then one day he met Sir Percival
And later on Sir Bors caught up to them.
The three rode on until they came unto
Sir Pelles' castle where they were received
With joy by all the people gathered there.
Late in the day, nine other knights
Arrived and were received by the good king.
And these twelve men by Christ's own hand received
The Holy Grail, and Christ Himself spoke to
Sir Galahad to tell him where to find
The holy dish wherein He ate the Lamb
At His last Meal, and sail with it
Unto another land. With his two knights,
Sir Percival and Bors, he found the ship
And sailed until they came to Sarras town.
The silver table, too, they took with them
Whereon was resting now the Holy Grail
And wrought a cure to prove the power it held.
The city's king, a tyrant was and bold;
He threw these knights into a dungeon cold.
They stayed there for a year until the king
Lay sick, and thought that he would die.
He sent for them and begged them to forgive
His tyranny. They did this with good grace,
And so he died. The people mourned but then
A voice bade them to choose Sir Galahad.
As king this knight built up a famous shrine
Around the table of the Holy Grail
And for one year with Percival and Bors
Said all his prayers kneeling at the shrine.
One day they saw a bishop kneeling there
Surrounded by celestial brotherhood.
And he spoke out, "Come forth, Sir Galahad,

The servant true of Christ, see that which long
Thou has desired to see." Then Galahad
Trembled in joy at vision of these things.
And said, "I thank Thee, Blessed Lord, for this
Which I now see unveiled before my eyes,
And if it please Your Will I now would die."
When this was done, he went to Percival
And to Sir Bors, commended them to God,
And to Sir Bors he said, "Commend me to
My father Lancelot and bid him to
Be mindful of the promise he has made."
Then he knelt down to pray before the Lord
And his pure soul departed unto Christ.

MARY
CLAYTON

NARRATIVE STRUCTURE IN POETRY—THE FABLE AND THE
LEGEND: Examine the verse fable, *The Serpent and the Mouse,*
and the verse legend, *St. Swithin.* Explain what characteristics
of the fable and the legend you find in them. Choose a prose
fable or legend that you know to reshape into a narrative poem
of your own.

The Serpent and the Mouse

TRANSLATED
BY
ARTHUR
W.
RYDER

Within a basket tucked away
In slow starvation's grim decay,
A broken-hearted serpent lay.

But see the cheerful mouse that gnaws
A hole, and tumbles in his jaws
At night—new hope's unbidden cause!

Now see the serpent, sleek with meat,
Who hastens through the hole, to beat
From quarters cramped, a glad retreat!

So fuss and worry will not do;
For fate is somehow muddling through
To good or bad for me and you.

St. Swithin

"Bury me," the bishop said,
"Close to my geranium bed;
Lay me near the gentle birch.
It is lonely in the church,
And its vaults are damp and chill!
Noble men sleep there, but still
House me in the friendly grass!
Let the linnets sing my mass!"
Dying Swithin had his whim
And the green sod covered him.

Then what holy celebrations
And what rapturous adorations,
Joy no wordly pen may paint—
Swithin had been made a saint!
Yet the monks forgot that he
Craved for blossom, bird and bee,
And, communing round his tomb,
Vowed its narrow earthen room
Was unworthy one whose star
Shone in Peter's calendar.

"Who," they asked, "when we are gone
Will protect this sacred lawn?
What if time's irreverent gust
Should disperse his holy dust?"
Troubled by a blackbird's whistle,
Vexed by an invading thistle
They resolved to move his bones
To the chaste cathedral stones.
But the clouds grew black and thick
When they lifted spade and pick,
And they feared that they had blundered
By the way it poured and thundered.
Quoth the abbot: "Thus, I deem,
Swithin shows us we blaspheme!
He was fond of wind and rain;
Let him in their clasp remain!"
Forty days the heavens wept,
But St. Swithin smiled and slept.

DANIEL
HENDERSON

DISCOVERY OF COMMON PATTERNS: Read this poem made from the fairy tale, *The Three Little Pigs*. **-a** Is the story as well told in the poem as it is in the fairy tale? **-b** What characteristics does the poem have that a fairy tale in prose does not have? **-c** Compare the story structure of *Three Billy Goats Gruff* with that of *The Three Little Pigs*. Be ready to tell the class about these story structures. **-d** What characteristics does the poem have which make it easily sung by a group?

The Three Little Pigs

Three little piggies lived in a pen,
Wee, win, wonnie.
Their mother died; what to do then?
Wee, win, wonnie.

The first little pig went into the town
Ree, rin, ronnie.
He found some straw and pitched it down,
Ray, rah, ronnie.

Out of that straw he built a warm house,
Ray, rah, ronnie;
And there he lived as snug as a mouse.
Ray, rah, ronnie.

The old wolf came by with a sly, wicked grin,
Chin, chin, chonnie,
"Little pig, little pig, let me come in."
Nay, nay, nonnie.

"Not by the hair of my chinny chin chin,
Chin, chin, chonnie.
Though sweet you may talk, I'll not let you in."
Chin, chin, chonnie.

So he huffed and he puffed with all of his might,
Huff, huff, honnie,
Till all of the straw blew way out of sight.
Huff, huff, honnie.

The little pig squealed, but the wolf held him tight,
Wee, wee, wonnie;
He boiled him and ate him for supper that night.
Wee, wee, wonnie.

The next little pig went out on the land,
Wee, wee, wonnie.
He found some wood and broke it by hand.
Wee, wee, wonnie.

Out of the wood he built a warm house,
Ray, rah, ronnie,
And there he lived as snug as a mouse.
Ray, rah, ronnie.

The old wolf came by with a sly, wicked grin,
Chin, chin, chonnie,
"Little pig, little pig, let me come in."
Nay, nay, nonnie.

"Not by the hair of my chinny chin chin,
Chin, chin, chonnie,
Though sweet you may talk, I'll not let you in."
Chin, chin, chonnie.

So he huffed and he puffed with all of his might,
Huff, huff, honnie,
And all of the wood blew way out of sight.
Huff, huff, honnie.

The little pig squealed but the wolf held him tight,
Wee, wee, wonnie;
He boiled him and ate him for supper that night.
Wee, wee, wonnie.

The third little piggy who had lots of pluck,
Wee, wee, wonnie,
Bought a big pile of bricks to try out his luck.
Ray, rah, ronnie.

Out of the bricks he built a warm house,
Ray rah, ronnie;
And there he lived as snug as a mouse.
Ray, rah, ronnie.

The old wolf came by with a sly, wicked grin,
Chin, chin, chonnie,
"Little pig, little pig, let me come in!"
Chin, chin, chonnie.

"Not by the hair of my chinny chin chin,
Chin, chin, chonnie,
Though sweet you may talk, I will not let you in."
Chin, chin, chonnie.

So he huffed and he puffed with all of his might,
Huff, huff, honnie,
But all of the bricks just held on tight,
Ray, rah, ronnie.

So he honeyed his voice, as he temptingly said,
Wee, wee, wonnie,
"There are some mighty fine turnips in yon turnip bed."
Nay, nay, nonnie.

"I'll meet you at nine in the morning," said he,
Chin, chin, chonnie,
"And we'll gather some turnips to have with your tea."
Nay, nay, nonnie.

But Pig Three rose early and was back home by eight,
Ray, rah, ronnie,
The wolf saw he was bested but held back his hate.
Woe, woe, wonnie.

So he honeyed his voice as sweetly said he,
Wee, wee, wonnie,
"There're some mighty fine apples on yon apple tree."
Nay, nay, nonnie.

"I'll meet you at six in the sweet morning dawn,
Ree, rin, ronnie,
And we'll gather some apples before they're all gone,"
Ree, rin, ronnie.

But Pig Three rose early and was back home by five,
Ray, rah, ronnie,
The old wolf was angry that Pig Three was alive.
Ray, rah, ronnie.

But he honeyed his voice with the utmost of care,
Woe, woe, wonnie,
As he said, "Little Pig, in the town there's a fair."
Woe, woe, wonnie.

"So let us rise early and if it's good weather,
Wee, win, wonnie,
We'll wander around on the fairgrounds together."
Nay, nay, nonnie.

But Pig Three rose early and went to the fair,
Ray, rah, ronnie,
And bought a fine churn before wolf got there.
Ray, rah, ronnie. ·

But the wolf watched his chance on the side of the hill,
Woe, woe, wonnie,
He was tired and hungry and set for the kill.
Woe, woe, wonnie.

Pig jumped in the churn and gaily rolled past,
Ray, rah, ronnie,
And frightened the wolf till he ran away fast.
Ray, rah, ronnie.

The old wolf was angry and stamped all his feet,
Wee, wee, wonnie,
And vowed that Pig Three would soon be wolf meat.
Chin, chin, chonnie.

Then up on the top of Pig Three's roof he sped.
Woe, woe, wonnie,
"I'll come down the chimney and eat you," he said.
Woe, woe, wonnie.

The pig built a fire and put on the pot.
Ray, rah, ronnie,
And said, "Come on in, this water is hot."
Ray, rah, ronnie.

Then the old wolf, the sly, wicked grinner,
Wee, wee, wonnie,
Ended his life as the little pig's dinner.
Ray, rah, ronnie.

MARY CLAYTON

Examine the structure of *Babylon*. Compare it with the structure of the fairy tale, *The Three Little Pigs*. Be ready to tell this story in class and to work out its story pattern.

Babylon

There were three ladies lived in a bower—
  Eh, wow, bonnie!
And they went out to pull a flower
  On the bonnie banks o' Fordie.

They had not pulled a flower but one,
  Eh, wow, bonnie!
When up started to them a banished man
  On the bonnie banks o' Fordie.

He's taken the first sister by her hand,
  Eh, wow, bonnie!
And he's turned her round and made her stand
  On the bonnie banks o' Fordie.

"It's whether will you be a rank robber's wife,
  Eh, wow, bonnie!
Or will you die by my wee pen-knife?"
  On the bonnie banks o' Fordie.

"It's I'll not be a rank robber's wife,
  Eh, wow, bonnie!
But I'll rather die by your wee pen-knife."
  On the bonnie banks o' Fordie.

He's killed this maid and he's laid her by,
  Eh, wow, bonnie!
For to bear the red rose company
  On the bonnie banks o' Fordie.

He's taken the second one by the hand,
  Eh, wow, bonnie!
And he's turned her round and made her stand
  On the bonnie banks o' Fordie.

"It's whether will you be a rank robber's wife,
  Eh, wow, bonnie!
Or will you die by my wee pen-knife?"
  On the bonnie banks o' Fordie.

"It's I'll not be a rank robber's wife,
  Eh, wow, bonnie!
But I'll rather die by you wee pen-knife."
  On the bonnie banks o' Fordie.

He's killed this maid, and he's laid her by,
  Eh, wow, bonnie!
For to bear the red rose company
  On the bonnie banks o' Fordie.

He's taken the youngest one by the hand,
  Eh, wow, bonnie!
And he's turned her round and made her stand
  On the bonnie banks o' Fordie.

Says, "Will you be a rank robber's wife,
  Eh, wow, bonnie!
Or will you die by my wee pen-knife?"
  On the bonnie banks o' Fordie.

"It's I'll not be a rank robber's wife,
  Eh, wow, bonnie!
Nor will I die by your wee pen-knife
  On the bonnie banks o' Fordie.

"For in this wood a brother I ha'e;
  Eh, wow, bonnie!
And if you kill me, it's he'll kill thee."
  On the bonnie banks o' Fordie.

"What's thy brother's name? Come tell to me."
  Eh, wow, bonnie!
"My brother's name is Baby Lon."
  On the bonnie banks o' Fordie.

"O sister, sister, what have I done!
  Eh, wow, bonnie!
O have I done this ill to thee!
  On the bonnie banks o' Fordie.

"O since I've done this evil deed,
  Eh, wow, bonnie!
Good shall never be my meed."
  On the bonnie banks o' Fordie.

He's taken out his wee pen-knife,
  Eh, wow, bonnie!
And he's twined himself of his own sweet life
  On the bonnie banks o' Fordie.

OLD
BALLAD

SOUND AND LANGUAGE—RHYTHM: Sound and language work together to help the poet shape his meaning. Before you begin to read the metrical tales and ballads that follow, spend some time studying the way poets use sound and language.

The regular movement that makes children jump rope in time to a chanted rhyme, couples dance in time to a polka, and stadium audiences stamp their feet in time to a march is what we call rhythm. It involves patterned movement.

Rhythm in the poetry you will read patterns on the basis of stressed and unstressed syllables. When a stressed syllable begins the pattern, it creates what we call falling rhythm, for the other syllables fall down from the stressed one. A stressed syllable followed by an unstressed syllable (/ x) and one stressed syllable followed by two unstressed syllables (/ x x) are falling rhythms. Falling rhythm may emphasize conviction:

> / x / x / x /
> "Bury me," the bishop said,
> / x / x / x /
> "Close to my geranium bed,"

Or it may rouse:

> / x / x / x /
> Who will shield the fearless heart
> / x / x / x /
> Who avert the murderous blade

Or it may command with delicacy and gentleness:

> / x x / x x
> Take her up tenderly,
> / x x /
> Lift her with care.

The words it joins with can make it do many things.

When the unstressed syllable or syllables rise up to the stressed one, they create what we call rising rhythm. An unstressed syllable followed by a stressed syllable (x /) and two unstressed syllables followed by a stressed syllable (x x /) are rising rhythms. Rising rhythm may calmly narrate:

> x / x / x / x x / x
> There were three ladies lived in a bower

Or it may confirm a resolution:

> x / x / x / x / x /
> To strive, to seek, to find, and not to yield

Or it may gallop:

> x / x x / x x / x x /
> I galloped, Dirck galloped, we galloped all three;

Like falling rhythm, it is merely a pattern of beats by itself, but in combination with words it creates mood and meaning. If you recognize the patterns of the two rising rhythms and the two falling rhythms, you will enjoy the simple rhythmic effects in ballads and metrical tales.

To practice sensing the rhythm of a poem, read *The Lady of the Tomahawk, Sea Lullaby, A Lady Comes to an Inn,* and *Lazybones.* Note the various sound patterns.

The Lady of the Tomahawk

Hannah was a lady,
　　She had a feather-bed,
And she'd worked Jonah and the whale
　　Upon the linen spread,
She did her honest household part
To give our land a godly start.

Red Injuns broke the china
　　Her use had never flawed,
They ripped her goose-tick up with knives
　　And shook the down abroad.
They took her up the Merrimac
With only one shirt to her back.

Hannah Dustin pondered
　　On her cupboard's wrongs,
Hannah Dustin duly mastered
　　The red-hot Injun songs.
She lay beside her brown new mates
Remembering the Derby plates.

She got the chief to show her
　　How he aimed his blow
And cut the white man's crop of hair
　　And left the brains to show.
The Lord had made her quick to learn
The way to carve or chop or churn.

The moon was on the hilltop,
   Sleep was on the waves,
Hannah took the tomahawk
   And scalped all twenty braves.
She left her master last of all,
And at the ears she shaved his poll.

Homeward down the river
   She paddled her canoe.
She went to her old cellar-place
   To see what she could do.
She found some bits of plates that matched,
What plates she could she went and patched.

She built her chimney higher
   Than it had been before
She hung her twenty sable scalps
   Above her modest door.
She sat a-plucking new gray geese
For new mattresses in peace.

ROBERT P.
TRISTRAM
COFFIN

1. Show how this poem is built on a sharp and mocking contrast between Hannah's normal activities and the Indians' normal activities. **2.** The rhythm is clipped and abrupt. Does it heighten or lessen the tragedy? Explain. **3.** Each stanza patterns on three actions. How does the rhythmic pattern vary among the three? Does it make any dramatic contribution to the movement?

Sea
Lullaby

The old moon is tarnished
With smoke of the flood,
The dead leaves are varnished
With color like blood,

A treacherous smiler
With teeth white as milk,
A savage beguiler
In sheathings of silk,
The sea creeps to pillage,
She leaps on her prey;
A child of the village
Was murdered today.

She came up to meet him
In a smooth golden cloak,
She choked him and beat him
To death, for a joke.
Her bright locks were tangled,
She shouted for joy,
With one hand she strangled
A strong little boy.

Now in silence she lingers
Beside him all night
To wash her long fingers
In silvery light.

ELINOR
WYLIE

1. There is mocking in this poem, too, but it is built on a different kind of contrast. Analyze the contrast and its patterning throughout the poem. **2.** Though the lines of this poem are very short, how does the rhythm help to lengthen them? **3.** The rhythm of this poem is very regular. Does its regularity reduce it to mere accompaniment to the meaning, or does the regularity of the rhythm enable it to make an important contribution to the meaning?

A Lady Comes to an Inn

Three strange men came to the inn;
One was a black man pocked and thin,
One was brown with a silver knife,
And one brought with him a beautiful wife.

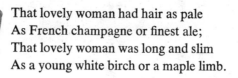

That lovely woman had hair as pale
As French champagne or finest ale;
That lovely woman was long and slim
As a young white birch or a maple limb.

Her face was like cream, her mouth was a rose,
What language she spoke nobody knows,
But sometimes she'd scream like a cockatoo
And swear wonderful oaths that nobody knew.

Her great silk skirts like a silver bell
Down to her little bronze slippers fell,
And her low-cut gown showed a dove on its nest
In blue tattooing across her breast.

Nobody learned the lady's name
Nor the marvellous land from which they came,
But no one in all the countryside
Has forgotten those men and that beautiful bride.

ELIZABETH COATSWORTH

1. In this poem, an air of mystery makes a frame around a core of interest that is patterned in very concrete details. Show how the lines fall into this shape. In what lines does the mystery invade the concrete description?   **2.** The rhythm of the lines varies: some are in falling rhythm, some in rising rhythm. Point out all the lines where the rhythm reverses, and analyze what special emphatic effect is created.

Lazybones   Of all the Tipsham lazybones
                The Yanceys took the cake,
             Only in blueberry time
                Did Mother Yancey bake.

And then it was but six or so
    Pies that had the pip,
And the soggy bottom crust
    Would sink an iron ship.

The Yancey boys went bare of foot
    Till the snowflakes flew,
And you could put in your right eye
    The corn Dan Yancey grew.

They were folks for whom the skies
    Were always low and murky.
They were always on hard-pan
    And poor as old Job's turkey.

One winter when the bay froze up
    From Whaleboat out to Ram,
The Yanceys did not have so much
    As a knuckle-bone of ham.

They sat around their dying stove
    And worried at the weather,
The neighbors went and got a cord
    Of seasoned birch together.

They brought it to the Yancey home
    Where seven tall sons sat
Round the last stick of their wood,
    Crowding out the cat.

"Here you are, Dan Yancey, this
    Will keep you for a spell."
They left the wood and went back home
    Feeling pretty well.

But there was not a sign of smoke
    From the Yancey flue
Going up that afternoon
    On the winter blue.

And when the dusk was coming on,

ROBERT P.   Dan came to Abel Leigh,
TRISTRAM   "Can't you send one of your boys
COFFIN   To saw my birch for me?"

1. The rhythmic pattern in this poem, as in *The Lady of the Tomahawk,* is short and clipped. Here, however, it creates a completely different effect. Analyze the difference. **2.** Show how this poem patterns in terms of exposition and development. **3.** Does the author seem more concerned here with telling a story or with making a point? Explain.

ASSIGNMENTS ON RHYTHM

1. Omit some of the adjectives in the poem *A Lady Comes to an Inn* and observe the effects on the movement of the lines. Determine the change in pattern and decide whether the effect is more or less pleasing.

2. Considering the following as first lines for narrative poems, choose the word that creates the best effect:

The (*great, bellowing, stampeding*) herd came (*crashing, retreating*) down the hill.

Three bodies (*lay, rotted*) in the grave.

The (*red-haired, dark*) girl fell from the tree.

On the top of the (*mountain, mountain trail*) there lived an old man.

King Arthur (*rode, galloped*) with all his men.

They ran up the (*stairs, stairway*) to get to the hall.

Around the bend the (*Dodge, Oldsmobile, Chevy*) roared.

The (*wren, robin, chickadee*) sat on the snow-covered branch.

The icy (*trees, bushes*) swayed in the cruel winter wind.

They crept through the grass on the (*large, immense*) vacant lot.

3. Convert each of the following to a rhythmic line:

There is an underwater treasure that is sought by many men.

There are five blackbirds sitting on a low branch of a tree and
all day they make the strange noise that is their song.

A boy, red-haired and freckled, is riding his bicycle up and down
in front of a girl's house.

A flash of lightning, accompanied a few minutes later by
thunder, lit up the whole sky.

The model 1929 car made a lot of noise as it came down
the street.

SOUND AND LANGUAGE—RHYME

Part of the sound you enjoy the most when you hear a poem
is rhyme. And this enjoyment is a natural human one. If you
doubt that it is, listen to how children at their happiest play
recite numbers or the alphabet or nonsense. Or listen to a
modern love song.

Most commonly in poetry, rhyme is end rhyme. In other
words, it occurs between words at the end of two or more lines.
For true rhyme, the stressed vowels and all the sounds that
follow must be alike, while the sounds that precede must be
unlike.

If the syllable with the stressed vowel is the only or the last
syllable of the words, the firmness created makes the rhyme
masculine:

glee — free   deny — reply
taint — paint   comprehend — will attend

If the syllable with the stressed vowel has other syllables following it, the lightness created makes the rhyme feminine:

tasteful — wasteful   duty — beauty
thinker — tinker   glimmering — shimmering

When the sounds are close but not exactly the same, we call
the result imperfect rhyme:

love — prove   out — sought
gloom — some   breathe — beneath

Some poems have sound patterns that include both end rhyme and internal rhyme. Shelley's *The Cloud* is an example of these two kinds of rhyme in the same poem.

> *I bring fresh showers for the thirsting flowers,*
> > *From the seas and the streams;*
> *I bear light shade for the leaves when laid*
> > *In their noonday dreams.*

Letters of the alphabet are used to show the pattern of end rhyme. Two successive lines that rhyme are marked **a-a**. This is how the rhyme scheme of a poem is usually indicated:

A gown made of the finest wool	**a**
Which from our pretty lambs we pull;	**a**
Fair-lined slippers for the cold,	**b**
With buckles of the purest gold.	**b**

Behold this living stone	**a**
I rear for me,	**b**
Ne'er to be thrown	**a**
Down, envious time, by thee.	**b**

Thy voice is on the rolling air;	**a**
I hear thee where the waters run;	**b**
Thou standest in the rising sun,	**b**
And in the setting thou art fair.	**a**

O who is this has done this deed,	**a**
This ill deed done to me,	**b**
To send me out this time of year,	**c**
To sail upon the sea!	**b**

ASSIGNMENTS ON RHYME

1. See how many adjectives you can rhyme with proper nouns.
EXAMPLES:

Plain Jane   Handy Andy   Surly Shirley

2. Prepare some pairs of rhyming lines that might be used in class as the openings for stories to be built up by the joint efforts of the class. EXAMPLES:

In terror I began to stare
When I saw who was standing there . . .

The tired year was almost spent
When there occurred a strange event . . .

I stood, a child unseen, unheard,
The night he spoke that fatal word . . .

3. Reread the narrative poems you've already studied. Try to discover and demonstrate how rhyme creates music, emphasis, and meaning.

Introduction to the Ballad

Ballads are a special kind of narrative poetry. In them story and song meet in a way that makes them different from any other folk type. About their beginnings, all we can be certain of is that they arose among the working people and were the kind of entertainment in which the whole group could participate. They are short because the people who sang them for entertainment had only the brief space of an evening between their chores and early bedtime.

In the folk ballads, place and time relations are vague. A story is told that presents one episode or situation centered around a conflict. From the conflict the story emerges. Tragic themes seem to be preferable, but their range is limited—rival suitors, an unkind stepmother, violent death, jealousy, revenge, a brave deed, a preternatural being who is either devil or witch. Human relations are of prime interest—family relationships, men in rivalry for love or power, men and women in relationships, of love or infidelity. Still, the actual relationship is not given importance. It is the tragedy it causes that makes the story, for ballads are concerned with effects, not causes.

Read the following ballads:

A Ballad of Marjorie

"What ails you that you look so pale,
    O fisher of the sea?"
" 'Tis for a mournful tale I own,
    Fair maiden Marjorie."

"What is the dreary tale to tell,
    O toiler of the sea?"
"I cast my net into the waves,
    Sweet maiden Marjorie.

"I cast my net into the tide
    Before I made for home:
Too heavy for my hands to raise,
    I drew it through the foam."

"What saw you that you look so pale,
    Sad searcher of the sea?"
"A dead man's body from the deep
    My haul had brought to me!"

"And was he young, and was he fair?"
    "Oh, cruel to behold!
In his white face the joy of life
    Not yet was grown a-cold."

"Oh, pale you are, and full of prayer
    For one who sails the sea."
"Because the dead looked up and spoke,
    Poor maiden Marjorie."

"What said he, that you seem so sad,
    O fisher of the sea?"
(Alack! I know it was my love,
    Who fain would speak to me!)

"He said: 'Beware a woman's mouth—
   A rose that bears a thorn.' "
"Ah, me! these lips shall smile no more
   That gave my lover scorn."

"He said: 'Beware a woman's eyes;
   They pierce you with their death.' "
"Then falling tears shall make them blind
   That robbed my dear of breath."

"He said: 'Beware a woman's hair—
   A serpent's coil of gold.' "
"Then will I shear the cruel locks
   That crushed him in their fold."

"He said: 'Beware a woman's heart
   As you would shun the reef.' "
"So let it break within my breast,
   And perish of my grief."

"He raised his hands; a woman's name
   Thrice bitterly he cried.
My net had parted with the strain;
   He vanished in the tide."

"A woman's name! What name but mine,
   O fisher of the sea?"
"A woman's name, but not your name,
   Poor maiden Marjorie."

DORA
SIGERSON

1. This ballad is a common type—the reported tragedy—in a common pattern, a question-answer one. **-a** How does this pattern heighten the effect of the poem? **-b** How does it make the story very definitely Marjorie's by a kind of indirection? **2.** Show which characteristics of a ballad, as described on page 369, operate in *A Ballad of Marjorie*.

Ballad
of
the
Huntsman

And "No" she answered to his plea;
  "We never can be wed
Though you ask me a hundred times," said she.
  "Or a thousand times," she said.

"Oh, then, farewell my golden dear,
  Farewell my stony-hearted.
I shall go away, far, far from here."
  Said she: "It's time you started."

"I shall go away with my bag and my gun
  To hunt and forget," said he.
"I shall put my woven jacket on
  And my boots that lace to the knee."

"It's time you left and I wish you luck.
  If you bag a grouse or a pheasant
Or a spotted quail," she said, "or a duck,
  Bring one to me for a present."

"Each time I aim into the blue
  Of the sky or the brown of the marsh,
I shall think I point my gun at you,"
  Said he, and his voice was harsh.

A day and a week and a month went by
  And again he stood at her door,
Pale and worn, with his cap awry,
  And stained were the clothes he wore;

Stained was his coat of woven wool
  And stained his boots of calf.
"But I've brought you a gift, my beautiful,"
  And he began to laugh.

"That's neither grouse nor spotted quail
  That you hide from me," she said.
"And why is your face so pale, so pale,
  And why are your hands so red?"

"Nor grouse nor quail nor duck I give,"
  He said, and spread apart
His hands, and there like a crimson sieve
  He offered his riddled heart.

**SELMA
ROBINSON**

1. Show how this poem is a variety of the reported tragedy in question-answer form. **2.** Is the tragedy of the huntsman's lady a greater one than that of Marjorie? Explain. **3.** Do the light comments of the lady lessen or heighten the tragedy? Explain. **4.** Show at what point and in what manner the characters reverse positions. Show that the poem patterns on this reversal.

Sir Patrick Spens

1.
THE
SAILING

The King sits in Dumferling Town
  Drinking the blood-red wine;
"O where will I get a good sailor
  To sail this ship of mine?"

Then up and spake an eldern knight
  Sat at the King's right knee.
"Sir Patrick Spens is the best sailor
  That ever sailed the sea."

The King has written a broad letter,
  And signed it with his hand,
And sent it to Sir Patrick Spens,
  Was walking on the sand.

"To Noroway, to Noroway,
  To Noroway o'er the foam;
The King's daughter to Noroway,
  'Tis thou must take her home."

The first line that Sir Patrick read,
  A loud laugh laughed he;
The next line that Sir Patrick read
  The tear blinded his e'e.

"O who is this has done this deed
  And told the King of me,
To send me out, this time of year,
  To sail upon the sea?

"Be it wind or weet, be it hail or sleet,
  Our ship must sail the foam;
The King's daughter to Noroway,
  'Tis we must take her home."

They hoisted their sails on Monday morn
  With all the speed they may;
And they have landed in Noroway
  Upon the Wodnesday.

2.
THE
RETURN

"Make ready, make ready, my merry men all!
  Our good ship sails the morn."
"O say not so, my master dear,
  For I fear a deadly storm.

"Late, late yestreen I saw the new moon
  With the old moon in her arm;
And I fear, I fear, my dear master,
  That we shall come to harm."

They had not sailed a league, a league,
 A league but barely three,
When the lift grew dark, and the wind blew loud,
 And gurly grew the sea.

The ropes they broke and the topmast snapt,
 It was such a deadly storm:
And the waves came over the broken ship
 Till all her sides were torn.

"O where will I get a good sailor
 To take the helm in hand,
Until I win to the tall topmast
 And see if I spy the land?"

"O here am I, a sailor good,
 To take the helm in hand,
Till you win up to the tall topmast,
 But I fear you'll ne'er spy land."

He had not gone a step, a step,
 A step but barely one,
When a bolt flew out of the good ship's side,
 And the salt sea it came in.

"Go fetch a web of the silken cloth,
 Another of the twine,
And wrap them into our good ship's side,
 And let not the sea come in."

They fetched a web of the silken cloth,
 Another of the twine,
And they wrapped them into that good ship's side,
 But still the sea came in.

O loath, loath were our good Scots lords
 To wet their cork-heeled shoon;
But long ere all the play was played,
 Their hats they swam aboon.

And many was the feather bed
　　That floated on the foam;
And many was the good lord's son
　　That never more came home.

O long, long may the ladies sit
　　With their fans into their hand,
Before they see Sir Patrick Spens
　　Come sailing to the land.

O long, long may the ladies stand
　　With their gold combs in their hair,
A-waiting for their own dear lords,
　　For they'll see them no mair.

Half o'er, half o'er to Aberdour
　　It's fifty fathom deep;
OLD　And there lies good Sir Patrick Spens,
BALLAD　　With the Scots lords at his feet!

1. *Sir Patrick Spens* is another common type of ballad—the request-response. Notice how minor question-answer patterns combine with it. 2. Plot the narrative structure of this poem and discuss how well the parts are tied together. 3. Find instances where the stress of the rhythmic pattern crowds out the natural accent of the words. Discuss the effect this has on the total poem. 4. Compare *The Sailing* and *The Return* in terms of the amount of meaning packed into few words.

Cerelle　There was a score of likely girls
　　Around the prairieside,
　　But I went down to Galveston
　　And brought me home a bride.

A score or more of handsome girls,
Of proper age and size,
But the pale girls of Galveston
Have sea-shine in their eyes.

As pale as any orange flower,
Cerelle. The gold-white sands
Were like her hair, and drifting shells,
White fairy shells, her hands.

I think she liked my silver spurs,
A-clinking in the sun.
She'd never seen a cowboy till
I rode to Galveston.

She'd never known the chaparral,
Nor smell of saddle leather,
Nor seen a round-up or a ranch,
Till we rode back together.

Shall I forget my mother's eyes?
"Is this the wife you need?
Is this the way to bring me rest
From forty men to feed?"

Cerelle—I think she did her best
All year, She'd lots to learn.
Dishes would slip from out her hands
And break. The bread would burn.

And she would steal away at times
And wander off to me.
And when the wind was in the south
She'd say, "I smell the sea!"

She changed. The white and gold grew dull
As when a soft flame dies,
And yet she kept until the last
The sea-shine in her eyes.

There are (I make a husband's boast)
No stronger arms than Ann's.
She has a quip for all the boys,
And sings among the pans.

At last my mother takes her rest.
And that's how things should be.
But when the wind is in the south
There is no rest for me.

MARGARET
BELL
HOUSTON

1. Stanzas 1, 6, 9, 10, and 11 of *Cerelle* provide the basic structural exposition and narration of this poem. Show how the main threads of meaning are joined in these stanzas. **2.** One common type of ballad is the prediction-destruction type in which the tragic end is announced at the beginning. Although the author of *Cerelle* does not make an announcement or prediction at the beginning, she very subtly prepares for the outcome. Analyze the patterning of this preparation.

ASSIGNMENTS ON THE BALLAD

1. Parody the first stanza of *Cerelle,* page 404. Choose your subject from one of the following:

the first high school dance
the election of a homeroom president
cheerleader tryouts
freshman football team
freshman initiation

2. Write an original ballad stanza that could be the opening of a ballad based on a movie you have seen.
3. Read the following ballad, which is meant to be a humorous mocking of ballad elements. If you really know and appreciate ballads, you can enjoy it more fully. Try to analyze which elements it mocks and how it does so.

The Ballad of the Oysterman

It was a tall young oysterman lived by the river-side,
His shop was just upon the bank, his boat was on the tide;
The daughter of a fisherman, that was so straight and slim,
Lived over on the other bank, right opposite to him.

It was the pensive oysterman that saw a lovely maid,
Upon a moonlight evening, a-sitting in the shade;
He saw her wave her handkerchief, as much as if to say,
"I'm wide awake, young oysterman, and all the folks away."

Then up arose the oysterman, and to himself said he,
"I guess I'll leave the skiff at home, for fear that folks should see;
I read it in the story-book that, for to kiss his dear,
Leander swam the Hellespont,—and I will swim this here."

And he has leaped into the waves, and crossed the
        shining stream,
And he has clambered up the bank, all in the moonlight gleam;
Oh, there were kisses sweet as dew, and words as soft as rain—
But they have heard her father's step, and in he leaps again!

Out spoke the ancient fisherman,—"Oh, what was that,
        my daughter?"
" 'Twas nothing but a pebble, sir, I threw into the water."
"And what is that, pray tell me, love, that paddles off so fast?"
"It's nothing but a porpoise, sir, that's been a-swimming past."

Out spoke the ancient fisherman: "Now bring me my harpoon!
I'll get into my fishing boat, and fix the fellow soon."
Down fell that pretty innocent, as falls a snow-white lamb;
Her hair drooped round her pallid cheeks, like seaweed
        on a clam.

Alas for those two loving ones! she waked not from her swound,
And he was taken with the cramp, and in the waves
        was drowned;
But Fate has metamorphosed them, in pity of their woe,
And now they keep an oyster-shop for mermaids down below.

OLIVER WENDELL HOLMES

REPETITION IN THE BALLAD: Because the early ballads were sung, if not created, by a group, you will find repetition in them commonly used as an artistic device. It is a natural means of choric interval that can be used variously to express emotion, to counteract the tension of the narrative, or merely to fill out the meter. When it recurs regularly as a line or group of lines, it is called a refrain. When it is exact, it is called simple repetition; when it is changed slightly to develop the meaning, it is called incremental repetition.

Study these ballads to discover how repetition helps the sung story of a ballad:

Edward, Edward

"Why does your brand sae drop wi' blude,
 Edward, Edward?
Why does your brand sae drop wi' blude,
 And why sae sad gang ye, O?"
"O I hae killed my hawk sae gude,
 Mither, mither;
O I hae killed my hawk sae gude,
 And I had nae mair but he, O."

"Your hawk's blude was never sae red,
 Edward, Edward;
Your hawk's blude was never sae red,
 My dear son, I tell thee, O."
"O I hae killed my red-roan steed,
 Mither, mither;
O I hae killed my red-roan steed,
 That erse was sae fair and free, O."

"Your steed was auld, and ye hae got mair,
 Edward, Edward;
Your steed was auld, and ye hae got mair;
 Some other dule ye dree, O."
"O I hae killed my father dear,

Mither, mither;
O I hae killed my father dear,
    Alas, and wae is me, O!"

"And whatten penance will ye dree for that,
    Edward, Edward?
Whatten penance will ye dree for that?
    My dear son, now tell me, O."
"I'll set my feet in yonder boat,
    Mither, mither;
I'll set my feet in yonder boat,
    And I'll fare over the sea, O."

"And what will ye do wi' your towers and your ha',
    Edward, Edward?
And what will ye do wi' your towers and your ha',
    That were sae fair to see, O?"
"I'll let them stand till they doun fa',
    Mither, mither;
I'll let them stand till they doun fa',
    For here never mair maun I be, O."

"And what will ye leave to your bairns and your wife,
    Edward, Edward?
And what will ye leave to your bairns and your wife,
    When ye gang owre the sea, O?"
"The warld's room: let them beg through life,
    Mither, mither;
The warld's room; let them beg through life;
    For them never mair will I see, O."

"And what will ye leave to your ain mither dear,
    Edward, Edward?
And what will ye leave to your ain mither dear,
    My dear son, now tell me, O?"
The curse of hell frae me sall ye bear:
    Mither, mither;
"The curse of hell frae me sall ye bear,
    Sic counsels ye gave to me, O!"

OLD
BALLAD

1. The question-answer pattern in this poem leads up to two climactic points. Analyze this movement. Discuss whether or not the second point is a letdown. **2.** There are three patterns of repetition in the poem, each with a different function. Show how the three differ. Which are simple and which incremental?

Binnorie

There were two sisters sat in a bower;
   Binnorie, O Binnorie!
There came a knight to be their wooer,
   By the bonnie milldams o' Binnorie.

He courted the eldest with glove and ring
But he loved the youngest above everything.

The eldest she was vexed sair
And greatly envied her sister fair.

Upon a morning fair and clear,
She cried upon her sister dear:

"O sister, sister, take my hand,
And we'll see our father's ships to land."

She's taken her by the lily hand,
And led her down to the river-strand.

The youngest stood upon a stone,
The eldest came and pushed her in.

"O sister, sister, reach your hand!
And you shall be heir of half my land."

"O sister, I'll not reach my hand,
And I'll be heir of all your land."

"O sister, reach me but your glove!
And sweet William shall be your love."

"Sink on, nor hope for hand or glove!
And sweet William shall be my love!"

Sometimes she sank, sometimes she swam,
Until she came to the miller's dam.

Out then came the miller's son,
And saw the fair maid floating in.

"O father, father, draw your dam!
There's either a mermaid or a swan."

The miller hastened and drew his dam,
And there he found a drowned woman.

You could not see her waist so small,
Her girdle with gold was broidered all.

You could not see her lily feet,
Her golden fringes were so deep.

You could not see her yellow hair
For the strings of pearls that were twisted there.

You could not see her fingers small,
With diamond rings they were covered all.

And by there came a harper fine,
To harp to the king when he should dine.

And when he looked that lady on,
He sighed and made a heavy moan.

He's made a harp of her breast-bone,
Whose sound would melt a heart of stone.

He's taken three locks of her yellow hair,
And with them strung his harp so rare.

He went into her father's hall,
And there was the court asembled all.

He laid his harp upon a stone,
And straight it began to play alone.

"O yonder sits my father, the King,
And yonder sits my mother, the Queen;

"And yonder stands my brother Hugh,
And by him my William, sweet and true."

But the last tune that the harp played then—
    Binnorie, O Binnorie!
Was, "Woe to my sister, false Helen!"
    By the bonnie milldams o' Binnorie.

**OLD
BALLAD**

1. The structure of this poem is rather loose. **-a** Which pattern of repetition seems to provide for choric accumulation without advancement of action? **-b** Which pattern of repetition is truly incremental? **-c** Which pattern of repetition unites beginning and end? **2.** The last part of the ballad provides revenge through a preternatural means. Is the device made believable in the poem? Discuss. **3.** Discuss in what ways this is a typical ballad and in what ways it is not.

Jesse James

Jesse James was a two-gun man,
    (*Roll on, Missouri!*)
Strong-arm chief of an outlaw clan.
    (*From Kansas to Illinois!*)
He twirled an old Colt forty-five,
    (*Roll on, Missouri!*)
They never took Jesse James alive.
    (*Roll, Missouri, roll!*)

Jesse James was King of the Wes';
   (*Cataracks in the Missouri!*)
He'd a di'mon' heart in his lef' breas';
   (*Brown Missouri rolls!*)
He'd a fire in his heart no hurt could stifle;
   (*Thunder, Missouri!*)
Lion eyes an' a Winchester rifle.
   (*Missouri, roll down!*)

Jesse James rode a pinto hawse;
Come at night to a water-cawse;
Tetched with the rowel that pinto's flank;
She sprung the torrent from bank to bank.

Jesse rode through a sleepin' town;
Looked the moonlit street both up an' down;
Crack-crack-crack, the street ran flames
An' a great voice cried, "I'm Jesse James!"

Hawse an' afoot they're after Jess!
   (*Roll on, Missouri!*)
Spurrin' and spurrin'—but he's gone Wes'.
   (*Brown Missouri rolls!*)
He was ten foot tall when he stood in his boots;
   (*Lightnin' light the Missouri!*)
More'n a match fer sich galoots.
   (*Roll, Missouri, roll!*)

Jesse James rode outa the sage;
Roun' the rocks come the swayin' stage;
Straddlin' the road a giant stan's
An' a great voice bellers, "Throw up yer han's!"

Jesse raked in the di'mon' rings,
The big gold watches an' the yuther things;
Jesse divvied 'em then an' thar
With a cryin' child had lost her mar.

The U. S. troopers is after Jess;
  (*Roll on, Missouri!*)
Their hawses sweat foam, but he's gon Wes';
  (*Hear Missouri roar!*)
He was broad as a b'ar, he'd a ches' like a drum,
  (*Wind an' rain through Missouri!*)
An' his red hair flamed like Kingdom Come.
  (*Missouri down to the sea!*)

Jesse James all alone in the rain
Stopped an' stuck up the eas'-boun' train;
Swayed through the coaches with horns and a tail
Lit out with the bullion an' the registered mail.

Jesse made 'em all turn green with fright,
Quakin' in the aisles in the pitch-black night;
An' he give all the bullion to a pore ole tramp
Campin' nigh the cuttin in the dirt an' damp.

The whole U. S. is after Jess;
  (*Roll on, Missouri!*)
The son-of-a-gun, if he ain't gone Wes';
  (*Missouri to the sea!*)
He could chaw cold iron an' spit blue flame;
  (*Cataracks down the Missouri!*)
He rode on a catamount he'd larned to tame.
  (*Hear that Missouri roll!*)

Jesse James rode into a Bank;
Give his pinto a tetch on the flank;
Jumped the teller's window with an awful crash;
Heaved up the safe an' twirled his mustache;

He said, "So long, boys!" He yelped, "So long!
Feelin' porely to-day—I ain't feelin' strong!"
Rode right through the wall agoin' crack-crack-crack,—
Took the safe home to Mother in a gunny-sack.

They're creepin', they're crawlin', they're stalkin' Jess;
  (*Roll on, Missouri!*)
They's a rumor he's gone much further Wes';
  (*Roll, Missouri, roll!*)
They's word of a cayuse hitched to the bars
  (*Ruddy clouds on Missouri!*)
Of a golden sunset that busts into stars.
  (*Missouri, roll down!*)

Jesse James rode hell fer leather;
He was a hawse an' a man together;
In a cave in a mountain high up in air
He lived with a rattlesnake, a wolf, an' a bear.

Jesse's heart was as sof' as a woman;
Fer guts an' strength he was sooper-human;
He could put six shots through a woodpecker's eye
And take in one swaller a gallon o' rye.

They sought him here an' they sought him there,
  (*Roll on, Missouri!*)
But he strides by night through the ways of the air,
  (*Brown Missouri rolls!*)
They say he was took an' they say he is dead;
  (*Thunder, Missouri!*)
But he ain't—he's a sunset overhead!
  (*Missouri down to the sea!*)

Jesse James was a Hercules.
When he went through the woods he tore up the trees.
When he went on the plains he smoked the groun'
An' the hull lan' shuddered fer miles aroun'.

Jesse James wore a red bandanner
That waved on the breeze like the Star Spangled Banner;
In seven states he cut up dadoes.
He's gone with the buffler an' the desperadoes.

Yes, Jesse James was a two-gun man
  (*Roll on, Missouri!*)
The same as when this song began;
  (*From Kansas to Illinois!*)
An' when you see a sunset bust into flames
  (*Lightnin' light the Missouri!*)
Or a thunderstorm blaze—that's Jesse James!
  (*Hear that Missouri roll!*)

WILLIAM
ROSE
BENÉT

1. Does this poem have a narrative structure in any sense? Discuss. **2.** How does the refrain fit the structure that is peculiar to this poem? **3.** What elements of the tall tale does this poem have? of the myth? of the romance?

De
Boll
Weevil

Oh, de boll weevil am a little black bug,
  Come from Mexico, dey say.
Come all de way to Texas,
  Jus' a-lookin' for a place to stay,
  Jus' a-lookin' for a home, jus' a-lookin' for a home,

De first time I seen de boll weevil,
  He was settin' on de square.
De next time I seen de boll weevil,
  He had all of his fam'ly dere,
  Jus' a-lookin' for a home, jus' a-lookin' for a home,

Boll weevil say to his wife:
  "Bettah stan' up on yo' feet,
Look way down in Mississippi,
  At de cotton we's got to eat,
  De whole night long, de whole night long."

Boll weevil say to de lightnin' bug:
  "Can I get up a trade wid you?
If I was a lightnin' bug,
  I'd work de whole night through,
  De whole night long, de whole night long."

De farmer take de boll weevil,
 An' he put him in de hot san';
De weevil say, "Dis is mighty hot,
 But I'll stand it like a man.
Dis'll be my home, dis'll be my home."

De farmer take de boll weevil
 An' put him in a lump of ice.
De weevil say to de farmer,
 "Dis is mighty cool an' nice,
Dis'll be my home, dis'll be my home."

De farmer take de boll weevil
 An' he put him in paris green;
De weevil say to de farmer
 "Best bed I ever seen;
Dis'll be my home, dis'll be my home."

Boll weevil say to de farmer:
 "You can ride in dat Fohd machine.
But w'en I get through wid yo' cotton,
 Can't buy no gasoline,
Won't have no home, won't have no home."

Boll weevil say to de doctah:
 "Bettah pull out all dem pills.
W'en I get through wid de farmer,
 Can't pay no doctah's bills.
I have a home, I have a home."

Boll weevil say to de preacher:
 "Bettah close up dem church doors,
W'en I get through wid de farmer,
 Can't pay de preacher no mo'.
I have a home, I have a home."

De merchant got half de cotton,
 De boll weevil got de res'—
Didn't leave de farmer's wife
 But one ol' cotton dress,
An' it's full of holes, an' it's full of holes.

De farmer say to de merchant,
  "We's in an awful fix;
De boll weevil et all de cotton up
  An' left us only sticks.
We's got no home, oh, we's got no home."

De farmer say to de merchant:
  "I want some meat an' meal!"
"Get away f'm here, yo' son-of-a-gun,
  You got boll weevils in yo' fiel';
Dey's got yo' home, dey's got yo' home."

Boll weevil say to de farmer,
  "I wish you all is well!"
Farmer say to de boll weevil:
  "I wish you wuz in hell!
I'd have a home, I'd have a home."

AMERICAN NEGRO BALLAD

1. Chart the overall structure of this poem to see if it has a true narrative pattern. **2.** Do any parts seem more accumulation than progression? **3.** Discuss the contribution of the repetition. **4.** Is this poem tragic or comic? What elements create the tone?

ASSIGNMENTS ON REPETITION IN THE BALLAD

1. Write a class poem built on the simple repetition of refrain (about three stanzas). Suggested topics are:

eighth grade graduation   school rules
lunch in the cafeteria   extra-curricular activities
my class tour or trip   Monday morning classes
assemblies   homeroom cleaning
school work (some specific phase like a tale of woe about
a heavy assignment)

Here is an example of a student poem with simple repetition. Notice how the refrain begins the stanza instead of ending it. Read this poem before the class tries a group ballad.

McGee

McGee was his name
And 'tis a well-known fact
That he's never been caught
For the safes he has cracked.

McGee was his name
As he crept to the door,
And he silently laid
All his "tools" on the floor.

McGee was his name
As he scratched his old back
And placed all the money
In his small brown plaid sack.

McGee was his name
As he polished the safe
Very careful was he
To leave never a trace.

McGee was his name
As he sat in his house,
And was feeding green cheese
To his little gray mouse.

McGee was his name
As he sat in his cell
For this wretched old being
Things have not gone too well.

TERRY
DERESZYNSKI

2. Decide with your class on a refrain to be used in an original ballad. Together, compose the first stanza, using the refrain. Now complete the ballad yourself. Compare your results with those of your classmates. SUGGESTED TOPICS:

Lincoln	the coming of the Ice Age
Napoleon's exile	Mary Stuart, her marriage
Nero's wife	Socrates drinking poison
Cleopatra	Henry VIII's wives
harp of Nero	beheading of Marie Antoinette
Al Capone	the mutiny against Columbus
stock market crash	short stature of Napoleon
Mayflower Compact	death of Shakespeare's son

3. Find a newspaper article that suggests good material for a ballad. Use it for an original ballad with incremental repetition. Before attempting to write the ballad, design the narrative incidents.

Introduction to the Metrical Tale

A poem in which story and verse combine is a metrical tale. Unlike the ballad, which has qualities that make it a unique type of narrative poetry, the metrical tale needs only a story and word music to qualify as a storytelling poem. Any short tale told in verse, unless it is a ballad, is a metrical tale.

Read *The Glove and the Lions, Casey at the Bat, The Highwayman,* and *The Battle of Blenheim,* with the following points in mind for class discussion.

1. Diagram the chain of incidents that makes the action line of each of the poems.
2. Compare the means each author uses to build suspense through these incidents.
3. Note the different rhythm for the different subject matter.

The Glove and the Lions

King Francis was a hearty king, and loved a royal sport,
And one day as his lions fought, sat looking on the court;
The nobles filled the benches, with the ladies by their side,
And 'mongst them sat the Count de Lorge, with one for whom
       he sighed:
And truly 'twas a gallant thing to see that crowning show,
Valor and love, and a king above, and the royal beasts below.

Ramped and roared the lions, with horrid laughing jaws;
They bit, they glared, gave blows like bears, a wind went with
       their paws;
With wallowing might and stifled roar they rolled on
       one another,
Till all the pit with sand and mane was in a thunderous smother;
The bloody foam above the bars came whisking through the air;
Said Francis then, "Faith, gentlemen, we're better here
       than there."

De Lorge's love o'erheard the King, a beauteous lively dame,
With smiling lips and sharp bright eyes, which always
       seemed the same;
She thought, the Count my lover is brave as brave can be;
He surely would do wondrous things to show his love of me;
King, ladies, lovers, all look on; the occasion is divine;
I'll drop my glove to prove his love; great glory will be mine.

She dropped her glove, to prove his love, then looked at
       him and smiled;
He bowed, and in a moment leaped among the lions wild;
The leap was quick, return was quick, he has regained
       his place,
Then threw the glove, but not with love, right in the lady's face.
"By heaven," said Francis, "rightly done!" and he rose from
       where he sat;
"No love," quoth he, "but vanity, sets love a task like that."

LEIGH HUNT

1. Does the immediacy of action in this poem prevent it from being a parable? Discuss. 2. This poem patterns on two locations—*above* and *below*—and two actions that bridge them. Show how valor, vanity, and love focus in these two places and these two actions both apparently and actually. 3. How does the slight use of internal rhyme heighten a major effect of the poem?

Casey at the Bat

The outlook wasn't brilliant for the Mudville nine that day:
The score stood four to two, with but one inning more to play,
And then when Cooney died at first, and Barrows did the same,
A pall-like silence fell upon the patrons of the game.

A straggling few got up to go in deep despair. The rest
Clung to that hope which springs eternal in the human breast;
They thought, "If only Casey could but get a whack at that—
We'd put up even money now, with Casey at the bat."

But Flynn preceded Casey, as did also Jimmy Blake,
And the former was a hoodoo, while the latter was a cake;
So upon that stricken multitude grim melancholy sat,
For there seemed but little chance of Casey getting to the bat.

But Flynn let drive a single, to the wonderment of all,
And Blake, the much-despised, tore the cover off the ball;
And when the dust had lifted, and men saw what had occurred,
There was Jimmy safe at second and Flynn a-hugging third.

Then from five thousand throats and more there rose a
        lusty yell;
It rumbled through the valley, it rattled in the dell;
It pounded on the mountain and recoiled upon the flat,
For Casey, mighty Casey, was advancing to the bat.

There was ease in Casey's manner as he stepped into his place;
There was pride in Casey's bearing and a smile lit Casey's face.
And when, responding to the cheers, he lightly doffed his hat,
No stranger in the crowd could doubt 'twas Casey at the bat.

Ten thousand eyes were on him as he rubbed his hands with dirt;
Five thousand tongues applauded when he wiped them on
        his shirt;
Then while the writhing pitcher ground the ball into his hip,
Defiance flashed in Casey's eye, a sneer curled Casey's lip.

And now the leather-covered sphere came hurtling through
        the air,
And Casey stood a-watching it in haughty grandeur there.
Close by the sturdy batsman the ball unheeded sped—
"That ain't my style," said Casey. "Strike one!" the
        umpire said.

From the benches, black with people, there went up a
        muffled roar,
Like the beating of the storm-waves on a stern and distant shore;
"Kill him! Kill the umpire!" shouted someone on the stand;
And it's likely they'd have killed him had not Casey raised
        his hand.

With a smile of Christian charity great Casey's visage shone;
He stilled the rising tumult; he bade the game go on;
He signaled to the pitcher, and once more the dun sphere flew;
But Casey still ignored it, and the umpire said, "Strike two!"

"Fraud!" cried the maddened thousands, and echo
        answered "Fraud!"
But one scornful look from Casey and the audience was awed.
They saw his face grow stern and cold, they saw his
        muscles strain,
And they knew that Casey wouldn't let that ball go by again.

The sneer has fled from Casey's lip, his teeth are clenched
        in hate;
He pounds with cruel violence his bat upon the plate.
And now the pitcher holds the ball, and now he lets it go,
And now the air is shattered by the force of Casey's blow.

Oh, somewhere in this favored land the sun is shining bright;
The band is playing somewhere, and somewhere hearts are light,
And somewhere men are laughing, and little children shout;
But there is no joy in Mudville—great Casey has struck out.

ERNEST LAWRENCE THAYER

1. In what sense is the narrative structure of this poem a tall tale? How does it differ? **2.** How does the difference between this poem and a true tall tale increase the humor of the poem? **3.** Analyze the effect of repetition wherever it occurs.

The Highwayman

PART ONE

I

The wind was a torrent of darkness among the gusty trees,
The moon was a ghostly galleon tossed upon cloudy seas,
The road was a ribbon of moonlight over the purple moor,
And the highwayman came riding—
    Riding—riding—
The highwayman came riding, up to the old inn-door.

II

He'd a French cocked-hat on his forehead, a bunch of lace at
        his chin,
A coat of the claret velvet, and breeches of brown doeskin;
They fitted with never a wrinkle: his boots were up to the thigh!
And he rode with a jewelled twinkle,
    His pistol butts a-twinkle,
His rapier hilt a-twinkle, under the jewelled sky.

III

Over the cobbles he clattered and clashed in the dark inn-yard,
And he tapped with his whip on the shutters, but all was
        locked and barred;
He whistled a tune to the window, and who should be
        waiting there

But the landlord's black-eyed daughter,
  Bess, the landlord's daughter,
Plaiting a dark red love-knot into her long black hair.

 IV

And dark in the dark old inn-yard a stable-wicket creaked
Where Tim the ostler listened; his face was white and peaked;
His eyes were hollows of madness, his hair like moldy hay,
But he loved the landlord's daughter,
  The landlord's red-lipped daughter,
Dumb as a dog he listened, and he heard the robber say—

 V

"One kiss, my bonny sweetheart, I'm after a prize tonight,
But I shall be back with the yellow gold before the morning light;
Yet, if they press me sharply, and harry me through the day,
Then look for me by moonlight,
  Watch for me by moonlight,
I'll come to thee by moonlight, though hell should bar the way."

 VI

He rose upright in the stirrups; he scarce could reach her hand
But she loosened her hair i' the casement! His face burnt
      like a brand
As the black cascade of perfume came tumbling over his breast;
And he kissed its waves in the moonlight,
  (Oh, sweet black waves in the moonlight!)
Then he tugged at his rein in the moonlight, and galloped
      away to the west.

PART TWO

I

He did not come in the dawning; he did not come at noon;
And out o' the tawny sunset, before the rise o' the moon,
When the road was a gypsy's ribbon, looping the purple moor,
A red-coat troop came marching—
  Marching—marching—
King George's men came marching, up to the old inn-door.

II

They said no word to the landlord, they drank his ale instead,
But they gagged his daughter and bound her to the foot of her
      narrow bed;
Two of them knelt at her casement, with muskets at their side!
There was death at every window;
   And hell at one dark window;
For Bess could see, through her casement, the road that *he*
      would ride.

 III

They had tied her up to attention, with many a sniggering jest;
They had bound a musket beside her, with the barrel beneath
      her breast!
"Now keep good watch!" and they kissed her. She heard the
      dead man say—
Look for me by moonlight;
   Watch for me by moonlight;
I'll come to thee by moonlight, though hell should bar the way!

 IV

She twisted her hands behind her, but all the knots held good!
She writhed her hands till her fingers were wet with sweat
      or blood!
They stretched and strained in the darkness, and the hours
      crawled by like years,
Till, now, on the stroke of midnight,
   Cold, on the stroke of midnight,
The tip of one finger touched it! The trigger at least was hers!

 V

The tip of one finger touched it; she strove no more for the rest!
Up, she stood up to attention, with the barrel beneath her breast,
She would not risk their hearing; she would not strive again;

For the road lay bare in the moonlight;
   Blank and bare in the moonlight;
And the blood of her veins in the moonlight throbbed to her
      love's refrain.

 VI

Tlot-tlot; tlot-tlot! Had they heard it? The horse-hoofs
      ringing clear;
Tlot-tlot, tlot-tlot, in the distance? Were they deaf that they
      did not hear?
Down the ribbon of moonlight, over the brow of the hill,
The highwayman came riding,
   Riding, riding!
The red-coats looked to their priming! She stood up,
      straight and still!

 VII

Tlot-tlot, in the frosty silence! *Tlot-tlot,* in the echoing night!
Nearer he came and nearer! Her face was like a light!
Her eyes grew wide for a moment; she drew one last deep breath,
Then her finger moved in the moonlight,
   Her musket shattered the moonlight,
Shattered her breast in the moonlight and warned him—with
      her death.

 VIII

He turned; he spurred to the Westward; he did not know who
      stood
Bowed, with her head o'er the musket, drenched with her own
      red blood!
Not till the dawn he heard it, his face grew grey to hear
How Bess, the landlord's daughter,
   The landlord's black-eyed daughter,
Had watched for her love in the moonlight, and died in the
      darkness there.

Back, he spurred like a madman, shrieking a curse to the sky,
With the white road smoking behind him, and his rapier
       brandished high!
Blood-red were his spurs i' the golden noon; wine-red was his
       velvet coat
When they shot him down on the highway,
  Down like a dog on the highway,
And he lay in his blood on the highway, with the bunch of lace
       at his throat.

 X

And still of a winter's night, they say, when the wind is in
       the trees,
When the moon is a ghostly galleon tossed upon cloudy seas,
When the road is a ribbon of moonlight over the purple moor,
A highwayman comes riding—
  Riding—riding—
A highwayman comes riding, up to the old inn-door.

 XI

Over the cobbles he clatters and clangs in the dark inn-yard;
He taps with his whip on the shutters, but all is locked
       and barred;
He whistles a tune to the window, and who should be
       waiting there
But the landlord's black-eyed daughter,
  Bess, the landlord's daughter,
Plaiting a dark red love-knot into her long black hair.

ALFRED NOYES

1. Discuss how the following poetic elements contribute to the
artistic patterning of this legend:

  -a rhythm
  -b rhyme

-c repetition (Though it fills out the rhythm pattern, does it ever do merely that?)

2. How does the author create the atmosphere of this legend:

-a through setting?
-b through characters?
-c through progression of action?

3. Could any stanzas or lines of this poem be exchanged or omitted? Explain.

The Battle of Blenheim

It was a summer evening;
    Old Kaspar's work was done,
And he before his cottage door
    Was sitting in the sun,
And by him sported on the green
His little grandchild Wilhelmine.

She saw her brother Peterkin
    Roll something large and round,
Which he beside the rivulet
    In playing there had found;
He came to ask what he had found,
That was so large, and smooth, and round.

Old Kaspar took it from the boy,
    Who stood expectant by;
And then the old man shook his head,
    And with a natural sigh,
" 'Tis some poor fellow's skull," said he,
"Who fell in the great victory.

"I find them in the garden,
    For there's many here about;
And often, when I go to plow,
    . The plowshare turns them out!

For many thousand men," said he,
"Were slain in that great victory."

"Now tell us what 'twas all about,"
    Young Peterkin, he cries;
And little Wilhelmine looks up
    With wonder-waiting eyes;
"Now tell us all about the war,
And what they fought each other for."

"It was the English," Kaspar cried,
    "Who put the French to rout;
But what they fought each other for,
    I could not well make out;
But everybody said," quoth he,
"That 'twas a famous victory.

"My father lived at Blenheim then,
    Yon little stream hard by;
They burnt his dwelling to the ground,
    And he was forced to fly;
So with his wife and child he fled,
Nor had he where to rest his head.

"With fire and sword the country round
    Was wasted far and wide,
And many a childing mother then
    And new-born baby died;
But things like that, you know, must be
At every famous victory.

"They say it was a shocking sight
    After the field was won;
For many thousand bodies here
    Lay rotting in the sun;
But things like that, you know, must be
After a famous victory.

"Great praise the Duke of Marlbro' won,
  And our good Prince Eugene."
"Why, 'twas a very wicked thing!"
  Said little Wilhelmine.
"Nay . . nay . . my little girl," quoth he,
"It was a famous victory.

"And everybody praised the Duke
  Who this great fight did win."
"But what good came of it at last?"
  Quoth little Peterkin.
"Why, that I cannot tell," said he,
"But 'twas a famous victory."

ROBERT
SOUTHEY

1. Does this poem have a true narrative structure? Does it resemble *Jesse James* in any way?   **2.** The repetition in this poem is very subtle. Is it completely essential to the effect of the poem? What contribution does it make? Is the effect cumulative or static?   **3.** In what sense does the contrast between the old man and the two children contribute to the same effect?

Reread *A Lady Comes to an Inn*, page 391. Discover what, besides a chain of incidents, builds up the structure of this poem between the opening and closing incidents. Explain what makes the poem narrative.

Re-examine *The Lady of the Tomahawk*, page 389. Compare this poem with the preceding one on the basis of plot structure and means of revealing the character of the lady.

SOUND EFFECTS—ONOMATOPOEIA: Sometimes the poet uses the sound effect called onomatopoeia. Here the sound of the word and the meaning are alike. Reread E. E. Cummings' poem on page 62. Notice the onomatopoetic power of words like: *twitchy, tinkling, hob-a-nob, hoppy, itchy, scuttling, rustle, ouch.* In fact, you will find that Cummings' poem would lose its meaning if it lost its sound pattern.

Read *Forest Fire* and *Out, Out*. Compare the structure of these two poems with the structure of *The Highwayman,* page 424, and *A Lady Comes to an Inn,* page 391.

Forest Fire

Whispers of little winds low in the leaves,
Rustle of warm winds through tall green trees,
A full resinous fragrance, rich, warm, sweet,
A sharp acrid odor, a hint of heat,
Snap, hiss, crackle, a faint blue smoke,
A whirl of black swept by tawny flame—
Deep in the forest the wild wind broke;
Fast in the wild wake the fire-wind came,
A soughing of branches swept sudden and strong
Like the rush and crash when the storm winds meet:
Crimson streams of fire flowed quickly along
The tall grey grasses and the spruce needles deep;
Red tongues of fire licked the tall pine trees,
Grey twigs fell as though shrivelled by disease;
Broad orange streamers floated everywhere
And bulging puffs of copper smoke filled the molten air.
A pitiable squeaking came from little furry creatures,
Chipmunks and marmots as they scurried helter-skelter;
Mountain sheep and mountain goats leaping to some shelter,
Warned by their instincts—grim, sure teachers—
And the suffocating stenches from the red relentless thing;
Like a plummet dropped a blue-jay with a burning broken wing;
The eagles screamed in anger from the smoke-beclouded skies;
A sudden rush of slender deer, dumb fright in liquid eyes . . .
Now burning brands seem missiles sent,
Projectiles hurled through space,
Now and then a chuckle, like mirth malevolent,
A sweeping beauty sinister, a dread and treacherous grace;
And conflagration with the sound of thunder
Has pulled a thousand tall trees under.
But men have come in purpose bent
To halt the fire's fierce race.

They fell great trees and dig deep lanes,
They smother out small flames;
With tools and chemicals and wit
At last they curb, they conquer it.
But fire that raged for half a day
Has burned a hundred years away.

EDNA DAVIS ROMIG

1. Both this poem and *The Highwayman* have narrative and descriptive qualities. Compare the two poems on the basis of how these two methods affect the structure and the artistic purpose of the poem. **2.** Trace the sound of the fire through the poem by lining up the instances of onomatopoeia and the repeated letters that make the onomatopoetic words echo through the lines. **3.** How does the chain of incidents depend on the setting of the poem? **4.** How does the use of onomatopoeia affect the emotional quality and the meaning of the poem?

Out, Out

The buzz-saw snarled and rattled in the yard
And made dust and dropped stove-length sticks of wood,
Sweet-scented stuff when the breeze drew across it.
And from there those that lifted eyes could count
Five mountain ranges one behind the other
Under the sunset far into Vermont.
And the saw snarled and rattled, snarled and rattled,
As it ran light, or had to bear a load.
And nothing happened: day was all but done.
Call it a day, I wish they might have said
To please the boy by giving him the half hour
That a boy counts so much when saved from work.
His sister stood beside them in her apron
To tell them "Supper." At the word, the saw,
As if to prove saws knew what supper meant,
Leaped out at the boy's hand, or seemed to leap—
He must have given the hand. However it was,
Neither refused the meeting. But the hand!

The boy's first outcry was a rueful laugh,
As he swung toward them holding up the hand
Half in appeal, but half as if to keep
The life from spilling. Then the boy saw all—
Since he was old enough to know, big boy
Doing a man's work, though a child at heart—
He saw all spoiled. "Don't let him cut my hand off—
The doctor, when he comes. Don't let him, sister!"
So. But the hand was gone already.
The doctor put him in the dark of ether.
He lay and puffed his lips out with his breath.
And then—the watcher at his pulse took fright.
No one believed. They listened at his heart.
Little—less—nothing!—and that ended it.
No more to build on there. And they, since they
Were not the one dead, turned to their affairs.

ROBERT FROST

1. Actually there is very little onomatopoeia in this poem. Most of the poem is written in a conversational style. In what sense does this fact increase the effect of the onomatopoeia? **2.** Compare this poem with *The Highwayman* for **-a** onomatopoetic effects **-b** approach to life **-c** narrative structure **-d** musical effect.

ASSIGNMENTS ON ONOMATOPOEIA

1. List ten words that give the impression of noise, ten that give the feeling of silence or stillness.

2. Write a four-line stanza using onomatopoeia to describe:

a boy diving into a pool   Chicago slaughter-house district
   a teen-age dance step   a threshing machine in operation
women in heels walking down the street   thunderstorms
   a racing shell taking off   washing dishes in a cafeteria

3. Write a sentence in which you use an onomatopoetic device to present:

   an angry snake   a gentle fall wind
      an old man laughing at the antics of a small granddaughter

a pile of burning leaves and twigs
a squirrel happy over his cache of nuts
a scavenger circling over the body of a dead animal
the sudden rush of a car down a quiet street
a beginning violin student

SOUND EFFECTS—ALLITERATION

Another kind of rhyme is initial rhyme, or alliteration. The early Anglo Saxon poets used this sound effect as a substitute for end rhyme. Their system of alliteration was an intricate and essential part of their sound pattern. Today we say words alliterate if either initial vowel sounds or consonant sounds are identical. Notice how the alliterative sound pattern supports the meaning of this poem by Ellen White.

Sea still, sea bound
From somewhere, water bound.
I never heard the wave-crash,
Fawn fall of light,
Rich rise of wind on sea
Until I met someone, close,
Not far from me.
Distanced by the sea—
An eye-catch sparkle salt,
Jewel bright, holding light
Of day and night in wave-cut prisms.

Reread *Forest Fire* and show the contribution made by alliteration to the effects you have already analyzed in the poem.

ASSIGNMENTS ON ALLITERATION

1. Become aware of alliteration in everyday speech or familiar poetry. EXAMPLES:

the long loneliness
silence of the seas
low buzz of bees

the great gray gulls
singing the same old song
Don Dirk of Dowdee

2. Bring to class examples of alliteration from newspapers and magazines.

3. Write an alliterative sentence on each of the following topics:

school cafeteria	old age
the reading room in the library	trees
building and construction	hose spray
summer air	ice melting

4. Write a paragraph in which alliteration and onomatopoeia are used. Describe what you would hear in certain places; for instance:

study hall	the typing room
kitchen	your brother's bedroom

5. Tell of an experience you had in which sound was very important. SUGGESTIONS:

your first dance	back stage during a play
a music lesson	doing the dishes
housecleaning	decorating a Christmas tree
picnic	roller skating
football game	gym locker room

IMAGERY—SIMPLE IMAGES: The imagination is the image-making power of man. Anything that can be perceived by the senses can be reproduced as an image in the mind. It is this image-making power that the poet uses when he creates poetry and which the capable reader uses when he reads it. The poet avoids abstract and general words because they appeal only to the intellect; rather he chooses words that make sense images of sight or sound or feeling or smell or taste. These are called simple images unless they involve a comparison with something else.

The poet who wrote *Truly Thy Speech* tells us of her delight in discovering St. Peter's power to create word images; and she expresses her pleasure through her own word images of sight. Notice that in this poem the reader can see through the medium

of words *a white dove wheeling, a wind-blown rose, sun-tanned
toes, a sunset that mends you, a star-sky that lends you aid
against your foes.*

Truly Thy Speech

*"Whereunto you do well to attend
as to a light that shineth in a dark place
until the day dawn
and the day-star arise in your hearts." (2 Peter 1, 19)*

I thought to read crude fisher words
in your epistle, Peter;
Instead, I find a poet's mind
with images and meter.

Before *He* came healing
did you know such feeling
for a white dove wheeling
or a wind-blown rose?

Tell me, will you,
did this wide world fill you
with delight and thrill you
to your sun-tanned toes?

Could a small child bend you
or a sunset mend you
or a star-sky lend you
aid against your foes?

Yes, you've walked with Truth and Goodness
and these have made you free,
but the Beauty walking with the Truth—
it's *this* that's made you *see*.

MARY O'CONNELL

For a further study of imagery, read the following poem.

A Shot at Night

A shot rings out upon the dreaming night.
Night shivers to pieces like a broken vase;
The stars are spangled on the sky like lace;
The moon is shedding a terrible cold light;
And, like the crystal running of a stream
Of water flowing from a broken jar,
Fear creeps across the earth, and every star
Stops moving, and a moment dulls the gleam
Of the ivory moon. The rustling boughs of trees
Are silent, and a rare and breathless chill
Falls on the world, and makes it very still.
Then the cocks crow, a watchdog barks ill ease
And is chorused by a hundred yapping curs.
Men turn in beds. A wind like weeping stirs.

IDELLA PURNELL

1. The cause which is stated in the first line of this poem starts a string of effects that pattern the entire poem. Is the order of the effects necessary or arbitrary? **2.** Each effect includes some simple imagery. Show all the ways that each two images are connected poetically—by sound, by suggested meaning, by contrast, etc. **3.** Show how each simple image is apt as an effect of a sound. **4.** Compare this poem to *Forest Fire*. Find the simple images and show to what sense each appeals. Discuss their contribution to the meaning of the poem.

ASSIGNMENTS ON SIMPLE IMAGERY

Recreate simple images of sense:

1. Smell
-**a** a smell connected with a memory
-**b** a smell that nauseates you
-**c** a smell that pleases you

2. Sight
-**a** a sight you can't forget
-**b** a sight that makes you sad
-**c** a sight that makes you angry

3. Taste
-**a** a taste that makes your mouth water
-**b** a taste that wrinkles your tongue
-**c** a taste you associate with family picnics

4. Sound   **-a** a sound at night
               -b a sound in the country
                     or in the woods
               -c a sound that suggests a story

5. Touch   **-a** the feel of something rough
               -b the feel of your pillow at night
               -c the feel of wet mud

SIMILES AND METAPHORS: Poets use another kind of imagery called figurative language or figures of speech. Like simple images, figures of speech let the reader see what the poet has already seen, hear what he has already heard, or perceive what he has already perceived through the use of any of his senses. The most common of the figures of speech are similes and metaphors.

These are more complex than simple images because two terms are needed to create them. That is why similes and metaphors are sometimes called figures of likeness. The two terms that make a simile or a metaphor are not alike in their total meaning. As a matter of fact, they are quite different if the image is a successful one. But a writer who has imaginative insight into the meaning deep down inside things discovers likeness in very different objects. And through his similes and metaphors he lets the reader share the delight of this imaginative insight.

You can easily distinguish a simile from a metaphor by the signs of likeness, *as* or *like*. In a simile the *as* or *like* is expressed; in the metaphor it is not.

Here are some examples of similes and metaphors written by freshmen:

SIMILES

The pianist played like a robot, unerringly but without
    interpretation.
The shaggy dog lay in the shade like a crumpled newspaper.

A dishonest person is like a hawk looking for prey.
Like nails drawn to a magnet, the crowd surrounded
   the fighters.
Time dragged by like a lead-footed trackman.
The dawn looked like an aging fisherman unfurling rosy sails.
The wind gnawed at the town like a dog chewing a bone.

METAPHORS

A coward is a turtle that slinks into its shell in the
   face of danger.
My pile of homework was a junior Matterhorn.
The waves were drums beating on the shore.
My pen was a tired old hound dragging along.
His similes were knives grown dull.

Read the following poems. After you have enjoyed them,
analyze the contribution that the similes make to the meaning.

The Destruction of Sennacherib

The Assyrian came down like the wolf on the fold,
And his cohorts were gleaming in purple and gold;
And the sheen of their spears was like stars on the sea,
When the blue wave rolls nightly on deep Galilee.

Like the leaves of the forest when Summer is green,
That host with their banners at sunset were seen;
Like the leaves of the forest when Autumn hath blown,
That host on the morrow lay withered and strown.

For the Angel of Death spread his wings on the blast,
And breathed in the face of the foe as he passed;
And the eyes of the sleepers waxed deadly and chill,
And their hearts but once heaved, and for ever grew still!

And there lay the steed with his nostril all wide,
But through it there rolled not the breath of his pride;
And the foam of his gasping lay white on the turf,
And cold as the spray of the rock-beating surf.

And there lay the rider distorted and pale,
With the dew on his brow, and the rust on his mail;
And the tents were all silent, the banners alone,
The lances unlifted, the trumpet unblown.

And the widows of Ashur are loud in their wail,
And the idols are broke in the temple of Baal;
And the might of the Gentile, unsmote by the sword,
Hath melted like snow in the glance of the Lord!

GEORGE NOEL GORDON, LORD BYRON

1. The most powerful motif in this poem is the idea of the movement of a whole made up of parts and of the breaking of a
whole into parts. **-a** How does the simple imagery express this
motif? **-b** How do the similes express it? **-c** How does the line
movement express it? **2.** How do the similes contribute to the
emotional effect of the poem?

The Wreck of the Hesperus

It was the schooner Hesperus,
    That sailed the wintry sea;
And the skipper had taken his little daughter,
    To bear him company.

Blue were her eyes as the fairy-flax,
    Her cheeks like the dawn of day,
And her bosom white as the hawthorn buds,
    That ope in the month of May.

The skipper he stood beside the helm,
    His pipe was in his mouth,
And he watched how the veering flaw did blow
    The smoke now West, now South.

Then up and spake an old Sailor,
    Had sailed to the Spanish Main,
"I pray thee, put into yonder port,
    For I fear a hurricane.

"Last night, the moon had a golden ring,
　　And tonight no moon we see!"
The skipper, he blew a whiff from his pipe,
　　And a scornful laugh laughed he.

Colder and colder blew the wind,
　　A gale from the Northeast,
The snow fell hissing in the brine,
　　And the billows frothed like yeast.

Down came the storm, and smote amain
　　The vessel in its strength;
She shuddered and paused, like a frighted steed,
　　Then leaped her cable's length.

"Come hither! come hither! my little daughter,
　　And do not tremble so;
For I can weather the roughest gale
　　That ever wind did blow."

He wrapped her warm in his seaman's coat
　　Against the stinging blast;
He cut a rope from a broken spar,
　　And bound her to the mast.

"O father! I hear the church bells ring;
　　Oh, say, what may it be?"
" 'Tis a fog bell on a rock-bound coast!"—
　　And he steered for the open sea.

"O father! I hear the sound of guns;
　　Oh, say, what may it be?"
"Some ship in distress, that cannot live
　　In such an angry sea!"

"O father! I see a gleaming light;
　　Oh, say, what may it be?"
But the father answered never a word,
　　A frozen corpse was he.

Lashed to the helm, all stiff and stark,
  With his face turned to the skies,
The lantern gleamed through the gleaming snow
  On his fixed and glassy eyes.

Then the maiden clasped her hands and prayed
  That savèd she might be;
And she thought of Christ, who stilled the wave,
  On the Lake of Galilee.

And fast through the midnight dark and drear,
  Through the whistling sleet and snow,
Like a sheeted ghost, the vessel swept
  Tow'rds the reef of Norman's Woe.

And ever the fitful gusts between
  A sound came from the land;
It was the sound of the trampling surf
  On the rocks and the hard sea-sand.

The breakers were right beneath her bows,
  She drifted a dreary wreck,
And a whooping billow swept the crew
  Like icicles from her deck.

She struck where the white and fleecy waves
  Looked soft as carded wool,
But the cruel rocks, they gored her side
  Like the horns of an angry bull.

Her rattling shrouds, all sheathed in ice,
  With the masts went by the board;
Like a vessel of glass, she strove and sank,
  Ho! ho! the breakers roared!

At daybreak, on the bleak sea-beach,
  A fisherman stood aghast,
To see the form of a maiden fair,
  Lashed close to a drifting mast.

The salt sea was frozen on her breast,
  The salt tears in her eyes;
And he saw her hair, like the brown seaweed,
  On the billows fall and rise.

Such was the wreck of the Hesperus,
  In the midnight and the snow!
Christ save us all from a death like this,
  On the reef of Norman's Woe!

HENRY WADSWORTH LONGFELLOW

1. **-a** Is this poem structured like a ballad or a simple metrical tale? **-b** Point out which elements of the form you select operate in the poem. **2.** Compare the contribution of the similes in this poem with that of the similes in *The Destruction of Sennacherib* on the basis of vividness, emotional effect, and contribution to meaning. **3.** Compare the relative effectiveness of these two poems on the basis of tight structure, patterning of religious sentiment, and contribution of rhyme to meaning.

The
Means
Massacre

King George raised his jewelled pen
And wrote *death* for a thousand men.

King Louis spoke a single word,
And overseas the forest stirred.

Naked bodies through the brakes
Slid like deadly copper snakes.

Thomas Means was hoeing corn,
His wife was lulling her last-born.

The father smiled to hear the tune
Of a lullaby at noon.

Chloris, Chloris, wooing doves
Are the sentries of our loves.

Maquoit Bay was a diamond's shine
Through the branches of the pine.

Jane and Mary, three-feet high,
Stared round-eyed at a dragonfly.

Baby James's eyes were tight
As morning-glories are at night.

Every bush along the rise
Held a pair of hungry eyes.

All the afternoon the swallows
Clicked their beaks along the hollows.

The afterglow of daytime brought
Peleg Anderson foot-hot.

"The Redskins have been seen at Gorham,
Houses are in flames at Shoreham.

"Take your family, Thomas, fly
To the blockhouse, and be spry!"

Thomas looked upon his crop
Fed by sweat in drop on drop.

Every cornstalk had its feet
In an alewife plump and sweet.

The Lord had exalted Thomas's horn,
His head was roofed in by his corn.

He had powder and two guns,
The Lord would look after his sons!

Thomas folded in his flock,
Dropped the bar and turned the lock.

Thomas sat on the settee,
His rifle lay across his knee.

The honey bees that sang all day
In his head still hummed away.

Thomas's chin sank lower, lower,
His heart hammered slower, slower.

Through the grass the snakes crawled nigher,
Their eyeballs were red coals of fire.

A whippoorwill cried hoarse with fright
To the four corners of the night.

A tree was coming up the hill
On twelve legs, stealthily and still.

Mistress Means was picking may
In Kent three thousand miles away.

The night split with the crack of doom,
The tree came through into the room.

Goodman Thomas sprang up blind,
A bob-cat leapt him from behind.

Mistress Means came back from dreams
To a world of children's screams.

She caught a brand up with a yell,
She stood upon the brink of hell.

At her feet a dusky spider
Was busy where a gash grew wider.

A horrible red spider spread
His fangs along her husband's head.

She brought the brand down on the thing,
She smelt the red flesh sundering.

The monstrous insect leapt aside,
The husband's eyes stared upward wide.

The curls were gone from baby's head,
He wore a fearful cap of red.

The mother heard a distant gun
And the shout of Peleg Anderson.

The serpents melted from the room,
Hissed, and vanished in the gloom.

The neighbor found the mother weeping
On son and mate forever sleeping.

She kept saying, "We were five,
And I am all the one alive.

"Father, Mary, James, and Jane—
I shall not hear them speak again."

The oven creaked, and Jane came out
And clasped her mother round about.

The churn's lid gave a sudden lift,
And Mary sprang out in her shift.

Mistress Means sat by her dead
With living tears upon her head.

Across the ocean dark and broad
King George played his harpsichord.

ROBERT P.
TRISTRAM
COFFIN

And Louis sat with mistresses
Leaning on his satin knees.

1. Analyze the way the introduction and conclusion frame the development of this narrative. How do they create unity, heightened emotion, power of contrast? 2. In a sense the proportion of the incidents is reversed. Universal action (the action of the kings) is given brief statement; personal action (the action of the characters) is given detailed description. Discuss the fitness of this reversal in relation to the total meaning of the poem. 3. Analyze the contribution of simple imagery and of similes to the poetic unity, to the atmosphere, and to the heightening of emotion.

ASSIGNMENTS ON SIMILES

1. Create a one-sentence simile for each of the following:

a gnarled bent tree	the wonder in the eyes of a
a shaggy dog	surprised child
a chattering child	a person beginning to get angry
a zig-zaggy stretch of road	a spirited horse
a sly person	a brilliantly colored car
an underhanded person	

2. Find ten similes in a magazine story. Write the complete sentence containing the simile. Underline the simile.

Read the following narrative poem, remaining alert to its sound patterns, sound effects, and imagery.

The Skater of Ghost Lake

Ghost Lake's a dark lake, a deep lake and cold:
Ice black as ebony, frostily scrolled;
Far in its shadows a faint sound whirrs;
Steep stand the sentineled deep, dark firs.

A brisk sound, a swift sound, a ring-tinkle-ring;
Flit-flit,—a shadow, with a stoop and a swing,
Flies from a shadow through the cracking cold.
Ghost Lake's a deep lake, a dark lake and old!

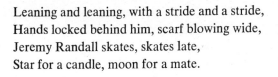

Leaning and leaning, with a stride and a stride,
Hands locked behind him, scarf blowing wide,
Jeremy Randall skates, skates late,
Star for a candle, moon for a mate.

Black is the clear glass now that he glides,
Crisp is the whisper of long lean strides,
Swift is his swaying,—but pricked ears hark.
None comes to Ghost Lake late after dark!

Cecily only,—yes, it is she!
Stealing to Ghost Lake, tree after tree,
Kneeling in snow by the still lake side,
Rising with feet winged, gleaming, to glide.

Dust of the ice swirls. Here is his hand.
Brilliant his eyes burn. Now, as was planned,
Arm across arm twined, laced to his side,
Out on the dark lake lightly they glide.

Dance of the dim moon, a rhythmical reel,
A swaying, a swift tune,—skurr of the steel;
Moon for a candle, maid for a mate,
Jeremy Randall skates, skates late.

Black as if lacquered the wide lake lies;
Breath is a frost-fume, eyes seek eyes;
Souls are a sword-edge tasting the cold.
Ghost Lake's a deep lake, a dark lake and old!

Far in the shadows hear faintly begin
Like a string pluck-plucked of a violin,
Muffled in mist on the lake's far bound,
Swifter and swifter, a low singing sound!

Far in the shadows and faint on the verge
Of blue cloudy moonlight, see it emerge,
Flit-flit,—a phantom, with a stoop and a swing . . .
Ah, it's a night bird, burdened of wing!

Pressed close to Jeremy, laced to his side,
Cecily Culver, dizzy you glide.
Jeremy Randall sweepingly veers
Out on the dark ice far from the piers.

"Jeremy!" "Sweetheart?" "What do you fear?"
"Nothing, my darling,—nothing is here!"
"Jeremy?" "Sweetheart?" "What do you flee?"
"Something—I know not; something I see!"

Swayed to a swift stride, brisker of pace,
Leaning and leaning, they race and they race;
Ever that whirring, that crisp sound thin
Like a string pluck-plucked of a violin;

Ever that swifter and low singing sound
Sweeping behind them, winding them round;
Gasp of their breath now that chill flakes fret;
Ice black as ebony,—blacker—like jet!

Ice shooting fangs forth—sudden—like spears;
Crackling of lightning,—a roar in their ears!
Shadowy, a phantom swerves off from its prey . . .
No, it's a night bird flit-flits away!

Low-winging moth-owl, home to your sleep!
Ghost Lake's a still lake, a cold lake and deep.
Faint in its shadows a far sound whirrs.
Black stand the ranks of its sentinel firs.

WILLIAM ROSE BENÉT

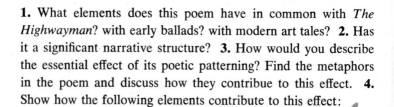

1. What elements does this poem have in common with *The Highwayman*? with early ballads? with modern art tales? **2.** Has it a significant narrative structure? **3.** How would you describe the essential effect of its poetic patterning? Find the metaphors in the poem and discuss how they contribue to this effect. **4.** Show how the following elements contribute to this effect:

-**a** rhythm

-**b** repetition

-**c** alliteration

-**d** onomatopoeia

-**e** rhyme

ASSIGNMENTS ON METAPHORS

1. Reread *The Highwayman*. Find the metaphors, and analyze each one to determine what it contributes to plot, setting, or character.

2. Write metaphors of your own to describe:

the highwayman's hat
 the bunch of lace at his chin
  his sweetheart's love knot
   Tim's face
    the red-coat troop

3. Write a stanza which will create the setting of a ballad. Use a metaphor in your stanza. SUGGESTIONS:

ballad of the kitchen	decorating for a school dance
ballad of Monday morning	a car accident on the way to a picnic
ballad of Friday (afternoon or night)	the Chicago fire
	final tests
ballad of the gym locker room	getting ready for a dance (home preparation)
Christmas shopping	

4. Write metaphors in the form of two rhyming lines on:

icicles	the grade school playground
an old horse	a piece of driftwood
factory windows	an inside pool
country fair or carnival	an ice-skating pond
a Ferris wheel	sumach trees in fall

IMAGERY—PERSONIFICATION: Personification is a figure of speech related to similes and metaphors. It, like them, is a figure of likeness. In this figure of speech, animals and inanimate objects are given the characteristics of people. Personification is sometimes called a dramatized figure of likeness.

In this lovely poem, the mist is treated as a person. It is personified. You will understand something of the power of personification to create rich poetic effects if you read this poem thoughtfully. You will also see that personification is a development of metaphor, for *mist walks in my garden* only because she is *a contemplative in white*.

Mist

a mist walks in my garden
a contemplative in white;
its frost-filled face is turned from me
yet it fills me with delight.

beyond the trees, immobile,
it gives no word or sign;
though the black-ribbed trees enfold it
i am certain it is mine.

at last it turns to leave me
as it trails its long white dress;
if it asked me to go with it
i'm quite sure that i'd say yes.

CATHERINE
BOCK

Read *The Creation*. Notice how the meaning of the poem is affected by the use of personification.

The Creation

And God stepped out on space,
And He looked around and said:
I'm lonely—
I'll make me a world.

And far as the eye of God could see
Darkness covered everything,
Blacker than a hundred midnights
Down in a cypress swamp.

Then God smiled,
And the light broke,
And the darkness rolled up on one side,
And the light stood shining on the other,
And God said: That's good!

Then God reached out and took the light in His hands,
And God rolled the light around in His hands
Until He made the sun;
And He set that sun a-blazing in the heavens.
And the light that was left from making the sun
God gathered it up in a shining ball
And flung it against the darkness,
Spangling the night with the moon and stars.
Then down between
The darkness and the light
He hurled the world;
And God said: That's good!

Then God himself stepped down—
And the sun was on His right hand,
And the moon was on His left;
The stars were clustered about His head,
And the earth was under His feet.
And God walked, and where He trod
His footsteps hollowed the valleys out
And bulged the mountains up.

Then He stopped and looked and saw
That the earth was hot and barren.
So God stepped over to the edge of the world
And He spat out the seven seas—
He batted His eyes, and the lightnings flashed—
He clapped His hands, and the thunders rolled—
And the waters above the earth came down,
The cooling waters came down.

Then the green grass sprouted,
And the little red flowers blossomed,
The pine tree pointed his finger to the sky,

And the oak spread out his arms,
The lakes cuddled down in the hollows of the ground,
And the rivers ran down to the sea;
And God smiled again,
And the rainbow appeared,
And curled itself around His shoulder.

Then God raised His arm and He waved His hand
Over the sea and over the land,
And He said: Bring forth! Bring forth!
And quicker than God could drop His hand,
Fishes and fowls
And beasts and birds
Swam the rivers and the seas,
Roamed the forests and the woods,
And split the air with their wings.
And God said: That's good!

Then God walked around,
And God looked around
On all that He had made.
He looked at His sun,
And He looked at his moon,
He looked at His little stars;
He looked on His world
With all its living things,
And God said: I'm lonely still.

Then God sat down—
On the side of a hill where He could think;
By a deep, wide river He sat down;
With His head in His hands,
God thought and thought,
Till He thought: I'll make me a man!

Up from the bed of the river
God scooped the clay;
And by the bank of the river
He kneeled Him down;

And there the great God Almighty
Who lit the sun and fixed it in the sky,
Who flung the stars to the most far corner of the night,
Who rounded the earth in the middle of His hand;
This Great God,
Like a mammy bending over her baby,
Kneeled down in the dust
Toiling over a lump of clay
Till He shaped it in His own image;
Then into it He blew the breath of life,
And man became a living soul.
Amen. Amen.

JAMES WELDON JOHNSON

1. Because most of the action in this poem is God's, there is
little occasion for personification. Find where it occurs, however,
and analyze how it fits in the pattern of God's action, both in
substance and in treatment. **2.** This poem is a Negro sermon.
What elements identify it as such? Does it remain narrative in
structure? **3.** Similes play an important role in shaping both
the beginning and the ending of the poem. Show the contribution
they make by their essential contrast to each other (one extends,
the other limits) and by their similarity to each other. **4.** Discuss
the irregularity of the rhythm and its contribution to the poem.

Reread *The Means Massacre* to see the essential difference
in effect between simile and metaphor and between metaphor
and personification. Retrace the figures of speech through this
poem. You will discover that they begin as similes, eventually
become metaphors, and end as personifications. Show how this
progression affects the meaning of the poem.   •

ASSIGNMENTS ON PERSONIFICATION

1. Creat as many images or personifications as possible by
giving these verbs inanimate subjects:

snarl	rollick	stutter	snatch	shiver
wheeze	tear	rummage	snore	pant

2. Write a paragraph personifying one of the following. Let all the verbs carry the personification through the paragraph.

a derrick	a train
a construction	a vegetable cannery
feet in a shopping center	a bulldozer
a study period	a beehive or an ant hill
lunch line in a cafeteria	a brass band

ADDITIONAL NARRATIVE
POEMS TO ENJOY

How the Helpmate of Blue-Beard Made Free with a Door

A maiden from the Bosphorus, with eyes as bright as phosphorus,
Once wed the wealthy bailiff of the Caliph of Kelat.
Though diligent and zealous, he became a slave to jealousy;
Considering her beauty 'twas his duty to be that.
When business would necessitate a journey he would hesitate,
But, fearing to disgust her, he would trust her with his keys,
Remarking to her prayerfully, "I beg you'll use them carefully.
Don't look what I deposit in that closet, if you please."
It might be mentioned casually, that blue as lapis-lazuli
He dyed his hair, his lashes, his mustaches, and his beard,
And, just because he did it, he aroused his wife's timidity;
Her terror she dissembled, but she trembled when he neared.
This feeling insalubrious soon made her most lugubrious,
And bitterly she missed her elder sister Marie Anne:
She asked if she might write her to come down and spend a
        night or two;
Her husband answered rightly and politely: "Yes, you can."
Blue-Beard, the Monday following, his jealous
        feelings swallowing,
Packed all his clothes together in a leather-bound valise,
Then, feigning reprehensibly, he started out ostensibly
By traveling to learn a bit of Smyrna and of Greece.
His wife made but a cursory inspection of the nursery,

The kitchen and the airy little dairy were a bore,
As well as big or scanty rooms, and billiard, bath, and anterooms,
But not that interdicted and restricted little door.
For, all her curiosity awakened by the closet he
So carefully had hidden and forbidden her to see,
This damsel disobedient did something inexpedient
And in the key-hole tiny turned the shiny little key.
Then started back impulsively, and shrieked aloud convulsively;
Three heads of maids he'd wedded—and beheaded—met
            her eye.
And turning round much terrified, her darkest fears were verified,
For Blue-Beard stood behind her, come to find her on the sly.
Perceiving she was fated to be soon decapitated, too,
She telegraphed her brothers and some others what she feared.
And Sister Anne looked out for them in readiness to shout
            for them
Whenever in the distance with assistance they appeared.
But only from her battlement she saw some dust that
            cattle meant.
The ordinary story isn't gory, but a jest.
But here's the truth unqualified: the husband wasn't mollified;
Her head is in his bloody little study with the rest!

The Moral: Wives, we must allow, who to their husbands will
            not bow,
A stern and dreadful lesson learn when, as you've read, they're
            cut in turn.

GUY WETMORE CARRYL

The
Cremation
of
Sam
McGee

There are strange things done in the midnight sun
    By the men who moil for gold;
The Arctic trails have their secret tales
    That would make your blood run cold;
The Northern Lights have seen queer sights,
    But the queerest they ever did see
Was that night on the marge of Lake Lebarge
    I cremated Sam McGee.

Now Sam McGee was from Tennessee, where the cotton
	blooms and blows,
Why he left his home in the South to roam 'round the Pole,
	God only knows.
He was always cold, but the land of gold seemed to hold him
	like a spell;
Though he'd often say in his homely way that "he'd sooner
	live in hell."

On a Christmas Day we were mushing our way over the
	Dawson Trail.
Talk of your cold! through the parka's fold it stabbed like a
	driven nail.
If our eyes we'd close, then the lashes froze till sometimes we
	couldn't see;
It wasn't much fun, but the only one to whimper was
	Sam McGee.

And that very night, as we lay packed tight in our robes
	beneath the snow,
And the dogs were fed, and the stars o'erhead were dancing
	heel and toe,
He turned to me, and "Cap," says he, "I'll cash in this trip,
	I guess;
And if I do, I'm asking that you won't refuse my last request."

Well, he seemed so low that I couldn't say no; then he says with
	a sort of moan:
"It's the cursed cold, and it's got right hold till I'm chilled clean
	through to the bone.
Yet 'tain't being dead—it's my awful dread of the icy grave
	that pains;
So I want you to swear that, foul or fair, you'll cremate my
	last remains."

A pal's last need is a thing to heed, so I swore I would not fail;
And we started on at the streak of dawn; but God! he looked
	ghastly pale.

He crouched on the sleigh, and he raved all day of his home
in Tennessee;
And before nightfall a corpse was all that was left of
Sam McGee.

There wasn't a breath in that land of death, and I hurried,
horror-driven,
With a corpse half hid that I couldn't get rid, because of a
promise given;
It was lashed to the sleigh, and it seemed to say: "You may tax
your brawn and brains,
But you promised true, and it's up to you to cremate
those last remains."

Now a promise made is a debt unpaid, and the trail has its own
stern code.
In the days to come, though my lips were dumb, in my heart
how I cursed that load.
In the long, long night, by the lone firelight, while the huskies,
round in a ring,
Howled out their woes to the homeless snows—O God! how
I loathed the thing.

And every day that quiet clay seemed to heavy and heavier grow;
And on I went, though the dogs were spent and the grub was
getting low;
The trail was bad, and I felt half mad, but I swore I would
not give in;
And I'd often sing to the hateful thing, and it hearkened
with a grin.

Till I came to the marge of Lake Lebarge, and a derelict
there lay;
It was jammed in the ice, but I saw in a trice it was called the
"Alice May."
And I looked at it, and I thought a bit, and I looked at my
frozen chum;
Then "Here," said I, with a sudden cry, "is my cre-ma-tor-e-um."

Some planks I tore from the cabin floor, and I lit the boiler fire;
Some coal I found that was lying around, and I heaped the
fuel higher;
The flames just soared, and the furnace roared—such a blaze
you seldom see;
And I burrowed a hole in the glowing coal, and I stuffed in
Sam McGee.

Then I made a hike, for I didn't like to hear him sizzle so;
And the heavens scowled, and the huskies howled, and the wind
began to blow.
It was icy cold, but the hot sweat rolled down my cheeks, and
I don't know why;
And the greasy smoke in an inky cloak went streaking down
the sky.

I do not know how long in the snow I wrestled with grisly fear;
But the stars came out and they danced about ere again I
ventured near;
I was sick with dread, but I bravely said: "I'll just take
a peep inside.
I guess he's cooked, and it's time I looked"; . . . then the
door I opened wide.

And there sat Sam, looking cold and calm, in the heart of the
furnace roar;
And he wore a smile you could see a mile, and he said: "Please
close that door!
It's fine in here, but I greatly fear you'll let in the
cold and storm—
Since I left Plumtree, down in Tennessee, it's the first time I've
been warm."

> There are strange things done in the midnight sun
> By the men who moil for gold;
> The Arctic trails have their secret tales
> That would make your blood run cold;

The Northern Lights have seen queer sights,
But the queerest they ever did see
Was that night on the marge of Lake Lebarge
I cremated Sam McGee.

The Rhyme of the Chivalrous Shark

Most chivalrous fish of the ocean—
  To ladies forbearing and mild,
Though his record be dark, is the man-eating shark,
  Who will eat neither woman nor child.

He dines upon seamen and skippers,
  And tourists his hunger assuage,
And a fresh cabin boy will inspire him with joy
  If he's past the maturity age.

A doctor, a lawyer, a preacher,
  He'll gobble one any fine day,
But the ladies, God bless 'em, he'll only address 'em
  Politely and go on his way.

I can readily cite you an instance
  Where a lovely young lady of Breem,
Who was tender and sweet and delicious to eat,
  Fell into the bay with a scream.

She struggled and flounced in the water,
  And signaled in vain for her bark,
And she'd surely been drowned if she hadn't been found
  By the chivalrous man-eating shark.

He bowed in a manner most polished,
  Thus soothing her impulses wild;
"Don't be frightened," he said, "I've been properly bred—
  And will eat neither woman nor child."

Then he proffered his fin and she took it—
  Such a gallantry none can dispute—

While the passengers cheered as the vessel they neared,
   And a broadside was fired in salute.

And they soon stood alongside the vessel,
   When a life-saving dinghy was lowered
With the pick of the crew, and her relatives too,
   And the mate and the skipper aboard.

So they took her aboard in a jiffy,
   And the shark stood attention the while,
Then he raised on his flipper and ate up the skipper
   And went on his way with a smile.

And this shows that the prince of the ocean,
   To ladies forbearing and mild,
Though his record be dark, is the man-eating shark
   Who will eat neither woman nor child.

WALLACE IRWIN

Tact

The Sultan was vexed by a dream
   That had troubled his slumbers;
For, feasting on lobsters and cream
   With half-ripened cucumbers
And lying with head to the South
   Gives the Night Mare full power:
He dreamed that the teeth of his mouth
   Tumbled out in a shower!
So, calling a sayer of sooth
   To interpret the vision,
He charged him to utter the truth
   With unflinching precision.

"Oh, Fountain of Justice and fear
   Of the infidel foemen,

The vision," expounded the seer,
  "Is of dolorous omen;
For Allah who governs this ball,—
  May his favor restore you!—
Decrees that your relatives all
  Shall drop dead right before you!"

The Sultan leaped up in a fit
  Of devouring fury.
He stayed not to issue a writ
  Or impanel a jury,
But, "Shorten this fellow!" he said,
  "And be rapid about it!"
So off went the soothsayer's head;
  He was wiser without it.

One sage in the discard, they sent
  To the mosque for another,
An augur of wilier bent
  Than his innocent brother.
"Now Allah be honored and praised!"
  Cried this shrewdest of mages,
"And high let your banner be raised,
  For the vision presages
That long shall your Majesty thrive
  Like the fertile plantations;
So long that my Lord shall survive
  E'en his youngest relations!"

The gratified Sultan expressed
  His delight beyond measure;
The prophet went home with a chest
  Overflowing with treasure.

Which proves,—'tis a principle still,
  Let the blunt-spoken weigh it,—
A person may say what he will
  If he knows how to say it.

ARTHUR
GUITERMAN

Matilda

Matilda told such Dreadful Lies,
It made one Gasp and Stretch one's Eyes;
Her Aunt, who, from her Earliest Youth,
Had kept a Strict Regard for Truth,
Attempted to believe Matilda:
The effort very nearly killed her,
And would have done so, had not She
Discovered this Infirmity.
For once, towards the Close of Day,
Matilda, growing tired of play,
And finding she was left alone,
Went tiptoe to the Telephone
And summoned the Immediate Aid
Of London's Noble Fire-Brigade.
Within an hour the Gallant Band
Were pouring in on every hand,
From Putney, Hackney Downs, and Bow
With Courage high and Hearts a-glow
They galloped, roaring through the Town,
"Matilda's House is Burning Down!"
Inspired by British Cheers and Loud
Proceeding from the Frenzied Crowd,
They ran their Ladders through a Score
Of windows on the Ball Room Floor;
And took Peculiar Pains to Souse
The Pictures up and down the House,
Until Matilda's Aunt succeeded
In showing them they were not needed;
And even then she had to Pay
To get the Men to go Away

It happened that a few Weeks later
Her Aunt was off to the Theatre
To see that Interesting Play
The Second Mrs. Tanqueray.
She had refused to take her Niece
To hear this Entertaining Piece:
(A Deprivation Just and Wise
To Punish her for Telling Lies.)
That Night a Fire *did* break out—
You should have heard Matilda Shout!
You should have heard her Scream and Bawl,
And throw the window up and call
To People passing in the Street—
(The rapidly increasing Heat
Encouraging her to obtain
Their confidence)—but all In Vain!
For every time She shouted, "Fire!"
They only answered, "Little Liar!"
And therefore when her Aunt returned,
Matilda, and the House, were Burned.

HILAIRE
BELLOC

Lochinvar

O, young Lochinvar is come out of the west,
Through all the wide Border his steed was the best;
And, save his good broadsword, he weapons had none.
He rode all unarmed, and he rode all alone.
So faithful in love, and so dauntless in war,
There never was knight like the young Lochinvar.
He stayed not for brake, and he stopped not for stone;
He swam the Eske river where ford there was none;

But, ere he alighted at Netherby gate,
The bride had consented, the gallant came late;
For a laggard in love, and a dastard in war,
Was to wed the fair Ellen of brave Lochinvar.

So boldíy he entered the Netherby Hall,
Among bridesmen, and kinsmen, and brothers, and all.
Then spoke the bride's father, his hand on his sword
(For the poor craven bridegroom said never a word),
"O, come ye in peace here, or come ye in war,
Or to dance at our bridal, young Lord Lochinvar?"

"I long wooed your daughter, my suit you denied;—
Love swells like the Solway, but ebbs like its tide;—
And now I am come, with this lost love of mine,
To lead but one measure, drink one cup of wine.
There are maidens in Scotland more lovely by far,
That would gladly be bride to the young Lochinvar."

The bride kissed the goblet; the knight took it up:
He quaffed off the wine, and he threw down the cup.
She looked down to blush, and she looked up to sigh,
With a smile on her lips, and a tear in her eye.
He took her soft hand, ere her mother could bar,—
"Now tread we a measure!" said young Lochinvar.

So stately his form, and so lovely her face,
That never a hall such a galliard did grace;
While her mother did fret, and her father did fume,
And the bridegroom stood dangling his bonnet and plume;
And the bride-maidens whispered, " 'Twere better by far
To have matched our fair cousin with young Lochinvar."

One touch to her hand, and one word in her ear,
When they reached the hall door, and the charger stood near;
So light to the croupe the fair lady he swung,
So light to the saddle before her he sprung!
"She is won! we are gone! over bank, bush, and scaur;
They'll have fleet steeds that follow," quoth young Lochinvar.

There was mounting 'mong Græmes of the Netherby clan;
Forsters, Fenwicks, and Musgraves, they rode and they ran;
There was racing and chasing on Cannobie Lee;
But the lost bride of Netherby ne'er did they see.
So daring in love, and so dauntless in war,
Have ye e'er heard of gallant like young Lochinvar?

SIR WALTER SCOTT

Lady Isabel and the Elf-Knight

There came a bird out of a bush,
  On water for to dine,
And sighing sore, says the king's daughter,
  "O woe's this heart of mine!"

He's taken a harp into his hand,
  He's harped them all asleep,
Except it was the king's daughter,
  Who one wink could not get.

He's leaped upon his berry-brown steed,
  Taken her on behind himsel',
Then both rode down to that water
  That they call Wearie's Well.

"Wade in, wade in, my lady fair,
  No harm shall thee befall;
Oft times have I watered my steed
  With the waters of Wearie's Well."

The first step that she steppèd in,
  She steppèd to the knee;
And sighing says this lady fair,
  "This water's not for me."

"Wade in, wade in, my lady fair,
  No harm shall thee befall;

Oft times have I watered my steed
  With the water of Wearie's Well."

The next step that she steppèd in,
  She steppèd to the middle;
"O," sighing says this lady fair,
  "I've wet my golden girdle."

"Wade in, wade in, my lady fair,
  No harm shall thee befall;
Oft times have I watered my steed
  With the water of Wearie's Well."

The next step that she steppèd in,
  She steppèd to the chin;
"O," sighing says this lady fair,
  "I'll wade no farther in."

"Seven king's daughters I've drowned there,
  In the water of Wearie's Well,
And I'll make you the eighth of them,
  And ring the common bell."

"Since I am standing here," she says,
  "This dreadful death to die,
One kiss of your comely mouth
  I'm sure would comfort me."

He leanèd over his saddle bow,
  To kiss her cheek and chin;
She's taken him in her arms two,
  And thrown him headlong in.

"Since seven king's daughters ye've drowned there,
  In the water of Wearie's Well,
I'll make you bridegroom to them all,
  And ring the bell mysel'."

OLD
BALLAD

The Cruel Brother

There was three ladies played at the ba',
With a hey ho and a lily gay.

There came a knight and played o'er them a',
As the primrose spreads so sweetly.

The eldest was baith tall and fair,
But the youngest looked like beauty's queen.

The midmost had a graceful mien,
But the youngest looked like beauty's queen.

The knight bowed low to a' the three,
But to the youngest he bent his knee.

The lady turned her head aside,
The knight he wooed her to be his bride.

The lady blushed a rosy red,
And said, "Sir knight, I'm o'er young to wed."

"O lady fair, give me your hand,
And I'll make you lady of a' my land."

"Sir knight, ere ye my favor win,
You maun get consent frae a' my kin."

He's got consent frae her parents dear,
And likewise frae her sisters fair.

He's got consent frae her kin each one,
But forgot to spier at her brother John.

Now, when the wedding day was come,
The knight would take his bonny bride home.

And many a lord and many a knight
Came to behold that lady bright.

And there was nae man that did her see,
But wished himself bridegroom to be.

Her father dear led her down the stair,
And her sisters twain they kissed her there.

Her mother dear led her through the close,
And her brother John set her on her horse.

She leaned her o'er the saddlebow,
To give him a kiss ere she did go.

He has ta'en a knife, baith lang and sharp,
And stabbed the bonny bride to the heart.

She hadna ridden half through the town,
Until her heart's blude stained her gown.

"Ride softly on," said the best young man,
"For I think our bonny bride looks pale and wan."

"O lead me gently up yon hill,
And I'll there sit down, and make my will."

"O what will you leave to your father dear?"
"The silver-shod steed that brought me here."

"And what will you leave to your mother dear?"
"My velvet pall and my silken gear."

"What will you leave to your sister Anne?"
"My silken scarf and my gowden fan."

"What will you leave to your sister Grace?"
"My bloody clothes to wash and dress."

"What will you leave to your brother John?"
"The gallows tree to hang him on."

"What will you leave to your brother John's wife?"
"The wilderness to end her life."

This fair lady in her grave was laid,
And a mass was o'er her said.

But it would have made your heart right sair,
To see the bridegroom rive his hair.

OLD BALLAD

Dives and Lazarus

As it fell out upon a day,
    Rich Dives he made a feast,
And he invited all his friends
    And gentry of the best.

Then Lazarus laid him down and down,
    And down at Dives' door;
"Some meat, some drink, brother Dives,
    Bestow upon the poor!"—

"Thou art none of my brother, Lazarus,
    That lies begging at my door;
No meat nor drink will I give thee,
    Nor bestow upon the poor."

Then Lazarus laid him down and down,
    And down at Dives' wall,
"Some meat, some drink, brother Dives,
    Or with hunger starve I shall!"—

"Thou art none of my brother, Lazarus,
    That lies begging at my wall;
No meat nor drink will I give thee,
    But with hunger starve you shall."

Then Lazarus laid him down and down,
    And down at Dives' gate:
"Some meat, some drink, brother Dives,
    For Jesus Christ His sake!"—

"Thou art none of my brother, Lazarus,
    That lies begging at my gate;
No meat nor drink will I give thee,
    For Jesus Christ His sake."

Then Dives sent out his merry men,
    To whip poor Lazarus away;
They had no power to strike a stroke,
    But flung their whips away.

Then Dives sent out his hungry dogs,
    To bite him as he lay;
They had no power to bite at all,
    But lickèd his sores away.

As it fell out upon a day,
    Poor Lazarus sicken'd and died;
Then came two angels out of heaven
    His soul therein to guide.

"Rise up, rise up, brother Lazarus,
    And go along with me;
For you've a place prepared in heaven,
    To sit on an angel's knee.'

As it fell out upon a day,
    Rich Dives sicken'd and died;
Then came two serpents out of hell,
    His soul therein to guide.

"Rise up, rise up, brother Dives,
    And go with us to see
A dismal place, prepared in hell,
    To sit on a serpent's knee."

Then Dives look'd up with his eyes,
    And saw poor Lazarus blest:
"Give me one drop of water, brother Lazarus,
    To quench my flaming thirst.

"Oh had I as many years to abide
    As there are blades of grass,
Then there would be an end, but now
    Hell's pains will ne'er be past.

"Oh was I now but alive again,
    The space of one half hour!
OLD   Oh that I had my peace secure!
BALLAD   Then the devil should have no power."

The Revenge
of Hamish

It was three slim does and a ten-tined buck in the bracken lay;
    And all of a sudden the sinister smell of a man,
    Awaft on a wind-shift, wavered and ran
Down the hill-side and sifted along through the bracken and
        passed that way.

Then Nan got a-tremble at nostril; she was the daintiest doe;
    In the print of her velvet flank on the velvet fern
    She reared, and rounded her ears in turn.
Then the buck leapt up, and his head as a king's to a crown
        did go

Full high in the breeze, and he stood as if Death had the form
        of a deer;
    And the two slim does long lazily stretching arose,
    For their day-dream slowlier came to a close,
Till they woke and were still, breath-bound with waiting and
        wonder and fear.

Then Alan the huntsman sprang over the hillock, the hounds
        shot by,
   The does and the ten-tined buck made a marvellous bound,
   The hounds swept after with never a sound,
But Alan loud winded his horn in sign that the quarry was nigh.

For at dawn of that day proud Maclean of Lochbuy to the hunt
        had waxed wild,
   And he cursed at old Alan till Alan fared off with the hounds
   For to drive him the deer to the lower glen-grounds:
"I will kill a red deer," quoth Maclean, "in the sight of the wife
        and the child."

So gayly he paced with the wife and the child to his chosen stand;
   But he hurried tall Hamish the henchman ahead:
       "Go turn,"—
   Cried Maclean—"if the deer seek to cross to the burn,
Do thou turn them to me: nor fail, lest thy back be red as
        thy hand."

Now hard-fortuned Hamish, half blown of his breath with the
        height of the hill,
   Was white in the face when the ten-tined buck and the does
   Drew leaping to burn-ward; huskily rose
His shouts, and his nether lip twitched, and his legs were o'er-
        weak for his will.

So the deer darted lightly by Hamish and bounded away to
        the burn.
   But Maclean never bating his watch tarried waiting below.
   Still Hamish hung heavy with fear for to go
All the space of an hour; then he went, and his face was
        greenish and stern,

And his eye sat back in the socket, and shrunken the
        eye-balls shone,
   As withdrawn from a vision of deeds it were shame to see.

"Now, now, grim henchman, what is't with thee?"
Brake Maclean, and his wrath rose red as a beacon the wind
hath upblown.

"Three does and a ten-tined buck made out," spoke Hamish,
full mild,
"And I ran for to turn, but my breath it was blown, and
they passed;
I was weak, for ye called ere I broke me my fast."
Cried Maclean: "Now a ten-tined buck in the sight of the wife
and the child

I had killed if the gluttonous kern had not wrought me a snail's
own wrong!"
Then he sounded, and down came kinsmen and clansmen all:
"Ten blows, for ten tine, on his back let fall,
And reckon no stroke if the blood follow not at the bite
of thong!"

So Hamish made bare, and took him his strokes; at the last
he smiled.
"Now I'll to the burn," quoth Maclean, "for it still may be,
If a slimmer-paunched henchman will hurry with me,
I shall kill me the ten-tined buck for a gift to the wife and
the child!"

Then the clansmen departed, by this path and that; and over
the hill
Sped Maclean with an outward wrath for an inward shame;
And that place of the lashing full quiet became;
And the wife and the child stood sad; and bloody-backed
Hamish sat still.

But look! red Hamish has risen; quick about and about turns he.
"There is none betwixt me and the crag-top!" he screams
under breath.
Then, livid as Lazarus lately from death,
He snatches the child from the mother, and clambers the crag
toward the sea.

Now the mother drops breath; she is dumb, and her heart goes
      dead for a space,
  Till the motherhood, mistress of death, shrieks, shrieks
      through the glen,
  And that place of the lashing is live with men,
And Maclean, and the gillie that told him, dash up in a
      desperate race.

Not a breath's time for asking; an eye-glance reveals all the
      tale untold.
  They follow mad Hamish afar up the crag toward the sea,
  And the lady cries: "Clansmen, run for a fee!—
Yon castle and lands to the two first hands that shall hook him
      and hold

Fast Hamish back from the brink!"—and ever she flies up
      the steep,
  And the clansmen pant, and they sweat, and they jostle
      and strain.
  But, mother, 'tis vain; but, father, 'tis vain;
Stern Hamish stands bold on the brink, and dangles the child
      o'er the deep.

Now a faintness falls on the men that run, and they all stand still.
  And the wife prays Hamish as if he were God, on her knees,
  Crying: "Hamish! O Hamish! but please, but please
For to spare him!" and Hamish still dangles the child, with a
      wavering will.

On a sudden he turns; with a sea-hawk scream, and a gibe, and
      a song,
  Cries: "So; I will spare ye the child if, in sight of ye all,
  Ten blows on Maclean's bare back shall fall,
And ye reckon no stroke if the blood follow not at the bite of
      the thong!"

Then Maclean he set hardly his tooth to his lip that his tooth
      was red,
  Breathed short for a space, said: "Nay, but it never shall be!
  Let me hurl off the damnable hound in the sea!"
But the wife: "Can Hamish go fish us the child from the sea,
     if dead?

Say yea!—Let them lash *me,* Hamish?"—"Nay!"—"Husband,
     the lashing will heal;
  But, oh, who will heal me the bonny sweet bairn in his grave?
  Could ye cure me my heart with the death of a knave?
Quick! Love! I will bare thee—so—kneel!" Then Maclean 'gan
     slowly to kneel

With never a word, till presently downward he jerked to
     the earth.
  Then the henchman—he that smote Hamish—would tremble
     and lag;
  "Strike, hard!" quoth Hamish, full stern, from the crag;
Then he struck him, and "One!" sang Hamish, and danced with
     the child in his mirth.

And no man spake beside Hamish; he counted each stroke
     with a song.
  When the last stroke fell, then he moved him a pace down
     the height,
  And he held forth the child in the heartaching sight
Of the mother, and looked all pitiful grave, as repenting
     a wrong.

And there as the motherly arms stretched out with the
     thanksgiving prayer—
  And there as the mother crept up with a fearful swift pace,
  Till her finger nigh felt of the bairnie's face—
In a flash fierce Hamish turned round and lifted the child in
     the air,

And sprang with the child in his arms from the horrible height
           in the sea,
   Shrill screeching, "Revenge!" in the wind-rush; and
           pallid Maclean
  Age-feeble with anger and impotent pain,
Crawled up on the crag, and lay flat, and locked hold of dead
           roots of a tree—

And gazed hungrily o'er, and the blood from his back drip-
           dripped in the brine,
   And a sea-hawk flung down a skeleton fish as he flew,
   And the mother stared white on the waste of blue,
And the wind drove a cloud to seaward, and the sun began
           to shine.

   SIDNEY
   LANIER

How the Great Guest Came

Before the Cathedral in grandeur rose,
At Ingelburg where the Danube goes;
Before its forest of silver spires
Went airily up to the clouds and fires;
Before the oak had ready a beam,
While yet the arch was stone and dream—
There where the altar was later laid,
Conrad, the cobbler, plied his trade.

Doubled all day on his busy bench,
Hard at his cobbling for master and hench,
He pounded away at a brisk rat-tat,
Shearing and shaping with pull and pat,
Hide well hammered and pegs sent home,
Till the shoe was fit for the Prince of Rome.
And he sang as the threads went to and fro:
"Whether 'tis hidden or whether it show,
Let the work be sound, for the Lord will know."

Tall was the cobbler, and gray and thin,
And a full moon shone where the hair had been.
His eyes peered out, intent and afar,
As looking beyond the things that are.
He walked as one who is done with fear,
Knowing at last that God is near.
Only the half of him cobbled the shoes:
The rest was away for the heavenly news.
Indeed, so thin was the mystic screen
That parted the Unseen from the Seen,
You could not tell, from the cobbler's theme,
If his dream were truth or his truth were dream.

It happened one day at the year's white end,
Two neighbors called on their old-time friend;
And they found the shop, so meager and mean,
Made gay with a hundred boughs of green.
Conrad was stitching with face ashine,
But suddenly stopped as he twitched a twine:
"Old friends, good news! At dawn today,
As the cocks were scaring the night away,
The Lord appeared in a dream to me,
And said, 'I am coming your Guest to be!'
So I've been busy with feet astir,
Strewing the floor with branches of fir.
The wall is washed and the shelf is shined,
And over the rafter the holly twined.
He comes today, and the table is spread
With milk and honey and wheaten bread."

His friends went home; and his face grew still
As he watched for the shadow across the sill.
He lived all the moments o'er and o'er,
When the Lord should enter the lowly door—
The knock, the call, the latch pulled up,
The lighted face, the offered cup.
He would wash the feet where the spikes had been;
He would kiss the hands where the nails went in;

And then at the last would sit with Him
And break the bread as the day grew dim.

While the cobbler mused, there passed his pane
A beggar drenched by the driving rain.
He called him in from the stony street
And gave him shoes for his bruiséd feet.
The beggar went and there came a crone,
Her face with wrinkles of sorrow sown.
A bundle of fagots bowed her back,
And she was spent with the wrench and rack.
He gave her his loaf and steadied her load
As she took her way on the weary road.
Then to his door came a little child,
Lost and afraid in the world so wild,
In the big, dark world. Catching it up,
He gave it the milk in the waiting cup,
And led it home to its mother's arms,
Out of the reach of the world's alarms.

The day went down in the crimson west
And with it the hope of the blesséd Guest,
And Conrad sighed as the world turned gray:
"Why is it, Lord, that your feet delay?
Did You forget that this was the day?"
Then soft in the silence a Voice he heard:
"Lift up your heart, for I kept my word.
Three times I came to your friendly door;
Three times my shadow was on your floor.
I was the beggar with bruiséd feet;
I was the woman you gave to eat;
I was the child on the homeless street!"

EDWIN
MARKHAM

Simon Legree—a Negro Sermon

Legree's big house was white and green.
His cotton-fields were the best to be seen.
He had strong horses and opulent cattle,
And bloodhounds bold, with chains that would rattle.
His garret was full of curious things:
Books of magic, bags of gold,
And rabbits' feet on long twine strings.
But he went down to the Devil.

Legree he sported a brass-buttoned coat,
A snake-skin necktie, a blood-red shirt.
Legree he had a beard like a goat,
And a thick hairy neck, and eyes like dirt.
His puffed-out cheeks were fish-belly white,
He had great long teeth, and an appetite.
He ate raw meat, 'most every meal,
And rolled his eyes till the cat would squeal.

His fist was an enormous size
To mash poor niggers that told him lies:
He was surely a witch-man in disguise.
But he went down to the Devil.

He wore hip-boots, and would wade all day
To capture his slaves that had fled away.
But he went down to the Devil.

He beat poor Uncle Tom to death
Who prayed for Legree with his last breath.
Then Uncle Tom to Eva flew,
To the high sanctoriums bright and new;
And Simon Legree stared up beneath,
And cracked his heels, and ground his teeth:
And went down to the Devil.

He crossed the yard in the storm and gloom;
He went into his grand front room.
He said, "I killed him, and I don't care."
He kicked a hound, he gave a swear;
He tightened his belt, he took a lamp,
Went down cellar to the webs and damp.
There in the middle of the mouldy floor
He heaved up a slab, he found a door—
And went down to the Devil.

His lamp blew out, but his eyes burned bright.
Simon Legree stepped down all night—
Down, down to the Devil.

Simon Legree he reached the place,
He saw one half of the human race,
He saw the Devil on a wide green throne,
Gnawing the meat from a big ham-bone,
And he said to Mister Devil:

"I see that you have much to eat—
A red ham-bone is surely sweet.
I see that you have lion's feet;
I see your frame is fat and fine,
I see you drink your poison wine—
Blood and burning turpentine."

And the Devil said to Simon Legree:
"I like your style, so wicked and free.
Come sit and share my throne with me,
And let us bark and revel."
And there they sit and gnash their teeth,
And each one wears a hop-vine wreath.
They are matching pennies and shooting craps,
They are playing poker and taking naps.
And old Legree is fat and fine:
He eats the fire, he drinks the wine—
Blood, and burning turpentine—

> *Down, down with the Devil;*
> *Down, down with the Devil;*
> *Down, down with the Devil.*

VACHEL
LINDSAY

Pershing at the Front

The General came in a new tin hat
To the shell-torn front where the war was at;
With a faithful Aide at his good right hand
He made his way toward No Man's Land,
And a tough Top Sergeant there they found,
And a Captain, too, to show them round.

Threading the ditch, their heads bent low,
Toward the lines of the watchful foe
They came through the murk and the powder stench
Till the Sergeant whispered, *"Third-line trench!"*
And the Captain whispered, *"Third-line trench!"*
And the Aide repeated, *"Third-line trench!"*
And Pershing answered,—not in French—
"Yes, I see it. Third-line trench."

Again they marched with wary tread,
Following on where the Sergeant led
Through the wet and the muck as well,
Till they came to another parallel.
They halted there in the mud and drench,
And the Sergeant whispered, *"Second-line trench!"*
And the Captain whispered, *"Second-line trench!"*
And the Aide repeated, *"Second-line trench!"*
And Pershing nodded: *"Second-line trench!"*

Yet on they went through mire like pitch
Till they came to a fine and spacious ditch
Well camouflaged from planes and Zeps
Where soldiers stood on firing steps

And a Major sat on a wooden bench;
And the Sergeant whispered, *"First-line trench!"*
And the Captain whispered, *"First-line trench!"*
And the Aide repeated, *"First-line trench!"*
And Pershing whispered, *"Yes. I see.*
How far off is the enemy?"
And the faithful Aide he asked, asked he,
"How far off is the enemy?"
And the Captain breathed in a softer key,
"How far off is the enemy?"

The silence lay in heaps and piles
As the Sergeant whispered, *"Just three miles."*
And the Captain whispered, *"Just three miles."*
And the Aide repeated, *"Just three miles."*
"Just three miles!" the General swore,
"What in hell are we whispering for?"
And the faithful Aide the message bore,
"What in hell are we whispering for?"
And the Captain said in a gentle roar,
"What in hell are we whispering for?"
"Whispering for?" the echo rolled;
And the Sergeant whispered, *"I have a cold."*

ARTHUR GUITERMAN

St. Brigid

Brigid, the daughter of Duffy, she wasn't like other young things,
Dreaming of lads for her lovers, and twirling her bracelets
      and rings;
Combing and coiling and curling her hair that was black
      as the sloes,
Painting her lips and her cheeks that were ruddy and fresh as
      the rose
Ah, 'twasn't Brigid would waste all her days in such follies
      as these—
Christ was the Lover she worshipped for hour after hour on
      her knees;

Christ and His Church and His poor,—and 'twas many a mile
        that she trod
Serving the loathsome lepers that ever were stricken by God.

Brigid, the daughter of Duffy, she sold all her jewels and gems,
Sold all her finely-spun robes that were braided with gold
        to the hems;
Kept to her back but one garment, one dress that was faded
        and old,
Gave all her goods to the poor who were famished with hunger
        and cold.
Ah, 'twasn't Brigid would fling at the poor the hard word like
        a stone—
Christ the Redeemer she saw in each wretch that was ragged
        and lone;
Every wandering beggar who asked for a bite or a bed
Knocked at her heart like the Man who had nowhere to shelter
        His head.

Brigid, the daughter of Duffy, she angered her father at last.
"Where are your dresses, my daughter? Crom Crauch! You
        wear them out fast!
Where are the chains that I bought you all wrought in red gold
        from the mine?
Where the bright brooches of silver that once on your bosom
        would shine?"
Ah, but 'twas he was the man that was proud of his name and
        his race,
Proud of their prowess in battle and proud of their deeds in
        the chase!
Knew not the Christ, the pale God Whom the priests from afar
        had brought in,
Held to the old Gaelic gods that were known to Cuchulain
        and Finn.

Brigid, the daughter of Duffy, made answer, "O father,"
        said she,
"What is the richest of raiment, and what are bright jewels
        to me?

Lepers of Christ must I care for, the hungry of Christ must
        I feed;
How can I walk in rich robes when His people and mine are
        in need?"
Ah, but 'twas she didn't fear for herself when he blustered
        and swore,
Meekly she bowed when he ordered his chariot brought to
        the door;
Meekly obeyed when he bade her get in at the point of
        his sword,
Knowing whatever her fate she'd be safe with her Lover
        and Lord.

Brigid, the daughter of Duffy, was brought to the court of
        the King,
(Monarch of Leinster, MacEnda, whose praises the poets
        would sing).
"Hither, O monarch," said Duffy, "I've come with a maiden
        to sell;
Buy her and bind her to bondage—she's needing such
        discipline well!"
Ah, but 'twas wise was the King. From the maid to the chieftain
        he turned;
Mildness he saw in her face, in the other 'twas anger
        that burned;
"This is no bondmaid, I'll swear it, O chief, but a girl of
        your own.
Why sells the father the flesh of his flesh and the bone of
        his bone?"

Brigid, the daughter of Duffy, was mute while her
        father replied—
"Monarch, this maid has no place as the child of a chieftain
        of pride.
Beggars and wretches whose wounds would the soul of a
        soldier affright,
Sure, 'tis on these she is wasting my substance from morning
        till night!"

Ah, but 'twas bitter was Duffy; he spoke like a man that
      was vext.
Musing, the monarch was silent; he pondered the
      question perplexed.
"Maiden," said he, "if 'tis true, as I've just from your father
      heard tell,
Might it not be, as my bondmaid, you'd waste all my substance
      as well?"

Brigid, the daughter of Duffy, made answer. "O monarch,"
      she said,
"Had I the wealth from your coffers, and had I the crown from
      your head—
Yea, if the plentiful yield of the broad breasts of Erin were mine,
All would I give to the people of Christ who in poverty pine."
Ah, but 'twas then that the King felt the heart in his
      bosom upleap,
"I am not worthy," he cried, "such a maiden in bondage
      to keep!
Here's a king's sword for her ransom, and here's a king's word
      to decree
Never to other than Christ and His poor let her in servitude be!"

DENIS A. McCARTHY

The
Vizier's
Apology

Sing, Muse, of the anger of Haroun the Caliph
    Aroused by complaints on the Sheik of Irak.
"The scoundrel!" he thundered, "we'll cast him in jail if
    We don't drop him overboard sewn in a sack!

"It seems he has robbed the imperial coffer,
    And witnesses charge him with every abuse.
And think of the rascal disdaining to offer
    Our Clemency even a shred of excuse!"

"It might be as well," said his minister, smiling,
    "To calm the imperial wrath for a time.
Excuses, like charges, are framed for beguiling;
    Besides, the excuse might be worse than the crime."

"What nonsense!" cried Haroun, that monarch effulgent,
    "A fault not as bad as the criminal's plea?"
"Perhaps," said the minister, blandly indulgent,
    "I'll prove to your Highness that such it may be."

The very next morning, superbly attended
    By eunuchs in dozens, and emirs in pairs,
With grandeur befitting the nobly descended
    The Caliph descended the glittering stairs.

Then, daring unspeakable woes and disasters
    And rage that devours its prey like pilaff,
The minister reached through the marble pilasters
    And wickedly pinched the imperial calf!

Aghast at an outrage unthinkably sinister,
    "Dog!" roared the Autocrat, "what do you mean!"
"What a mischance!" wailed the profligate minister;
    "Pardon, your Highness, I thought 'twas the Queen!"

And so, by another experience wiser,
    The Caliph with graciousness truly sublime
Admitted the truth that his faithful adviser
    Had made an excuse that was worse than the crime.

ARTHUR GUITERMAN

Johnnie Armstrong

There dwelt a man in fair Westmoreland,
    Johnnie Armstrong men did him call;
He had neither lands nor rents coming in,
    Yet he kept eight score men in his hall.

He had horse and harness for them all,
    Goodly steeds were all milk-white;
O the golden bands about their necks,
    And their weapons, they were all alike.

News then was brought unto the king
    That there was such a one as he,
That livèd like a bold outlaw,
    And robbèd all the north country.

The king he wrote a letter then,
    A letter which was large and long;
He signèd it with his own hand,
    And he promised to do him no wrong.

When this letter came Johnnie unto,
    His heart was as blythe as birds on the tree:
"Never was I sent for before any king,
    My father, my grandfather, nor none but me.

"And if we go the king before,
    I would we went most orderly;
Every man of you shall have his scarlet cloak,
    Laced with silver laces three.

"Every one of you shall have his velvet coat,
    Laced with silver lace so white;
O the golden bands about your necks,
    Black hats, white feathers, all alike."

By the morrow morning at ten of the clock,
    Towards Edinborough gone was he,
And with him all his eight score men;
    Good Lord, it was a goodly sight for to see!

When Johnnie came before the king,
    He fell down on his knee;
"O pardon, my sovereign liege," he said,
    "O pardon my eight score men and me."

"Thou shalt have no pardon, thou traitor strong,
    For thy eight score men nor thee;
For tomorrow morning by ten of the clock,
    Both thou and them shall hang on the gallow-tree."

But Johnnie looked over his left shoulder,
    Good Lord, what a grievous look looked he!
Saying, "Asking grace of a graceless face—
    Why, there is none for you nor me."

But Johnnie had a bright sword by his side,
    And it was made of the mettle so free,
That had not the king stept his foot aside,
    He had smitten his head from his fair body.

Saying, "Fight on, my merry men all,
    And see that none of you be ta'en;
For rather than men shall say we were hanged,
    Let them report how we were slain."

Then, God knows, fair Edinborough rose,
    And so beset poor Johnnie round,
That four score and ten of Johnnie's best men
    Lay gasping all upon the ground.

Then like a madman Johnnie laid about,
    And like a madman then fought he,
Until a false Scot came Johnnie behind,
    And ran him through the fair body.

Saying, "Fight on, my merry men all,
    I am a little hurt, but I am not slain;
I will lay me down for to bleed a while,
    Then I'll rise and fight with you again."

News then was brought to young Johnnie Armstrong,
    As he stood by his nurse's knee,
Who vowed if e'er he lived for to be a man,
    On the treacherous Scots revenged he'd be.

OLD BALLAD

Barbara Allen

In London City where I once did dwell, there's where I got
       my learning,
I fell in love with a pretty young girl, her name was
       Barbara Allen.
I courted her for seven long years, she said she would not
       have me;
Then straightway home as I could go and liken to a dying.

I wrote her a letter on my death bed, I wrote it slow
       and moving;
"Go take this letter to my old true love and tell her
       I am dying."
She took the letter in her lily-white hand, she read it slow
       and moving;
"Go take this letter back to him, and tell him I am coming."

As she passed by his dying bed she saw his pale lips quivering;
"No better, no better I'll ever be until I get Barbara Allen."
As she passed by his dying bed, "You're very sick and
       almost dying,
No better, no better you will ever be, for you can't get
       Barbara Allen."

As she went down the long stair steps she heard the death
       bell toning,
And every bell appeared to say, "Hard-hearted Barbara Allen!"
As she went down the long piney walk she heard some small
       birds singing,
And every bird appeared to say, "Hard-hearted Barbara Allen!"

She looked to the East, she looked to the West, she saw the
       pale corpse coming
"Go bring them pale corpse unto me, and let me gaze upon them.
Oh, mama, mama, go make my bed, go make it soft
       and narrow!
Sweet Willie died today for me, I'll die for him tomorrow!"

They buried Sweet Willie in the old church yard, they buried
            Miss Barbara beside him;
And out of his grave there sprang a red rose, and out of
            hers a briar.
They grew to the top of the old church tower, they could not
            grow any higher,
They hooked, they tied in a true love's knot, red rose around
            the briar.

**OLD
BALLAD**

The Mermaid

'Twas Friday morn when we set sail,
And we were not far from the land,
When the captain spied a lovely mermaid,
With a comb and a glass in her hand.

CHORUS:
O, the ocean waves may roll, and the stormy winds may blow,
While we poor sailors go skipping to the tops,
And the land lubbers lie down below, below, below,
And the land lubbers lie down below.

Then up spake the captain of our gallant ship,
And a well-spoken man was he:
"I have married a wife in Salem town.
And tonight she a widow will be."

Then up spake the cook of our gallant ship,
And a red-hot cook was he:
"I care much more for my kettles and my pots,
Than I do for the depths of the sea."

Then three times around went our gallant ship,
And three times around went she;
Then three times around went our gallant ship,
And she sank to the depths of the sea.

OLD BALLAD

Geary's
   Rock

Come all you true-born shanty-boys, wherever you may be,
I hope you'll pay attention and listen unto me.
It's all about some shanty-boys, so manly and so brave.
'Twas on the jam on Geary's Rock they met their watery grave.

'Twas on one Sunday morning as you shall quickly hear,
Our logs were piled up mountain-high, we could not keep
       them clear,
"Turn out, brave boys," the foreman cried, with a voice devoid
       of fear,
"And we'll break the jam on Geary's Rock and for Eagletown
       we'll steer."

Some of the boys were willing, while the others hid from sight.
For to break a jam on Sunday, they thought it was not right.
But six American shanty-boys did volunteer to go
To break the jam on Geary's Rock with their foreman,
       young Monroe.

They had not rolled off many logs before the boss to them
       did say,
"I would you all to be on your guard, for the jam will soon
       give way."
He had no more than spoke those words before the jam did
       break and go,
And carried away those six brave youths with their foreman,
       young Monroe.

Now when the news got into camp and attorneys came to hear,
In search of their dead bodies down the river we did steer,
And one of their dead bodies found, to our great grief and woe,
All bruised and mangled on the beach lay the corpse of
          young Monroe.

We took him from the water, smoothed back his raven-black hair,
There was one fair form amongst them whose cries did rend
          the air,
There was one fair form amongst them, a girl from Saginaw
          town,
Whose mournful cries did rend the skies for her lover that
          was drowned.

We buried him quite decently. 'Twas on the twelfth of May,
Come all you jolly shanty-boys, and for your comrade pray.
We engraved upon a hemlock tree that near his grave
          did grow—
The name, the age, and the drownding date of the foreman,
          young Monroe.

His mother was a widow living down by the river side.
Miss Clark she was a noble girl, this young man's promised bride.
The wages of her own true love the firm to her did pay,
And liberal subscription she received from the shanty-boys
          that day.

She received their presents kindly and thanked them every one,
Though she did not survive him long, as you shall understand;
Scarcely three weeks after, and she was called to go,
And her last request was to be laid by her lover, young Monroe.

Come all you true-born shanty-boys, who would like to go
          and see
Two green mounds by the river bank where grows the
          hemlock tree;
The shanty-boys cut the woods all round. These lovers they
          lie low—
'Tis the handsome Clara Clark and her true love, brave Monroe.

LUMBERJACK BALLAD

Lord Randal

"O where hae ye been, Lord Randal, my son?
O where hae ye been, my handsome young man?"—
"I hae been to the wild wood; mother, make my bed soon,
For I'm weary wi' hunting, and fain wad lie down."

"Where gat ye your dinner, Lord Randal, my son?
Where gat ye your dinner, my handsome young man?"—
"I dined wi' my true-love; mother, make my bed soon,
For I'm weary wi' hunting, and fain wad lie down."

"What gat ye to your dinner, Lord Randal, my son?
What gat ye to your dinner, my handsome young man?"
"I gat eels boil'd in broo'; mother, make my bed soon,
For I'm weary wi' hunting, and fain wad lie down."

"What became of your bloodhounds, Lord Randal, my son?
What became of your bloodhounds, my handsome
          young man?"—
"O they swell'd and they died; mother, make my bed soon,
For I'm weary wi' hunting, and fain wad lie down."

"O I fear ye are poison'd, Lord Randal, my son!
O I fear ye are poison'd, my handsome young man!"—
"O yes! I am poison'd; mother, make my bed soon,
For I'm sick at the heart, and I fain wad lie down."

**OLD
BALLAD**

SUMMING UP

I. Identify these terms:

—A

narrative poetry	couplet
story pattern	rhythm
metrical tale	rhyme
ballad	refrain
ballad stanza	simple repetition

—B

simple image	personification
denotation	animation
connotation	rhythm pattern
simile	rhyme pattern
metaphor	quatrain

—C

sound patterns	onomatopoeia
nonsense refrain	rising rhythm
consonance	assonance
falling rhythm	legend
alliteration	fable

—D

myth	tall tale
saint's legend	feminine rhyme
parable	masculine rhyme
hero story	imperfect rhyme
fairy tale	stock response

II. Know each poem in terms of

    —A story structure

    —B classification

    —C characteristics

    —D summary of story with characters

Grammar and Usage

SUPPLEMENTARY EXERCISES

Part of the challenge of becoming a student is to be able to analyze your own learning problems and to work at solving them. The following exercises will help you acquire understandings and habits you may be lacking in certain areas of usage and grammar.

Grammar and Usage

SUPPLEMENTARY EXERCISES

Predicating

SENTENCES—NATURE: Number your paper from one to ten. After each, write COMPLETE if the group of words is a sentence and INCOMPLETE if it is not.

EXERCISE A

1. Does Mary really know her lesson
2. The storm frightened Bob and his friends
3. Her coming to help me
4. Has the committee started another drive
5. Under the circumstances he cannot come
6. About to begin the process of simplification
7. The rain kept falling lazily all day
8. Over-production causes enforced leisure
9. Henry, driving at fifty miles an hour
10. Is her original idea included in this new theory

EXERCISE B

1. The men were ordered to defend the fort until death
2. To carry out the order quickly and effectively
3. The inquest indicted the entertainment committee
4. Speaking of twenty-four student leaders
5. Will be asked to help those who need it
6. There is no better way to accomplish this purpose
7. Where do all the profits go
8. The final struggle for the bridge has started
9. Many officers and men were freed
10. When will the council begin to act

EXERCISE **C**

1. Glancing up in order to see the road
2. After the shower had begun
3. The steamship company would not permit it
4. Suddenly the wind changed
5. A good imagination is an admirable quality
6. What holds your interest in the story
7. Examples of bad sportsmanship on the football field
8. There are many historical references in his writings
9. Acquiring a good vocabulary after years of practice
10. The pattern which Mary had originally used

SENTENCES—SUBJECT AND PREDICATE: Number your paper from one to ten. In each exercise, write the subject and the predicate of each sentence.

EXERCISE **A**

1. The careless spendthrift died in poverty.
2. The rising sun glittered on the snow-capped hills.
3. Influenza is killing thousands of people.
4. The western sky is massed with golden clouds.
5. Spring rains are a menace to our local bridges.
6. Ceaseless snow sifted into the valleys and ravines.
7. The storm littered the coast with wreckage.
8. The beautiful city was almost completely destroyed.
9. The raging fire spread from the barn to the house.
10. Morning found us stranded on an island.

EXERCISE **B**

1. Laughter is a tonic for the gloomy.
2. The grassy slopes looked lovely in the moonlight.
3. Kind words consoled the sensitive child.
4. Scarred forests are reminders of the awful war.
5. All creation reflects order and purpose.
6. True valor is often unrecognized.
7. The general entered the building cautiously.
8. Fitful light shone on the mass of wreckage.
9. The unhappy man found no pleasure in his money.
10. The neglected poor have the heaviest burden.

1. Every boy felt proud to be in the school.
2. In outward circumstances he was less happy than Jim.
3. All his books were torn and ragged.
4. The cry for help was flashing across the country.
5. Freedom had exacted its price from this forsaken dog.
6. For half an hour the bell continued to sound.
7. Lightning and storm were believed by the Romans to be a prediction of danger.
8. Count the game already lost.
9. No one could realize her sudden change in disposition.
10. There was a bulky manuscript lying on the table.

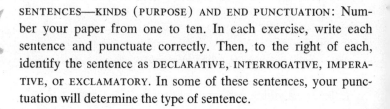

SENTENCES—KINDS (PURPOSE) AND END PUNCTUATION: Number your paper from one to ten. In each exercise, write each sentence and punctuate correctly. Then, to the right of each, identify the sentence as DECLARATIVE, INTERROGATIVE, IMPERATIVE, or EXCLAMATORY. In some of these sentences, your punctuation will determine the type of sentence.

EXERCISE **A**

1. Are Mary and June in the library
2. Thoughtlessness often brings dreadful disaster
3. Enter at the right and leave at the left
4. Do the girls know their papers are due
5. What in the world shall I do
6. Who can help me now
7. Beware of the dog
8. Listen to the record while there is yet time
9. Truth will ultimately triumph over error
10. Live justly and have no fear

EXERCISE **B**

1. The proud man knows no happiness
2. When did you finish your work
3. A little child shall lead them
4. Do not let yourself be misled

5. Liberty is responsibiity
6. Linda prefers riding to swimming
7. True happiness is found in little things
8. When will we learn the things that are vital to our peace
9. Peace is the fruit of justice
10. Love justice and fight evil

EXERCISE **C**

1. Under the spreading chestnut tree the village smithy stands
2. Gather the flowers while you may
3. What will be the effect on the person who reads that book
4. Scientific magazines have educational material
5. Our class ought to develop interest in European problems
6. Have you given much thought to possible future careers
7. The drawbridge dropped with a surly clang
8. How happy is he whose only armour is simple truth
9. Above the orchard the clouds were slowly drifting
10. Hear the tolling of the bells

SENTENCES—KINDS (STRUCTURE): In each exercise, number your paper from one to ten. After each number write SIMPLE, COMPOUND, COMPLEX, or COMPOUND-COMPLEX according to the number and kind of clauses each sentence contains.

EXERCISE **A**

1. After all the cards had been sorted, we stacked them alphabetically.
2. Jane wanted to run for class president, but her mother thought the office would be too great a responsibility.
3. If all of us go, the crowd will be too large.
4. Into every life some rain must fall.
5. The boys who were on the team were dismissed, but everyone else stayed until 3:30.
6. Can you tell by looking at this whether it will hold our books or not?
7. John is not only the fastest runner on the team but also the highest jumper.

8. Our school received a high rating last year, but we are anxious about this year's report.

9. Close the door, Jane, or the mosquitoes will get in.

10. To be a good secretary, one must be accurate, dependable, friendly, and observant.

EXERCISE **B**

1. At the time of Agamemnon's murder, Orestes is hustled away to safety by his sister, Electra.

2. Orestes grows up in exile, and Pylades, son of King Strophius, becomes his inseparable companion.

3. Because she remains loyal to her father's memory, Electra is treated as a slave by her mother.

4. When he has grown to manhood, Orestes returns and, with the help of Pylades, kills Aegisthus and Clytemnestra.

5. Pylades marries Electra, and they live happily together for some time.

6. Because he killed his mother, Orestes is pursued by the Furies, and he appeals to Apollo.

7. Apollo tells him to go to the land of the Taurians and bring back "the sister," so he sets off with Pylades to the strange land.

8. Orestes thinks he is to bring back a statue of Apollo's sister Artemis.

9. Just as Pylades and Orestes are being made sacrifice-victims, the priestess recognizes Orestes as her brother, and they escape together.

10. These are just a few of the many stories found in Greek literature relating the tragedies of the house of Atreus.

EXERCISE **C**

1. Since you insist on perfection, I will do this lesson again; but don't rush me.

2. Along the riverbank some rare plants and flowers can be found.

3. Are all members who are eligible going to compete for the prize?

4. The boys will have only five minutes to complete the exercise, but the girls will have six minutes.

5. Getting into college today takes foresight, ambition, perseverance, and money.

6. After we won the game, both teams came to our cafeteria for a run-down.

7. Now that you know the facts you can decide for yourself who is guilty, but try to avoid prejudice.

8. Mary promised not only to wash the dishes but also to set the table.

9. Send the letter airmail, dear, or it will not reach him in time.

10. Janet proposed that the girls plan a surprise party for Mrs. Curtis.

VERBS—NATURE AND KINDS (ACTION—LINKING): Write each of the sentences in these three exercises and underline the verbs. Then, to the right, write **A** if the verb expresses *action;* write **L** if it is a *linking* verb.

EXERCISE **A**

1. General agreement is difficult to reach.
2. The majority approve of this name.
3. The order applies to city employees.
4. Civil servants are satisfied.
5. The act reduced the number of applicants.
6. The new members demand new rights.
7. Government policies change with administrations.
8. The audience was eloquent in praise of the symphony.
9. Caracarra conducted with great artistry.
10. The first production of the play drew a large crowd.

EXERCISE **B**

1. The play will be a great success.
2. The music emphasized the beauty of the words.
3. The professor referred specifically to the Greek poem.
4. The governor's daughter was one of the applicants.
5. They sent us word of the meeting.
6. The message is not very clear.
7. The question bothered the council for a long time.
8. This attitude leads inevitably to failure.

9. The girls behaved like college boys.

10. I led the group successfully.

EXERCISE **C**

1. Her family was steeped in cultural traditions.

2. The result of our conversation is given in this document.

3. Education was another topic under consideration.

4. My employer hailed me with exaggerated cordiality.

5. Academic and scientific men, in turn, puzzled Anderson.

6. His sister writes his letters for negotiating with publishers.

7. The library contained many rare volumes.

8. Prominent artists brought their influence to bear on the situation.

9. He made his first lecture tour in 1937.

10. Does this plan correspond with your original idea?

VERBS—KINDS (TRANSITIVE—INTRANSITIVE—LINKING): Write the sentences in these three exercises, skipping every second line. Underline each verb. Above each verb write its classification: TRANSITIVE, INTRANSITIVE, or LINKING.

EXERCISE **A**

1. If all of us go, the crowd will be too large.

2. Our team won the state championship last year, but we are expecting stronger competition this year.

3. Pylades marries Electra, and they live happily for some time.

4. Helen said that she would go to the game with us.

5. Close the door, Jane, or the mosquitoes will get in.

6. John is the only boy in his class who is going to M. I. T.

7. Before we tackle that problem, I suggest that we settle this one.

8. The woods are lovely, dark and deep, But I have promises to keep.

9. You are not responsible for what others have done.

10. She is the type of person who wants everything in order.

1. I am confident that we can reach a settlement.

2. Stop that noise, children, or we will send you upstairs.

3. The river is swollen and almost ready to overflow.

4. Unless we put sandbags along the banks, we shall have a flood by tomorrow.

5. Did Mother send for the dress that she wanted?

6. I will consider well what you have said.

7. A true lover is constant, even when the one whom he loves is faithless.

8. All at once they heard a melodious sound.

9. *The Canterbury Tales* is a collection of stories which Geoffrey Chaucer wrote in 1387.

10. There are twenty-four tales in the collection, but the prologue and the links between the stories are as good as the tales.

1. When I took the first survey of our project, I saw that there was a great deal of work ahead of us.

2. "What is truth?" said jesting Pilate, and would not stay for an answer.

3. *Hamlet* is the most controversial play ever written; even its bibliography fills a large volume.

4. But most readers will agree that *Hamlet* is the most fascinating of all plays; indeed it must have been Shakespeare's favorite, for he revised it more than once.

5. Tell me not in mournful numbers/Life is but an empty dream.

6. Will you go on the trip with us, or will you stay home tomorrow?

7. I thought he said she is his sister.

8. When you have done all that you can, stop at my room and tell me how she is.

9. Milk is a perfect food; it contains a great deal of protein.

10. We would be very happy if you would come to our house for supper.

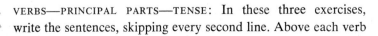VERBS—PRINCIPAL PARTS—TENSE: In these three exercises, write the sentences, skipping every second line. Above each verb

write **R** if it is a regular verb and **I** if it is an irregular verb. To the right of each sentence write the present, past, and past participle of the verb.

1. That country chooses its foreign ministers carefully.
2. John brought his bicycle here for repairs.
3. By law I possess the right to vote.
4. You have lost much of your facility.
5. Alfred certainly speaks frequently during the discussion.
6. Very seldom she shrinks from duty.
7. His book gives us a greater appreciation of poetry.
8. Poets say everything most beautifully.
9. The welfare worker seeks to alleviate the sufferings of the poor.
10. A picture sometimes teaches better than words.

EXERCISE **B**

1. This fantasy has an ironic situation.
2. My sister took her orchestral practice seriously.
3. It required great effort to acquire an education.
4. We appreciate America in many ways.
5. He made an attempt to acquaint himself with our rules.
6. Mr. Ross swims three times daily.
7. Louise always forgets her lines.
8. By their very nature men desire to live socially.
9. The class discusses all these points individually.
10. Children are easy imitators of their teachers.

EXERCISE **C**

1. Kindness draws human beings together.
2. At twenty-one man becomes an adult citizen.
3. The body needs its calories and vitamins.
4. We both hold the idea to be impractical.
5. Man seeks for the beautiful, the true, and the good.
6. Poets share with readers their experience.
7. Composers see nature as a source of inspiration.
8. I know the handwriting is Mary's.

9. The artist chose a vivid scene.

10. Miss Jakon gave us so little time to complete the work.

Naming

NOUNS—NATURE AND FUNCTION: In these three exercises write each sentence, skipping every second line. Underline each noun. Above each write its use in the sentence: SUBJ., DIR. OBJ., IND. OBJ., SUBJ. COMPL., APPOSITIVE, OBJ. COMPL., OBJ. OF PREP.

EXERCISE **A**

1. The site of the Oklahoma Public Library has been approved by the donors.

2. The dark green clump of trees attracted the tourists as they drove toward the park site.

3. As Ethel entered her homeroom, she saw her little green parakeet fly through the open window.

4. Where is the young lady with the neat hair-do and pleasant smile?

5. Bill is a tall, robust, sandy-haired individual who loves football and spends a good part of his time on the practice field.

6. Miss Degler, the librarian at the Chicago Public Library, gave Jean the correct history text.

7. The devoted parents, Mr. and Mrs. John J. Hill, named their child Mary.

8. Here is the very case which I have tried to buy since Mrs. Barry saw me last year.

9. Did the principal of McKinley High School attend the forum on Latin America?

10. Where could Marie have filed her set of papers when the office was being painted?

EXERCISE **B**

1. Mark Smith, that level-headed freshman of 204, has joined the debate group for the coming year.

2. When Irene walked into my study, Tom spied his friend and offered to take him home.

3. Although tennis and sailing are his favorite sports, Don also enjoys baseball.

4. Mother could have sent Anne her package if we had known her address.

5. As soon as Miss Doherty finishes the last number, she will dismiss the sopranos.

6. The honesty of the girl impressed the group to such an extent that she was invited to become a member of their club.

7. Gusts of rain blurred the vision of the drivers.

8. The principles set down by the remaining officers were carefully followed.

9. Such a variety of trees and flowers add special beauty to the college grounds.

10. An increased interest in art will continue in her life.

EXERCISE **C**

1. Mr. Hansen, the president of the Canadian Air Lines, will preside at the last meeting for jet pilots at McCormick Place.

2. The guest insisted that Mary should accept the package.

3. Captain Becker directed Tom to the nearest gas station.

4. To the amazement of Mr. Burg, Tim and Terry received the coveted government jobs.

5. Wheat, an important grain, is used in many breads today.

6. Erosion has destroyed much valuable land which the country needs.

7. Upon her arrival, Rose joined her group at the beach.

8. Should Mr. Ludwig investigate the new trends?

9. The science experiment must prove his point.

10. Sharon became the dearest child of the entire group.

NOUNS—PUNCTUATION OF APPOSITIVES: Most of the following sentences contain appositives. Write each one with the correct punctuation.

EXERCISE **A**

1. Margaret an unusually poor speller a slow reader and a hasty thinker had a talk with her English teacher.

2. Mr. Radigan head coach at Township High teaches history.

3. Chicago the greatest railroad center in the world is strategically located in the Midwest.

4. Shirley Nichols the famous poet is also renowned for her beautiful prose.

5. Dickens' great novel *A Tale of Two Cities* gives dramatic insight into the French Revolution.

6. My uncle Joe and my brother Bill went fishing up north with Al Collins a neighbor.

7. Have you read Dickens' great autobiographical novel *David Copperfield?*

8. Earling a little town in Iowa competes in various ways with its neighbor town Westphalia.

9. The Pullman car porter was most willing to assist three important passengers the President of the United States his wife and the Vice-president.

10. Have you read these three novels by Dickens *Great Expectations David Copperfield* and *Bleak House?*

EXERCISE **B**

1. In a few days we received an answer a most courteous reply explaining the oversight.

2. After the class was over, we all went up to Mr. Brown our very energetic history teacher to ask two favors an extension of time on the assignment and a postponement of the test.

3. The main character Silas Marner becomes a miser because human friendship has failed him.

4. Some people think that co-education the favorite American system does not give girls a true education.

5. My cousin Edward is very annoying, but Walter my favorite uncle can always silence him.

6. The porter an elderly man was most courteous and thoughtful, observing all our needs before we asked.

7. Some sophomores can't even spell the word *sophomore.*

8. Calculus a very complicated branch of mathematics attracts students who like numbers.

9. Bill Stevens a newcomer to York has three hobbies photography coin collecting and whittling.

10. Scrabble our own American word game differs in many ways from dominoes an imported game.

EXERCISE **C**

1. John the brother of the president of the senior class is entering high school this year.

2. His favorite nieces Joan Martha and Lenore will all work in his office after graduation.

3. Chicago the largest city in Illinois is not the capital.

4. Have you met Robert Frost a famous American poet?

5. In February many sports fans are attracted by the Ice Capades a favorite winter entertainment.

6. Joe Louis the former heavyweight champion struggled against poverty in his youth.

7. He returned the overdue novel *The Friendly Persuasion*.

8. Although Bill enjoyed activity, he could find delight in fishing the poor man's sport.

9. Overcoming many obstacles, Glenn Cunningham a great track star achieved the success he desired.

10. The poet Sarett was born in Chicago.

NOUNS—NATURE AND KINDS: Number your paper from one to ten. Write all the nouns of these exercises. After each common noun write the letter **C** and after each proper noun write the letter **P**.

EXERCISE **A**

1. The area around the Black Sea is important.

2. The Americas are trying to establish closer alliance.

3. The group includes many prominent figures.

4. There is a sharp disagreement as to method.

5. The enemy is retreating on all fronts.

6. Our destiny is in the hands of God.

7. A virtuous life is our only security against ultimate disaster.

8. Americans sell their products at low prices in Canada.

9. The climate of the extreme West is delightful.

10. The girls do not work on Monday.

EXERCISE **B**

1. We all love the balmy days of spring.

2. Three generals participated in the debate.

3. The captain sailed the seven seas.

4. We know that General Waters was present.

5. We listened attentively while the professor explained his theory.

6. There are many who do not agree with his theory.

7. One of the cold months is January.

8. Their case for higher wages is sound.

9. Have you heard about the Wage Act?

10. The Mesley twins often go skating together.

EXERCISE **C**

1. Mr. Nichols is a prolific writer of both verse and prose.

2. Padraic Colum, the poet, is Irish by birth, education, and culture.

3. Mary had an intense devotion to science from her earliest years.

4. Did you complete your education at Holdstam University?

5. Gerald was born in Paris, where his parents were then visiting.

6. Harry is the kind of boy who loves excitement more than study.

7. Benito Mussolini ruled Italy as a dictator.

8. If suffering is endured, it can become ennobling.

9. We always judge events according to our own experience.

10. Frank developed his ability during his college days at Lehigh.

NOUNS—RULES OF CAPITALIZATION: In these exercises, number your paper from one to ten. Look at each sentence carefully. If any word which should begin with a small letter is capitalized, or if any word that should be capitalized begins with a small letter, write that word correctly after the proper number.

EXERCISE **A**

1. My uncle went to the west to regain his health.

2. Our guide had told us to turn West at the first crossing.

3. My mother knew she must obey doctor Taylor's instructions.

4. The French ambassador was conspicuous by his absence.

5. Have you studied any European History?

6. The republican Assembly met on the thirteenth of June.

7. A group of spanish dancers toured the British Isles last year.

8. the wind was a torrent of darkness among the gusty trees,
the moon was a ghostly galleon tossed upon cloudy seas.

9. *I believe* was written by Douglas Hyde.

10. All through the winter the basketball equipment was much in demand.

EXERCISE **B**

1. Reading some English literature does promote literary appreciation and knowledge.

2. There is much cotton produced in the south.

3. I have never been to a democratic Convention.

4. My brother is studying the french language very diligently.

5. The audience grew restless as the senator from Maine continued his speech.

6. the curfew tolls the knell of parting day,
the lowing herd winds slowly o'er the lea,

7. No reason could be discovered for lieutenant Patterson's disastrous action.

8. *American men of science* is a directory of brief biographies.

9. We thought our boat was drifting steadily to the East.

10. March twenty-first is the first day of Spring.

EXERCISE **C**

1. One of my most difficult courses in school was taught by miss Blackstone.

2. At our next meeting the president will preside.

3. Do you ever read The *New York Times?*

4. This Summer we will be able to use the tennis courts more frequently.

5. The first half of the eighteenth century marked a rapid expansion to the west.

6. Her brother joined the marine corps recently.

7. the world is too much with us; late and soon,
getting and spending, we lay waste our powers;

8. Our school has duplicate copies of *the fundamentals of astronomy.*

9. As Miller traveled South on highway 12, the landscape became more and more beautiful.

10. It was hard for the ambassador to adapt himself to chinese customs.

NOUNS—NUMBER: Number your paper from one to ten for each exercise. Write the plural of each of these nouns.

EXERCISE **A**

1. pulley	**4.** brush	**7.** herd	**10.** peach
2. scout	**5.** fox	**8.** policeman	**11.** echo
3. pansy	**6.** prayer	**9.** chief	**12.** cry

EXERCISE **B**

1. box	**4.** piano	**7.** mass	**10.** case
2. donkey	**5.** society	**8.** leaf	**11.** buffalo
3. bundle	**6.** tomato	**9.** button	**12.** berry

EXERCISE **C**

1. wharf	**4.** garden	**7.** cookie	**10.** branch
2. diary	**5.** chorus	**8.** dress	**11.** soprano
3. brush	**6.** crowd	**9.** ox	**12.** church

NOUNS—NUMBER (AGREEMENT): Number your paper from one to ten. If the verb agrees with its subject, write the word COR-RECT next to the number; if it does not agree, write the correct form.

EXERCISE **A**

1. Her hair are her most attractive feature.

2. The instruction, with particular details, were repeated over the communication system.

3. That group of students were not present for the last lecture.

4. Is this the table on which the scissors was found?

5. This sort of apples is very edible.

6. Either Amy or her sister are capable of taking over the class in your absence.

7. There are no end to the complaints about Robert's work.

8. In the last edition the bibliography and the index is in small type.

9. The mob were forced back onto the narrow bridge.

10. Kevin don't think it necessary to observe the rules.

EXERCISE **B**

1. This kind of books are interesting reading.

2. Either the painting or the sketch are going to be exhibited.

3. Because of the limited time the topic, with its many subdivisions, were not discussed.

4. Your sister's hair are not as dark as yours.

5. The large scissors is preferable for cutting woolen material.

6. In our course for this semester that school of musicians are not included.

7. Our class agree on that debatable question.

8. After one has studied physics, meteorology and astronomy does not present insurmountable difficulties.

9. There are no correct list of rules accompanying the game.

10. The assignment don't have to be completed by Monday.

EXERCISE **C**

1. Our class is disagreeing about the new auditorium.

2. Has this type of verbs been studied?

3. The scissors is in the second drawer.

4. Either her mother or her father send her books on her birthday.

5. Observation and careful experimentation forms the basis of that report.

6. The problem of reconstruction, with its many difficulties, are the responsibility of the whole world.

7. Are your hair going to be arranged differently tonight?

8. There is no data to sustain your proof.

9. That display of fruit baskets were presented by convalescent patients.

10. Mary don't answer for anyone's safety.

NOUNS—POSSESSIVE CASE: How many possessive nouns are you able to find in the following exercise? Write each sentence and draw a circle around each one. If it is used *correctly,* write CORRECT to the right; if it used *incorrectly,* write the correct form.

EXERCISE **A**

1. The photographer specializes in childrens' portraits.
2. That story brings out this authors' favorite themes.
3. Mary's and Lou's mother is very ill.
4. Poets' observations are not always true to factual reality.
5. This is exclusively a womens' store.
6. The babies' portraits were arranged across the mantelpiece.
7. The secretary and the treasurer's reports were accepted.
8. Helen's record is good, but her sisters is better.
9. The animal's teeth are sharp and its claws are long.
10. When the boys' father refused his exaggerated claim, his mother conceded.

EXERCISE **B**

1. The states jurisdiction begins with its laws.
2. Will the army's entrance into town relieve our allies?
3. The workmen are redecorating the juniors' and seniors' lunchroom.
4. The clothiers and the carpenters' unions admitted new members at the beginning of last month.
5. Womens' interest in political affairs has gradually become more apparent.
6. Teacher's conventions meet in the last week of September.
7. The oxens' carts were heavily loaded.
8. The boys' hat was pulled down low.
9. The Country Club closed the season with a ladies' golf tournament.
10. Our friends are likewise Marys' friends.

EXERCISE **C**

1. The shopkeeper left the childrens' school supplies in the window longer than usual.
2. Is the new invention in the owners possession?
3. Harrys and Williams experiments were both successful.

4. Tuesday is the junior's day for entertaining.

5. The thieves scheme admitted of no flaw.

6. Here is an account of that new reporters' achievements.

7. Many interruptions disturbed the gentlemens' discussion.

8. The two mices' tails were caught in the trap.

9. Ted's and Fred's tool chest has been ordered.

10. Jame's is the solution we finally used.

NOUNS—PHRASES AND CLAUSES: In these three exercises, write each sentence. Underline each noun clause or noun phrase. To the right explain the use as SUBJECT, OBJECT OF VERB, OBJECT OF PREPOSITION, SUBJECTIVE COMPLEMENT, or APPOSITIVE.

EXERCISE A

1. That Africa is a large continent is a well known fact.

2. It is not true, however, that Africa can be considered as one large land.

3. Many people do not realize that Africa is made up of many countries which vary in size from small to large.

4. Whoever visits Africa today will find very restless but determined people.

5. Today Africans are looking for education and for whatever else the free peoples of the world possess.

6. For whoever dabbles in legend and printer's ink, the Africa of the safari and the witch doctor is rich but ancient history.

7. The new Africa belongs to whichever form of government proves most attractive to the people.

8. What is unquestionable is that Africa is constantly changing.

9. What the future of Africa will be we cannot predict.

10. That future, however, will be whatever the people themselves choose to make it.

EXERCISE B

1. Imagine that you are traveling along a new toll road.

2. There is something, whatever it is, in the distance.

3. Your driver, wiser than you, identifies what is ahead as the toll station.

4. You are astonished. Can he mean what he says?

5. It's true. Whoever drives up to the station stops and pays.

6. You, of course, must do what they are doing.

7. You brace yourself for what seems to you an incredible act of bravery.

8. Your friend wonders that you should be frightened at a mechanical toll station.

9. "Toll! Good heavens! What you were saying, I thought, was 'troll.' "

10. "I have never been able to forget what I read in a book of fairy tales about that terrible troll who lived under the bridge."

EXERCISE **C**

1. Give the box to whomever you find in the office.

2. I knew what the note contained, and I was not too happy to receive the command.

3. After the game we plan to make sundaes.

4. Going to the beach is my favorite summer diversion.

5. I don't understand how Mary writes so well.

6. Deliver the message to whoever comes to the door.

7. The fact that she was popular gave her no special privileges.

8. A good swim in Lake Michigan is perfect for keeping cool on a hot day.

9. Can "after the game" be used as an adjective?

10. That two plus two equals four is not a matter of faith but of fact.

NOUNS—PUNCTUATION OF DIRECT QUOTATIONS: In these three exercises, write the sentences and punctuate them correctly.

EXERCISE **A**

1. She's not at home the voice on the telephone answered

2. Mary I insisted you've got to clean your own room

3. I heard her say Did you ever see such a child

4. The crowd began to chant We want a touchdown

5. Who first said the words We are such stuff as dreams are made of

6. Can you tell me she asked the way to Bond Street

7. Where are you going John demanded Let me go with you
8. In a rage he screamed Give me back my balloon
9. There are two ways to sail the Captain retorted and I know both of them
10. Where can I meet you he inquired

1. I hardly know how to begin Joan faltered
2. If only his mother grieved he had taken my advice.
3. They shouted that they had found the stream
4. What sort of men the boy asked were the pioneers
5. Fourscore and seven years ago is the beginning of the Gettysburg Address
6. Really, Tim his sister said you could be fair about that pie
7. Will they never learn to punctuate the teacher wondered
8. The old man roared Get off the grass
9. Lucy's favorite expression is Good grief, Charlie Brown
10. If you leave Dad insisted be sure to lock the door carefully

1. I am constantly being warned Don't do this or Don't do that
2. It's amazing the coach declared what that boy can do with a basketball
3. Since I can't sew anyway A stitch in time saves nine doesn't help me much
4. The trouble with me she wept is that I forgot all the answers
5. What does one do he inquired when one has two hours in which to do four hours of homework
6. Read the fable to which Thurber attaches the following moral Don't count your boobies until they are hatched
7. Don't pretend innocence Mom scolded This time I saw you reach for the cookie jar
8. The new groom announced Mother-in-law trouble has begun already
9. What good does it do she asked the chairman to prepare all this food beforehand
10. The old proverb says Rolling stones gather no moss

PRONOUNS—NATURE: Number your paper from one to ten. After each number, write the pronouns that occur in each sentence of these exercises. Ignore possessive pronominal adjectives like *his* in the phrase *his book*.

EXERCISE A

1. He died before his eighteenth birthday.
2. She worked her way through our college.
3. To her Harry owed his accomplishments.
4. We do not value our challenges sufficiently.
5. Anyone may take his choice.
6. You are requested to place your offering here.
7. Our sincere thanks are for you.
8. America is our land and we are her citizens.
9. He says that their work is satisfactory.
10. Their advice has brought success to us.

EXERCISE B

1. Each is asked to do his share.
2. Someone is responsible for our trouble.
3. Few knew the depth of her sorrow.
4. Whoever asks will receive his share.
5. He cannot expect his pay.
6. Whom are you asking to see?
7. Whose books did they find on the floor?
8. Who can rely on his friends in need?
9. We need our friends and they need us.
10. Their work freed them from anxiety.

EXERCISE C

1. Many are called but few are chosen.
2. Will this course benefit me in my present position?
3. Each made some contribution to the bazaar.
4. Study of the weather is essential to them.
5. Have you visited the Field Museum?
6. Everyone knows that he is a very competent accountant.
7. We have enjoyed the beauty of a peaceful summer evening.
8. They will attend the art classes this season.

9. Some of us should be able to assist him.
10. Neither of us would venture first from the fishing craft.

PRONOUNS—NATURE AND KINDS: Write each of the sentences in these three exercises and underline the pronouns in each. To the right of each sentence, tell whether they are PERSONAL, RELATIVE, or INTERROGATIVE.

EXERCISE A

1. The lady seemed so nice that I wondered who she was.
2. Give him the book before he asks for it.
3. What is it you wanted to know?
4. There are no books here which you can read.
5. Did you notice the man who walked out just now?
6. This is my friend Tim, whom you met last evening.
7. I heard you ask what right we had to be here.
8. Who was finally elected?
9. "What's the use?" is John's favorite expression.
10. "I will not," she insisted, "say what was done."

EXERCISE B

1. They are the people who will regret that decision.
2. Can you distinguish me from my twin sister?
3. What do you suppose they will do to us?
4. I am too tired to ask.
5. What do you plan to study?
6. Have you decided to study?
7. Mary was determined she would never be late again.
8. Ione invited Mary and me to her cocktail party.
9. By whom was the speech delivered?
10. Did he ask you to carry his book?

EXERCISE C

1. What has he done with that new lamp?
2. John wondered to what he would be driven next.
3. They are the very people for whom I was looking.
4. Who will help me move these books?
5. Which is the better of the two pictures?

6. He refused to see her until she apologized.
7. Whose jacket are you wearing?
8. There are no boys here whom I can trust.
9. She spoke to them with great reluctance.
10. He is the sort of person whom I admire.

PRONOUNS—CASE—NUMBER (SUBJECT PERSONAL): Number your paper from one to ten. After each number, write only the subject pronouns and the pronouns in the nominative case after linking verbs. After each pronoun write its person and its number. Indicate the person by **1**, **2**, or **3**; and indicate the number by **S** if the pronoun is singular and by **P** if it is plural. EXAMPLE: *It is Mary.* IT **3-S**.

EXERCISE **A**

1. I am of the opinion that Mary is correct.
2. Do you, Sue and Jo, know what time it is?
3. He did his work satisfactorily.
4. We are convinced of the necessity of co-operation.
5. They concluded the debate hurriedly.
6. Several persons were waiting. Who were they?
7. She practiced for eleven hours.
8. The ball has disappeared. Where is it?
9. Who are we to question your integrity?
10.. Mary remarked that one of the group was she.

EXERCISE **B**

1. Are you really charter members?
2. The judge knew they were the guilty ones.
3. Can he be of any help?
4. When will we learn to accept the responsibility?
5. They are courageous who face reality.
6. The teacher knows that you are a diligent student.
7. Shall I always be satisfied with mediocrity?
8. Can you see it from this distance?
9. Where did she acquire such facility?
10. John and he remained to the last.

1. We never contact others without influencing them.
2. In his attempts at reformation he was apparently tireless.
3. It is not reasonable that we should remain unsupporting.
4. We learned that others had been admitted before us.
5. Can he ever repay so great a debt?
6. They promised to consider the matter.
7. To understand his life you need historical background.
8. They strongly upheld the principles of popular sovereignty.
9. She was the cause of my unusual experience.
10. I trembled under the sense of my responsibility.

PRONOUNS—CASE—NUMBER (OBJECT PERSONAL): In these exercises some of the personal pronouns are subject pronouns and some are object pronouns. Number your paper from one to ten. After each number, write each object pronoun; after it, indicate its person by **1**, **2**, or **3**; and indicate the number by **S** if the pronoun is singular and by **P** if it is plural. EXAMPLE: *We would like to see her.* HER **3-S**.

EXERCISE **A**

1. They are interested in him.
2. We are inclined to believe her.
3. Are you sure they will listen to us?
4. You are the only one who supports me.
5. She is in the library reading for them.
6. Mary and they are going to see her.
7. Do you think they will see us?
8. It is they who have ruined it.
9. He and his father are listening to us.
10. We will do our best for you.

EXERCISE **B**

1. When will she learn to recognize them?
2. You are the only one who knows me.
3. I agree with you, Harry, on that point.
4. We are held by the ties of friendship for them.
5. Who are you to condemn him?

6. It is she who will free them.

7. We can only pray for him and them.

8. Do you know that we gave it to them?

9. What can she and her mother do for us?

10. You and they alike are hostile to me.

EXERCISE **C**

1. Anna and I knew her during her student days.

2. He has imposed his will upon them by violence.

3. They had great confidence in us.

4. Vincent enjoyed history because he understood it.

5. To undertake it they must have had great courage.

6. She impressed them by her simplicity and candor.

7. When the speaker stopped, we began to question him.

8. She refused me even the ordinary marks of courtesy.

9. Through his powerful canvases, he speaks to us of justice.

10. It was this moment for which we had tried to prepare him.

PRONOUNS—CASE—NUMBER (POSSESSIVE PERSONAL): Number your paper from one to ten. After each number, write the possessive pronouns the sentence contains. Indicate the person by **1**, **2**, or **3**, and write **S** after the pronoun if it is singular and **P** after it if it is plural.

EXERCISE **A**

1. Where are Mary's books? John has his.

2. Ida's papers are here. I cannot find mine.

3. John and I are getting the skates. Where are yours?

4. Do me a favor when you get Al's coat. Get mine, too.

5. We have two notebooks. Have you and Mary yours?

6. Where have you put Mary's books? They have theirs.

7. Did she ask for Teresa's work? Helen has hers.

8. Do you see Jane's mother? I see mine.

9. He bought a new house. Did he buy ours?

10. They said that theirs is the first house in the block.

EXERCISE **B**

1. We know that ours will last longer than yours.

2. Mary believes that hers is the longest story.
3. We admit that yours is the better of the two.
4. Theirs and ours are the oldest houses in the town.
5. He asked us if his were the better bargains.
6. We informed them that theirs were too old.
7. Let us help her when hers is difficult.
8. We say that ours is the finest country.
9. I tell you that his will last the longest.
10. We gave them some paper when they lost theirs.

EXERCISE C

1. These are my copies. Don't you have yours?
2. My experiments could never be compared with hers.
3. I can remember his criticism of mine.
4. Mr. McLoy always consults his first, then ours.
5. Will you bring mine along the next time?
6. Ruth considered hers to be the only possible solution.
7. I think yours is the more interesting.
8. They inquired if we would like to use theirs.
9. Ours was really the most advantageous position.
10. Was hers the prize-winning contribution?

PRONOUNS—CASE (PERSONAL—RELATIVE): In these exercises, write each sentence and underline all the pronouns. To the right of each sentence write the word CORRECT if the pronoun is used correctly; if it is used incorrectly, write the correct form.

EXERCISE A

1. Mary thought the girl was I.
2. Harriet completed the work faster than me.
3. The librarian notified Gerald and I.
4. The class is open to whoever is interested.
5. Henry and myself played a duet.
6. The only competition is between Helen and I.
7. We musicians all heard the broadcast.
8. The shouting disturbed whoever was in the next classroom.
9. No one but I answered the advertisement.
10. The assignment was given to Helen and I.

1. The work should be completed between you and I.
2. The analysis can be made by whomever is in the laboratory.
3. Us club members are adept at discussion.
4. The valedictorian of this class will be me.
5. Who did the captain appoint?
6. Arnold and himself were the two chosen.
7. Would the girls do the job better than them?
8. John gave permission to Harold and I.
9. Popular as the book was, no one had read *Silas Marner* but Jane and she.
10. Uncle John objected to you're traveling.

EXERCISE **C**

1. Mary and myself met the visitors at the train.
2. Mary gave the theater pass to Jane and she.
3. The course was of practical importance for we seniors.
4. The professor decided John was him.
5. The student's sketch portrayed Emily and she.
6. Each member of the group but Harry and he had given an extra report.
7. The dean enlisted whomever was willing to write an essay.
8. Helen would give the speech as well as John or me.
9. Complete harmony exists between the class and they.
10. Whomever Mary suggests will be the person Alice will choose.

PRONOUNS—AGREEMENT: Number your paper from one to ten for each of these exercises. Examine the sentences to see if there is proper agreement between pronouns, antecedents, and verbs. If there is not, rewrite the sentence correctly. If there is, write CORRECT after the number.

EXERCISE **A**

1. Everyone don't like to go to movies.
2. Neither he nor I were chosen.
3. No one except you are coming over soon.
4. You was not in bed on time.

5. Everybody brought his bathing suit, but it rained.

6. Not one of us is willing to do the work.

7. Each of the girls have money for candy.

8. Had anyone lost their lunch by the time the group arrived at the picnic grounds?

9. Any of these old cars are good for scrap metal.

10. Some of the boys were absent on Tuesday.

EXERCISE **B**

1. Neither of them have been here for a long time.

2. Everyone brought their tennis shoes on the day of the game.

3. Most of the students have their books at school.

4. Most of the peanut butter that was in the jar yesterday is gone today.

5. Each of us were happy when he came home.

6. Each child must have their own book.

7. Everyone of them who heard the lecture were enthusiastic about this new idea.

8. If each club member insists on their own ideas, we will not succeed as a group.

9. He, as well as all of his friends, are going.

10. Someone will be glad to lend you their sunglasses.

EXERCISE **C**

1. The performance of each of them were extremely arresting and entertaining.

2. Each of the judges lost their vote.

3. Neither one of us have an opportunity to get to a public library.

4. All of the candy was eaten.

5. Neither of the jobs are open any longer.

6. Every one of the buildings were designed by Frank Lloyd Wright.

7. Not one of my friends are coming for the commencement exercises.

8. She, with her husband and entire family, are planning to spend the week at the lake.

9. Every one of you have a duty to vote in this election.

10. Neither the Cubs nor the Cardinals were a threat to the other teams in the league that year.

Modifying

MODIFICATION—DESCRIPTION—LIMITATION: In these exercises, write each sentence and skip every second line. Underline all the single word modifiers. If the modifier describes, write **D** above it; if it limits by telling *how many* or by *pointing out what is spoken about,* write **L** above it.

EXERCISE **A**

1. This letter is the longest one I have received.
2. Fifty sailors watched the beautiful sunset on the ocean.
3. We can see that old lighthouse from here.
4. That fine antique lace is expensive.
5. We recognize this accurate expression of thought.
6. Who can measure this unselfish devotion?
7. This book distinguishes between new meanings and old.
8. The champion speller won this valuable prize.
9. I believe that two dollars will be enough for this book.
10. Where can I find that interesting story?

EXERCISE **B**

1. The weekly publication of this paper is imperative.
2. Today there is an even greater demand for this type of heroism.
3. It is the purpose of this group to establish a permanent fund.
4. A few commuters sat in the cold train.
5. Money from this fund will be given to poor refugees.
6. We see how modernism is destroying culture in these parts.
7. Those who work for a lasting peace in all parts of the world are admirable.
8. These and many others are willing to help a young nation.
9. We will have a regular meeting for all members.
10. He let himself be swayed by public opinion.

EXERCISE **C**

1. Complete living implies awareness of the good things of life.

2. Alfred Lord Tennyson died in 1892 after a long life of literary successes.

3. Mary certainly must have been in good spirits when she wrote this letter.

4. Only one answer would satisfy the old gentleman.

5. Isn't this the teacher's own personal manuscript?

6. In idleness alone is there perpetual despair.

7. He whose body is a ready servant of the will has had a liberal education.

8. There was one manuscript copy with original illustrations.

9. John's deep convictions account for the sincere tone in which he speaks.

10. An outstanding trait of the Italian is love for the beautiful.

ADJECTIVES—NATURE: Number your paper from one to ten. List all the adjectives in these exercises. To the right write the adjective and the noun or pronoun it describes. Do not consider articles.

EXERCISE A

1. He was vigilant in watching.

2. They rejected the essential truth.

3. The lawyer proceeded with the greatest caution.

4. These tragic events were enacted throughout the Lowlands.

5. A crushing defeat was inflicted on them.

6. Repeated attempts failed to reconcile them.

7. The uncompromising methods of Elmer saved us.

8. The stage was ready for a new conquest.

9. Vulgar luxury brought him into contempt.

10. Bad manners are offensive.

EXERCISE B

1. She placed selfish interests above generosity.

2. Important territories were taken.

3. The frenzied outcry was of no avail.

4. The new arrangement was acceptable.

5. They saw in this a further extension of power.

6. Strong protests stormed the council.

7. Thirty members of the group were there.

8. The keen eyes reveal nobility.

9. He daily strengthened his frail body.

10. They were easily aroused to reckless enterprise.

EXERCISE C

1. There was literary atmosphere about her home.

2. Recently millions of dollars have been devoted to scientific research.

3. Robert Browning is one of England's greatest poets.

4. My aunt suffered partial blindness late in life.

5. Ruth used to spend numberless hours in the library.

6. Nancy's outstanding trait is her love for poetry.

7. Was any of her work published in the college magazine?

8. Put the name on the reverse side of the page.

9. The little girl was deeply influenced by Mary's conduct.

10. Such an odd combination would certainly attract attention.

ADJECTIVES—COMPARISON: Number your paper from one to ten. For each sentence write correctly the degree of comparison which the meaning requires.

EXERCISE A

tall	1. John is the _____ of the two Smith boys.
beautiful	2. I must find a _____ picture than that one for this room.
shady	3. Can't we find a _____ spot in which to eat our lunch?
quiet, slight	4. In a _____ room the _____ noise sounds very loud.
quiet	5. Girls are usually _____ than boys.
old	6. Is Frank or Bill the _____ of the Kleins?
interesting	7. I found *A Tale of Two Cities* —— than *David Copperfield*.
little	8. There is —— danger of his drowning than of his getting poison ivy.
much	9. Larry did the _____ work of all the boys.
capable	10. Is John or Ed the _____ of winning?

cheerful
1. Of the three friends, Hank is the _____.

bad
2. Your excuse was _____ but mine was _____.

good
3. Which of the two is the _____ writer?

famous
4. Hamlet is the _____ of Shakespeare's heroes.

slow
5. The *Arrow* is a slow train, but the one we took was even _____.

honest
6. That was the _____ compliment I've heard today.

happy
7. Jane is growing _____ every day, but Betty is already the _____ child I know.

bad
8. This is the _____ storm we've had this year, but there are _____ ones coming.

difficult
9. When given a choice, Fred always takes the _____ problem.

rapid
10. Is car, bus, or train the _____ means of getting there?

quick
1. Joanne always does a _____ job than her twin.

good
2. If your singing isn't any _____ than that, I think you should give up the lessons.

skillful
3. Ken's driving is _____ than Loren's, isn't it?

fast, safe
4. Loren's driving is _____ than Ken's but Ken's is _____.

high
5. Bob has a _____ jump than Clarence, but Ray has the _____ jump of them all.

little
6. Grace told her story with the _____ conviction of all those in the group.

often
7. Uncle Jack's visits were _____ this year than last year.

stealthy
8. Each step of his was _____ than the last.

late
9. Her arrival seems to be _____ every day.

happy
10. The little ones' playing was _____ when there were no older children to distract them.

ADJECTIVES—PHRASES: In these exercises, write each sentence. Underline each prepositional phrase used as an adjective. Then circle the noun or pronoun it modifies.

EXERCISE **A**

1. The books on this shelf are all very interesting.
2. After the game between the Cubs and the Braves, we saw a movie.
3. Is the girl in the blue sweater your sister?
4. Comments of that kind are better unsaid.
5. He looked around the room for that lost jewel of hers.
6. Books about adventure are usually most attractive to high school boys.
7. Exploration of space has replaced medical research in the minds of many students.
8. My choice of book differs greatly from hers.
9. I attended all of the concerts given at school.
10. The winner of the prize will be awarded a free trip to Washington.

EXERCISE **B**

1. My uncle bought a boat with an outboard motor.
2. The purpose of this meeting is to clarify the principles of our club.
3. A letter of recommendation should be sent to the principal.
4. We explored under the old bridge on Third Avenue.
5. The automobile in the garage is a Rambler.
6. The recent flood was one of the worst disasters in the history of our town.
7. The clown in the center of the ring howled with glee.
8. On the new carpet lay a little white dog with black ears.
9. When the free day was announced, the students responded with shouts of joy.
10. The fragrant smell of roses filled the morning air.

EXERCISE **C**

1. With the graceful strokes of an experienced swimmer, Sandy swam across the pool.
2. The horses galloped with the speed of frightened animals.

3. Between the rows of tulips grew several lilac bushes.

4. New Orleans, located on the Gulf of Mexico, is a great center of domestic and foreign trade.

5. Some people seek a magic formula for happiness.

6. In the box were pearls of great beauty.

7. The mother cat with her kittens paraded proudly before us.

8. The President strode with poise to the center of the stage.

9. The white birch bent under the weight of the glistening ice.

10. The canoe swerved dangerously around the bend at the forest clearing.

ADJECTIVES—NATURE AND PUNCTUATION OF ADJECTIVE CLAUSES: Some adjective clauses in the following sentences are restrictive and some are nonrestrictive. Write the sentences, underline each adjective clause, and punctuate correctly.

EXERCISE **A**

1. The men who have worked here ten years will receive a bonus at Christmas.

2. Clarence Jones who has lived here twenty years is still considered a newcomer in town.

3. My only brother who likes his vacations simple and restful is planning a fishing trip in the North Woods.

4. Later, the man who had threatened to ruin John went bankrupt himself.

5. The F.B.I. which had begun the manhunt earlier brought it to a sudden halt for no apparent reason.

6. It is evident that no one who contradicts Frank is considered worthy of mention by him.

7. The girls who finally qualified for membership refused to apply to the Top Teen Club because of the expenses and obligations of membership.

8. Man who is physically diminutive compared to the universe has conquered vast areas of its power and mystery.

9. Carp shooting which he does with a bow and arrow is his favorite sport.

10. Anyone who follows directions and applies himself to daily practice can type well in six weeks.

EXERCISE **B**

1. Bill was glad that he learned to drive in a car which has a hand shift.

2. Everyone agrees that the Johnsons' party which was a very informal affair was a real success.

3. Mr. Jones my next door neighbor who happened to see the accident occur swore that Benson was passing in a no-passing lane.

4. Some people mistake conversation which is fifty percent good listening for a "talk-a-thon."

5. An education which is worth the name teaches a man about himself first of all.

6. Graham who had insured the woman heavily planted a home-made bomb in her suitcase.

7. The Pep Club whose members go to all the basketball games have proved their loyalty to the school.

8. Anyone who practices as Kelly does deserves to win.

9. I knew that Don who paid his last penny to buy the car had forgotten about paying insurance, gas, and maintenance.

10. A man who likes others finds himself easier to accept.

EXERCISE **C**

1. Ricky who is only five explained his theory of self-defense— "If a big guy hits you, hit him back; if he does it again, you do it again."

2. John Hersey who is an author of real insight points out that the crime of war is not death multiplied but death in itself.

3. The class insisted that anyone who had no afterschool job should volunteer to work on the float.

4. Those who had abandoned all they owned during the flood were reimbursed by a special collection from a near-by city.

5. Slowly, uncertainly, but courageously, her youngest child who had lain paralyzed for three years began to walk again.

6. Many scientists accept Darwin's concept of evolution which is still only a theory as a basic generalization.

7. The team quarrel among themselves when they discuss a member who may qualify for All-State.

8. I will agree that men like Harris who break training and show up at games out of condition should be knocked off the team list.
9. Spelling which many class with the magic arts is a simple matter of intelligent application.
10. A reel which is an absolutely necessary piece of equipment for trout fishing costs more than I can afford.

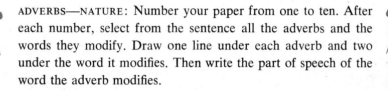

ADVERBS—NATURE: Number your paper from one to ten. After each number, select from the sentence all the adverbs and the words they modify. Draw one line under each adverb and two under the word it modifies. Then write the part of speech of the word the adverb modifies.

EXERCISE **A**

1. Her class responded immediately.
2. He reported extremely cold weather.
3. The excited dog barked continually.
4. The rope was dropped from a very high cliff.
5. The professor was greatly annoyed by the response.
6. The girl wrapped the package carefully.
7. This instrument is too delicate for general use.
8. The bridge was completely destroyed.
9. The boy entered the room cautiously.
10. This sentence is not punctuated properly.

EXERCISE **B**

1. Harry worked carefully.
2. Edison secured his patent easily.
3. It was an unusually lovely garden.
4. Red Heron is a dangerously deep lake.
5. She grasped the rope frantically.
6. Mary's dress was of extremely thin material.
7. This color is too dark.
8. Completely new ideas are few.
9. The badly frightened child cried.
10. The man looked up angrily.

EXERCISE **C**

1. I moved the mossy stone cautiously.

2. The hourly report was quickly transmitted to the surrounding stations.

3. Harry did not expect to attain his end cheaply.

4. Their emotions are too deep to express in words.

5. Her attitude was the least tolerant I had encountered.

6. Instantly there was the sound of soft, steady footsteps through the open doors.

7. The symbolism of the poem is based primarily on nature.

8. Eleanor was intensely interested in music from her earliest years.

9. He put down the brush hastily as I rose to leave.

10. She was extremely sensitive to the depth and beauty of classical music.

ADVERBS—USAGE, DISTINCTION FROM ADJECTIVES: In these exercises, write each sentence, skipping every second line. Underline all the adjectives and adverbs. Write ADJ. above each adjective and ADV. above each adverb. If an adjective or adverb is used incorrectly, write the correct form at the right.

EXERCISE **A**

1. Mary sure waited long for the reply.

2. Mary is the brightest of the twins.

3. Her new dress is more suitable than any one in her wardrobe.

4. There were less than thirty girls at her home.

5. We pretty near finished the assignment in two hours.

6. The theme was written beautiful.

7. The doctor said that she would be good enough to leave in two weeks.

8. He does not appreciate these kind of books.

9. Whereabouts is the recital to be held?

10. Most all the typewriters were cleaned recently.

EXERCISE **B**

1. My mother feels very good in the morning.

2. Pretty near all of the students worked for the award.

3. That investment will bring more profits than any one you could make.

4. Less people came in the afternoon than in the evening.

5. Which of the two portraits do you value most?

6. That kind of tree is very hard to raise in this soil.

7. Most all colloquial expressions are suitable for use in informal essays.

8. Whereabouts is that dog?

9. The twins sing very beautiful.

10. This author sure portrays rural life well.

EXERCISE **C**

1. Most all the writers used many unnecessary words.

2. He pretty near finished the biology experiment.

3. That kind of explanation will not be sufficient.

4. He played tennis and golf, but he enjoyed tennis most.

5. My brother wanted to know whereabouts my bicycle was.

6. The club profits were fewer than ours.

7. I sure appreciated the gift.

8. Do you think John looks good now?

9. The professor spoke beautiful that particular morning.

10. Virginia enjoys her Latin class more than any student does.

 ADVERBS—COMPARISON: List the adverbial forms in all degrees of the adjectives in Exercises **A**, **B**, and **C** of *Adjectives—Comparison,* page 531.

 ADVERBS—DISTINCTION OF ADVERBIAL FROM ADJECTIVE PHRASES: Number your paper from one to ten. After each number, write the prepositional phrases found in these sentences. After each write ADJ. if the preposition shows relationship between its object and a noun or pronoun; or ADV. if it shows relationship between its object and a verb, adjective, or other adverb.

EXERCISE **A**

1. The plans directed us to the new routes.

2. The areas of interest are expanding.

3. Apply all requests to the central bureau.

4. Transportation on a mass scale is proposed.

5. The largest plane is the last one on the list.
6. The size of this aircraft is astounding.
7. The difference between these two cars is slight.
8. The speed of the largest plane is increased.
9. The airplane has opened gateways of commerce.
10. The job was done by specialists.

EXERCISE **B**

1. My young brothers were entranced by his exciting stories.
2. His teaching knowledge resulted from first-hand experience.
3. The editions without prefaces were printed more cheaply.
4. Each morning the applicants stood before his door.
5. A man's responsibility to the members of his family was the chief topic discussed.
6. A different style marked his departure from the established tradition.
7. We ate under the old oak.
8. His long struggle against injustice had finally been rewarded.
9. Melvin's experience with the new automobile had been rather unfortunate.
10. We had long discussions about relativity.

EXERCISE **C**

1. Long ago a mighty Hebrew king, David, put his thoughts into psalms.
2. All the heavens tell of God's glory.
3. The whale is the largest creature in the sea.
4. Have you ever listened to sea shells' mysterious sounds?
5. For centuries the word "gypsy" has spelled mystery.
6. The more you know about animals the more you appreciate and enjoy them.
7. Courtesy is man's acknowledgment of the rights of others.
8. All law is grounded in human rights.
9. Man's material needs are supplied by nature and labor.
10. Through conversation we share one another's ideas.

ADVERBS—DISTINCTION OF ADVERBIAL FROM ADJECTIVE CLAUSES: In these exercises, write each sentence, skipping every second line. Underline each dependent clause (be sure you have the clause, the whole clause, and nothing but the clause). Circle the word the clause modifies. Above each clause write ADJ. or ADV. according to its use in the sentence.

EXERCISE A

1. We will send the package wherever you like.
2. The story that took first place was a beautiful fantasy about a mythical kingdom.
3. Although the staff was small, they put out an excellent paper.
4. When the committee asked for suggestions, only three people responded.
5. The party, which was over by eleven, was one of the best this year.
6. An adverbial clause is a clause which modifies a verb, an adjective, or another adverb.
7. It is rare to find a clause which modifies an adverb.
8. Frank rarely goes out because he loves solitude.
9. People who love solitude are usually either bookworms or hobbyists.
10. That book I gave you can be returned whenever you have read it.

EXERCISE B

1. The game which we played against St. John's was an exhibition of real skill.
2. Whenever you have time, you may read these books which I have just purchased.
3. We trust that you will locate Mr. Waite wherever he may be.
4. This novel, which was recommended by our book club, is a delightful reading experience.
5. The boys were detained after school because they were tardy this morning.
6. Although the fruit appeared to be ripe, it was bitter.
7. Marge treated her pet as though it were human.
8. After she had written the letter, Phyllis regretted her hasty decision.

9. The paper that I just completed took me several days to write.
10. Sales increased after the manager lowered the prices.

1. You must pay the penalty because you completely disregarded the regulation.
2. The boy I met yesterday is a student at St. Patrick's.
3. The girls who typed these reports did an excellent job.
4. I gave the book to Jerry, whom I met at the library.
5. If you follow the directions carefully, you cannot fail to have a successful experiment.
6. If you carefully view the situation which caused his dismissal, you will consider it a serious affair.
7. A man can scarcely achieve success unless he learns self-discipline and moderation.
8. The student who led the discussion could not be heard unless he used a microphone.
9. Because he loves sports, Bob seldom misses a baseball game.
10. The class illustrated Wordsworth's *Daffodils,* which is a nature lyric.

ADVERBS—PUNCTUATION OF ADVERBIAL AND ADJECTIVE CONSTRUCTIONS: Write each of these sentences and insert the proper punctuation marks.

1. The electoral college in my opinion should be abolished.
2. We attended a Broadway play when we went to New York.
3. When we sat in the back row we could hardly understand the speaker.
4. By the way I still think you should go.
5. For six hours of anxious waiting beside the battered car they looked for help to come.
6. Nero fiddled while Rome burned.
7. People burdened by debts avoid bills and bill collectors.
8. Whatever you do don't fail to consider the advantages of a year in college.
9. As every one knows a cat may look at a king.
10. The telephone rang just as we sat down to dinner.

1. If Americans widely agree that the electoral college should be reformed why has no action been taken?
2. I enjoyed watching the last few students dashing toward the classroom door after the bell had rung.
3. Hoping to arrive ahead of the teacher the last few members of the class dashed down the corridor.
4. Although the weather was cold the party was a success.
5. While Mary put a hat on her husband waited patiently in the car.
6. The policeman as far as I can see will never catch the thief at that pace.
7. I won't go unless you do.
8. Although Frank is not exceptionally bright he gets high marks because he applies himself.
9. With her simple and unaffected manner of meeting people and conversing she attracts many otherwise shy people.
10. She was greatly disappointed when no answer came.

1. According to recent surveys made throughout the country a patent has a fifty-fifty chance of being put into use at some time during its seventeen-year life.
2. Because their star quarterback had been injured the players lacked confidence.
3. Although Mary works very hard to have proper human relations she has never been a popular student.
4. Though she likes to eat food disgusted her at the moment.
5. At the time we flew to Paris from London.
6. You can in fact get Vitamin D by consuming fish-liver oils.
7. For example you address the chair as "Mr. Chairman."
8. His father wanted to see him riding the new bicycle.
9. Through her membership in the Future Teachers of America she has had several opportunities to conduct classes.
10. Don't lose your new hat while you're running to catch the train.

Joining

CONJUNCTIONS—NATURE AND KINDS: In these exercises write each sentence, skipping every second line. Underline every conjunction. Above each write CO-ORD., SUBORD., or CORREL. according to its use.

EXERCISE A

1. Two of the all-time athletic greats were Babe Ruth and Knute Rockne.

2. Neither Ruth nor Rockne became famous as a golfer.

3. Because he spent so many successful years there, Rockne is always linked with Notre Dame.

4. While Rockne was a member of the faculty at Notre Dame, he was popular with both the faculty and the students.

5. Neither work nor hard effort deterred Babe Ruth; baseball would be his career.

6. Baseball is popular not only in America but also in Europe.

7. Football is enjoyed in some parts of France, but the *Tour de France* is most popular.

8. Inasmuch as both Rockne and Babe Ruth were great men, they were inspirations for many teenagers.

9. Babe Ruth was great in baseball and Rockne was great in football.

10. Because Rockne worked hard, he succeeded.

EXERCISE B

1. Whenever a pep rally roused the students, the cheerleaders felt rewarded.

2. Neither the team nor the manager was aware of the mounting interest in the bleachers.

3. The school band paraded during the half, since this was the homecoming game.

4. While Pat dashed to make the final touchdown, the crowd cheered wildly.

5. After the third quarter of the game was lost, the opponents neither cheered nor followed the team.

6. St. Mary's lost the game, but the team put up a fight.

7. The winning team would make a tour to the State College or they would entertain at a school dance.

8. Both the student body and the faculty were proud of the team.

9. The members of the team were neither arrogant nor self-satisfied after they won their sixth game.

10. After the school paper carried the headlines of victory, the players were awarded their letters.

EXERCISE **C**

1. Mary and Ruth were on their way to the library when they met two friends.

2. A visit to the Louvre is both fascinating and memorable.

3. Although reproductions of the *Mona Lisa* or *Winged Victory* are common in art galleries, to see the originals in the Louvre is overwhelming.

4. Both the *Mona Lisa* and the *Winged Victory* are great master-pieces.

5. Some visitors admire the *Winged Victory* more than they do the *Venus de Milo*.

6. When visitors come to the Louvre, they often ask to see the *Mona Lisa*.

7. The Louvre was a royal palace before it became a museum.

8. If the weather permits, the two girls plan to walk from the Louvre to Notre Dame.

9. Two American boys attending the Sorbonne visited the Louvre whenever they had an opportunity.

10. While they studied in France, the boys worked hard because they were eager to become good artists.

CONJUNCTIONS—PUNCTUATION OF CO-ORDINATE ELEMENTS: Write each sentence and punctuate it correctly.

EXERCISE **A**

1. I wanted to see the play that everyone has been raving about but it was impossible to get tickets.

2. It is not only inconvenient to practice tonight it is almost impossible.

3. Bill finds mathematics very difficult nevertheless, he has carried a B average.

4. Children were screaming vendors were calling and people were chattering however, in spite of the confusion, there was a happy atmosphere in the air.

5. As we rounded the curve, we expected to see the bridge ahead of us but we had made a wrong turn.

6. We were detained after school consequently, we missed football practice.

7. In most schools home economics is taught .however, this school does not offer the course.

8. I will join the chorus the band or the orchestra but I haven't time to do all three.

9. Apples cookies fruit and candy were sent to the orphanage.

10. Mary talked to Jean for an hour to convince her to join their combo group, which included Bill Perry piano Sue Bogan saxophone Betty Harris clarinet Phil Serlo bass and John Morton drums.

EXERCISE **B**

1. Is golfing really the healthful exercise that many people claim it to be or is it only a current fad?

2. In sophomore year I registered for biology Latin English and history but besides those I will take physical education.

3. Cleaning the house preparing the meals and caring for the children kept Ellen busy all summer.

4. I had a party for the new Student Council officers: John Murphy president Joan Belo vice-president Mary Convers secretary-treasurer.

5. Bill had worked hard to complete the assignment on time and he hoped Mr. Johnson would appreciate his effort.

6. Helen had been ready for her date at seven o'clock nevertheless, she kept Bill waiting when he came.

7. Joan Bill and Mary Jane were ready to leave but Alice and Tom had not yet arrived.

8. Mr. Reed, the bank president, will speak about finances at the same assembly Miss Lee, the civics teacher, will speak about budgeting.

9. The student doesn't think he should hand in late assignments nor does the teacher think they should be accepted.

10. Don't touch the baby robin or its mother will object.

EXERCISE C

1. We are going by train to New York and from there we will fly to London.

2. My uncle my aunt and my three cousins are visiting us now but they will leave next week.

3. I find jig-saw puzzles card games and bingo a waste of time but many people seem to enjoy them.

4. Joan drinks no milk eats no fruit and devours candy yet she expects to remain healthy.

5. You lost your book you have no assignment and you are tardy can you still expect me to be patient?

6. Judy is generous with her time but Anne refuses to help the committee.

7. The games were ready the refreshments were prepared and the committee was waiting but where were the guests?

8. If the bell rings, we will be late but if we hurry, we can get there in time.

9. You can help me or Mark can.

10. We went as fast as we could but the time was too short to include Chicago Illinois Philadelphia Pennsylvania and Brooklyn New York.

PREPOSITIONS—NATURE, DISTINCTION FROM ADVERBS: Number your paper from one to ten. After each number, write the prepositions and adverbs contained in the sentence. After each preposition write **P** and after each adverb write **A**.

EXERCISE A

1. Jackson forced the horse over the ditch.

2. The boys rode beyond the river.

3. He stood outside.

4. Gertrude placed a chair before the table.

5. Mary threw the paper into the basket.

6. Harry hurried from school.

7. She applauded for her friends.

8. We live near the church.

9. We study during the evening.

10. The books are underneath.

1. The boy's little dog was lying under the hedge.
2. Didn't Agnes leave after the first act?
3. The author's ability to describe is apparent in all his works.
4. Flowers were placed all about.
5. Miss Larch, the science instructor, lectured until two-thirty.
6. I tripped over the little toy truck.
7. His results have been duplicated by our experiments.
8. We went to the library to use this reference material.
9. The opera lasted for two hours.
10. The committee members walked around.

EXERCISE **C**

1. We went under the shelter to fish.
2. I think you should go with the children.
3. Harvey's contributions ended with his scholarship.
4. His achievements have been acclaimed by the people.
5. The King sacrificed everything that he might bring succor to unfortunate people.
6. They preferred to remain without.
7. We followed the same route we had traveled before.
8. The children all clambered through.
9. Great marvels result from this invention.
10. The boys and girls played beside the waterfront.

PREPOSITIONS—NATURE, DISTINCTION FROM CONJUNCTIONS, USAGE: Write each of these sentences, skipping every second line. Underline every preposition and conjunction. Write **P** above each preposition and **C** above each conjunction. If a preposition or conjunction is used incorrectly, write the correct form to the right.

EXERCISE **A**

1. Jane gave a cry of delight as her brother stepped off of the train.
2. The telegram stated that Morris arrived last Wednesday.
3. Our project must be completed inside of a week.
4. He could not help from being depressed at the news.

5. We read on the bulletin board where the meeting was postponed until this afternoon.

6. Our library will be of no use to you except you know how to use it.

7. To venture in the dark building required much courage.

8. She discovered that his beliefs were not fundamentally different than hers.

9. John was faced with a difficult situation like he had expected.

10. Too extensive for one person, the research was divided among Peter and Matthew.

EXERCISE **B**

1. Do the work as perfectly as you can inside of the allotted time.

2. All the honors were divided between the three highest ranking students.

3. How could the principal help from deciding against her?

4. My aunt Helen read in the paper where the stores will be closed because of the holiday.

5. Except you trade with a reputable dealer, you are not certain of obtaining good material.

6. Last Tuesday the tourists attended a lecture in Patterson Galleries.

7. His approach to the subject is different than his predecessor's.

8. Just as I opened the door, he walked in the elevator.

9. Like she had promised, she returned my brief case before the end of the week.

10. He collected the coal which had fallen off of the truck.

EXERCISE **C**

1. We find the simple enjoyment of music different than a critical appraisal of it.

2. Final preparations were completed during the week.

3. Except you are familiar with the original, you cannot appreciate the beauty of the translation.

4. In a vain effort to recover the package, he leapt off of the speeding train.

5. His influence was very powerful, like I had been told.

6. Believing the cause lost, she could not help from giving way to despair.

7. Did you read in the letter where Phillip's roommate might accompany him?

8. His tremendous fortune was distributed between his various relatives.

9. Inside of a few more days the halls will be deserted and the classrooms empty.

10. The registrar walked in the building before Mark could attract his attention.

Non-Grammatical Elements

PUNCTUATION—REVIEW OF ALL RULES, DIRECT ADDRESS, INTRODUCTORY WORDS, DATES, AND ADDRESSES: Write each of these sentences and punctuate them correctly.

EXERCISE **A**

1. Although the students were tired they visited the museum the Art Institute and the Adler Planetarium

2. Reluctantly John queried Are you going to the Benoit dance

3. Francis will you help set up the stage for the program

4. George Washington who led our country in its fight for independence and Abraham Lincoln who signed the Emancipation Proclamation are considered great men

5. The girls lockers were located in the annex to the main building at Carlsfort Terrace

6. Students who do not do assignments will probably not gain their credits

7. In the beginning of the school year students eagerly plan to attend all social activities

8. Why I will certainly help you arrange the art exhibit

9. Dickens wrote *Great Expectations Bleak House* and *David Copperfield*

10. On June 7 1962 he plans to move the office to 1632 S Oakdale Boulevard Kankakee 13 Illinois

EXERCISE **B**

1. Because he was miserable Joe gloomily snubbed his friends they however merely teased him

2. Russia a country with great spiritual potential is now governed by materialistically minded politicians

3. Well it might be advisable to take advanced algebra if you plan to study chemistry

4. John or Mark or Paul will be elected to represent the class at the student council meeting

5. On December 7 1941 Japanese planes bombarded Pearl Harbor Hawaii

6. He planted roses lilies and zinnias in the patio garden

7. Breathing heavily Martin climbed the stairs to his dingy cluttered attic flat

8. The Story of Ruth Francine will give you some knowledge of ancient Hebrew traditions

9. The seniors enjoyed their trip to Denver for the scenery and Western hospitality impressed them

10. If you sell your quota of tickets explained the class president you will help the school pay for the new library equipment

EXERCISE **C**

1. During the Avignon Captivity, the popes resided at Avignon France but were persuaded to return again to Rome Italy

2. Yes I intend to join chorus and will volunteer to be in the school play

3. She planned to read the article entitled Design in Home Furnishings in *Better Homes and Gardens*

4. In April, after the rains the ground is ready for ploughing

5. The Persians I believe were one of the few ancient peoples who lived by a high moral code

6. My friend Mary and I chose Emily Dickinson and Sara Teasdale and Elinor Wylie as our favorite poets

7. Please close the door Joseph

8. Central High School a co-educational school is situated in Springfield Montana

9. Walt Whitman was not accepted as a poet in his early youth but today his influence is seen in many modern poets

10. His new address is 2134 W Sheridan Road Chicago Illinois

GLOSSARY

Abridged–shortened or condensed —often used in reference to the dictionary

Accent–a vocal force giving prominence to one syllable of a word over adjacent syllables

Accumulative tale–a story made up of a series of episodes arranged in logical order and related by a cadence that is repetitional

Action–the smaller and larger movements of the events of a story through time and place

Aesthetic myth–a myth believed to have been created to amuse or to delight men rather than to explain the universe

Allegory–an extended metaphor in which objects, persons, or actions in a narrative (prose or verse) represent meaning on a level beyond the literal

Alliteration–the close recurrence of an initial sound in words or stressed syllables

Allusion–a figure of speech which makes a passing reference to a famous literary or historical event or figure

Anecdote–a brief narrative of an interesting event

Animation–a figure of speech like personification, in which inanimate objects are given animal life

Antagonist–in drama or fiction, a character or force in conflict with the main character or protagonist

Anticlimax–events arranged in descending order of importance, or a drop in interest at a point where a rise of interest is expected

Antonym–a word of opposite meaning to another

Appendix–matter added to a book which is not essential to its completeness

Art ballad–a modern imitation of a folk ballad

Art epic–a long, dignified, narrative poem, carefully structured by an individual, which contains the ideals of a people expressed through a superhuman hero

Art tale–a modern tale that imitates a folk tale

Association–everything that the mind and imagination connect with a word

Assonance–as part of the sound structure of a poem, the recurrence of a vowel sound with different consonants following the vowel

Atlas–a collection of maps in a volume

Ballad–a short narrative poem, originating among the common people, which is composed to be sung and which develops one episode dramatically

Ballad stanza–alternating iambic tetrameter and trimeter lines rhyming *abxb,* appearing most often in a quatrain but occasionally in couplet form

Beast story–an allegorical tale in which animals are the main characters

Bibliography–a list of writings relating to a given subject or author

Card catalogue–a definite arrangement of cards of uniform size in drawers, each card usually identifying a single publication in a library

Causality–the necessary connection between events or the incidents of a plot, to establish cause and effect

Characterization–in literature, the projection of a person—his actions, his thoughts, his manners, his speech

Characters–the actors in a story

Chivalry–the system of customs, manners, and morals operative in the feudal system

Colloquialism–a word or expression acceptable and appropriate in ordinary informal conversation

Conflict–in drama or fiction, the struggle within an individual arising from the need to make a decision, or the struggle between the individual and opposing forces

Connotation–the associations a word has for an individual, or meanings suggested by words

Consonance–a sound device in which the consonants of two or more words or stressed syllables agree while the vowels differ

Copyright–the exclusive right to reproduce, publish, and sell the matter and form of a written work

Couplet–two lines of verse with end rhyme used as a unit or as part of a poem

Credibility–in a fictional piece, intervolvement of characters and incidents as can be accepted as believable

Cross reference–a specific direction of the user's attention from one part of a book, index, or catalogue to another part

Denotation–the exact meaning of a term

Derivation–the formation or development of a word from its original elements; also the tracing or statement of the process

Dewey decimal system–a numerical system of classifying the fields of knowledge, devised by Melvil Dewey for library books

Diacritical marks–a mark attached to a letter to distinguish its sound from that of another

Dialect–a characteristic way of speaking limited to a locality

Dictionary–a book which lists the words of a language

Encyclopedia–a work in which the various branches or fields of learning are treated in separate articles, usually arranged in alphabetical order

Endpaper–a sheet of paper folded and pasted to the first or last leaf of a book to provide an extra flyleaf, or a sheet pasted to the inside cover

Epic–a long, dignified poem which contains the ideals of a people expressed through a superhuman hero

Epic simile–an extended simile

Etymology–the history of a word, showing its source and its development in form and meaning; sometimes synonymous with derivation

Explanatory myth–a myth believed to represent the attempt of primitive people to answer the questions: What is the world? and What is man?

Fable–a tale, pointing out a moral, in which animals talk and act like human beings

Fairy tale–a folk tale in which the the world of make-believe and the world of reality meet in a romantic story

Farce–a comedy depending on improbable situations, word play, and physical humor, in which action is contrived by situation and the characters are types

Feminine rhyme–a rhyme in which the correspondence in sound is in two syllables, one stressed, the other unstressed

Folk ballad–a short narrative poem originating among the common people, which is composed to be sung and develops one episode dramatically

Folklore–the traditional stories, customs, beliefs, songs, and entertainment of the common people

Folk tales–stories that have their origin from the folk of ancient times rather than from the individual artist conscious of literary form

Foreshadowing–the process by which a writer hints at events which follow

Foreword–see **Preface**

Frontispiece–an ornamental figure or illustration, sometimes found facing the title page of a book

Giants–huge, mythical manlike or monstrous beings, more than mortals but less than gods

Glossary–that part of a book which lists explanations of words and passages included in the book

Grammar–the study of the classes of words, their means of indicating relation to each other, and their functions and relations in the sentence, according to established use

Handbook–a guidebook

Hero tale–a tale, the action of which is centered about a superhuman hero

Homonym–a word having the same pronunciation as another, but differing from it in origin, meaning, and, often, in spelling

Hyperbole–a figure of speech based on exaggeration and used for emphasis or literary effect

Hyphenation–use of a punctuation mark (-) for syllabic division and for compounding of words

Imperfect rhyme–rhyme in which there is the substitution of consonance, assonance, or a similar device for exact or perfect rhyme

Initiating incident–that happening or event in a plot structure or tale which sets the main action into motion

Internal rhyme–the repetition of rhymed words within a line of verse

Introduction–the opening situation in a narrative; that part of a book which leads into the main part

Legend–a story told as truth but which has only a small core of fact, if any

Library–a collection of books, manuscripts, etc., kept for study and reading but not for sale

Masculine rhyme–a rhyme in which the correspondence in sound is in final accented syllables

Metaphor–a figure of speech based on analogy in which each term expands the meaning of the other

Meter–in prosody, the arrangement of words into patterned rhythmic groups of stressed and unstressed syllables

Metrical romance–a romance told in verse

Metrical tale–any poem that tells a story, but specifically a story poem that is not in the form of epic, romance, or ballad

Minstrel–an entertainer of the Middle Ages who composed and recited poems for the nobility

Motif–a subject or theme that lends itself to literary structure, or a conventional situation used repeatedly in folk and modern literature

Myth–a story believed to be primitive man's explanation of the world and man's life in it

Mythology–a system or body of myths which explain through the actions or intentions of the gods of a people why the world is what it is and why things happen as they do

Narration–the relating of events or actions that have occurred or could occur in time

Narrative poem–a verse structure in which story and sound fuse

Newspaper–a paper printed and distributed at stated intervals to convey news, advocate opinions, and carry advertisements and other matters of public interest

Nonsense refrain–a refrain of a ballad made up of meaningless words

Obsolete–no longer in use

Onomatopoeia–the matching of sound and sense in a word

Parable–a story in which the anecdote that is shaped on the literal level parallels a moral or religious situation on the symbolic level

Patterning–designing with literary elements

Personification–a figure of speech by which human characteristics are attributed to inanimate objects or to abstractions

Phonetic–pertaining to speech sounds

Plot–the complete action of story within which single events arranged in causal relationship to character and to each other receive their meaning

Preface–something written as introductory to a book, usually by way of explanation of the object of the book, sources of information, and methods of treatment; often used interchangeably with foreword

Prefix–a letter or a combination of letters or syllables placed before a root word to modify the meaning

Preternatural–beyond the natural

Preternatural being–a mysterious being, neither human nor divine, not necessarily miraculous but strange and unexplainable

Pronunciation–manner of giving correct sound and accent to a word

Readers' Guide to Periodical Literature–an index containing author, title, and subject treated in magazines and referring the reader to the specific issue in which the article was printed

Reference book–a book intended primarily to give specific information on certain subjects rather than to provide page by page reading

Refrain–a group of words repeated in the same position in relation to the successive stanzas of a poem

Restrictive label–indication given in the dictionary to identify usage or vocabulary proper to specific fields

Rhyme–the matching sounds of the last accented syllable or syllables of two or more lines of poetry

Rhyme pattern–the sequence of rhyme sounds occurring in a stanza or poem

Rhythm–the regular recurrence of stress and time patterns

Rising rhythm–the iambic and anapestic meters

Romance–a loose narrative, sometimes in prose, sometimes in verse, that tells of knightly adventures

Root word–the simple element from which new words are derived by phonetic change or by one or more extensions of various kinds, such as the addition of prefixes and suffixes

Saga–an Icelandic or Scandinavian story from the medieval period that records heroic legendary adventures of members of aristocratic families

Saints' legends–apocryphal lives of the saints

Setting–the time and place in which the action of a story occurs

Simile–a figure of speech in the form of an analogy, the likeness between the two terms being indicated by *like* or *as*

Simple repetition–in a ballad, the recurrence of a word or group of words for the sake of song pattern and dramatic effect

Stanza–in a poem a unit of organization in which a pattern of lines is established

Stock phrase–a trite expression or a cliché

Stock response–the conventional response of readers to the connotation of a word

Suffix–a letter or a combination of

letters or syllables added to a root word to modify its meaning

Superstition–something that fear or coincidence seems to make true

Syllabication–methods of dividing words into separate speech sound units of one or more letters, each unit containing at least one vowel with or without consonants

Synonym–one of two or more words having the same or nearly the same essential meaning

Tale–a narrative consisting of a single episode in which story interest is dominant

Tall tale–a story combining the characteristics of myth and leg-end that is told by the use of hyperbole

Thesaurus–a guide to word selection in terms of synonyms, antonyms, and related words

Title page–the page of a book in which is given the full title, author's and publisher's names, and date and place of publication

Unabridged–complete; often used in reference to a dictionary

Variant spelling–different spelling

Vertical file–a special case in which a librarian files pamphlets, pictures, and clippings of current interest

Vocabulary–the sum or stock of words one can use and understand

INDEX of AUTHORS, Titles, and *First Lines*

Set in Linotype Times Roman by Brown Bros. Linotypers, Inc.
Format by F. Sadlier Dinger
Text printed by Mercury Litho Sales Corp.
Covers printed by Mercury Litho Sales Corp.
Bound by F. M. Charlton Company
Published by William H. Sadlier, Inc., New York and Chicago